HANS STURM

HANS STURM

A SOLDIER'S ODYSSEY ON THE EASTERN FRONT

GORDON WILLIAMSON

FONTHILL

Learn more about Fonthill Media. Join our mailing list to find out about our latest titles and special offers at:
www.fonthillmedia.com

Fonthill Media Language Policy

Fonthill Media publishes in the international English language market. One language edition is published worldwide. As there are minor differences in spelling and presentation, especially with regard to American English and British English, a policy is necessary to define which form of English to use. The Fonthill Policy is to use the form of English native to the author.

Fonthill Media Limited
Fonthill Media LLC
www.fonthillmedia.com
office@fonthillmedia.com

First published in the United Kingdom and the United States of America 2015
Reprinted 2015

British Library Cataloguing in Publication Data:
A catalogue record for this book is available from the British Library

Copyright © Gordon Williamson 2015

ISBN 978-1-78155-393-0

Typeset in 10pt on 13pt Sabon
Printed and bound by CPI Group (UK) Ltd, Croydon, CR0 4YY

Connect with us
 facebook.com/fonthillmedia   twitter.com/fonthillmedia

CONTENTS

Dedication

This book is respectfully dedicated to the memory of Hans Sturm.

When I suggested to him that I wanted to create a book about his experiences for the English-speaking reader, more detailed and accessible than a previous, 70-page publication in which they appeared in Germany in the 1960s, he willingly agreed to put pen to paper for me.

Over a period extending into years he would send me reminiscences and epistles, which I would translate, collate, and pull together into book format. The process was almost like reading an adventure novel: I always found myself anxiously waiting for the next chapter to arrive—only this was not fiction, but real life.

In adapting the material for the English reader, I have kept the text as true to Sturm's original notes to me as possible, only making changes when an alternative term was required where the original German had no direct English equivalent.

I am honoured that Sturm allowed me to carry out this task, and to present his story to a wider audience.

Sadly, the publishers I approached some years ago felt that the time was not right for the memoirs of ordinary German soldiers, only famous generals or fighter aces seeming to be 'in vogue'. Tastes have changed in recent times and now many biographies and autobiographies of common German soldiers are making their way onto the bookshelves. I am delighted that, thanks to Fonthill Media, I can keep my promise to Hans Sturm: his story—that of an incredibly brave young soldier—will not go untold.

Gordon Williamson

Foreword

I was pleasantly surprised when my friend Hans Sturm and Gordon Williamson, the noted author of several excellent books and articles on Second World War history, asked me to write a few words as an introduction to this work. Of course, I was only too honoured to agree to such a request on behalf of Hans, a soldier of the 'Old School' and a true gentleman. His accomplishments, both on and off the battlefield, are worthy of our respect and study.

As one who entered military service in 1978, I will never be able to fully comprehend the hardships, privations, and physical pain Hans endured during both the Second World War and the subsequent years in Soviet captivity. However, I can admire Hans's dedication to duty, loyalty to his comrades, and heroism on the battlefield, for these are the ideals that every person who serves his country strives to fulfil. Events beyond his control threw Hans, like millions of other young men of his generation, into a global conflict. With thoroughness and candour, Mr Williamson relates how Hans strove to do his duty as best he could and return home to his family.

It is through Mr Williamson's words in relating to us Hans's ordeals as a combat soldier that we should pause and rise above the politics of the Second World War in order to draw lessons for the future. Only then will all the suffering and destruction the world experienced not have been in vain. Regardless of their nationality, soldiers like Hans Sturm endeavoured to display both moral and physical courage. Hans's heroism was deservedly recognised by his being awarded Germany's highest decoration for bravery, the *Ritterkreuz* of the Iron Cross. More than 15 million men saw service in the German military between 1939 and 1945; however, only approximately 7,300 men were to become *Ritterkreuzträger*. Hans told me that he wore this coveted award in remembrance of his fellow soldiers whose sacrifices went unrecognised and for those who paid the ultimate price in battle.

The Second World War was the defining event of the twentieth century, and the Cold War that it ushered in caused an Iron Curtain to descend between East and West.

That curtain is now thankfully gone. Germany is once again a united country. Russia and the now freed countries of Eastern Europe are pursuing democracy and market economies. Yet, in the waning euphoria over the end of the Cold War, the world remains a dangerous place. As Hans so admirably displayed more than fifty years ago, integrity, loyalty, sacrifice, and bravery must remain the touchstones for defenders of peace-loving countries around the world.

David L. Sims
Lieutenant Colonel
United States Air Force

Introduction

My first contact with Hans Sturm was the result of a fortuitous accident.

At the time I was carrying out research into the famous *Großdeutschland Division* and had thought I was writing to a *Ritterkreuz*-winning soldier from this unit with the same name.

Despite the obvious case of mistaken identity, this Hans Sturm wrote back a very polite and friendly letter enclosing a signed copy of a wartime photograph showing him in uniform and wearing his *Ritterkreuz*, as well as a brief '*Lebenslauf*' or summary of his military career.

I was intrigued to read that he had not only won this high decoration as a mere *Gefreiter*, or Lance-Corporal, but had in fact been awarded a whole string of military decorations over a period of just a few months of service on the Eastern Front. My curiosity was roused and I wrote back asking for more information. This was to be just the beginning of a long period of pen-friendship in which I gradually grew to know more and more about this fascinating character. One of the items sent to me was a copy of the German veterans' magazine *Der Landser*, in which was contained a narrative report of the exploits which won this gallant young soldier the *Ritterkreuz*. I was warned, however, that the author of the piece had used some artistic license in his writing, which was not entirely accurate.

In 1991, my wife and I were able to take up Hans Sturm's gracious offer to visit him in his Dortmund home. By a happy coincidence we arrived on his birthday, 29 July, and were made to feel extremely welcome as he and his charming family celebrated his 75th.

The great admiration I had already grown to feel for this man could not fail to be enhanced by meeting him in person. No one, in fact, who encountered Hans Sturm could fail to have been impressed. He was quite simply one of the kindest and most pleasant fellows I have ever had the privilege to meet, possessed of a charming personality and wonderful sense of humour. Despite extreme discomfort following hip replacement surgery, he insisted in being our guide as well as our host and ensured our trip was one which would never be forgotten.

Following my suggestion that the story of his military exploits warranted a fuller study that that presented in *Der Landser*, it was agreed that he would provide me with details of his military career from his enlistment in 1940 until his release from Soviet captivity in 1953. His habit of collecting autographs and dedications from those he encountered during the course of his duties in several hardbound volumes has left him with a superb record of dates, places, and personalities relating to most of the major events in his military career, allowing him to recall and describe these events with great accuracy.

Sturm's story is an incredible one. From a simple infantry soldier to a commissioned officer mixing with some of the Third Reich's top brass, his range of experiences in combat and on the home front was much greater than could ever be the case for any normal combat soldier. During this traumatic period in history, Hans Sturm managed to retain his own strong sense of personal honour and integrity, and never hesitated to speak his mind and speak truthfully, despite the dangers inherent in the paranoid atmosphere of Hitler's regime.

Hans Sturm's military awards are testimony enough to his own personal gallantry. The *Ritterkreuz* of the Iron Cross was a multi-faceted award. It could, for instance, be awarded to a fighter pilot for downing a specific number of enemy planes—in which case it could reasonably be equated with the Distinguished Flying Cross—or bestowed upon a senior officer for inspired leadership of troops—in which case it might equal the DSO. However, it was otherwise awarded for personal gallantry above and beyond the call of duty in the face of the enemy. In such a case, and certainly in the case of Hans Sturm, there can be no doubt that the nearest equivalent would have been the Victoria Cross.

This is not just the story of one brave soldier, but of the triumph of the human spirit over adversity. I am proud to have counted Hans Sturm as a personal friend and it is my privilege to present his story.

Gordon Williamson
Livingston, Scotland
2013

A keen keyboard player, Sturm relaxes at his Dortmund home after his retirement.

Lebenslauf

Military Ranks

Schütze	
Gefreiter	August 1941
Unteroffizier	September 1942
Fahnenjunckerfeldwebel	February 1944
Leutnant	September 1944

Awards

Iron Cross Second Class	29 July 1941
Iron Cross First Class	1 August 1941
Wound Badge in Black	22 August 1941
Infantry Assault Badge	December 1941
East Front Medal	Early 1942
German Cross in Gold	26 August 1942 (received 5 November 1942)
Wound Badge in Silver	14 September 1942
Ritterkreuz of the Iron Cross	26 September 1942
Anti-Partisan Badge in Bronze	1944
Wound Badge in Gold	1 May 1945

Wounds

Hand Grenade Shrapnel	22 August 1941
Shell Splinters, Bullet Wound	23 August 1941
2 and 3 Degree Frostbite	February 1942
Shrapnel, Shell Splinters, Severe Concussion	14 September 1942

Shell Splinters   29 April 1945
Shell Splinters   1 May 1945

Units

Infanterie Ersatz Bataillon 289   3 October 1940 to 28 October 1940

Infanterie Regiment 473   29 October 1940 to December 1942

Infanterie Ersatz Bataillon 473   January 1943 to February 1944

Grenadier Regiment 871   February 1944 to May 1944

Kriegsschule Hagenau   June 1944 to August 1944

Grenadier Ersatz Bataillon 88   September 1944 to October 1944

Grafenwöhr Training Grounds   November 1944 to January 1945

Führungsstab Deutscher Volkssturm   February 1945 to 2 May 1945

Soviet Captivity   2 May 1945 to 10 October 1953

PART ONE

The Making of a *Ritterkreuzträger*

1

Enlistment

Hans Sturm was born in Dortmund on 29 July 1920, the son of an engineer, and bearing the same name as his father. After attending *Volksschule* and a one year term at *Oberrealschule*, Sturm left education without his *Abitur*, having had difficulty with foreign languages. He then went on to study artistic and constructional metal working.

As well as his trade training, Sturm undertook a course of evening classes in technical training, taking his final examinations in 1939.

On 3 September 1939, Sturm was apprenticed to the firm of Dortmunder Hüttenunion. Because of his apprenticeship, he was excused service in the *Reichsarbeitsdienst*. The RAD was a compulsory labour service organisation in which German males were expected to spend six months before going on to military service. It was a uniformed organisation, structured along military lines with strict discipline, preparing its members for life in the armed forces. Most of the work undertaken was of a physical nature, such as road building *etc*. For young men such as Sturm, the technical skills he would acquire during his apprenticeship were considered more important than carrying out unskilled labouring work, and he was thus excused the usual six months' RAD service.

Sturm worked for three months in the company's workshops before commencing training as an engineering draughtsman, involved in the design of wheels for gun carriages and artillery pieces. He was called up for military service on 3 October 1940.

As a young boy of 12, Sturm had joined the *Deutsche Jungvolk* in October 1932, before Hitler's accession to power and the organisation's ultimate absorption into the Nazi youth movement, the *Hitlerjugend*. Shortly thereafter he was to discover the realities of the darker side of the Nazi regime.

Sturm had had a very close school friend, who had shared the same bench seat with him in class, the two of them always getting up to some mischief or other. The other lad was a Jew.

Sturm had always worn his *Jungvolk* uniform with considerable pride. One day, as Sturm made his way to the bike shed after school, he came upon his friend being bullied by a number of other boys. Sturm immediately went to his aid and, back to back, they held off the other boys until a schoolmaster arrived to investigate the cause

A family photograph with the young Sturm in the far right, wearing his sailor's suit.

Sturm as a young boy with two of his pets.

of the commotion. All were taken before the headmaster and severely reprimanded, reports of the incident being sent to the boys' parents. As a young boy, Hans Sturm had conducted himself with the same spirit and sense of comradeship to his friends that he would later display in his military service, in captivity, and in his private life.

By March 1933, Sturm was a platoon leader in the youth movement and was shocked to discover that his *Fahnleinführer*, or troop leader, was being expelled from the *Jungvolk* because it had been discovered that he was half-Jewish. The boy's father was a renowned Dortmund businessman who had been a highly decorated officer during the First World War. Sturm knew the boy's parents, as they lived in the same district as he did.

Disgusted at the treatment of his young comrade, Sturm resigned from the Jungvolk in protest, thus incurring the wrath of his teacher, an ardent Nazi. The latter was also the leader of the school orienteering group, and enrolled all of his pupils into the *Deutsche Jungvolk* and eventually the *Hitlerjugend*. Eventually, after pleas from his other comrades and those of his parents and worried at the possible consequences of this act, Sturm agreed to remain but would long remember the disgraceful treatment of his young friend.

At the start of 1934, Sturm joined the *Marine-Hitlerjugend*, taking his A Certificate in Haltern and his B Certificate in Kiel. There he also took part in the state championships, his boat achieving second place.

For the C Certificate it was necessary to take part in a world cruise on one of the Navy's sail training ships. Naturally, this meant considerable time off work being granted by his employer. Parental consent was also required for this undertaking, but Sturm's father would not agree, insisting that his engineering training must take priority.

As well as achieving a number of qualifications in sports such as in judo, Sturm gained his qualifications at basic, intermediate, and advanced level in Lifesaving.

The demands of his trade training led Sturm to request leave of absence from the *Marine-Hitlerjugend*. But because the *Marine-Hitlerjugend* tried to make difficulties for him in this matter, Sturm simply resigned his membership and thus never became a party member. (Membership of the *Hitlerjugend* lasted until the youth's eighteenth birthday. On reaching adulthood, he would have been strongly encouraged by his *Hitlerjugend* superiors to join the Nazi Party.)

Sturm discovered that some former naval signals personnel were giving training lessons in the main Post Office on Saturday evenings. He attended regularly and, after two years' training from 1937 to 1939, Sturm gained his signaller's qualification. He achieved superb speed in both sending and receiving, and learning much in the way of signals theory.

Sturm felt confident that he would eventually make himself a career as a naval signals officer, though he would first have to complete his apprenticeship. With A and B Certificates from the *Marine-Hitlerjugend* plus his signals training, this assumption seemed a fairly reasonable one. When he eventually went along to register for enlistment into military service, the mustering officer was a major from

A family portrait showing Sturm with his mother and father.

Sturm as a young man prior to military service.

the Dortmund anti-aircraft detachment. He encouraged Sturm to join his own unit, but Sturm was not interested. The *Luftwaffe* major was not put off by Sturm's reluctance and persisted with his attempts to persuade the young man to join his Flak unit. Sturm grew more and more irritated at this *Luftwaffe* officer. He was determined on a career in the Navy, and insisted that his signals training would be most useful there.

'But we can also use your signals skills,' insisted the major.

The naval representative, whom Sturm recognised as a former colleague from the *Marine-Hitlerjugend*, said nothing in support of Sturm's argument, but simply warned him about his unsoldierly behaviour towards the major. This was too much for Sturm.

'Soldier, yes I'll be a soldier, but never a *Schlipsträger* with the Flak.'[1]

'Get out!' roared the major. Thus it was decided that Sturm would become neither an airman nor a sailor, but an infantryman.

2

Infantryman

Sturm's service with the infantry began in October 1940, when he joined *Infanterie Ersatzbataillon 289*, in Herford. The recruitment training there lasted only three weeks. A request had been received for volunteers, who had completed their basic preparatory training, as battle casualty replacements for a front-line unit serving in France. Sturm was one of the volunteers.

After a three-day train journey through Holland, Belgium, and France, he arrived at the town of Vitry-le-François on 29 October 1940. The town had been almost completely destroyed in German bombing centred on the cathedral district. It was said to be a retaliatory raid following the French bombardment of the university town of Heidelberg, which the French had twice captured and destroyed in 1689 and 1693. Despite the bombing raid, however, Sturm found the locals, with only a few exceptions, not to be particularly unfriendly to the *Landsern*.[1]

After a brief period of further training in France, the volunteer recruits from Herford joined *1 Bataillon, Infanterie Regiment 473*, a component of the German Army's *253 Infanterie Division*.

In 3 Company, to which Sturm was posted, there were already a few comrades who wore decorations won during the campaign in France. Those from Herford, the 'new boys', were the first replacements to arrive, and because of their very brief period of training were considered unfit and unready for combat service by the rest of the company, and were treated accordingly.

In Sturm's case, this soon changed. The particular proficiency he displayed, especially in weapons training with the MG34 machine gun and with the carbine, meant he soon found himself selected as Number 1 in a machine gun crew.

Shortly before the unit was due to be transported from France to East Prussia, a company social was held to allow the men time to relax and enjoy a few drinks. The festivities began at 18.00 hours, but before attending, Sturm and his comrade Heinz Sandkühler had to complete a spell on patrol, from 18.00 to 20.00 hours. Both had trained at Herford and been posted to the same company on reaching France.

The noise and laughter from the canteen in which the function was being held reached the kitchens where Sturm and Sandkühler were enjoying their meal after finishing their duty. As the two comrades entered the hall, they were struck by the atmosphere of good humour and greeted by calls from their friends, who had been making the most of this pleasant evening. Space was made for them at the table, and Sturm and Sandkühler each found themselves a glass of Schnapps before joining their friends. They had some catching up to do before they could indulge in the same good mood as their comrades.

As Sturm was about to have a drink, he was nudged by one of the 'old boys' who had already had too much. He pushed Sturm aside, saying that Sturm had taken his place at the table. He was a *Gefreiter* who already wore the Iron Cross Second Class, and was normally a nice enough chap when he was sober.

Because '*Herr Gefreiter*' was obviously drunk, and Sandkühler and the others nearby were winking at Sturm, he ignored the challenge, took up his glass, and went to take a sip.

On seeing this, the drunken NCO came at Sturm again, pushing him and knocking the glass from his hand. 'Hey, youngster, you shouldn't be drinking Schnapps. Not until we make a soldier of you!'

Sturm's reaction was immediate. He grabbed the *Gefreiter* by the collar. As his comrades struggled to hold him back, Sturm pronounced the fateful words, 'What makes you think you are so special? Just because you are a *Gefreiter*, or because you have the Iron Cross! Maybe I could be a *Gefreiter* with the Iron Cross too, if I had had the chance to fight in the French campaign!'

The *Gefreiter* threw a punch at Sturm's face. Sturm avoided it easily and caught the *Gefreiter* off balance, throwing his own punch which caught and threw him over onto the next table.

Suddenly the company commander appeared. After a few curt questions to the two of them and to others in the vicinity, he summoned Sturm and his opponent to his office.

The platoon leader of 3 Platoon, *Feldwebel* Kionke, who had be sitting at the table and seen what had happened, said a few words on Sturm's behalf, but they were of little help.

The company commander did not punish Sturm. Worse, however, than a formal punishment was the way in which he was treated by the men of the company. In their opinion, he had insulted the other soldier's Iron Cross, and abused the man who had won it. This had not been Sturm's intention; he had only said what he felt inside. He could see that his words must have appeared arrogant, but couldn't bring himself to apologize.

It was *Feldwebel* Kionke who gave Sturm some courage. He pointed out that Sturm was the best Number 1 on any machine gun crew in the company. This was praise indeed, because all of the other machine-gunners were veterans of the French campaign with a battle-proven unit. Heinz Sandkühler was his Number 2. Sturm and Sandkühler were the best in the company in terms of speed in changing barrels and ammunition belts, and accuracy.

Many in the company and also in his own platoon had taken offence at Sturm's behaviour in the canteen, and held it against him for some time. Even his section leader and platoon commander made their displeasure abundantly clear to him, especially during weapons drill. Sandkühler, as his Number 2, also had to suffer alongside Sturm.

It was hardly an auspicious start for the new soldier.

The journey from France to East Prussia in April 1941 was a memorable experience. Sturm had volunteered to guard the transport train. Sandkühler, who was initially all against the idea, eventually had to admit that they, along with two other machine-gunners, were better off than the men in the wagons. The machine gun, with a belt of ammunition fitted and ready, was sited on a platform on an open wagon. As the train passed through various stations and under foot bridges, small gifts were often thrown by the civilian populace, generally into the open wagons! There was also much more room for those in the open wagon to stretch out and sleep under the gun platform when they were off watch.

The months in East Prussia went by very quickly. The *Gefreiter* (named Kröger) who had had the altercation with Sturm in the canteen came to Sturm one day and apologised. Having made their peace, the two men sealed their new friendship with a mouthful of Schnapps.

Often pushing his luck, Sturm on one occasion returned to the quarters well after last parade. *Feldwebel* Kionke caught him, but didn't report him, as this would have resulted in three days' close confinement for Sturm.

Once, after a generous ration of alcohol won in the course of a competition, Sturm got so drunk that he gate-crashed a celebration held by the officers of the battalion and some local dignitaries. Only at the formal request of the civilians did Sturm escape severe punishment. He was beginning to get quite a reputation as a bit of a rascal.

On the next day, the section and platoon leaders made sure that the alcohol was worked out of Sturm's system. He was put through countless weapons drills until he was so exhausted he could hardly crawl.

Sturm had to admit that, from a strictly military viewpoint, his actions were sometimes impossible! 'You should just call yourself "Stur" and drop the "m" from the end of your name,' summed up his friend Sandkühler. (In German, the word 'stur' means stubborn and obstinate.)

Baptism of Fire

Infanterie Regiment 473, along with *253 Infanterie Division*, moved over to the border into Russia during the evening of 22 June, meeting no response from the enemy. An advance party would, however, be involved in the opening battles.

The Germans were to meet an enemy which, in respect to their state of training and the quality of their weapons, was ill equipped for conflict with the *Wehrmacht*. Where the Russians did make determined stands and cause the Germans considerable difficulties, it was thanks more to the dogged and determined mentality of the common Russian soldier. Wherever he was well led, the Russian soldier gave an outstanding performance.

In view of the lack of tanks, planes, cannon, and mechanised troops with which to oppose the Germans, the Russian leadership had no choice but to throw every available man into the fray and use the one weapon that it did have—sheer volume of manpower!

Infanterie Regiment 473 was among the second assault wave of the invasion force. For five weeks Sturm's company marched towards the sound of the guns. At night the muzzle flashes of the artillery could be seen in the distance as the front line moved inexorably forward. Many of Sturm's comrades were concerned that they would arrive too late. At the rate that the German spearheads were moving, they would soon be in Moscow and then—well, then the war would be over of course.

The front ahead of *Infanterie Regiment 473* was advancing at the rate of 10 to 30 km daily. The spearhead of *Kampfgruppe Guderian* was *Infanterie Regiment 215*, a component of *78 Infanterie Division* which was then fighting under the command of *General* Walter Nehring's *18 Panzer Division*.

The Russians to their front first began to make attempts at a defensive stand in the Bialowiezaer Forest, in which units of the Russian Fourth Army had dug themselves in.

The speed of the advance had resulted in many well-armed Russian units seeking shelter in the vast woodlands and being by-passed. The task of Sturm's regiment was to 'clean up' these areas. This was rarely achieved with total success. Such incidents were the germ-cell from which the deadly partisan war would grow.

The baptism of fire for Sturm came at a bend in the road during the advance through this so heavily wooded area.

His section formed the infantry spearhead of the regiment, as the point of a wedge formed with 2 Platoon of 3 Company. 2 Section moved along the right side of the road, while the left side along the forest edge was covered by 3 Section; 50 m behind them followed 3 Platoon, led by *Feldwebel* Kionke.

The march through the forest required a heightened state of alertness. The bend in the road had almost been reached when Sturm noticed movement in a copse of bushes within the woods. His warning shout came too late, as machine gun fire rang out and the Germans flung themselves into the ditches which ran either side of the road.

Sturm had thrown himself into the ditch on the left, followed by Sandkühler with the ammunition boxes. *Gefreiter* Kröger landed immediately behind them. Two wounded comrades lay on the road. One was laboriously crawling his way towards the ditch to be dragged into cover by his comrades, while the other lay calling for help. A third soldier was still ominously prostrate on the road.

Sturm quickly brought his machine gun into position and began firing towards the bushes. A stream of bullets from the opposition forced him to take cover again, however.

Comrades from the other platoons had now joined in and were returning the enemy fire with firearms and hand grenades.

'*Sanitäter*!' cried the wounded soldier once again.[1]

'Give covering fire Hans,' called Kröger, and leapt up onto the roadway.

Sturm renewed his fire on the forest edge in an attempt to halt the enemy fire. Two other machine guns from 3 Platoon joined in. The bullets zipped into the woods shaking trees and bushes, and ricochets spun off in all directions. Kröger had picked up the wounded man, run back, and was about to drop him into the ditch. Just then Kröger himself was pitched forward by a blow to his back, and both men fell forward at the edge of the ditch. Kröger was dead, his still open eyes seeming to stare directly at Sturm. Kröger hadn't had the chance to wear his Iron Cross for long.

Sturm would never forget this sight. They had not long since settled their differences and become friends, and now this man lay dead over there in the other ditch. Rage swept over him. He did not stop to think that, of course, the Russians were only defending their own land and their own lives.

In situations such as these, it was possible for a small group of enemy troops, well positioned in the forest, to hold up an entire regiment.

'Damn! It's too far for hand grenades, but we have to try something,' Sturm heard Sandkühler say. He took Kröger's machine pistol and some hand grenades. 'I want to try to work my way around to the right,' he said. 'Fire at whatever you can see, and keep the Russian's noses to the ground. Stop firing when I have thrown the hand grenades.'

Sturm saw him speak with the section commander. The message was passed on to the other sections and to the platoon leader, *Feldwebel* Kionke, over in the other ditch where, beyond the bend in the road, the Russians were firing at every incautious movement.

While Sturm and the others gave covering fire with every available weapon, Sandkühler, the section commander *Unteroffizier* van der Kerkhof, and two other men dashed from the cover of the ditch. The dense terrain gave them good cover and they made fast progress as their comrades kept up the covering fire. As the last hand grenades flew threw the air, the covering fire halted abruptly and the four sprang back into the cover of the ditch as the hand grenades detonated. Machine pistol fire into the wood from the Germans ensured that those Russians not killed by the grenades were forced to flee.

German losses were two killed and two wounded. Another company took over the point, and the regiment marched onwards.

Sturm went over to Sandkühler and offered him his hand with the words, 'You did well there, Heinz!'

'Do you think I'd let them get me so easily?' replied Sandkühler, astonished. 'I admire Kröger for what he tried to do, but it was pointless, Linker over there on the road was already dead,' he continued, none the worse for wear. 'Anyhow, we couldn't lie here for ever.'

Later, Sturm would often come to admire Sandkühler, because he never showed any fear and was often very foolhardy. He was a real daredevil who dealt quickly with any danger, whereas Sturm had to force himself to overcome his own fears first. He was afraid of death of course, but even more so of being wounded and ending up a cripple. Surmounting these demons was in of itself testimony of Sturm's courage.

The actions in the second line of the assault became a difficult period for *Infanterie Regiment 473*. The advance in the direction of the front lines was continually interrupted by battles in the forests, in which groups of Russian soldiers as well as partisans had installed themselves. These groups defended themselves with great determination and were only overcome at considerable cost to the Germans in terms of casualties and fatalities.

Sturm considered that fighting for the small villages and even individual houses was easier than fighting in the forests, with their hilly terrain and where none of the regiment's heavy weapons could be brought into play. The troops had to be wary of snipers in the trees, of well concealed mines and of well camouflaged and constructed bunkers and foxholes. The forward reconnaissance troops were often allowed to pass unhindered, then the Russians would open fire on the unsuspecting soldiers who followed.

For *Infanterie Regiment 473*, the delay to its advance caused by having to deal with such fragmented enemy units in the dense forests was a terrible burden.

Never again, not even during the rainy season (known as the *Schlammzeit*, or 'Muddy Season'), did Sturm witness such demands being made on both men and material. The march to the front line, which often extended to between 30 and 60 km a day, was embarked on with full pack and in soaring temperatures: it took the men over and above the limits of endurance.

During the march, Sturm had to carry, among other things: the machine gun; a spare barrel in its holder; a tool kit for the machine gun on his belt; a holstered pistol; a *Zeltbahn*; a haversack; a gasmask in its steel canister; and his steel helmet.[2]

As Number 2 on the machine gun, Sandkühler carried two spare barrels in a metal container, and two cases of ammunition.

Regardless of the needs of their own people, the Russians had poisoned all the wells with the carcasses of dead animals as they retreated. This was on the direct orders of Stalin, part of his directive for the conduct of the partisan war and within his well known scorched earth policy.

4

Bloody Conflict at Kikino

Stalin had laid down rules for the conduct of the war in a speech on 30 June 1941. From the outbreak of hostilities until that day, he had locked himself in his study as he decided his strategy.

In the middle sector of the front it fell to the Russian General Jeremenko to implement these measures. The German public and the men at the front had of course no knowledge of the Russian plan. It is uncertain whether generals such as Guderian, Hoth, and Manstein, or even the commander in chief of the *Wehrmacht*, knew of Stalin's intentions to deprive the German invaders of any possibility of obtaining sustenance from the land. The cost to Soviet civilians was immaterial.

The advance of *Infanterie Regiment 473* took it past Mariampol and the area around Newel towards Welikije Luki. After a 40-km night march, *I Batallion, Infanterie Regiment 473* was loaded onto trucks and transported 20 km further towards the Front. The men were highly suspicious of this development, and the use of such a scarce commodity as motorised transport to move them.

It was in the early morning hours of 27 July when Sturm and his comrades reached their destination and the men jumped down from the trucks with mixed feelings. The regiment had marched for hundreds of kilometres forwards and back, to and fro in the continuing battle against enemy stragglers and partisans. Their own losses were certainly not as high as they would have been had the regiment been at the Front, but had nevertheless been enough to dampen the initial enthusiasm for battle that many had had.

Sturm jumped down from the truck behind *Unteroffizier* van der Kerkhoff, and the various sections of the company quickly formed up. Thick fog obscured their view, but away to the left could be heard the distant sounds of battle. In front of Sturm's battalion, however, all seemed quiet.

3 Company (to which Sturm belonged) was sent into the line to the left of 2 Company, with 1 Company bringing up the rear as the German infantrymen marched off into the heavy mist which lay over the meadow.

Was this to be the real combat action for which they had waited so long?

The men marched off as they had been taught on the training grounds. With the growing daylight, the sun first appeared as a pale yellow disc, before changing into a

Sturm relaxes with a comrade just after the award of the Iron Cross.

fiery red ball. Sturm could not help thinking of the soldier's rhyme, 'Morning red—sooner dead'.

He could make out the houses on the edge of the village of Kikino which was to be their objective. No one could know that they would see almost four weeks of unbroken, hard fighting for this insignificant looking village.

It was assumed that the lead elements of the company would, under cover of the morning fog and without a preliminary softening up bombardment, be able to take the enemy by surprise.

2 Company had almost reached the first of the houses and was ready to make its dash at the enemy when it was surprised by a burst of fire from a Maxim machine gun, which hit the men with devastating effect. All over the meadow, hand grenades began to detonate. The attack was halted, with 2 Company suffering the greatest toll of dead and wounded.

Sturm quickly made ready his machine gun and opened fire. At the head of the first section from 2 Platoon, and with Sandkühler's support, he found a good position behind the edge of a ditch, giving him a good field of fire over the whole edge of the village. A Maxim machine gun positioned in the sauna building just in front of him had caused the greatest losses. Sturm dealt with it swiftly with his machine gun.

Sandkühler pointed out fresh targets, and the other machine guns from 2 and 3 Companies which could still be used joined in, firing at targets indicated to them by Sturm using tracer bullets.

The attack by 1 Company brought a degree of relief to 2 Company's beleaguered troops, but it was clear that the objective of the assault could not now be achieved.

The cries of the wounded began to play on the men's nerves. Medical orderlies gave first aid, and helped by men from 1 Company dragged all the wounded men into cover behind bushes and in gullies before moving them to the rear.

The company commander of 2 Company, *Oberleutnant* Becker, was very seriously wounded. A machine gun bullet had scored a direct hit. He was courageous soldier, and had led his company from the front, just like on training exercises in France, where he had headed the training company with which Sturm and Sandkühler had completed a short training course. The problem was, here the enemy used live ammunition.

Oberleutnant Becker cried, 'Help your company commander!' That help came from *Unteroffizier* Meier, who lay beside Becker having himself sustained a horrendous abdominal wound. The *Unteroffizier* administered the coup de grace to his fatally wounded commander before turning his pistol on himself. The promising career of this brave officer, the son of a general, was over.

The so-called 'surprise attack' had been an unmitigated disaster. The deaths and wounding of so many men on this day were the consequence of a flawed assessment of the situation on the ground. The battle was cruel and one-sided, because the enemy were firing from well established positions in good cover.

The greatest losses were suffered by 2 Company, but 3 and 1 Companies had suffered too. The foolhardy daredevils were much quieter now!

The order to retreat and dig in was given. With entrenching tools the soldiers began to dig and after a short time seemed to have disappeared into the earth. At the onset of nightfall, the darkness gave sufficient cover for the men to improve their dugouts.

The next day, 28 July, passed without incident. Both sides were quiet excluding activity from snipers.

On 29 July, Sturm's platoon was given a special task and during the night was attached to 1 Company, which was preparing for action.

Feldwebel Näckert explained the situation. 'We have been tasked with breaking into the enemy's forward positions. The enemy are around 300 m in front of us, on the edge of the village of Kikino. Armaments are probably one heavy machine gun, three light machine guns, and some rifles. Beyond the area which slopes down from here, there are three crests between us and the enemy. 1 Company will lead the attack. Our heavy company has its weapons zeroed in on the enemy positions.'

'Synchronize watches! It is now 04.30 hours. At 04.40, we go over the first crest. Our mortars and the heavy guns of 13 Company will open fire, and will cease fire again at 04.45.'

The whipping of machine gun fire, the plop, plop of the mortars, and the booming of the guns shattered the stillness of the morning. Then, the attack began.

Sturm and his comrades were ready to make the dash, his machine gun prepared and with a belt of ammunition fitted. He leapt up, ran over the crest and down the slope .The platoon reached the second crest without drawing enemy fire. Two more crests to go and they would be in among the enemy, thought Sturm. The most dangerous part would be the final dash; after that there would be no going back, and the breakthrough would have to be carried on.

Then came the command for the second leg of the dash towards the enemy. Just after they reached the highest point of the next crest, the platoon was hit by Russian machine gun and rifle fire, not from the front—from where it might have been expected—but from the right flank. This unexpected fire came from the nearest positions of the neighbouring regiment. The Russians had infiltrated the positions there during the night and no one had realised what had happened, leaving the assault wave in a perilous position.

The various sections of the platoon threw themselves back over the crest but found they were still coming under direct fire. The screams of the soldiers who had been hit were terrible. Others lay ominously still. Immediately, some of the comrades of the wounded men sprang forward and dragged them into what little cover was available.

Sturm, who with Sandkühler, had been the first to reach the third crest, brought his machine gun swiftly into firing position and let off a burst in the direction of the enemy machine gun which had caused the worst of the casualties. His well aimed shots pinned the enemy down, while his comrades moved into better cover.

Only one of the other three machine guns in the platoon was still in operation and joined in the battle, but it suddenly stopped, its crew presumed hit. The squad leader, *Unteroffizier* van der Kerkhoff, threw himself down behind Sturm, and with the upper part of his body raised pointed towards some Russians who were trying to bring another machine gun into position.

Sturm soon spotted the enemy and fired a burst in their direction, forcing them to crawl back into cover leaving their machine gun, some of them perhaps wounded.

'Men, don't build yourselves a tombstone here!' Sandkühler shouted to the squad leader, still raised enough to make himself an ideal target. But it was too late, enemy machine gun bullets zipped past. Van der Kerkhoff was knocked backwards and almost fell across Sturm and the machine gun. He had been hit in the head and neck and killed instantly. Sturm and his machine gun were splattered with blood and brain tissue from van der Kerkhoff's shattered skull. Sandkühler pushed the NCO's body over to the front of their position, using it as cover from the enemy fire.

Sturm knew he would have to move, for the enemy had obviously spotted him. He made his way along the upper edge of the crest until he found a position with a good field of fire and opened up anew at fresh targets, while Sandkühler brought more cases of ammunition.

Below in the gully, the remnants of the platoon tended the wounded.

By calling out to their comrades, the Germans eventually managed to establish the number of casualties. Thus far, eight were dead and seven wounded, some seriously.

The platoon commander, *Feldwebel* Decker, himself only lightly injured, had had a nervous breakdown. His place was taken by his deputy, *Unteroffizier* Hertel, who now had to take over responsibility for the platoon.

Unteroffizier van der Kerkhoff was dead and *Unteroffizier* Kurz severely wounded.

Only *Unteroffizier* Ückert remained. The two other machine guns in the platoon had fallen silent.

'Good field of fire Hans, but not much cover,' shouted Sandkühler during a brief pause in the firing.

No one gave any further thought to their original objectives. Were they still attainable? Their own heavy weapons had renewed their fire upon the positions they were supposed to have taken. There was only one more crest to go, but because of all the losses, no one had taken it upon themselves to give the order. Neither the remainder of Sturm's company nor any of their neighbours had realised the seriousness of the situation. The enemy's penetration of their open flanks was neither anticipated nor even noticed until it was too late.

The Russian attack had achieved complete surprise and given the Germans no chance. In spite of the firepower available to the platoon, it had been impossible to neutralize the Russian threat. The enemy lay only 200 m or so to the right, but were well established, whereas the Germans had virtually no cover.

Then from the Russian lines came a soft 'plop' sound. 'Mortars!' came the cry. The first salvo arrived, landing between the Germans and their objective. The Russians had anticipated the German intention and were waiting for the attack, having re-sited their heavy weapons to meet the threat.

'We must go back!' called Sturm. 'Where is *Unteroffizier* Ückert, Heinz?'

'Down below in the gully,' growled Sandkühler. 'He is waiting until a mortar shell lands right in there beside him, or the Russians overrun us.'

'Maybe he has been wounded,' suggested Sturm. Grasping the initiative, he called out, 'Everyone listen! We'll move back in short dashes. Each group of three men is to carry one of the wounded, laid on a *Zeltbahn*, one to the front and two at the rear. I have a good position here and will try to keep that machine gun over in the cowshed pinned down. Everyone fire until it's their turn to go. All unused machine gun ammunition to me.'

Unteroffizier Ückert should have taken the initiative in view of the situation. Sturm didn't know what had happened to him, but all the NCOs bar Ückert had been killed or wounded.

'Heinz, you go with the first group and report back to the company commander!'

Sandkühler looked doubtful. He had no wish to leave his friend alone in this perilous situation.

'Go on, move! Leave the spare barrels here!'

Sturm opened fire again, moving his point of aim back and forward between the Sauna and the cowshed. Those men still in position supported him with rifle and machine gun fire. The first group was already back over the crest and clear, and a second group quickly followed.

In the meantime it had grown very hot. The July sun was high in the sky, blazing down unmercifully. The meadow, overgrown with grass, weeds and bushes, shimmered in the heat.

Machine gun bullets forced Sturm to take cover. Seeing that another group was ready to make the dash back, Sturm quickly moved position then opened fire again. The high-pitched zip of the German machine gun, with its breakneck rate of fire, contrasted with the slower rattle of the Russian Maxim.

The group ran back, reached the crest and threw themselves down onto the reverse slope. All of them made it to safety. Two more groups followed and also reached safety.

The sounds of battle died away and left only an oppressive silence. Sturm could hear only faint noise and voices in the distance. A severely wounded comrade cried out as he was laid onto a *Zeltbahn*.

It was a difficult situation. Sturm cursed as he thought about the enemy machine gun on the edge of the village. Nevertheless, he had to give the Russians credit for halting the powerful German assault force.

Suddenly, Sturm sensed movement behind him. It was Sandkühler, crawling towards him with two cases of ammunition.

'What's up Heinz?' asked Sturm.

'*Unteroffizier* Überkert has given a situation report to the company commander.'

There had been no need for Sandkühler to return with this message, but he had not been prepared to leave his friend in the lurch. No words were necessary for this to be understood, a measure of the bond between the two comrades.

Sturm saw a group of Russians moving between the sauna and the cowshed and sent a well aimed burst of fire towards them, forcing them back. At first, two lay still as if hit, while the others slowly crawled back into cover.

Once again, another group appeared ready to make the dash to safety. Was it the rest of his own platoon? Sturm didn't know, but sent another burst of fire at the cowshed and sauna to keep the enemy pinned down. As he did so, the last group sprang up and ran to the rear. One of the men was hit by a single shot and collapsed to the ground. He tried to get up, but couldn't.

'Hans, fire, fire!' cried Sandkühler. From the corner of his eye, Sturm saw his friend run back to help their wounded comrade.

Fire from Sturm's machine gun blasted towards the enemy, but now they too had his position well marked and returned fire. A machine gun bullet hit the stock of Sturm's gun, slamming it against the side of his head and sending him flying backwards. The following bullets flew over his head towards the rear or zipped into the dirt around him. Despite the sound of the enemy gunfire, he heard Sandkühler call to him. Only slowly did the feeling of dizziness subside. He saw Sandkühler, with the severely wounded soldier over his back, make it to the safety of the other side of the ridge.

Sturm shook his head. In front of him lay the bloodied body of *Unteroffizier* van der Kerkhoff, his platoon leader. In the full glare of the blazing sun, a host of flies were making a grizzly meal of his corpse. Nausea overcame Sturm, and his mouth quickly filled with the contents of his stomach. He covered the disfigured body with a *Zeltbahn*. Sandkühler had already removed the paybook and ID tag.

In the gully all was now quiet. No more shots rang out. Despite the stillness, the sunny summer day was deceptive. Away in the distance, the sound of firing from both sides could be heard. Of this little argument in the gully, they knew nothing.

Sturm checked his machine gun. It was still operational, only the stock being damaged. He saw the Russians over yonder, but nothing of any significance seemed to be going on.

He fitted a new belt of ammunition into his machine gun, then took the weapon and crouched down in the gully.

'Is anyone still here? Shout if there is anyone still here,' he called out, keeping his voice down as low as possible. Apart from his dead compatriots and some abandoned weapons and equipment, there was nothing.

So it appeared that he would be the very last who would have to make the sprint to safety. The task he had taken upon himself, to cover the retreat of his comrades, was now over. It was time for him to go.

Cautiously, Sturm slid himself over towards the upper part of the slope. Would the Russians believe that all of the Germans had either been killed or fled, or...? He had to choose a path over the open terrain, one which would have to be as short as possible. Seconds could mean the difference between life and death. That was one lesson he had quickly learnt in the three days in the front lines.

With a bound he was up and running, and already enemy bullets were whirred past him. Instinctively he threw his arms up as if hit, and fell to the ground. His machine gun held tight to his body, he rolled sideways and slid into a depression in the ground. The enemy fire flew harmlessly over his head towards the rear.

Sturm was now more frightened than he had ever been before. A splitting headache and raging thirst tormented him. The Russians would assume that he had at least been severely wounded, but would they come after him?

He slid himself along the ground, the sight of so many dead Germans making him shudder. Sturm forced himself to calm down and think. He had not the courage to try another dash up and over the crest of the ridge. Further to the left, however, was a drainage ditch which he could perhaps use to reach safety. But to reach the ditch he would first of all have to expose himself to enemy fire. He pushed himself along through the tall grass. Insects buzzed around, flies pestered him. Soaked in sweat, he slowly forced himself along. The machine gun was a hindrance but he wouldn't leave it behind and, lengthening the carrying strap, he dragged it along behind him.

After minutes which seemed like hours, he reached the drainage ditch.

Centimetre by centimetre, he worked his way along. His movements felt as heavy as lead and thirst crazed him. Eventually, he reached the crest and stopped. He was totally exhausted and unable to move a centimetre further. Then he sensed someone's approach and quickly pulled the machine gun to himself, before recognizing a German steel helmet. It was Sandkühler, with two other comrades. Sturm was overwhelmed with relief. He tried to smile but could manage only a grimace through his dried and cracked lips.

'Man, Hans, we were on our way to fetch you!' Sandkühler took the machine gun from him while the others helped him up and offered him a bottle of water. This small drink worked wonders, and Sturm felt the tension ease from his body. Safe at last, he followed Sandkühler to the company commander.

'*Schütze* Sturm, reporting back from the assault group.'

'Thank you Sturm. *Unteroffizier* Ückert had told me that it is thanks mainly to you that the Russians did not inflict even greater losses.'

After reporting back, Sturm had the chance to lie down. The excitement and strain of the foregoing hours ebbed away only slowly. He couldn't eat or drink, and managed only a restless sleep.

Next morning, Sturm was awoken by Sandkühler.

'Hey, wake up—congratulations!'

Confused, Sturm came to from his slumber. 'What do you want, what is it?'

Heinz said nothing, but handed him his water flask, relishing the look of bafflement on Sturm's face.

'Man, it's your birthday! Had you completely forgotten in all the commotion?'

Now the penny dropped. He thanked Sandkühler, and both took a long slug.

'Who gave you this wonderful stuff?'

Heinz grinned. 'The cook had four bottles of it in his kitchen locker—I relieved him of three.'

'That was a good move,' nodded Sturm.

'Ach, these fat cats always have a private reserve,' he replied laconically. 'They hadn't used it and it will do us good.'

Obergefreiter König, their new squad leader, jumped into their foxhole.

'What's going on here? The place stinks of alcohol!'

'It's Hans's birthday,' said Heinz, and offered König the bottle.

'Congratulations Hans. You were born in 1920? Of course, our youngster is twenty-one and all grown up now!'

'Cheers Georg,' answered Sturm. 'But this is one 29th of July I would rather be spending at home!'

Georg nearly choked on his drink. 'Did you say 29th July? Today is the 30th!'

'Ach, dear God,' gulped Heinz. 'And you already had such a great time celebrating yesterday!'

5

The Iron Cross

For the whole of 30 July 1941, *Infanterie Regiment 473* was on stand-to. After the front was straightened out from the German side, the Russians found themselves holding Kikino, having successfully defended the eastern and north-eastern edges of the village in the previous few days. Elements of the neighbouring regiments were moved and dug themselves in a few hundred metres further to the south-west. Patrols were mounted by units of *Infanterie Regiment 473*.

Russian units which had broken through were engaged behind the front lines and either captured or destroyed. The quickly mounted counter-attacks saw several enemy units cut off in *Infanterie Regiment 473's* rear. The German transport and supply units had these enemy troops to contend with, and suffered a number of dead and wounded.

The entire night of 31 July was punctuated with the sound of small arms fire.

Here, around Welikije Luki, the enemy had dug himself in and was determined to stop the German advance at last. It seemed as if he might actually succeed. What the Russians and the German Infantry lying on the outskirts of Kikino did not know was that German panzer units to the left and right of the Russian defence lines around Welikije Luki were simply by-passing them, in a move to encircle the enemy by a massive pincer movement.

On the night of 1 August, Sturm and his comrades lay in their foxholes which they had set about improving and strengthening in the heat of the preceding day. Well aimed single shots fired by the Russians at each apparent mound of freshly turned earth or careless gesture showed that the enemy were as watchful as ever. The most dangerous of all was mortar fire which slammed down here and there along the front line, intended simply as nuisance which would prevent the Germans getting any sort of rest.

Sturm and Sandkühler got very little sleep, although they relieved each other of duty on the machine gun. At this time of year it only became dark late in the evening. Any hopes of a night's rest were dispelled by the appearance of the company commander, *Oberleutnant* Bauer, who arrived with the platoon commander at 23.30 hours.

'Get yourselves ready! The company is moving to new positions, further to the right, about 400 m from Kikino.'

As Bauer went off to brief the next platoon, *Oberfeldwebel* Winter called all the squad leaders to him. Five minutes later, König returned.

'Grab your weapons and equipment. No unnecessary noise. Communicate by hand signals or whispers only!'

Sturm grabbed his machine gun, the last spare barrel holder, and a box of ammunition. In single-file the squad moved cautiously rearwards, then towards the right and onwards in the direction of Kikino. Whispers could be heard, then the clinking of metal against metal, prompting soft curses.

In the darkness a figure appeared before them. He was one of the troops they had come to relieve and who had come to guide them to their new positions.

'König's squad?' he asked.

'Yes, the King and his retinue,' growled the squad leader.[1]

'Follow me, but don't make a sound, the Russians can hear a flea cough!'

Sturm and Sandkühler reached an exposed spot where their guide pointed out a spot for their machine gun.

'The squad must set up positions towards the right, here.' Then he disappeared into the darkness.

Hans and Heinz settled themselves into their position after digging it a little deeper. Recesses had to be dug in the sides of the dugout for their ammunitions boxes, hand grenades, and machine gun pouches, none of which had been done by the previous occupants.

'I'm sick of this stupid digging,' Heinz grumbled. 'You've hardly got the time to dig in at one spot before you get moved to another. We've been crawling around this village for five days already.'

'Calm down Heinz, better digging in one time too often than one time too few, otherwise you're a long time dead.'

Sturm set about digging, but Sandkühler took the spade from him. 'You keep look out, Hans.'

His misery was understandable. Since 27 July, the regiment had lain in front of Welikije Luki, constrained to static warfare and with little opportunity for rest. The front was in a perpetual state of flux, yet nothing much seemed to be achieved.

The summer night of 1 August was short. Heinz had worked hard and at last their position was finished and well concealed with large pieces of turf. Heinz was dog-tired. Sturm took the first watch despite his own exhaustion. Their construction efforts had been encouraged by the appearance of great thunderclouds above them, driven by strong winds.

Directly above Kikino, Sturm could make out the Pole Star. At mid-day, he calculated, he would have the sun to his back. That was something, for the enemy would be blinded if they attacked.

It grew lighter. Heinz should have taken over the watch, but Sturm let him sleep on. Their position lay on the left spur of a crest which sloped upwards towards the right. To the front and to the rear the ground fell away in a gradual slope, and to the left quite steeply to where 1 Platoon were located. The weapons of 1 Platoon would have little effect in this dead ground, and the same would apply to Sturm and his machine gun. Mines and barbed wire would have to be set out down there after dark, it occurred to him.

In the early morning mist, Sturm could make out a large meadow in front of his position. There were several gullies which would offer good cover to any attackers.

His was a fortuitous position in that it had an ideal field of fire, but as it lay on the highest point on the ridge, it would also be conspicuous in daylight. Sturm would stick out like a sore thumb once he opened fire.

Sturm looked towards the right. He could see the mounds of freshly turned earth where the others in his platoon had dug themselves in. Still further to the right, near 3 Platoon, someone crawled out of his dugout. Did the damned fool want to pick flowers for his grave? A shot rang out from the village, and with a leap the imprudent soldier disappeared.

Sturm knew that, after the sound of a shot, it was usually too late to help. The bullet travels faster than the sound.

With binoculars, he surveyed the village of Kikino. It was well marked with battle scars from previous engagements. Some houses were burned or shell-damaged. Saunas and cowsheds were raised to the ground. Of the Russians there was nothing to be seen. Nevertheless, occasional shots rang out from the village.

The less than effectively camouflaged German positions were as obvious as a thorn in the eye to the Russians. Sturm crouched lower—perhaps his position had already been spotted.

Despite the rising sun, it was still quite cool. Half asleep, Sandkühler crawled out from under his *Zeltbahn*. 'What! Four o'clock already! Why didn't you wake me up to take over watch?'

'Because I love the sound of your snoring so much. Now you can take over watch.'

'I will, but lend me your mirror first.'

'What do you want a mirror for? I can tell you what you look like—absolutely filthy and depraved!' Neither had washed or shaved for several days.

Heinz took the mirror. 'If my girlfriend could see me now, she would run away in terror,' he said with a grimace. 'Man. man, what have they done to us?'

Sturm didn't bother asking which girlfriend he meant, Heinz had so many. He had given Sturm a photo of one of them saying, 'Hans, you are my best friend. I can confide in you. Write her a nice letter for me. She is a lovely girl, but she won't let me go to the football match.'

Yawning, he took the binoculars from Sturm. 'Now, what's going on?'

'I suggest you get a grip of yourself. Give yourself a shake and waken up!' said Sturm. 'And be careful, the Russians are firing at all the new positions!'

'It'll be okay, now off you go.'

Afterwards, Sturm gave some thought to the situation and reckoned they would have to dig themselves a new position. This foxhole was good for fighting at night, but during daylight it was far too dangerous. 'You must be crazy,' he complained to no one in particular. 'Maybe by tomorrow we will be over to the other side of the village.'

Heinz stood up and stretched himself. In one hand he held the binoculars and with the other he scratched his head. Another shot rang out from the village.

'Did you hear that Heinz? I told you!' Hans scolded Heinz, and then curled up and covered himself with the *Zeltbahn.*

'Damn it. And what if I did hear it? Shit. Anyway, it's only a scratch.'

Sturm shot out from under the *Zeltbahn.* Heinz squatted there, holding his left hand.

'You bloody fool, didn't I warn you!' yelled Sturm.

He looked at the wound. The bullet had only grazed the top of the hand and there wasn't much blood. Sandkühler could still move his fingers freely.

'You're acting like a raw recruit. What were you waving your hands around at the enemy for?'

'Stop bleating and lighten up. If it was a choice of being hit in the hand or the head, I'd rather it was the hand,' Sandkühler said licking at his wound. 'Give me a dressing. That will sort it out and then everything will be fine.'

'It will only be fine once the doctor has given you a tetanus shot,' said Sturm, bandaging the hand. 'As soon as it gets dark, you go to the rear.'

Sturm scanned the landscape. Shortly afterwards, Sandkühler leapt out of the foxhole. No one fired. Within a few metres of the foxhole he was back into cover. Sturm heard him speak to the squad leader.

'Hans,' called out *Obergefreiter* König. 'I'll send Kronenberger over.'

Alfons Kronenberger was Number 3 on the machine gun team.

'No Georg,' called back Sturm. 'It's too dangerous now—perhaps later.'

That was a big mistake. A machine gun position must have at least two soldiers manning it at all times.

The sun rose ever higher in the skies behind Sturm. Against its glare, the Russians couldn't see the German positions so clearly. From time to time he looked cautiously over the area in front of the village. He was dog-tired but daren't sleep. He was sure Sandkühler would return, but by nightfall there was still no sign of him.

To keep himself awake, Sturm checked and re-checked all the components of his machine gun, the ammunition belt, and the ammunition in the boxes. The bullets glittered in the sunshine—a dangerous yet, for him, soporific sheen. His hand grenades lay ready to throw with their primer caps unscrewed. The machine gun was ready and could cover a wide field of fire.

The heat grew ever greater, and the metal parts of his weapon seemed to glow. No fire could be heard throughout the whole sector, and for this brief respite Sturm was grateful. After the heavy fighting of the last few days both sides needed at least one short spell of rest. Sturm found it harder than ever to keep his eyes open, and his head sank lower into the crook of his arm. He wondered what could have happened to Heinz. Certainly by now he should have been back from the medical officer. Little did Sturm know that Sandkühler was already on his way westwards, being evacuated from the Front in an ambulance.

The heat was becoming unbearable. His eyes hurt from a combination of the searingly bright light and of his utter exhaustion. He had a blinding headache and simply couldn't take any more.

Sturm understood from calls from the squad leader that he should take a rest. Georg König promised to keep watch for him. Sturm withdrew into his dugout and covered himself with his *Zeltbahn.*

How long his eyes had been closed, he could not tell. This was no natural sleep. It was almost as if he had been anaesthetised; no doubt an effect of the stress of the preceding five days. He suddenly found himself in a dreadful dream, he was being attacked by the Russians. His machine gun fire ripped through the oncoming enemy, but they would not fall and kept coming closer and closer, growing larger with each step.

The detonation of a hand grenade brought Sturm back to consciousness with a yelp. The tiredness evaporated in an instant. The roaring and cracking of small arms fire shattered the stillness of the afternoon.

Sturm threw himself behind his machine gun, cocked it, and fired off the whole of the first belt of ammunition at random, before he had even begun to gather his senses or grasp what was happening. Then he saw the Russians. The foremost group was only around 80 m from the German positions. He had soon expended a full box of ammunition, then drew the machine gun back to fit another belt.

Sturm noted that the sudden entrance of his machine gun into the fray had made a devastating impact on the enemy. Whether wounded by his bullets or simply in a state of terror, all of the Russians within his field of fire lay still on the ground. Some then tried to crawl backwards towards their own lines, only to be met by others still trying to crawl forward. The ground offered little cover, and the brown flecks began to come closer again, using the bodies of their fallen comrades for cover.

The assault had only been temporarily halted, not wiped out. Sturm cautiously stood higher in his foxhole to get a better view. His estimation was that the Russians were in at least company strength. A group of the brown uniformed enemy were tried to advance, rushing forward in short dashes. The assault seemed aimed principally at 2 Platoon, where the Russians had detected a weak point in the German lines.

Machine guns chattered and rifle shots cracked out all long the front line.

'Urrah! Urrah!' Along the width of the entire sector, Russian troops leapt up and charged. Over their heads flew mortar shells from the German lines, some landing in their midst and ripping them asunder.

Sturm desperately wanted to squeeze the trigger so tightly that it would break, but he forced himself to hold his fire so as not to betray his position, hoping to achieve the same success as he had against the preceding assault wave. He had no alternative position to move to and was stuck in this damned hole in the ground, with his body exposed from the shoulder upwards.

He began to experience the first feelings of panic as he saw, away off to the right, some of his comrades from 2 Platoon abandon their positions and retreat. What was up? Had a retreat been ordered? Maybe he should go too…?

His calls to the squad leader brought no response.

The detonations of the German mortars continued. Shrapnel sporadically slammed into the ground around him. The Russian mortars had joined in too.

Now the Russians immediately in front of him leapt up, determined to make a breakthrough. They were almost upon him.

Rattattattattattat. Sturm took the enemy completely by surprise, sweeping the machine gun from right to left.

'Damn it,' yelled Sturm as the thing jammed. He would need to change the barrel. Feverishly he went through the drill he had gone through a thousand times before. Just a few seconds could be decisive. He scalded his fingers on the barrel's hot metal as he removed it from the gun and tossed it behind him into the foxhole.

Whoom! Hand grenades exploded nearby.

Finished! Ready to fire! Sturm brought his machine gun back into position and fired at the nearest Russian, who immediately responded by throwing a hand grenade which landed right in front of Sturm among the pile of his machine gun's empty shell cases. Sturm swiftly grabbed it and threw it back at the Russian.

A Russian storming up towards Sturm was hurled backwards by the explosion. He was dead before he hit the ground, but another quickly took his place.

Sturm fired off the entire box of ammunition and reached for a fresh one. Before he could fit a new belt into the breech of his machine gun, another Russian appeared. He had fallen alongside the one who had thrown the grenade and had feigned death. Now he sprang up and ran directly towards Sturm.

Sturm tried to reach his machine pistol, which lay just a metre behind him. But he had no time to reach it, so he raised his machine gun high to ram the charging Russian. In that instant a shot rang out. Sturm heard it clearly through the surrounding noise. The Russian dropped to the ground in front of him. A bullet fired by one of Sturm's comrades had hit him as he leapt at Sturm.

Swiftly, he fitted the new belt of ammunition and opened fire again. The Russians were being more cautious now, advancing only either one by one or in small groups. Russian reinforcements were coming from the village and attacking along the whole length of the ridge.

Sturm noticed a small cluster making their way forward towards the gully to his left. He fired on them, but once again his gun jammed. This time it was the extractor pin. He changed the lock and the barrel, but vital seconds were being wasted. To his left a hand grenade exploded and shrapnel swept along the parapet of his foxhole. He heard the enemy's cries of 'Urrah' coming from that direction.

At last his weapon was ready for action again. As Sturm stood and prepared to fire, he saw the first Red Army soldier to reach the gully. Only a few metres more and he would be out of Sturm's field of fire. Sturm raised himself even higher, his feet in the recesses cut into the walls of the foxhole for the ammunition boxes. He raised the machine gun high, swung it round towards the enemy, and fired off a long burst from the hip. He had now exposed the whole of his upper body to enemy fire.

From the rear, two more German machine guns joined in. This was too much for the Russians, who had already suffered serious losses. Some let their weapons fall and raised their hands in surrender. Others ran back towards their own lines, shooting as they went. Many of the fleeing Russians were killed as they retreated, and still shots rang out from Kikino.

It seemed it was all over, and Sturm felt like simply letting himself fall back into the foxhole as the adrenaline rush of battle began to subside—but abruptly he felt a sharp impact against his left arm. He let the machine gun fall and drooped back into the foxhole. He could move his arm without pain, then saw that a bullet had hit his wristwatch and destroyed the casing. The watch was kaput, but his arm was unharmed. Fortune had smiled on Sturm once more.

Relieved, he exhaled slowly. He was about to pick up his machine gun when someone jumped into the foxhole behind him. Sturm whirled around. His fist lashed out and smashed into the stomach of none other than König!

'Hey, are you quite finished?' groaned the squad leader.

'I thought it was an Ivan.'

'I thought you were badly wounded, the way you dropped back into the foxhole.' König looked over its edge towards Kikino. 'The Russians have disappeared. They have had a nose full. What was wrong with you?'

'Here look, my watch is ready for the bucket. It was just a grazing shot—but the Russian there nearly finished me off,' said Sturm, pointing to the corpse just in front of his foxhole.

'Then I stopped him with a direct hit,' grinned Georg.

'Thanks,' said Sturm, and gave the squad leader his hand.

Sturm saw that his comrades from 2 and 3 Platoons were returning to their dugouts. It had become noticeably quiet. No shots were fired from either side. This pause lasted around an hour, and was unique among the Germans' experiences so far. They were able to move around safely outside their foxholes, and the Russians medics were able to come right up in front of the German positions and retrieve their dead and wounded.

Sturm checked his weapon and ammunition. The squad leader, who had already left, returned bringing Alfons Berg with him. He had been Number 3 on the gun and was now to be Number 2. Both of them were carrying boxes of ammunition. Sturm gave his new partner the defective lock and the barrel with the ejector pin to take to the armourer NCO.

'Hans, answer me one question,' enquired Georg. 'What was up with you, when the Russians attacked?'

'Nothing was wrong, I fired.'

'Fired? Man, don't be stupid. The Russians had almost overrun us. How could you wait so long before opening fire?'

'Calm yourself, Georg. I didn't wait at all, I opened fire as soon as I woke up.'

Georg looked at him quizzically. He waggled his finger in his right ear. 'Am I hearing you right? Say that again, please!'

'You heard right. I only really woke up after a hand grenade detonated just beside me and the first bullets were already leaving my gun. The Russians were already so close.'

'So our youngster really wasn't awake. Well, I suspected as much my dear Hans,' George grinned. 'It was me who threw the hand grenade beside your foxhole as an emergency alarm call, so to speak. Rattle your shutters.'

'Many thanks, my dear "alarm call", but my mother has pleasanter ways of waking me up.'

'Your mother would have clipped you round the ear if she had seen what you did. You never even put your steel helmet on.'

Actually, Sturm's steel helmet still lay in the corner. He had been using it as a pillow and in the heat of the moment had forgotten to put in on. He picked it up, then put it down again and sat on it. He realised how very fortunate he had been.

Georg had been watching Hans. 'The shock of it all will catch up with you later. Alfons can take over watch—I don't think we will be seeing Heinz for some time.'

'Why not? He only took van der Kerkhoff's pistol. You know Georg, I can't get used to the fact that Heinz—'

'Ach, don't be so selfish! If you are really his friend, be happy that he is out of all this shit—give me your things.'

The squad leader emerged slowly from the foxhole and said, 'It looks like the fighting is over, for today at least.'

Without haste he moved off to the rear, as Alfons reappeared with the machine gun barrel. No Russians fired.

The losses on the German side were small compared to the Russians'. In Sturm's squad, only one was seriously wounded and two lightly wounded, or so Georg had said. In 2 and 3 Platoon, casualties had been greater.

A hand grenade had landed right inside the machine gun post of 5 Squad, instantly killing both the machine-gunners. Eichler, Number 1 on 6 Squad's machine gun, was seriously injured. Sturm thought back to the comrades he had seen retreating—it must have been because of the casualties.

Sturm discussed the situation with the machine gun posts with Alfons Berg. 'We must dig new positions on the reverse side of the slope for use during the day, and only use those on the crest at night.'

Alfons took up a spade right away and started to dig at the spot chosen by Sturm. Alfons was a student of theology. His hair was red, and his face would go red too if anyone told a crude joke. Little by little, the senseless teasing had faded. The men had respect for him. Everyone had found that Alfons, although of frail appearance, could work as if he had the strength of a bull.

Martin, from the company HQ Squad, jumped into the foxhole with a summons: 'Hans, you have to come to the company commander right away.'

'Me, to the old man? Have you any idea what it's all about?'

'No, but the battalion commander is with the boss. He has specifically asked for you.'

'The battalion commander has asked for me? You're joking!'

Sturm took his steel helmet and set it properly on his head. 'I think the extractor claw on the machine gun lock was broken. Maybe I can bring it back with me.'

He nodded to Alfons and Georg, who had joined them by this point, and left the dugout. Sturm reported to the platoon commander, *Oberfeldwebel* Winter, who told him he thought that the only thing the battalion commander would want to see him about was the Russian attack.

It was certainly unusual for them to have summoned a machine-gunner from his post. Thinking of his machine gun, he cursed to himself. Had they noticed how late he was in opening fire?

Sturm made his way along the ridge to the company command post. Looking back he could see Alfons behind his machine gun. Georg waved to him.

From this vantage point above the action, the Russian attack and the German defence must have appeared a diverting yet gruesome training exercise in the sandbox. (Theoretical training exercises were held based on scale models of the terrain fashioned from clay or sand in a wooden frame—the 'sandbox'.)

Looks like trouble, thought Hans, as he arrived at the company commander's post. It was very busy there. A group of pioneers was building a bunker. That implied a long stay. Sturm saw the armourer NCO and asked him about the machine gun lock.

'You can take it with you when you go back, as well as a case of tracer ammunition.'

Nearby stood the company commander, *Oberleutnant* Bauer, and the battalion commander, *Hauptmann* Dreier.

Sturm reported to the Bauer: '*Schütze* Sturm, reporting as ordered!'

'So you are *Schütze* Sturm,' answered the *Hauptmann*. 'How old are you, and what is your trade?'

'Twenty-one years old, *Herr Hauptmann*. I was still at school, learning to be an engineer.'

Dreier nodded and looked at Bauer. Both officers examined Sturm in silence. Then the battalion commander gave the company commander a signal.

'*Schütze* Sturm, give us a report on how the attack and the defence went, from your own point of view.'

'Sturm had anticipated this question. He hesitated for a second. Should he tell the truth or not? Then he began: 'Shortly before twelve o'clock, the Russians attacked in the sectors held by 2 and 3 Platoons in reinforced company strength. I opened fire on the enemy at short range and, supported by my section, kept firing until the attack was beaten off.'

'That was a clear, concise report, *Schütze* Sturm.' The commander offered Sturm his hand. 'Thank you for your gallant action. I could see you clearly from up here during the decisive moments.'

Happy that the moment of danger was past and the thorny question of his late entry to the fray averted, Sturm blurted out before he could stop himself, 'The heavy machine gun returned fire just in time, otherwise the Russian breakthrough would have succeeded.'

'The gully down there will be secured by the pioneers by this evening.'

At this point, a battalion runner arrived. He delivered a signal, together with a small brown packet. 'Signal from regiment, *Herr Hauptmann*.'

Dreier took the signal, gave it to Bauer, and looked at Sturm.

'*Schütze* Sturm, three days ago, you were recommended for the Iron Cross Second Class for your gallant behaviour with the unsuccessful assault group. Today, I am recommending you for the Iron Cross First Class.'

He took the signal back, and said, 'Listen up everyone! I want to thank *Schütze* Sturm, in the name of the regiment, for his gallant behaviour on 29 July 1941, and wish him continued soldier's good fortune. *Oberst* Schütz, Regimental Commander.'

After reading out the signal, *Hauptmann* Dreier took from the little brown packet an Iron Cross Second Class and fastened the ribbon into the buttonhole of Sturm's tunic.

Still overwhelmed, Sturm thought, why was I worrying myself about the delay in firing? The decoration now glittered against his chest.

'*Schütze* Sturm,' interrupted the battalion commander after some deliberation, 'I will give you my own Iron Cross First Class to wear, until you receive your own.'

With this, he pinned the award which he had won during the French campaign, onto Sturm's tunic. 'In consideration of this day, which has been particularly significant not just for you, I want to express my thanks to all those who fell, or were wounded.' With this he shook Sturm's hand once again.

Sturm didn't know what to say, everything had happened so quickly. Congratulations sounded from the company commander and all those present. Felix, the company runner, appeared with a glass of Schnapps in his hand and gave it to Sturm, though he did not fail to look at *Oberleutnant* Bauer and ask, 'Is it permitted, *Herr Hauptmann*?'

Bauer nodded, chuckling and grinning at Sturm. 'So that the hero can keep his strength up!'

Relieved laughter all round encouraged Sturm to examine at his chest. The Iron Cross Second Class hung from his buttonhole, and the First Class glittered on his left breast pocket. It was no dream.

'*Schütze* Sturm, the entry of your machine gun into the action came very late,' *Hauptmann* Dreier said to Sturm. 'We thought you had been injured.'

This remark swept over Sturm like a cold shower. He froze rigid. Should he now tell the truth of what had really happened?

'I ... I was late in noticing the Russian attack, *Herr Hauptmann*.'

What do you mean by that?' The question was reflected in the curious expressions on everyone's faces.

'In the early morning, my Number 2, Heinz Sandkühler, was lightly wounded on the hand. First of all, I believed that he would return after a simple tetanus shot. I remained on watch, although I had had no rest in over 30 hours. By midday, I could hardly keep my eyes open. I informed the section leader and he promised to keep watch for me. When the Russians attacked, I was asleep. Then the section leader threw a hand—I mean he woke me up."

Fortunately, Sturm had stopped himself before mentioning the hand grenade 'alarm clock'.

The *Hauptmann* looked from Sturm to the company commander. 'What the devil!!? … you…!? Man, Man!' he roared. 'The machine gun post must always be manned by at least two! Well, we all hope that in future you will always manage to wake up at the right moment. You can go back to your post.'

'*Jawohl, Herr Hauptmann*!' said Sturm, thankful to be on his way.

On the way back to the armourer, he met Felix again.

'Tell me Hans, couldn't you have just given an excuse—the gun had jammed, for instance? The battalion commander had barely calmed down after his speech about your awards and then you come out with the story about your "sleeping sickness".'

'I don't understand,' was Sturm's answer.

'You should have heard him just now, tearing a strip off *Feldwebel* Kionke and *Oberfeldwebel* Winter.'

'Why?'

'Why, man? Didn't you see, that a lot of the guys over by 3 Platoon and your own 2 Platoon had bolted when it seemed the Russians would break through? The battalion commander had seen it all because he was up here at the company command post to find out what was happening, with all that machine-gun fire and hand grenades going off!'

'No, I had enough on my own plate to think about. Besides, I thought they were just following an order for them to pull back.'

'I wish I could be as cool as you,' said Felix. 'Why didn't you get out as well then? The 5th section in your platoon bolted first, as if the machine gun crew had been killed by a direct hit. *Hauptmann* Dreier went absolutely crazy when the attack wasn't an immediate success. I've never seen him in such a fury. All that was missing was for him to try to hold the front line by himself with nothing but his pistol.'

'You are mad, Felix! With a pistol?'

'Hans, don't I know it? You couldn't see as much of the whole picture as I could. We should be grateful if an official report isn't made about this.'

'Who would be the judge?' asked Sturm. 'That was the first time that the company had experienced a massed attack from the Russians. The losses and the stress over the last five days has played on everyone's nerves.'

'Maybe, Hans, but you could cope with it.' Felix dug in his pocket and pulled out a roll of sweets. 'Here, Hans, a gift for you.' He turned, shaking his head, and walked off.

Sturm's gun parts and ammunition were ready for him to collect, and handing them over, the armourer NCO added his own congratulations.

As Sturm got back to his own position, *Oberfeldwebel* Winter and some others were working on the dugout. They stopped their digging and came to offer their felicitations. He tried to answer all their questions.

Just in front of his foxhole, he met the section commander. He had almost finished the new foxhole on the reverse side of the slope, which would meet the requirements of the situation much better. He grabbed Hans with both hands and hugged him.

'Man, Hans! What a surprise! Congratulations!'

'Now then, what's that that's sparkling so?' called Alfons, his head appearing over the parapet of the foxhole. 'Now that lot over there will have something to aim at. He sleeps through half the attack and gets the Iron Cross First Class for it!'

'*Hauptmann Dreier* has only loaned me this Iron Cross until mine is approved. Maybe he'll get into trouble, because only the divisional commander can authorize this award.'

Georg saw that Hans was undoing the Iron Cross Second Class ribbon from his button hole. 'Leave it where it is,' he called out. 'You can only remove it after the first twenty four hours!'[2]

Sturm removed the Iron Cross, popped it into his pocket, and retied the ribbon into his buttonhole, riposting, 'You can keep your humour to yourself Georg, I'm not in the mood for it—the Commander knows I slept through the first attack.'

'What did you say?—how does he know?'

'I told him, but he had already pinned on my decorations. By coincidence he happened to be at the command post when the circus began. He said he thought I was late in joining in the fight. They thought it was some sort of special tactic I was using.'

'Tactics, schmactics. What does it matter? The Russians were beaten, that's the main thing! Why did you tell him? I covered for you and woke you up!'

'I said nothing about your "alarm call", but I did say that the section and especially you played a decisive part.'

'Very kind of you, Hansi.'

'No, I don't think so, because I'm worried that the old man might punish you because the machine gun wasn't manned by two.'

'Well, I was ready to spring into your foxhole and help, but your quick action meant that I didn't have to.'

'Well, if there is no punishment, there is always a chance—,' Hans saw Georg look at him, 'that the old man has recommended you for promotion to *Unteroffizier*, and for the award of the Iron Cross Second Class in recognition of the achievements of the section.'

Georg was obviously taken aback. 'To hell with decorations. My mother had some of my father's medals in a drawer. He was so proud of them. Shortly before the end of the war he was shot by fifth columnists. My mother wanted to throw his medals in the dustbin. Only her love and respect for my father stopped her. She was pregnant when she got the bad news. She had it tough, looking after herself and five kids. She had four boys and a girl to raise. At 8 years old, I was the oldest. Maybe you can understand how I learnt to hate war and everything to do with it.'

Georg had never said so much about himself before. Sturm gave him his hand. 'Forgive me Georg, I didn't mean to hurt or offend you,' he said. 'Your Hansi is still just a boy.'

'Well be happy then, digging won't be so hard on you. Alfons has blisters on his hands already. We must get these positions dug, and I have to go to the toilet!'

Hans took the spade and started to dig the next layer. His mind was on Georg. The big, quiet man was a good comrade, and such a solid character that he inspired confidence in people who had only just met him. He was held in great affection by the whole company.

His dislike of the Communists was well known. Labour service and military service up to 1939 had seen him ripe for wartime action. Poland, France, Russia. He had, as he had clearly expressed, already had a bellyfull of it. To him, being an *Obergefreiter* meant only one thing—extra pay. In 1940, he had forfeited a promotion to *Unteroffizier* in the aftermath of a crazy drinking session.

In civilian life, Georg was a smith. To him, military service was a troublesome necessity which he wanted to put behind him as quickly as possible. Six years of service had already gone by. In his opinion, these were lost years.

After their unsuccessful attack on 1 August 1941, the Russians appeared to have had a rough time of it. They withdrew back into Kikino, and for several weeks made no new attempts to launch any further attacks. The Germans contented themselves with consolidating their positions.

The front appeared paralysed in this sector of Welikije Luki, with only light recce units from either side seeing any action. Only careless exposure provoked shots from the other side.

Sturm brought his machine gun into position in a gap on the crest of the ridge. During daylight hours he had built a good position on the reverse slope, which gave him the advantage of the enemy being unable to see his position. The land to the front was well covered by the machine guns of the other sections. Only mortars posed any real danger. Heavy artillery pieces, meanwhile, sought their important targets in the hinterland, so Sturm and his comrades were rarely in any danger. When they heard the artillery fire, however, they instinctively ducked—one never knew. In due course, everyone developed an ear for where 'luggage' was fired from and at what the deadly freight was aimed.

6

The Battle Continues

For many weeks the situation remained peaceful. There was little shooting. The troops became tanned in the warm summer weather. Letters, newspapers, and embellished radio reports informed them of what was happening in the great, wide world, especially here in Russia, which they loved and admired so much.... The fighting was carried forward with great diligence and effort, not only in this sector of the Front.

In Sturm's company, only a few still had any lust for battle. The flame of enthusiasm from the first days of the campaign now flickered only faintly.

Alfons Berg delivered the post. 'Here Hans, it's from Sandkühler. He is with the replacement troops in Aachen, waiting until we have taken this damned village!'

Hans read the few lines and laughed to himself. Seeing the eager expressions on the faces of those around him, he read out loud: 'Here with the replacement crowd, I have received the Iron Cross Second Class and the Wound Badge. Coming soon. Will help you clear out that louse's nest you've been hanging around outside for the last three weeks!'

'Is it three weeks already?' asked one of the section leaders.

Georg drew on his pipe. He was trying to solve a crossword puzzle.

'Today is the 21 of August boys. You know we're going for it early tomorrow morning. There is nothing left for our gallant Heinz Sandkühler to do.'

König puffed a thick cloud of smoke from his pipe. Then he noticed Alfons.

'You have studied. Tell me, what would this be? Five letters, starts with 'W' and ends with 'H', tells the time.' He winked at his comrades.

'Ah, that's too difficult,' groaned Alfons.

Whoosh, crump! Whoosh, crump! Instinctively the men ducked down, as two mortar shells flew over their heads and crashed to the ground somewhere to the rear.

The Russian harassing fire achieved its intended aim of making sure the Germans could never fully relax.

'If we make a feint attack on Kikino tomorrow, the enemy will take a real hammering, from all our available heavy weapons. I wouldn't like to be in their shoes!' said Georg, and tapped out his pipe.

'Feint attack! Rubbish! What could our four infantry and two pioneer sections achieve?' Sturm shook his head. 'That would be a suicide mission!'

'Tactics lad, tactics! The main attack will come from the north.'

The section leader went off to the platoon commander for a briefing. The six sections lay ready on the reverse slope. It wasn't light yet. Kikino and the land around it lay in the morning haze which would soon be burned back by the rising sun. The outline of the village slowly became visible. Nearby sat the fence which led down into the area—almost certainly mined—which was the objective of König's squad. Fifty metres beyond it lay a well concealed machine gun position. After a weeks' careful observation, the locations of the enemy weapons had been detected. This knowledge made the dangers only too clear.

'How late is it, Georg?'

'Ten minutes to four, Hans. Now we must—'

Suddenly the fire from the heavy 10.5-cm infantry cannon began. The heavy bombardment made the earth shake. Heavy machine guns sent streams of tracer fire soaring over the heads of the men. At 04.20 hours, the 5-cm and 8-cm mortars joined in. This was the squad's signal to attack.

'Man, they are firing smoke shells! Great!'

'Go!'

Swiftly yet without undue haste, the soldiers slipped from their positions. In a wide chain they moved towards the village, each squad with its own objective. The artificial smoke drifted like a shimmering wall before the settlement, eliminating the enemy's visibility.

But the Russians, in spite of being bombarded by the concentration of German heavy weapons, responded to the attack with rifle and machine gun fire, even if they could only guess as to where the Germans were. Worse for Sturm and his comrades were the detonations of their own mortars, which forced them to move more speedily. The pioneers cut through the enemy barbed wire and cleared paths through the minefield.

'Charge!' sounded out all along the line. Hand grenades were thrown, and detonated. The heavy weapons ceased firing.

Sturm dashed forwards and fired at the enemy muzzle flashes. The enemy fire ceased, or at least lessened. Some of the leading men were hit and fell to the ground. The main body of troops, however, reached the enemy positions and burst into the enemy trenches with loud yells.

The enemy had already suffered heavy casualties from the German artillery, mortar fire, and hand grenades thrown by their attackers; nevertheless, they fought back desperately, but were overcome in fierce hand-to-hand combat.

'Quick, Hans, get through the enemy positions with your machine gun and prevent any counter-attack!'

Sturm ran on further. He saw two Russians suddenly appear from cover but, before he could bring his machine gun round, Walter Irrmler despatched them with his machine pistol.

Sturm ran on a few metres further, but was forced to take cover when he began to draw enemy fire. He spotted a good position for his machine gun and, throwing himself behind his weapon, he fired at Russians who were setting up a machine gun some 100 m further on. The gunner was hit and the others tried to flee, but didn't stand a chance.

Sturm had just set up his machine gun when a terrified yell from Alfons Berg reached him. He saw that a Russian, arm raised in the act of throwing a grenade, had suddenly appeared just to his right. Half a metre away, the grenade fell to the ground. Hans would later be unable to recall exactly what happened in the next few seconds. He didn't dare pick up the grenade and throw it away, so he leapt up and flung himself to the rear, the devilish device detonating as he did so.

He seemed to have been lucky, but only later noticed that he had been hit four times by shrapnel. Behind him, a shot cracked out. The Russian who had thrown the grenade fell back into his foxhole. His rifle aimed at Sturm, he had emerged from cover, intent on seeing if his hand grenade had worked. He wanted this treacherous enemy dead at all costs. Alfons Berg shot him with his pistol.

Walter Irrmler and Alfons Berg had each saved the life of Hans Sturm in these few minutes. The shrapnel from the hand grenade had struck the stock, handgrip, and breech of the machine gun. Sturm's injuries were fortunately only slight. Would they inform the next of kin that this brave, fallen Russian had sacrificed his life in order to damage an enemy machine gun?

Red! White! Green! Three flares, the pre-arranged cue for withdrawal.

'Back, lads!' squad leader König called out.

The Germans fired as they zig-zagged back from cover to cover, running more or less doubled over until they got back. Two dead and eight wounded were carried back. Twenty-six prisoners, some wounded, were also ferried off. Shellfire and grenades covered the retreat.

Sturm brought back his damaged machine gun just as if it were a wounded comrade. Of the four shrapnel wounds Sturm had suffered, only two had penetrated the skin. These were easily removed at the dressing station, and after a tetanus injection he returned to his section. He was issued a replacement machine gun from the supply unit.

The operation had gone according to plan. Twenty-six prisoners were taken, enemy weapons captured, and the enemy had suffered losses. Own losses: two dead and eight wounded.

The report which was sent back would have sounded innocuous. To the divisional staff, it was enough that the diversion had succeeded. Two fatalities would be considered acceptable collateral, as would the three of the eight wounded who subsequently died.

'What bloody idiocy. If *Generalleutnant* von Knobelsdorf's 19 Panzer Division was still here we wouldn't still be hanging around.'

'Are they already in Welikije Luki then, Alfons?'

'They were in the city by 18th of July, while we were still crawling along behind them. At that point the enemy tried to throw the division back over the River Lovat, but they held on as firm as iron. And do you know why?'

'No, but I can see you know and are going to tell us anyway!'

'Correct!' Alfons straightened his glasses and grinned.

'Welikije Luki was a key Russian supply centre, and our comrades in 19 Panzer Division first had to use up all the champagne and caviar that they liberated. That's why they held on with such determination.'

'Alfons, you're crazy. And why have they evacuated the city again?'

'Orders from LVII Army Corps. They want to tie down as many Russians as possible down here. Besides, the division belongs to 3 Panzer Group, and because its operations strayed so far north it was coming into the area of operations of the Sixteenth Army. The gentlemen on the staff feared that Sixteenth Army would grab the division for themselves.'

'You must have inside information, Alfons. Where did you get all this?'

'Connections, connections—the signallers know much more than we do!'

'And now we are stuck here,' moaned Walter Irrmler.

Oberfeldwebel Winter came towards them. 'But that's the worst part over. In the morning the whole regiment goes over to the attack.'

The other squad leaders were also present now, including *Unteroffizier* Ückert, who had returned from the dressing station. He wanted to be with the company when it eventually entered Welikije Luki. He had therefore foregone the opportunity to be evacuated to a hospital back in Germany. The left side of his face was covered with a large plaster.

He also brought the bad news that three of that morning's wounded were already dead. Sturm tried, from his position, to hear what the *Oberfeldwebel* was saying. He felt his stomach tense. This made sense of what he had overheard at the supply unit that morning. Tomorrow they had to press on again, and again there would be more killed and wounded. Perhaps he would be one of them.

Winter looked at his men. 'This is what is in store for you. You have seen, or heard about, the rocket launchers being set up behind our positions. These are a new type of weapon, the *Stuka zu Fuss*, so called because they are still being fired from wooden frames. They will start off the attack.[1] The company will then go in as follows: to the left, 1 Platoon; to the right, 3 Platoon; behind 1 Platoon on the left, 2 Platoon; and bringing up the rear will be König's squad as reserve.'

'And the other companies, Karl?'

Winter looked at his notes, then nodded to Ückert. '1 Company to the left of and in front of us, 2 Company to the right. The Pioneer Platoon goes behind 1 Platoon to clear any obstacles. The heavy company, 4 Company, follows 300 m behind.'

He looked at the tense faces watching him. 'Take it in turns to sleep,' he added. 'You need to be fresh for the morning.'

No doubt about it, the great attack on Welikije Luki was imminent. Sturm thought about being wounded. Maybe he could have wangled an evacuation in the ambulance if he had handled things better, maybe if he had moaned and groaned a bit more.

He watched as Georg stuffed his pipe with tobacco. Walter's face was contorted into a grimace, while Alfons looked at the heavens. A former pastor, perhaps he was trying to contact another kind of superior. None were as confident as the war correspondents always implied in their reports.

Those who didn't have any guard duties tried to sleep. However, they were constantly awoken by the sounds of shellfire and explosions. Conversations were held in hurried snippets.

With a horrific growl the rocket projectiles howled over the heads of the men of *I Batallion, Infanterie Regiment 473* at 04.10 hours. Streaks of flame flitted through the dark sky as the projectiles streaked into Kikino, hammering into the Russians, throwing earth, smoke, and flames into the air, and turning the village into a fire-spewing inferno. Again and again, loud and terrifying, the shells and projectiles of the infantry cannon and divisional artillery from the rear roared overhead.

'Move off,' yelled *Oberfeldwebel* Winter, as flares soared into the dawn sky. They ran towards the village along the planned route, through a gully. Sturm held his machine gun cocked and ready.

Along a front some hundreds of metres wide, the regiment moved forward with the companies which had been appointed to spearhead the attack taking the lead. Only a few individual shots rang out. On the right flank they could hear the slow rattle of a Maxim machine gun. Otherwise, it was surprisingly quiet once the rocket fire had died away. Only the firing of artillery in the hinterland could be heard.

'They're surrendering!' yelled *Unteroffizier Ückert*. 'There, they're coming out of their foxholes!'

Demoralised by the destruction and clamour of the rockets, the Russians were abandoning their positions. The first had already reached the foremost assault troops. The slightly injured were helping their more seriously wounded comrades. They had discarded their weapons and were calling, 'Kamerad, woina kaput, woina nix gutt—Stalin kaput. Spasiba!' ('Friends, war finished, war no good—Stalin kaput. Please!')

Some Russians passed close to Sturm. The experience of the barrage showed in their terrified eyes and twisted faces.

3 Company had reached Kikino and advanced through the ruined houses and overgrown gardens. Dead Russians, weapons, and equipment lay strewn all around. But certainly, some of the Russians would have escaped. They could be dug in all over. Once, 2 Platoon came under fire from a cellar. Stoof, the machine-gunner from 3 Squad, fired at the movement, and another threw two grenades into the cellar window. The enemy fire was silenced.

The platoon reached the exit from the village. König's squad had to cross a patch of scrub. From in front of them, machine gun fire suddenly rang out from a ditch on the flank of the squads from 1 Platoon.

Sturm fired from the hip in the direction of the enemy and then threw himself to the ground as the enemy fire swung round towards him. The first burst of enemy fire sliced through the shrubs behind which the men of the section had flattened themselves.

Suddenly Sturm had the enemy in sight. His shots hit the armoured shield of the Maxim. Three or four Russians tried to flee, but were cut down by other men of Sturm's squad.

'Welikije Luki! Still, only 2 km to go, we can rest later!' called König.

On and on they went, the undulating countryside favouring their rapid advance. The next kilometre was crossed without any enemy contact. The neighbouring companies were almost level with them. *Oberleutnant Bauer* came over to them from 1 Platoon.

'Well done men. Keep going in this direction. We are striking for the south of Welikije Luki!' he said, before running off towards 3 Platoon and disappearing from sight into the next gully.

'Looks well battered, *Herr Oberfeldwebel*,' called Sturm to his right. 'I think the Russians have been firing on that gully in front of us. These fresh mortar shell craters are not ours.'

Winter came running over to Sturm.

'*Herr Oberfeldwebel*, this gully in front of us falls away and opens up not just to the front but to the left too. If the Russians have dug themselves in there, they can hit us in the flanks.'

'Perhaps so,' said Winter, 'but they have all been pulled back into the city already. Anyway, 1 Company went that way—move on, move on,' he urged before running off to the right again.

The squad leader looked at Hans. 'I think you could be right about these craters. We'll go along the upper edge of the gully. We'll be in less danger from shrapnel there.'

They moved onwards, machine guns and rifles ready. The sun, meanwhile, was climbing higher, and blazed mercilessly down on them. The men could feel its intense heat through their clothing. Sweat poured from their bodies. The foremost squad of the platoon had crossed through the gully.

Suddenly, shots and machine gun fire rang out along the entire line of the advance. The enemy had camouflaged themselves well and were now counterattacking. They had allowed the first of the German troops to pass through unharmed in order to trap the bulk of the Germans in a perilous position and destroy them.

From over yonder the men could hear the 'plop' of mortars being fired. The first shots landed. Walkenhorst, from 3 Squad, vanished in an explosion. He lay there on his back, with multiple shrapnel wounds. Others, hit by rifle fire or shrapnel, cried out for medics.

Sturm could see that, even as some of his comrades in front were hit and lay still, others were returning fire at the enemy. The Russians were firing from positions which gave them good cover. Now they sprang up and charged into the attack. Sturm fired off his entire belt of ammunition, in short bursts, at the points of apparent greatest danger. It was clear to him that he didn't have a particularly good field of fire from this position. If the Russians tried to break through again, he could only play a limited part in the battle. Glancing behind him, he spotted a much better position, with an excellent field of fire but without any cover.

'Quick, Alfons, give me the ammunition box. As soon as I have fired it off, bring me another then get back into cover.'

Sturm seized the box from his hand and ran the few metres to the new position he had chosen, throwing himself down behind the machine gun. He hesitated a few seconds. This was a tricky position. There was no cover for him. Once he started to fire he would draw the enemy's attention to himself. In that instant, and just as Sturm's finger closed over the trigger, the Russians renewed their attack. The brown hordes ran forward in thick packs. Sturm's fire hit them along the entire line as far as 2 Platoon's positions. Nevertheless, many reached his comrades and bitter hand to hand fighting broke out between the Russians and *Oberfeldwebel* Winter and his men.

Sturm knew only that he had to halt the charging enemy. He fired sustained bursts at the area between 1 and 2 Platoons, as Alfons Berg crept back towards him with another ammunition box.

'Hans, you should come down and get under cover quickly. They'll pick you off as if they were shooting a rabbit.'

'Get back,' yelled Sturm. He saw the squad leader call and wave his fist. A burst of fire whipped past him and his machine gun. Behind him, the bullets ripped into the slope behind him, hurling up earth and stones. He moved a few metres to the side and saw that fresh groups of Russians were springing up near his squad. A hand-to-hand battle erupted in which König and his squad became embroiled.

Sturm fired again in sharp bursts. His bullets zipped past a hair's breadth over the heads of his comrades and into the enemy. He could only hope that none of them would hit his own men. In this critical moment, reinforcements arrived led by *Feldwebel* Kionke. The Russians, almost on the point of breaking through, were beaten back by the combined efforts of 2 and 3 Platoons.

'*Oberfeldwebel* Winter! *Oberfeldwebel* Winter!' A runner came over the crest. For a couple of seconds he was thrown to the ground as a mortar shell landed. Then he dived forwards and gasped for breath beside the platoon commander, who had straightened himself up and nodded at the runner.

'What is it then?'

'*Oberleutnant* Bauer has been seriously wounded. *Leutnant* Kaufmann from 1 Platoon, has taken over command of the company. The Company is to pull back 100 m to the rear.'

'Understood, thank you.'

The platoon commander passed on the message to pull back. Felix Meier, the runner, ran back, ducking and weaving.

'Disengage!' König called up to Sturm, and pointed towards the rear.

Sturm had spotted that some Russians were preparing to attack again, perhaps having realised that the Germans were about to withdraw. He grabbed his machine gun and an ammunition box and made ready, once again in his dangerously exposed position.

Scarcely had the first shots rung out when an enemy soldier fired a burst at him with an automatic weapon. The bullets zipped past him and into the dirt in front of his machine gun. He had been spotted. The next bullet would certainly hit him. With this in mind he rolled sideways; bullets once again zipped through the air, all around him. One shot hit his machine gun's bipod. Another bullet clanged against his steel helmet. The impact stunned him. A head wound! Now they've got you, he thought. As he lay stunned, he saw Alfons and Georg approach.

He was dragged over the rough ground, his head bumping over a stone, then taken to cover. Both hands pressed to his helmet, Sturm simply lay there.

'You stupid idiot!' snapped König. 'All this is your own fault.'

Alfons took Sturm's helmet off, and looked for the wound.

'Here is your wound.'

The squad loader held up the steel helmet, which now had a long dent on the left side. The strap from his haversack, which Sturm had tied round his helmet to hold camouflage, was torn up.

'Man, you were lucky!' cried Alfons.

Now and for the first time, Sturm felt a searing pain in his left shoulder. He took off his tunic.

'Hey, I wouldn't go sunbathing here,' cautioned König. 'Quickly, we're getting ready to pull back.'

'Our hero has been lucky. Only a flesh wound. The bullet was deflected over his shoulder.'

'Only a swelling, and the skin a little scratched,' confirmed Alfons.

'Man, we haven't time for this. He's still alive but not for much longer if we don't get out of here!'

Walter Irrmler had taken the machine gun and set it up in position. He fired at the pursuing Russians. The company moved back step by step. The troops took turns at giving each other cover as they moved. Some carried the seriously wounded, the dead too.

Whoof! Hans and his comrades threw themselves to the ground as a mortar shell crashed down onto the slope of the ridge, barely 10 m in front of them. The shrapnel was flung over their heads to their rear, missing most, as they lay in a hollow which gave them some cover. Irrmler flinched, the only one struck.

'Quick men, we are the last to go,' called the squad leader.

The Russians made them hurry. The enemy didn't press their attack any further, but their mortars and guns had done enough damage.

A stinging pain made Sturm wince—shrapnel in his left foot. He could still move it, however, and was able to keep up with the others.

2 Company had by now dug itself in and established a new forward line, while 3 Company, in which Sturm served, was able to go into cover behind a slope. They had many injuries, mostly from shrapnel as opposed to bullets.

Sturm removed his boots. He was able to pull out the splinters of shrapnel, the movement of his foot unaffected. A plaster would be sufficient. Alfons helped him.

Georg looked at his foot and shoulder. 'Hans you are a lucky lad. Two wounds in one day and one yesterday from that hand grenade. You are ripe for a trip home.'

Sturm reflected on the dangers that he had survived without any serious injury. He felt relief that he had come through it all, and that now he could rest for a while. No more attacks, mortars mines, or machine gun bullets.

The bullet which had been deflected from his helmet had ripped his tunic, straps, and shirt. There was an 8-cm long, reddened swelling, the end of which was blooded. The bullet had also penetrated the shoulder, and could have done much worse. Sturm found the bullet later in his rolled up *Zeltbahn*. He threw it away.

Sturm heard soldiers from another squad talking.

'Damn it!' cursed one out loud. 'If the Russian surprise attack hadn't been halted by that machine-gunner, we would all have been done for.'

Obergefreiter König drew himself up. 'There is the machine-gunner,' he said, and pointed to Sturm. He had risked his head and neck, and some of the troops came over and thanked him, patting his shoulder.

The troops lay in their newly dug foxholes and in the old trenches of the former Russian positions. *Oberfeldwebel* Winter spoke with many of them, especially the wounded.

'Sturm, you and the other wounded are to be sent back to the rear with the supply truck,' he decided. 'I will make sure the paperwork is taken care of,' then he disappeared.

Sturm simply had to wait until the truck turned up with the next issue of supplies, among which were chocolate, cigarettes and tobacco, schnapps, and other luxuries. All were given extra portions, too. Where there is good fighting, there should also be good living, was the mantra. The field kitchen issued double rations—noodles with goulash.

Some comrades, however, would need rations no more. These included the battalion commander, *Hauptmann* Dreier. He had fallen in battle with 1 Company, killed by a direct hit from friendly artillery shell. This tragic incident occurred either as a result of incorrect target co-ordinates or the company moving too fast and losing contact with the rear.

A host of crosses were erected in the area around Welikije Luki. They stood singly and in groups. Corpses were rolled in their gas sheets and buried, or at least what was left of them was. It was often the case that a leg, an arm, or even a head was missing.

Those comrades who had fallen during the assault on 29 July, including the squad leader *Unteroffizier* van der Kerkhoff and seven others, could only now, several weeks later, be laid to rest. They had been killed just in front of the enemy positions and had lain in No Man's Land. The burial detail had to wear gasmasks when carrying their rotting remains. The men drank a fair amount of schnapps before carrying out this duty. They lay now in their hero's graves, the soldiers and their Captain, decorated with a cross, a steel helmet, and bunches of sunflowers.

The regimental commander spoke over the grave of *Hauptmann* Dreier, about his sacrifice not being in vain among other things. He spoke with the dignity expected of a man of his rank, reassuring his men that their comrades would continue to fight alongside them in spirit. Sometimes, when the air was thick with lead, it seemed astonishing that some of these comrades were not hit multiple times.

When Sturm arrived at the supply unit, he was taken into a hospital tent. His bandages and plasters were renewed and he was allowed to sleep on a litter. The medical sergeant who had given him a tetanus injection earlier in the day came in with the medical officer and woke him.

'*Schütze* Sturm! Three minor wounds in two days—that earns you a trip home. Or, you could decide to stay here since the injuries are already healing,' said the doctor, and looked at the medical sergeant.

'The choice isn't difficult, *Herr Oberstabsarzt*. I'll go home. I've been ready for it for some time now.'

'Well, yes. But you would be going home soon anyway, on leave. What I mean is that it would be better if we first let the more seriously injured go. You can go to the supply unit first of all and take it easy there. You can go home on the next transport.'

'Do you really mean that I will be going home then, *Herr Oberstabsarzt*?'

'Of course,' pronounced the doctor with conviction. 'That would be in order.'

The days with the supply unit flew past. Sturm's wounds were healing fast. The supply troops spoiled him from beginning to end. Everyone wanted to celebrate the hero who had won the Iron Cross Second and First Class in just four days, and who, despite his wounds, had wanted to stay with his mates!

Sturm enjoyed this role. The Wound Badge in Black was presented to him and he was promoted to *Gefreiter* for gallantry in the face of the enemy. Sturm got the impression that life was good here at the base, just behind the muzzles of the guns which made up the front line.

7

Return to the Front

The stalemate at Welikije Luki weakened after 23 August 1941, and on the 26th was eventually broken. The soup in the great cauldron of the Waldai heights was consummate, and a great battle won.

At the beginning of September, Georg König appeared at the dressing station with a slight injury and was then sent to the supply troop. Sturm could hardly believe his eyes when he saw the braid around his collar and the ribbon of the Iron Cross Second Class in his buttonhole.

'Man, you're a squad leader now! It looks good, except for the bandage on your arm. What's up, what's been happening?'

'Ach, I've hurt my shoulder a little. Anyway, I must pass on greetings from the boys. We are dug in around the airfield at Welikije Luki. Practically a rest area. When you are ready, I'll take you back with me.'

Georg was looking at him rather doubtfully. But Sturm needed no further encouragement to return to his friends.

'What do you expect me to do? You talk about the boys and about a rest area. Quick, let's find the *Oberstabsarzt* and get me discharged!'

They were successful. Hans got his discharge papers, and was recommended for early leave. A little later, the pair got a lift back to the Front in an ammunition truck.

It came a great surprise to the squad when König appeared with Sturm, and the greetings which were offered were warm and sincere.

Alfons Berg, who had taken over on the machine gun while Sturm was away, jested: 'I suppose we will now have to address the *Herr Gefreiter* more formally!'[1]

Gefreiter Walter Irrmler clapped Sturm on the shoulder and asked, 'What are you doing here? Why didn't you get home leave with that wound of yours?'

Sturm waved his hand dismissively. 'There are only a few scratches left, the damage wasn't so bad and after a few days with the supply troops, I felt much better. I've been told I'll get home leave soon anyway!'

Sturm retrieved his machine gun from Berg, who then went off to serve as a gunner in another squad. Heinz Sandkühler was to be Number 2 on the machine gun, having just returned to the unit on 15 September with the first batch of replacements from home.

Hans and Heinz had agreed that whoever got back home to Germany first would visit the other's family. On his convalescence leave, Heinz had travelled to Dortmund to call on Sturm's parents and pass on his greetings, laughing when Sturm's parents had shown him a letter recently received from their son. Sturm had written that he was serving with the divisional supply troops as a driver, a relatively safe job. His paternal grandmother, a devout Catholic, took a great interest in her grandson, and his subterfuge was intended to save her any worry about his well-being. She was a wonderful woman, who regularly prayed for Sturm's safety at church and had made him the gift of a rosary on his departure for the Front. (Sturm carried it always and even managed to retain it during his captivity in Russia. When he was searched after his capture, the Soviets made abusive remarks about this religious item, but did allow him to keep it.) Once on home leave, Sturm intended to come clean and tell his parents the truth.

Sturm's intentions, however, were pre-empted by Sandkühler. Highly amused at Sturm's cover story, he could not help himself from revealing all to Sturm's astonished parents—that their son was in fact a real daredevil, who had already earned the Iron Cross in both Second and First Classes as a combat machine-gunner, and had been wounded in action. Sandkühler could tell from their reaction that Sturm's father was intensely proud of his son's achievements. His mother and grandmother, on the other hand, were aghast, and prevailed upon his father to write a sternly worded letter to him. In it he admonished Sturm for his foolhardiness, telling him he should think of his family and cease playing this mad, dangerous game. In any case, he argued, the recent entry of the USA into the war meant that Germany would certainly lose.

The military censor was enraged at these dangerously seditious remarks, which might have had serious consequences for his father and for Sturm himself. Their well-meaning but defeatist sentiment prompted an angry reaction from Sturm, who wrote a stinging reply. His father was told that those back at home could not possibly imagine what it was like at the Front, where everyone did his duty. His father was not a soldier, and therefore not in a position to comment on such things. (This wasn't strictly true. As a Sudeten German, his father had been called up for the Czech Army during the First World War, but was discharged after a few weeks due to illness. His engineering background was put to good use when he was made manager of a section of the Skoda armament works in Pilsen, making cannons.) Sturm's father responded in a similarly sharp tone, reminding Sturm of that those on the home front did their duty too, speaking of the women working in heavy munitions factories who released male workers for war service, and of the constant danger from air raids and so forth. Before Sturm had the chance to write back, he discovered that his father had been appointed to manage a bridge-building team serving in the central and southern sectors of the Eastern Front. Now Frau Sturm had lost both her son and her husband to the military.

After the successful conclusion of the battles at the Waldai Heights and Welikije Luki, Hans and his comrades believed that the war would soon be over. They had deluded themselves in the extreme, but at that point could not have foreseen the disaster which would soon overtake the Germans at the very gates of Moscow.

The foreign press was full of reports of the German invasion of Russia, though some correctly predicted a similar fate to that which befell Napoleon Bonaparte over a hundred years before. For months, the German infantry—including Sturm's company—slogged its way through the mud, freezing, filthy and hungry, only to be halted in December outside the capital. They had not realised that the German armies had poured into Russia like doomed rats into an open sack. When sufficient numbers were in, the Russians would close the neck and destroy the desperate German armies without mercy.

8

Welikije Luki

In September 1941, the company lay in its positions on the outskirts of Welikije Luki, on the edge of the large open expanse of an airfield area. The ruins of the airfield buildings lay to the right of Sturm and his comrades. It was a relatively peaceful interlude, undisturbed by any major Soviet or German operations. The company was billeted in houses abandoned by their inhabitants during the Soviet withdrawal. Guard posts were established to secure the area, and the weary *Landsern* now rested up as best they could as they awaited battle casualty replacements from home. All the while the Front moved further east, as the mighty *Wehrmacht* continued on its victorious path. It did not need the aid of this humble infantry company.

Each squad had a machine gun post. Directly in Sturm's field of fire lay the wide open plain of the airfield. Behind the airfield was a heavily wooded area. It was strongly suspected that the woods were infested with partisans, but that it was in any case the responsibility of another unit. Every civilian was considered suspect. All movement back and forth had to be controlled, restricted by papers being checked by patrols and guard posts. Only express written orders could secure permission to leave the town.

Much of the civil population had been evacuated, while the rest escaped at the last moment along with the fleeing Red Army. Now some of these returned, anxious to discover what had happened to their homes, often to find German troops billeted in them. Naturally, they blamed the Germans for any and every damage, whether inflicted in their attack or the Soviets' defence. Looting or pillaging by German occupying troops was expressly forbidden, and those caught were severely punished.

Most highly valued by the remaining civilians were the few surviving chickens and other livestock. Inevitably, however, many German soldiers became experts at 'organizing' extra rations for themselves and their comrades. Thus, much of the surviving livestock fell prey to sticky fingered soldiers. Hardly anyone remained totally innocent, most had at least some complicity in these unauthorised 'acquisitions'.

For now, Sturm and Sandkühler stood on watch in their machine gun post, with little to observe in the bare landscape in front of their position. They volunteered for guard duty, the lack of activity giving them plenty of time to chat at length about

Sandkühler's trip home on leave to Germany. Sandkühler was a real chatterbox and Sturm found it difficult to get a word in edgeways. Any time he did, Sandkühler would soon turn the conversation back to himself and his exploits on leave.

As the day wore on towards noon, Sandkühler carried out a strip down inspection of the machine gun with Hans, grumbling at everything he found. As far as he was concerned, everything was either dirty or rusty. After reassembling the weapon, he moaned, 'It makes me wonder if anyone would be able to fire this thing, it's ruined!'

Somewhat niggled by Sandkühler's complaining, Sturm retorted slowly and with emphasis: 'It would be fine by me if I could take this machine gun, wrap it up, and throw it in Dortmund harbour.' At the bewildered expression on Sandkühler's face, he continued. 'I think you should get a grip of yourself, tomorrow the war could be over and the machine gun may never be needed to fire again.'

'But Hans, that would leave me with nothing to do, and I have been so happy here!' joked Sandkühler.

'You are an incorrigible fool Heinz! Every day at least 2,000 Germans bite the dust—twice as many if you believe the enemy's claims. For you the war is like some stupid game. Well, it's a shitty kind of game. If we don't achieve a quick victory, we'll end up in conflict with half the world, especially if, like my father says, the Americans join in!'

'You shouldn't say such things, and you certainly shouldn't write them down. That could cost you your head! The *Führer* knows what he is doing and his successes prove his plans are correct!'

'Oh, the son of the *Sturmbannführer* has spoken. You've got some———!'[1]

'And you have no grounds for getting at me! You were in the *Hitlerjugend* for long enough, and—Hans, look over there, a cart!'

Sturm looked over to the right of the airstrip. At the reins of a cart sat a Russian civilian and behind him, apparently guarding him, a soldier. Conspicuously, he was avoiding coming near Sturm's position, or the other machine gun post about 300 m away.

'Probably going for hay for the horses or suchlike,' said Hans, 'but we'd better have a word with them. After all, orders say at least two Germans must accompany anyone leaving town.'

Hans stood up out of cover, shouted as loud as he could, and signalled to stop. The cart continued on its way. Either its occupants hadn't heard him or were just being stubborn. Hans drew his pistol from its holster, fired a shot in the air, and started to move towards the cart, about 180 m away.

The cart stopped but made no attempt to change direction and move towards their post. When he drew to within around 80 m of the cart, he could clearly see the soldier tap his temple with his finger and wink. Perhaps he was trying to suggest it was the fault of the simpleton of a driver that they had not halted when called. In any case, Sturm was having none of it when the cart started to move off again. He fired a second shot in the air as the cart moved off again, the horse breaking into a trot.

Hans turned and signalled to Sandkühler, then threw himself to the ground out of the line of fire as the machine gun fired a long warning burst.

Still the cart continued, its occupants ignoring the warning. That settled matters: Sturm signalled Sandkühler to aim for the cart. Its driver could be seen clearly at the reins, urging the horses to greater speed.

Once again the machine gun opened up, and this time it did the trick. The driver was hit and threw himself to the ground. The 'German' soldier ran for cover, ducking and weaving. The machine gun fired again.

The squad leader, König, and two of his men appeared behind Sturm. They saw the fugitive attempting to reach the cover of the woods, but in vain. Sandkühler was signalled to cease fire—they wanted this man alive.

In any case, their position was no picnic, with the machine gun behind them firing so close over their heads. The neighbouring squad, however, was determined to join in the manhunt and its machine gun opened up, hitting the quarry, and dropping him like a stone.

The fugitive lay on the ground severely wounded. He tried to turn around and shoot at Sturm as he approached, with a pistol he had concealed in his tunic. Then he put the pistol to his own head and was about to fire when it was kicked out of his hands. Under his German tunic he wore civilian clothes. He had been hit several times and looked certain to die unless he got first aid treatment post-haste. Despite suffering what must have been tremendous pain, he stifled his groans and refused to answer any questions.

He would have killed himself given the chance, thought Sturm. He must have sneaked into town during the night and somehow got hold of a cart and a driver to help him escape with his load—a single chest which must have been of great value to the Soviets. The dead horse was unhitched and the cart taken back with the two wounded prisoners.

The Soviets had clearly thought themselves very clever, sending a dangerous spy to outwit the Germans with this great ruse. They must have laughed over the presumed stupidity of the enemy—well, this was one insolent game they had lost.

The cart driver was an inhabitant of the town. Lamenting his fate and loudly protesting his innocence, he insisted that his wound—a simple flesh wound to the hip—should be punishment enough for the aid he had, willingly or not, given to the spy. Heinz nudged him and said, 'You should have stopped when you were called, then I wouldn't have shot your belly full of holes!'

The Russian misunderstood, knowing little or no German. He feared that Sandkühler meant to shoot him now, but the gift of a cigarette and a conciliatory pat on the shoulder finally reassured him.

The cart was moved back to the company billets. *Leutnant* Kaufmann, the company commander, arrived with an interpreter—a young Russian who had been captured. He too, however, failed to get any answers from the spy, who refused offers of a cigarette or a drink of water. Sturm found himself wondering at this man's obstinate tenacity and admired his bravery. Despite having failed in his task and been wounded and taken prisoner, he refused to give any information or to betray his side. What significance the contents of the chest might have for the Germans, Sturm could not fathom.

'Only papers and such rubbish,' said Sandkühler, 'certainly nothing to eat in there.' He had a gift for reducing everything to its most basic level.

As the cart was taken away, however, he pulled Sturm behind the house.

'Hans, I did manage to capture something though,' he said, drawing a small folded cloth from behind a chest. 'I'll use this to cover myself up in the winter and stop my bones from freezing,' he joked.

Hans was amazed. 'Man, it's a flag.'

It was a fine quality red fabric, beautifully embroidered with the globe, Cyrillic lettering, and the instantly recognizable hammer and sickle emblem. They agreed the flag must be quite a prize, both to the Russians and the Germans. It was too valuable to try to conceal, and Hans rapidly reached a conclusion. 'Heinz, we've got to hand it in!'

'And where do you think it will end up, as the "souvenir" of some senior commander? I'll tell you what, if you promise you won't hand it in, I'll give it to you!'

Quickly, the flag disappeared into Sturm's rucksack. He would take it home and one day it would decorate his room. In fact, the flag was destined to remain in Russia. Before the retreat of 1942, the entire baggage of the company was destroyed by fire: Sturm's momento of this remarkable day went up in smoke too.

The operation which the Germans began in late autumn 1941 was codenamed 'Typhoon'. No doubt the name was chosen to symbolize the speed and *élan* with which the drive on Moscow would be carried through. After the great initial success of the invasion of the Soviet Union, the leadership now set its sights on Moscow. Once their capital city had fallen, the morale of the Russians would be sure to crumble. They had seen devastating losses and defeats at Kiev, Bryansk, Wyasma and Orel, which Stalin's order of 'stand or die' had failed to deflect. The first phase of Typhoon was complete.

Yet the muddy season and early onset of winter brought severe difficulties to the Germans: not only did these conditions hinder the capture of Moscow, but they also caused considerable technical and supply problems.

Infanterie Regiment 473 of 253 Infanterie Division fought at the end of September, from Welikije Luki in the direction of the Waldai Heights and past the town of Toropec. The motorised units often met little if any resistance as they sped along the roads, but the infantry following had to advance cross-country, over open plains and through dense forests, invariably encountering scattered enemy units and bands of partisans.

During June and July they were engaged in many such actions against enemy units, which always defended their locations with grit. It was on the edge of the village of Kolina that Sturm and his comrades met with similarly determined defenders. This forest village had been battered by German mortars and artillery, and now lay in ruins. Flames leapt from the damaged shacks as the fire devoured its way through the dried-out wooden frames, spitting and crackling through the thatched roofs. Smoke not only aggravated breathing, but obscured vision too.

The squad under *Unteroffizier* König was ready to move. Sturm spotted Red Army soldiers at the corner of a shattered house and let off a burst, giving covering fire to his comrades as they rushed forward throwing grenades. As they reached the building, Sturm picked up his machine gun and ran after them—but the shallow trenches and bunkers were empty. The Germans looked at each other in bewilderment. Nothing? How had they disappeared so quickly? They couldn't have gone into the house, it was a blazing inferno.

'Look out, they're behind us!' yelled Heinz.

Instantly, machine pistols rattled and rifle shots cracked. Grenades detonated as the *Landsern* ran into the trenches just evacuated by the Soviets. One, however, wasn't quite quick enough. A Soviet machine pistol bullet hit him, and he pitched forward with an agonised yell and lay still. Sturm spotted the Russian who had fired and shot him. The others fired away madly, without any real attempt to select targets, into the smokey murk until the squad leader yelled at them: 'Pay attention, or you'll end up shooting our own men! Only fire at identified targets!'

'*Halt*!' a voice called out, as three brown-clad figures ran towards the house clutching charges of hand grenades taped together. A German soldier opened fire and the first of the group was hit by a machine pistol shot and fell to the ground, his face contorted into a grimace of agony. Fear of death flickered in his eyes, but also a fanatical fury and desire to kill. With his last remaining strength, he drew back his arm in readiness to throw his charge. Then a second German shot him, his body jerking with the impact of the bullet. The charge dropped right beside him and exploded a second later.

The Germans gasped as pieces of his body flew through the air. The other two Russians were also killed in the blast.

Another warning cry rang out, 'Enemy behind us!'

Then they came, ten or more Russians with smoke-blackened faces, howling, 'Urrah, Urrah!'

Sturm fired short, controlled bursts with his machine gun. The squad leader retained his presence of mind, trying to get a grip on the situation.

'Quick, counter-attack!' he cried, his voice breaking with the tension. The Germans, some of whom were inexperienced replacements, were not exactly eager to leave their foxholes and cross swords with the fanatical enemy.

'Get out of here, quick, they are attacking your foxholes,' screamed Sandkühler at his comrades. Rising to meet their fear, they leapt out of their dugouts and ran to the attack, screaming at the tops of their lungs.

They clashed in a great melee. German and Russian rifle butts alike were clubbed against helmeted heads, bayonets plunged deep into yielding flesh. Desperate, bare hands tried to choke the life from enemy throats and boots stamped into faces. Only one thought prevailed—kill the enemy before he kills you! It was hand-to-hand combat at the peak of its cruelty, with no end to it in sight.

In Kolina, the sound of battle cries was mingled with the piercing shrieks of the wounded. Orders were bawled out amid the crackle of machine pistol fire and the heavier rattle of belt fed machine guns.

Sturm's heavy machine gun could hardly be classified as the appropriate weapon for close-quarter battle, so he didn't have much chance to become involved in the struggle. Now, however, he saw more Russians running in from the left flank. Sturm had only a few bullets left on the ammunition belt, but Sandkühler arrived just in time with a fresh ammunition box. He pointed in the direction of the assault, only to see the enemy reach then overwhelm another squad from their platoon in a pincer movement. Sturm had no chance to fire at the enemy before they were mingled with German soldiers and the risk of hitting his own men was too great.

After a furious barrage from the regimental artillery, *II Bataillon* moved into the attack northwards from Kolina and penetrated the centre of the village.

The Soviet commander and his formation—which roughly consisted of a battalion of rapidly assembled, miscellaneous troops, in reality little more than a disorganised rabble—had not the strength to regroup. Before the start of the attack, he had read out an order to his men that each must fight and die holding his allocated position. It was, in fact, the only reasonable tactic: by this method he ensured that the Germans' advance would become time-consuming, heavy in casualties, and excruciatingly slow in its progress. In effect the Germans did, quite literally, advance metre by metre.

In the hours after the beginning of the attack, *I Batallion* struggled to defend its hard-won positions on the edge of the village.

Winter

Mud! Everywhere mud. Filth, damp, rain, and a barrier of clouds. The infantry companies and their horse-drawn transport rolled—no, dragged themselves through. The roads were nothing but ribbons of mud, laced with treacherous furrows and potholes. Clean, wide roads were utterly lost from sight in this sea of sludge. Drivers everywhere desperately sought firmer ground to take the weight of their vehicles. Motorcyclists were totally encased in mud from head to toe. Infantrymen trudged wearily along, sinking up to their boot tops with each step through the glutinous mire. Exhausted horses constantly had to stop for a few moments' rest. The rain drummed down in a steady rhythm, but not even it could rinse off the layer of greasy morass which clung to everyone all the way up to their steel helmets. This filth even found its way in between their teeth.

A large Büssing-Nag truck thundered by at full speed, splashing through a huge pothole, spewing stinking fumes from its exhaust. Yet more trucks sped by, their drivers trying to build up momentum for the incline they had to negotiate.

The infantry came behind, sprayed with mud by every vehicle which passed. Two squads, under König and Ückert, were tasked with securing the supply route, for the regiment was constantly coming under harassing attacks from partisans. Unexpected and sudden ambushes from the brown-clad and black-faced enemy frequently seemed to rise up out of nowhere on either of the retinue's flanks.

For Sturm and his comrades, securing the supply routes was a source of constant tension and fear. It was, in many ways, worse that combat action in the front line. Attrition in men and horses hampered the advance considerably, and the dangerously stretched supply routes required every more security to make them safe.

The heavy cart horses which had been drawing the company wagons were finding it harder and harder to cope. The supply unit therefore decided to outfit itself with Russian Panje wagons and horses—small but immensely strong, and quickly adaptable to the worst of conditions. The conversion of the supply unit took place in a large town between Toropec and Andreapol, in the Waldai Heights. The operation was only achieved with difficulty and sacrifice, due to interference by armed Russians and partisans. On the bright side, the company made use of this rare opportunity for the men to be de-loused, showered, and issued with clean underwear. Entertainment was provided in the evenings with stage performances and cinema shows. Supplies were plentiful. War correspondents arrived to film and interview the troops. Sturm couldn't help but suspect that all this was leading up to some major engagement for the regiment. The squad, meanwhile, was brought up to strength with replacements.

One camera team filmed the unit for the weekly cinema newsreels. The platoon marched past for the cameras, led by the machine-gunners. Sturm, on the right flank, was clearly visible, a cynical grin playing across his face. (A copy of the film strip was presented to Sturm as a gift after the award of his *Ritterkreuz*.)

Infanterie Regiment 473 marched onwards through the Waldai Heights. Two combat groups from *I* and *II Battaillon* formed the infantry spearhead. They pressed on through almost primeval terrain, its huge forests interspersed with vast, open plains, often defended by determined Russian stragglers.

Oberfeldwebel Winter, the previous commander of 2 Platoon, had now, being a career soldier, been promoted to *Oberleutnant* and given command of *3 Kompanie* following the death of *Leutnant* Kaufmann from his wounds. Winter checked out Hill 218 through his binoculars, relaying his observations of the terrain to the squads who lay in readiness to move via the platoon commander.

Feldwebel Ückert's 2 Platoon could not use the narrow pass which led towards the hill, despite its inviting appearance (with excellent cover), as it would almost certainly have been mined, and the regimental pioneers were away off to the right flank with 1 and 2 Companies. Sturm could hear explosions off in the distance, probably the result of the pioneers clearing mines. The hectic sounds of battle seemed stronger in that direction.

König's squad emerged from the tree line, giving up the cover of the last few trees and bushes. A shell from a Soviet '*Ratsch-Bumm*' exploded in the trees, showering the area with steel, wood splinters and dirt, but no one was injured. The 7.62-cm enemy canon got its nickname from the way the impact from its shell was felt before the sound was heard.

From the heights above came the rattle of a Maxim machine gun, recognisable by its 'Rattattattattat'.

Sturm spotted an enemy machine gun and immediately directed a burst of rapid fire towards it, while the squad worked its way forward using whatever cover it could find. Flickering light from tracer bullets illuminated the early morning skies, which were growing lighter by the minute. From over to the right came the sounds of the men of 2 Company engaging the enemy.

'Go,' came the command from *Oberleutnant* Winter.

Sturm fired in the direction of the crest of a rise, where Red Army soldiers had been spotted, and the *Landsern* ran onwards, reaching the foot of the slope and trying to find cover.

From above, Russian snipers had hit some of the Germans. The medic NCO, *Unteroffizier* Karl Sippel, ran over to one soldier who had just been hit. He could see the injured man was beyond help upon observing the gaping, ragged-edged exit wound of a bullet in his neck. Karl Sippel had already proven himself one of the war's unsung heroes, constantly risking his life under fire to tend to wounded comrades or to drag an injured man into safety. He was perpetually drawn back into the danger zone by the cries for help from one bloodied and mutilated soldier or another. On the Eastern Front, the stakes were raised all the more by the refusal of the Soviets to respect the Red Cross. From 21 June to 31 December 1941, 12.5 per cent of medics were killed in action, as opposed to 12 per cent of infantrymen!

Sturm pulled his trigger and sent a burst of fire towards the enemy. Before the Russians could return fire, he had thrown himself flat, face pressed into the ground, and it passed harmlessly over him as Sandkühler tossed a grenade into the Soviet machine gun nest. The enemy were eliminated, save for one, who survived the detonation. Sturm could see that blood was spurting from a wound in his neck, and leaping to the Russian's side applied a field dressing to it. The look of terror in the Russian's eyes as Sturm approached turned to gratitude, although his injuries were far too serious for Sturm to be able to do anything but comfort him as his life ebbed away. Abruptly rearing himself up, the Soviet soldier toppled and fell back dead. Sandkühler clapped Sturm on the shoulder.

'Come on, the company is moving on.'

They saw several squads of soldiers spring up and bound towards the next dip, then go charging up the slope. The enemy machine gun that had fired at them could no longer reach them. Sturm and Sandkühler ran on and soon reached the overgrown top of the hill. They joined in the battle, pushing the Russians back.

The Germans leapt into the enemy communications trench and rolled up the opposition with machine pistols and hand grenades. Of the *Ratsch-Bumm* canons there was nothing to be seen. The Soviets had withdrawn them in good time.

The lonely landscape looked abandoned and desolate. As the day wore on, the moon made its appearance, creeping furtively behind the clouds. The fading light was soon lost in a velvet-black darkness. It seemed that more snow was on its way. In the distance flickered Very lights, to the ominous rumble of artillery fire.

König's squad had been tasked with carrying out reconnaissance missions behind a dense stretch of forest about 1 km deep, and, if possible, bring back a prisoner. They moved into the trees, which stood before them like a solid black wall.

I've got a bad feeling about this, thought Sturm, as he and Sandkühler moved into the unknown. It was only possible to follow one route through the trees, due to the density of the undergrowth on either side of the path.

The route grew narrower the deeper they penetrated into the inky blackness, with visibility at best no more than a few paces. Only the occasional reflection of moonlight on a patch of freshly fallen snow helped to light their way. The unnatural stillness seemed almost tangible when the squad from time to time stood absolutely still to listen for any suspicious noises.

Then the path petered out and the squad stumbled and slipped their way forward over a mass of thick roots, deep furrows and water filled ditches. The trees stood like a solid wall along both sides, their branches reaching almost to the ground and impeding progress even further as the men ducked down low to avoid them. What lurked beyond the trees was a threatening, black unknown.

It was some compensation to the men to think that the Russians had clearly thought that no one could penetrate this deep thicket without making conspicuous amounts of noise. Previous reconnaissance had shown that the enemy had established his defence line just beyond the forest.

The squad approached a fork in the route, with a clearing from which another path led off to the left.

Suddenly, shots rang out. Bullets slapped into the mud close to Sturm while others slammed into the tree trunks. The muzzle flashes from the enemy guns could be clearly seen in the inky darkness.

Sturm quickly unslung his machine gun and fired off a burst from the hip before throwing himself to the ground alongside his comrades.

Abrupt commands in Russian echoed through the woods as the entire squad fired their weapons and threw hand grenades in the direction of the enemy.

Then came cries of wounded men. Russian curses. The dull thud of running, booted feet. Cracking wood. The Russians rushed away and suddenly all was still. König and a few men advanced into the clearing and along the other path. They found three Russians. One was dead, the second died as they reached him and the third was unconscious, merely stunned by a minor head injury.

Sturm and his comrades were fortunate, none were injured, but the terror of the surprise attack still gripped them.

The enemy must have spotted König and his squad as they moved and set up an ambush. Their big mistake had come when at least one of them had lost his nerve and fired too soon.

The squad quickly secured its perimeter. It was now only a few hundred meters to the enemy positions. The original task—to infiltrate the enemy positions undetected and return with a prisoner—was now impossible. The enemy would be alerted by the noise of battle from the woods and by the return of those Russians who had fled.

The squad leader ordered their return. The wounded Russian was laid out on a *Zeltbahn* and carried back. At least the second part of their task had been accomplished.

The subsequent questioning of the Russian revealed that he was the commander of the enemy group, and they had bolted when they had lost their leader. Because of his decent treatment, after initial hesitation, he had given information about his unit, its strength, positions, and the enemy's intentions to pull back on the following day.

By mid-October, weather conditions had worsened considerably. All roads were rapidly becoming impassable. The supply troops battled constantly against the deteriorating weather to bring at least the most essential provisions to the fighting troops, with growing losses in both men and vehicles.

Whereas Germans knew insurgents behind the line as partisans, the Russians referred to them as 'Forest Brothers'. They were mainly civilians, but among them—

especially in the early phase of the war against the Soviet Union—were a number of Red Army stragglers. Some were sworn fanatics, to whom the almost impenetrable forests offered thousands of hiding places, and who knew how to fight with cunning and determination. Moscow recognised the effectiveness of these partisan groups against the German supply lines, and Stalin ordered the operations at the Front to be co-ordinated with their actions.

The partisans often hit the Germans with what amounted to 'pin-prick' tactics, sometimes attacking individual German soldiers, supply lorries in the areas behind the Front, railway tracks, and other important lines of communication. In the course of the war in the east, as their strength grew, so did the danger they posed. They were equivalent to a 'second front' in the rear of the German troop formations.

The partisan's share in the victory of the Red Army in the Great Patriotic War would be well earned, though whether or not their actions were consistent with internationally accepted rules of conduct in war would always remain a point of contention. In some respects, they were fervent patriots. They considered Germans 'Hitlerists' and 'Fascist invaders' to be exterminated. They came predominantly from farming communities who had lost everything in this conflict, and thus were consumed with hatred. Fuelled by propaganda, they conducted themselves in a cruel and vicious manner.

The activities of the Forest Brothers were noted at *Führer* Headquarters, but little significance was attached to them. The troops at the Front saw the reality of the situation, however. They noticed the shortages of ammunition, supplies, and fuel for the motorised and armoured units, and of course the lack of any suitable winter uniforms. The *Landsern* still wore the same lightweight summer uniforms, now shabby and soaked, and through which the cold cut like a knife. They had no thick gloves or winter overcoats with which to protect themselves from the unpredictable elements—frost, rain, wind, snow, and frost again. Frostbite of all sorts was on the increase.

'By Christmas the war in the east will be over! The Russian bear is on the ground and is now making his last desperate efforts.'

No one would believe a winter in Russia. *Führer* Headquarters believed that the war in Russia need only be on the same scale as the campaigns in Poland, in the West, and in the Balkans. Now the vision of the demise of Napoleon's *Grande Armée* in 1812 haunted the German military experts.

On the home front, a collection of winter clothing for the troops was begun, as the leadership sought to compensate for this misjudgement by improvisation. The clothing collected lay in storage warehouses or in goods wagons in railway sidings in Warsaw or Breslau, but there were not enough locomotives to transport them, so the soldiers continued to freeze.

In the meantime, it was becoming bitterly cold. Many wounded soldiers developed light or even serious frostbite, presenting just about the worst cases that the medics saw in those days. They witnessed many a young lad's foot being entirely frozen and turned into a black stump, or their hands, noses, and ears simply rotting away. Everyone who saw it was filled with horror.

'If we don't get out of this cold soon, we're done for!'

Sandkühler pointed to the little village from which smoke spiralled upwards, evidence of warmth.

'Yes, if we could get in there—but the Russians are already there,' said Poldi, anxiously.

The men crouched together in their snow-hole. The east wind whirled waves of swirling powdery snow and smarting particles of ice into their faces each time they looked up. As *Unteroffizier* König had heard no response from Vogel, who lay just behind him, he raised himself up to take a look. In the twilight gloom he could see the nose and ears of his comrade appeared white.

'Man, Vogel! Rub, rub!'

Vogel whimpered. König crawled over to him, took off his gloves, and started to rub Vogel's face, ears, and nose. After a few minutes he began to lose the feeling in his hands. Yet still there seemed to be no colour in Vogel's nose, and König knew what that meant.

He crept over to *Feldwebel* Kionke, who lay perhaps 30 m to the side of their position.

'Kionke, we must get into that village!'

'Are you drunk, Georg, we have no orders to attack!'

'No, we haven't, but it's the 4th of December and at least thirty below. If we stay here, by morning, we won't have a single man left from the team.'

'So, it's a damned mess. No winter gear and no felt overboots. And the Russians have everything. And if they cross over the ice of Lake Seliger, they will only have to swing round to the south and they'll have trapped the regiment in a sack!'

Kaufmann, recently promoted to *Oberleutnant*, came trudging through a snowdrift towards them. He threw himself in the snow behind Kionke as a machine gun began to chatter from the village and tracer zipped through the darkening sky.

'What is it Kionke?'

'3 Platoon already has seven men with frostbite, *Herr Oberleutnant*. If we don't get into cover tonight and get some warmth, we are finished."

Kaufmann rubbed his ears. He nodded, then looked towards the men in the trench.

'How are things, Kionke, König, Sturm? Should we throw the Russians out of there? That way we'd also have a better position to start the assault towards Ostaschkow.'

'Yes, the sooner the better, *Herr Oberleutnant*,' said Sturm. He felt the cold eating through his clothes. In the moonlight he could see his breath freeze, and he felt his eyes begin to sting. From time to time he pulled his balaclava over his mouth, but then it became moist with his breath and froze, endangering the skin on his face.

And so they all froze. During the muddy season in September and October, they had penetrated all the way from Welikije Luki through Nasimowo, Toropjetz, Rogowka, and Dubowka up to the Volga. Through the impenetrable mud, they had forced a route through to the south bank of Lake Seliger and the large village of Ostaschkow, where a long, narrow finger of the lake reached out to the south.

'We must get out of here,' said Sandkühler once again. 'If the Russians attacked us now, we wouldn't be able to shoot back, the weapons are all frozen!'

'I'll send a runner to battalion and advise them that we will attack in an hour. Make yourselves ready. Check all the machine guns. Keep your weapons warm, with your own body heat if necessary, so that they'll function.'

No one was against the idea. They all worked feverishly to get ready. The prospect of getting into Ostaschkow, and into one of the small cottages where they warm up at last, was enough to drive all other thoughts from their minds. They thought nothing of the danger, only of getting out of the cold that had been burning its way into their bones for several days now.

While in Welikije Luki, Sturm had 'organised' a bottle of oil. It was found in a closet in a factory building. It was no good for frying potatoes, but Sturm had found that, mixed with a little sulphur powder, it made an excellent antifreeze treatment. He had kept a small bottle in his machine gun pouch, and the mechanism of his machine gun was always ready for action. The other gunners had also made use of Sturm's 'magic mixture'.

Finally, all was ready. *Oberleutnant* Kaufmann gave the signal to attack. The three platoons worked their way forward, well separated from each other, and through the snow towards the houses on the edge of the village.

'Not so loud, they'll hear us!' cursed König under his breath, as Poldi stumbled and fell into a snowdrift. Two men pulled him to his feet. The trees and the brambles either side of the hollow were transformed by their thick covering of snow into a solid barrier. No one would see them here. The frosted snow covering crunched under their feet as they made their approach.

Vogel staggered onwards behind *Unteroffizier* König. His face was numb with cold. He had no strength left to carry his rifle and it fell from his hands and lay in the snow. Sturm closed in behind him, stooped, and picked up his rifle. Heinz Schaller came from behind and took it from him. To his rear, Sturm could hear Sandkühler's panting. They worked their way forward as if in a stupor, yet with an imperturbable will to reach the village.

Further to their right, a machine gun spluttered out and the night was illuminated with yellow fire. From the village, a Maxim machine gun chattered and, once again, Sturm felt a lump in his throat as apprehension came over him—but the thought of the warmth which lay within spurred him onwards.

'Forwards!' cried *Unteroffizier* König.

They ran onwards. Sturm fired on the run. After a short burst, however, his weapon stopped. He ran on. Shots rang out and bullets whipped into the snow. Sturm stumbled into a ditch. Cries rang out in the darkness.

Then, Sturm's machine gun was clear once again. He fired off two full belts. As the third fitted into the breech, he sprang up and ran forward with the others. Sandkühler left an empty ammunition box lying behind in the snow. As he ran, he primed a hand grenade and, as the enemy fired again, threw it over the wall. A dull crack was heard and the enemy machine gun fell silent.

They reached the wall and swung themselves over. *Unteroffizier* König and two others threw grenades after the retreating Russians. They exploded in their midst and hurled the enemy to the ground. Right in front of them now lay the first of the Russian farmers' huts.

'Take cover,' someone screamed as something flashed at one of the windows. Scarcely anyone paid any attention to the warning, but simply ran onwards towards the warmth. Sturm reached the door at the same moment as Sandkühler. They kicked the door open. Sturm poked the muzzle of the machine gun in through the open door and a stream of fire burst through the darkness. A loud detonation threw the men to the ground. Sturm saw three or four shadowy figures, and from the centre of this group a burst of machine pistol fire rang out. In the confines of the room, everything sounded much louder than usual. Bright flames ripped through the gloom.

A Russian ran directly at Sturm, who hit him in the torso with his machine gun. From the entrance sounded out a German machine pistol. The next burst of fire brought the business to an end. Sandkühler cried out something, then all was still, though the sounds of battle from the other houses were clearly audible.

'Onwards, keep going!'

Sturm groped for his machine gun. He found it, half concealed by the body of the dead Russian who had run at him, and picked it up. With Sandkühler he reached the other door, which opened out towards the rest of the village.

'There, over there, Hans!' called König as they ran onwards. They rushed forwards, but were forced to drop to the ground by a burst of machine gun fire. Behind them they heard the bullets rip into a snowdrift. Sturm shoved himself through it. He lay down and, without taking the time to extend the bipod on his weapon, opened fire immediately at the enemy position. The slow rattling of the Maxim machine gun rang through the night. Hand grenades burst asunder. Voices called out from house to house—Russian orders, and curses. Everything merged together in an orgy of death and destruction.

All the men from the company were well aware that the capture of the village was essential to their own survival. If they stayed just one more night in the open, they would all be finished, or at the very least crippled—like Büderich, whose two feet were badly frostbitten.

Sturm reached the position that he had spotted earlier. The squad had closed up and fired with all their weapons. Now the enemy machine gun responded in kind. A pair of shadows were discernible in the glare of the muzzle flashes. Sturm fired too, spraying bullets to the left and to the right into the enemy position. Steel clashed against steel. A hand grenade was thrown and incandescent white flame erupted from the spot where the enemy machine gun had been.

Sturm's comrades now leapt up and ran onwards. Sandkühler came to Sturm. He fitted a new belt of ammunition to the machine gun and pointed forwards.

'There, Hans!'

Again Sturm fired. Sandkühler ran forwards, and safely reached the cover of a well on the northern edge of the village. Sturm and some others from the squad ran over to him. Further in front, a hand grenade detonated. The machine gun of another squad began to fire. Like glow-worms, the tracer bullets flashed through the darkness. Sturm reached Sandkühler, who had picked up a couple of more boxes of ammunition from the Number 3 on the machine gun team.

These last houses on the edge of the village were obstinately defended by the Russians. *Feldwebel* Kionke, *Unteroffizier* König and others from the platoon threw hand grenades. Some burst through the windows and exploded inside the houses. The men then stormed them, Sandkühler and Sturm with them. Inside the Russians, some of them wounded, gave themselves up; several were already dead.

From the window Sturm looked outside and saw more of the enemy, in their thick felt boots, run off over the snow. He fired, leaning his machine gun against the window frame, and the enemy fell dead in the snow.

The firing ceased. One hand grenade cracked, after which all was quiet. Then this silence was pierced by the calls and cries of men of 3 Company, excited cries to each other, in which Sturm and Sandkühler joined in. They had done it! Soon, they would have warmth and shelter from the biting wind.

No one had yet taken consideration of the dead and wounded, who had paid this penalty for the sake of a little warmth. What insanity! But better not to think of it.

'König's squad!'

Unteroffizier König left the house and reported to the *Oberleutnant*.

'Here, *Herr Oberleutnant*!'

'You stay in the house there on the northern edge of the village. We must prepare defensive hedgehog positions.'

'Yes, *Herr Oberleutnant*, but the main thing is that we have some warmth now!'

'One more thing, König. As soon as the men have the chance, tell them all to rub their faces and feet, even use snow as an abrasive, to get the circulation going. Understood?'

'Understood, *Herr Oberleutnant*.'

Oberleutnant Kaufmann hurried over to Übel's squad, who were over on the east edge of the village, and König went back into the house. He was well aware of the risk of serious frostbite injuries.

'Now, rub your faces and check your feet!'

He went over to Vogel and his eyes widened with horror. Vogel's right eye was missing. The soldier took off his boots. He moved his feet, covered with socks and cloth bindings towards the fire to try to warm them.

'I have no feeling in my legs, it's as if they're dead.'

Sandkühler helped him to unwind the binding cloth. Then he took the socks off. His nose was immediately assailed by the stench.

'Damn it!' said Sandkühler, unable to control himself. 'You got your feet wet yesterday and didn't do anything about it, did you?'

'I couldn't, you know that, it was so cold yesterday!' stammered Vogel.

Vogel suddenly gulped loudly and began to cry. The young lad's crying cut through to the hearts of the men in the hut.

'Be quiet!' shouted Bollmann, who couldn't bear it any more. 'You've got a ticket home now! You'll be fine. Always warm and always food to eat.'

'But my legs!'

'I'll go out and tell the old man that he will have to send a sledge for you.'

Sandkühler picked up his machine pistol and left. Through the window Sturm saw him dash across the open space. He ran hunched over, holding his weapon ready to fire. As he reached the other side safely, Sturm breathed a sigh of relief. Ten minutes later, Sandkühler returned again. He smiled quietly at Vogel.

'The old man has already ordered up a sled. There are still a couple of men over there with frostbite. The best thing is for us to take you over there too, and get you loaded on to the sled and off to hospital as soon as possible.'

A few days later, *Unteroffizier* König issued the mail. He gave each man his letters and packets. At the end there was one letter left. It was addressed to the squad and came from a field hospital in Poland. Vogel had written. He confirmed what Sandkühler had reckoned would happen. They had amputated both of Vogel's lower legs. This youngster from Bielefeld was now a cripple, because he had once forgotten, or hadn't had the chance, to dry his wet feet and put on fresh socks and bindings.

The company had had two dead after the attack on the village, plus one seriously wounded, three lightly wounded, four with mild frostbite, and one with serious frostbite—a high price for a little warmth.

Freezing is, they say, a pleasant death. One falls asleep, loses consciousness, and has no more pain. But who wants to be dead?

10

An Unusual Encounter

3 Company dug themselves well in in Ostaschkow, and the houses, damaged by shellfire or by burning, were repaired as best they could be. Failing that, their rubble was used in the building of bunkers. The supply section, with its field kitchens, offices, *etc.* were moved up and established themselves. None of the company knew how things were progressing at the Front as a whole, but it seemed to them as though they had already had to endure it for an age. Perhaps now they would also have to celebrate Christmas here, too.

The supply of provisions had been problematic. The various companies in the regiment had, in the meantime, to bake their own bread and improvise their own meals. Extras such as sausage, cheese, honey, and marmalade were in very short supply and had to be rationed. Letters and packages from home could not get through any more, and warm winter clothing remained a dream.

Despite the fight for the village, some Russians had hidden themselves in cellars and holes in the ground. Others came back from the forests to give themselves up. They had little or no food. So far as was possible, the meagre rations available to the company were shared with the Russian prisoners. A drink of hot soup from the field kitchen and slices of bread cut from the German soldiers own allowance. It was bread made from corn which the supply troops had seized from a supply depot.

Sturm got to know Tanja, a young Russian girl. She was pretty, but not as pretty as his own young girlfriend Ursula, who had died at the age of seventeen from a lung infection. Tanja was attractive in a different way. She was more robust, with wide cheekbones in a deeply tanned face and a shapely figure under her quilted jacket. This, it was supposed, was the result of her continuous chewing on sunflower seeds, which many German soldiers also maintained made the teeth of the Russian women and girls so even and white. Tanja was a student, and had learnt German. She was able to converse with Sturm. Her fiancée had fallen in battle against the Germans and her brother was missing in action. During his talks with Tanja, Sturm thought of the uncertain fate of soldiers on both sides, and the innumerable hopes and fears of wives and mothers, some never to be fulfilled. He imagined all the tears shed for men who had fallen somewhere, or had yet to fall, or who in the inconceivable vastness of Russia would go missing, or become POWs. Sturm went to great lengths to console Tanja, and also her father, the village elder, that they would soon hear news of her brother. He had probably only been wounded, or taken prisoner, he comforted them.

Then came a regimental order. Yet again, *I Batallion* was to move to another sector of the Front. Hans Sturm and his comrades were livid at having to give up the winter quarters that they had spent so much time and effort on.

Sturm's company, came to a slope, just before the location of their new positions, which led down to a frozen brook. The biting wind pierced their inadequate clothing, and left their ears, noses, and mouths tingling. Balaclavas pulled over their mouths and moistened by their breath froze solid. They had to remove them and rub their faces to encourage blood flow.

Some slid on the newly fallen snow covering the slope and got up, cursing, only to fall down again and knock down their comrades in the process. On the ground lay the vestiges of many horses, unhitched wagons, and Russian soldiers, their arms and legs already buried in the snow.

König's squad saw three men approach. They were all officers, identifiable by the piping on their field caps. They wore long, fur-lined greatcoats, their collars turned up to shield their bearded faces. None of the officers wore shoulder straps, so it was impossible to tell their rank. Sturm thought them to be either artillery or reconnaissance officers.

Sandkühler, in front of Sturm, had slipped. One of the officers came forward and helped him to his feet.

'Well, comrade, how goes it with you?' he asked.

'Just as you'd expect for someone who has just fallen on his arse!' answered Sandkühler.

Sturm was bitter over the unexpected relocation from Ostaschkow—partly because he was being separated from the lovely Tanja.

'They ask how things go with us, yet they are standing here in warm winter clothing while we are freezing our arses off!' he grumbled in annoyance.

The officer with the frost-covered, unshaven stubble showed astonishment at Sturm's outspokenness. His eyes fixed on Sturm, though not with hostility; in fact, he seemed somewhat amused, unlike one of his companions, who seemed intent on rebuking Sturm. A wave of the hand from the bearded officer stopped his colleague. He turned to Sturm. 'Now then, *Gefreiter*,' he said, 'tell me how things are with you!'

'We were pulled out of a good defensive position and brought to this place, which we know nothing about. We feel we are being taken for a ride!'

You call it being taken for a ride, but the circumstances made it necessary,' replied the officer.

'Circumstances! We are treated like stupid donkeys—the circumstances won't be improved by moving us here. The supply situation is getting worse, we can only dream about getting any kit from the stores, and the *Feldpost* is almost non-existent!"

'Now then, *Gefreiter*, who are you?' asked the officer. 'Which unit do you belong to?'

'You must know that I cannot tell you my unit, I don't even know who you are!'

'Good, but you can tell me your name.'

'*Gefreiter* Sturm!' he answered, taking a few steps forward and listening hard as the officer spoke quietly to one of his colleagues. 'Write that down, Kröger!'

'Yes, *Herr General*,' Kröger replied.

Sandkühler nudged Sturm with his elbow.

'Man, Hans, now you've really dropped yourself in it. That was our divisional commander, *General* Schellert!'

'Why should I care! What else can happen to me that's worse than I have already had to put up with? Will they punish me, lock me up?'

They walked back to towards König.

'What's up?' the *Unteroffizier* asked.

'Ach,' said Sandkühler laughing, 'nothing special—Hans here has just given our divisional commander a piece of his mind!'

'That was our general?' asked König in amazement. 'I wouldn't have recognised him either.'

'From now on we'll have to keep Hans well to the rear when we see an officer, but the general was quite friendly, really,' said Sandkühler.

The three then struggled on, trying to catch up with the rest of the squad. After wading through snow drifts which reached up to their chests, and snow holes which suddenly opened up under their feet, they were just about at the end of their strength.

Gasping and out of breath, the company reached the top of the slope, and on the other side reached a network of trenches connecting defensive bunkers. These had just been given up by another company, which was being withdrawn towards the rear after the squad, platoon, and company commanders had completed their hand-overs. Immediately in front of the German positions lay a dark forbidding forest.

The bunker, with its strong shoring beams secured deep into the earth, provided good protection from the cold and wind. König's squad settled in as best it could. In the bunker's crude earthenware stove, burning wood crackled and snapped. Guards coming off watch would enter the bunker, their clothing sparkling with frost, and stand shivering as the heat slowly penetrated them.

The thought of Vogel and his so recently lost legs played in the minds of the squad.

The Whole Squad on Guard

The squad leader came into the bunker, stamping his feet and brushing the snow from his greatcoat. He had come from the company command post and the men wordlessly eyed him with mixed feelings.

'Listen up. Fresh orders from the regiment!'

'Shit, already? You can bet it won't be good news,' said Sandkühler.

'Well, sometime yesterday in the sector held by *II Batallion*, an entire squad was snatched by a Russian patrol. It must have been as the guard changed at 22.00 hours.' The news came as a shock. Now the men knew what the outcome of occupying these positions for many hours in the cold night could be.

'This is what we will do,' said König. 'Two men at a time stay on guard until they are relieved. One of them then goes into the bunker to wake the next two to go on duty, then they can get their heads down.'

They all knew that this would be strictly against regulations. Sandkühler's deep voice broke the silence which followed. 'We'll manage alright.'

Sandkühler grinned as he saw the tension ease from the others' faces.

'So, today we spoke with our general, who has been inspecting the positions. Hans didn't recognise him, but the officer explained that our supplies are poor and we have no stores. It's still possible that our situation might improve.'

'Are you mad?' exclaimed Sturm. 'We should be keeping our heads down. If we are going to flout orders and do our own thing with the night guard, we'll end up drawing everyone's attention to ourselves!'

'Do you really think we will get a single crumb more of provisions?' asked another.

'I don't know,' replied Sturm taciturnly. 'I don't know why I said it. But if you want to have a go at me, I'll understand.'

'This business with the night watch…. Everyone outside in this cold is pretty shitty,' began Sandkühler, 'but maybe we can console ourselves with the thought that Hans's outburst will have some effect and the general will help us!'

'Yes, I bet you believe in Father Christmas too,' leered König. 'The general will have long forgotten about Hans.'

'Just be patient. He did look a bit like Father Christmas, with his beard and his long fur overcoat, but I trust him, and I think he will help—if he can.'

A Night with Serious Consequences

The supply situation did improve and some materiel arrived which had been obtained from older reserve stores from the time the division had been in France.

'We should really be satisfied,' said Sepp Hollerer. 'It is warm here in the bunker. If you think about it, in that last village, we weren't any better off than in these houses. We had more than enough bed bugs there to last us until the damned war was over.'

Sepp was an experienced skier. He was born in Garmsich-Partenkirchen and often returned there to visit his family. His trade as a motor mechanic had taken him to Bochum to find work. Sturm had taken his holidays in Garmisch-Partenkirchen from 1936 to 1940, so the two had plenty to talk about.

Sturm drew back the sack which covered the vision slot in the bunker and looked out. Through the snow he saw the trench which led to the camouflaged bunker. It was narrow and almost the height of a man, thus allowing the men to remain out of sight of the enemy when the guard changed. The two men on night guard duty had tested it. If the entire squad had gone on guard from 22.00 hours, it wouldn't have taken long before they were too exhausted to be of any use. The platoon leader, *Feldwebel*Ückert, knew of their wangling the guard duty, but of course 'officially' knew nothing.

Of the seven men in the squad (including the squad leader), two men were on guard. One remained awake in the bunker, alert and ready to wake the next two who were to change the guard every hour. This way, four men could sleep at any one time.

'This time, you go out with Hollerer,' Sandkühler said turning to Sturm. 'I'll stay on watch in here until you are both relieved.'

'Okay, Heinz.' Sturm looked at his watch. 'Come on, Sepp!' he said, and led the way out of the bunker.

They moved along the trench towards the forward position. In the time it took them to walk the 30 m or so towards their post, the cold had already easily made it through their clothing. They reached their position and took over from their predecessors.

'Anything happening, Georg?' Sturm asked König.

'Nothing special. Only once, I thought I saw a movement, way out in front, beside the two ruined trees. Something cracked and then everything went quiet again.'

Unteroffizier König made his way back to the bunker again, with Ede Bollmann following him.

'They are lucky. They can warm themselves up and have a kip,' murmured Hollerer.

'And you've already had your kip. Now, check and make sure your hand grenades are ready and the primer cap unscrewed.'

Hollerer made work to keep himself occupied. Simple routine tasks, such as checking the rounds in the ammunition boxes. Meanwhile, Sturm could have sworn he was turning into a block of ice. He moved the bolt of the machine gun and the belt of ammunition. Then he beat his arms against his chest to try to muster some warmth. His breath billowed in white clouds over their position. From somewhere in front he heard a loud crack, perhaps from a broken branch. He and Hollerer held their breath, listening intently. They could see and hear nothing.

'It must have been the frost, Hans.'

'Could be.'

Sturm and Hollerer stared into the night. The full moon was mostly obscured by clouds, which were thrown into silhouette against its brightness. Further to their right came the sound of a German machine gun. A flare shot into the night sky, seeming to momentarily hang there, as if weightless, before bursting asunder and shooting white stars from its centre.

The hour was soon over. Sturm noticed that his feet were stiff. He moved them. Somewhere on firm ground, packed snow crunched. The night was then still again. The minutes crept by, one after the other. He looked at his watch. He felt a peculiar tension building up inside him, and couldn't shake it off.

'Watch out, Sepp!' he said quietly, only just loud enough for his comrade to hear.

'They should have been here by now,' whispered Hollerer at length.

They scanned the terrain in front of them. There was nothing to be seen. The Russians, however, as both men knew, could move themselves through the snow like moles through soft soil.

Sturm looked at his watch. It was 02.00 hours. Any moment now, the bunker door should open. Why hadn't they heard anything? What was up in that bunker? Had the person who was supposed to wake up the next watch fallen asleep himself?

'Where is the relief?' asked Hollerer, rubbing his hands and face.

'Give them another minute,' said Sturm. 'They know we cannot leave our post.'

They waited one, five, ten minutes, and still no one came to relieve them. The wind, was agonising.

'Damn it! Someone will have to have a look,' decided Sturm. 'Quick, Sepp, go back.'

'No, you go, Hans!'

'If you like, but watch out. If you seen anything at all, holler as loud as you can!'

At first hesitatingly, then faster with each step, Sturm ran back over the densely packed snow. The soles of his boots slid. He reached the bunker door, paused a second to listen, then entered. He let out a loud curse, as he saw Sandkühler sitting with his head laid on the table in front of him, fast asleep. He was beside him within two steps, lifted his head, and let it bang down against the surface of the table with a thud. Sandkühler leapt up.

'Man, why didn't you wake the relief? We are freezing our arses off out there.'

Sturm didn't wait for an answer, as he saw the relief begin to get themselves ready. 'Hurry up, I'm going back out there!'

Sturm rushed back out the guard position, an overpowering sense of unease growing stronger by the second. Somewhere out to his front came cracking and snapping noises. He called out to Hollerer—no answer.

With long strides, he reached the post. Of Hollerer and the machine gun there was nothing to be seen. Except for a trail through the snow, there was no sign of a struggle. Panic overwhelmed Sturm. Where were the Russians? Would they suddenly appear over the edge of the foxhole and grab him, too? Without hesitating he grabbed some hand grenades which lay ready in the foxhole. The primer caps were already unscrewed. He threw the first grenade out to his front, then a second, third, and fourth. Sturm yelled out wild, unarticulated screams. He clamped the butt of his machine pistol to his shoulder and fired off a burst. Behind him he heard the calls of the relief guard.

Seconds later he sprang over the edge of the foxhole and ran in the direction of the enemy. From left and right came the rapid fire of machine guns. It was probably just the terror of the noise of Sturm's hand grenades and machine pistol fire which caused them to join in, and not the actual sighting of the enemy.

Flares rose into the night sky.

How much time had elapsed since Sepp had gone missing—one minute, two? The Russians must have already been close enough to their foxholes to have grabbed Hollerer in the few moments Sturm had been away at the bunker.

About 80 m away, Sturm could make out some Russians, ducking and dodging amid fallen trees and bushes over at the edge of the forest. He stood fast and fired off the entire magazine of his machine pistol, fitted a fresh magazine, then had to dive head first into the snow when a Russian returned his fire. Instinctively, Sturm fired back, aiming for the middle of the yellow stream spurting from the enemy machine pistol. The enemy fire abruptly stopped.

Sturm ran forward again. He yelled with all his might, totally oblivious to what he was doing so. Ice-cold air filled his lungs as he fired off another long burst. A Red Army soldier lay dead where he had fallen. Two others rushed at Sturm. One lunged at him with his bayonet but Sturm fired again, bringing the Russian down on the spot, then ran after the other who had dived into the forest. Again he let fly a burst of fire and ran on, finally reaching a motionless, crumpled figure. It was Hollerer. His machine gun lay nearby. From behind him, Sturm could hear the heavy firing coming from the German positions, all of the guards now fully awakened.

'Are you wounded, Sepp?'

'They stuck me in the back, Hans.'

'Can you stand? Come on, I'll help you back.'

Sturm kneeled beside his wounded comrade, who put his arm around Sturm's neck and slowly stood up. With the machine gun in his left hand, and supporting Hollerer with his right arm and hip, Sturm slowly retraced his steps. Another figure came hurrying forward. It was König, who helped Sturm bring Hollerer back.

Eventually, they reached their own position and set up the machine gun again to be taken over by the next two on guard duty, while others carried the wounded man into the bunker. Hollerer was unconscious by then. They lay him on a cot, and used this as a stretcher to carry him. Sandkühler held up a lamp to examine the stab wounds in his back.

'Shit, damn it!' growled Ede Bollmann. 'He'll have to be taken to the rear right away. It looks as though the bayonet pierced his lung.'

With every exhalation of breath, fine red blood bubbled from his lips. He began to come round.

'How do you feel, Sepp?' asked König.

'Well, a little better. At least Hans has got me back. God knows what they would have done with me!'

'How come you were asleep, Heinz? Why didn't you wake up the relief guard?' Sturm asked Sandkühler.

'I let them sleep because they were both frozen through and Ede had probable got a fever,' said Sandkühler. It sounded like an apology, but was really just an explanation. He knew that, on guard, no man should be asleep. König and Bollmann felt themselves partly to blame, and clapped Sandkühler on the shoulder.

'That won't help,' said König. 'Now we must all suffer the consequences.'

Sturm knew that he would receive the greatest blame for what had happened that night. He should never have left his post. In this situation, he should have fired a few shots in the air, and if this hadn't helped, perhaps thrown a grenade over towards the bunker in the hope the detonation would have aroused his sleeping comrades. It was, after all, a hand grenade thrown by König which woke him up and led to him being awarded the Iron Cross! On the other hand, Sturm also knew that all of the guard posts in this sector were extremely nervous after the Russians had snatched an entire squad. Had he fired a single shot, the whole sector would have erupted into a mad shooting gallery and questions would have been asked at regiment. They would have found out about the squad ignoring standing orders over the number on watch.

Feldwebel Ückert came into the bunker.

'Georg, we have to report to the company commander. First, we have to make a clean breast of it regarding our guard arrangements.'

'Just hold on a moment. That is my responsibility alone.'

'What was up with you, König? What were you shooting at, at night out there?' asked *Oberleutnant* Winter.

König reported what had happened in few words, including his guard arrangements to avoid all of his comrades freezing. After he had finished, there was silence for a few moments. The company commander was not inspired by what he heard, even though he recognised the personal actions of Sturm. He looked pensively at Ückert and König; they had all been friends together in the French campaign, even if their ranks had now seen a certain distance grow between them.

'You know that I must make a report of this.' The field telephone rang as he uttered the words.

'*3 Kompanie, Oberleutnant Winter.*'

'*Major* Gröber, here.' It was the battalion commander, urgency ringing in his voice. 'Why do we have a combat alarm along the whole line?'

Winter, who for a few months had been Ückert and König's platoon commander as an *Oberfeldwebel*, replied briefly. He explained in concise sentences, how the action in his sector had come about.

'Fine mess this. Tomorrow morning, have Sturm and König report. We'll send an ambulance for Hollerer. That's all!'

Only the fact that Sturm had followed the enemy assault troop, killed some of them, and brought back both his comrade and the missing machine gun prevented the entire squad from being severely punished. But in future the entire guard would be on duty at night. No more warm bunker for them. Sturm was embarrassed, as he was portrayed as the hero of the hour.

An examination of the terrain next morning revealed that the Russians had dug a small trench through the snow leading right up to the foxhole.

'Hans,' said Sandkühler, 'we are damned lucky that no report has been sent up the line about this situation. If it had been, we would all be in the shit!'

'Why didn't you wake the relief guard?' Sturm asked his friend once again.

'Now, if I had awoken them at the right time, then the Russians would perhaps have grabbed both of them, and it would have been another full hour before we knew anything was amiss. Possibly they would have crept up on the bunker and attacked it with hand grenades or captured all of us, if we survived their initial attack—you too,' was the reply from Sandkühler, who always seemed to have an excuse ready.

The battalion commander hadn't reported the circumvention of the Regimental orders in his own report. Nevertheless, Sturm's spontaneous actions on that night did seem to have reached the ears of the Regimental and even Divisional commanders, as he was later to discover.

13

The Attack on Moscow Fails

In mid-December 1941, replacements arrived from *Ersatz Battalion 473* in Aachen. Some of these men were evacuated comrades who, their wounds successfully healed, were returning to the Front. They had come from spells of recuperation or regular leave with their families, and having to say goodbye once again to their loved ones had left them decidedly gloomy in demeanour. Ten of the soldiers allocated to Sturm's company were novices, with no front-line experience whatsoever.

One of these was *Gefreiter* Günther Bieler, a reservist officer candidate (*Reserveo ffizierbewerber*, or ROB) whose home was in Monschau in the Eifel region and who had come to the Front to gain combat experience. By chance he was allocated to König's squad, and Sandkühler took an instant dislike to him.

'Can you lead a squad?' he asked in a cynical tone.

'Of course, it's quite simple when you have a basic understanding of tactics!' was Bieler's reply.

'Man, watch your mouth,' snarled Sandkühler. 'You have been lucky up to now, you haven't had your nose in the dirt like us, but that can soon be altered! Tactics indeed, what do you know about tactics!'

'Tactics are the doctrine of junior leadership in battle!' hissed the *Gefreiter* in a fury. 'Do you think so, eh?' yelled Sandkühler. 'That's just parroting what it says in regulations. It's rubbish—just war games theory!'

'Well then, just what are your ideas on tactics then?' asked Bieler spitefully.

'Reach the enemy, get wise to his tricks, outwit him, treat his men with respect, bring everyone back if possible, keep your head, don't walk straight ahead if a grenade has just landed there, carry your wounded comrade back, dress his wounds, share your last cigarette—these are my tactics . With your tactics, you won't last a week, and neither will the men under you!'

'Heinz,' cautioned Sturm, 'I don't think you should be so hard on the lad. Surely we all have to learn the difference between what regulations say and what happens in the real world!'

The new lads had brought newspapers with them, and were also up to date with the latest reports from all fronts. Soldiers who were coming into the front line for the first time after training were nothing like as enthusiastic as those who had marched into Russia on 22 June 1941. The situation had substantially worsened since 1939. The war unleashed against Poland on 1 September 1939, intended to settle the question of the status of Danzig and the Polish Corridor, had provoked declarations of war by England and France against the Reich. The blitz against Denmark, Norway, France, Belgium, Holland, and Luxemburg in 1940, and against Jugoslavia and Greece in April 1941, had served to further Hitler's quest for *Lebensraum*. Opposition to the punitive terms of the Versailles Treaty was but a pretext; and it was simultaneously clear to the other great powers, especially England, that Germany would ultimately become too strong and draw them into another great conflict. Despite the initial successes of the campaign against the USSR, Hitler's armies came to a halt on the outskirts of Moscow on 5 December 1941. The much vaunted *Blitzkrieg* had failed.

The newly arrived comrades from *Ersatz Bataillon 473* brought bad tidings. Japan, which had been at war against China since 1937, had now decided to expand further into South-East Asia, and on 7 December attacked the US Naval Base at Pearl Harbor. The US declaration of war on Japan followed the very next day. Although not obliged to do so by any formal treaties with Japan, Hitler responded by declaring war on the United States on 11 December. The reactions to this news within König's squad were mixed.

'Now we've really had it,' declared Sandkühler in his thick Westphalian accent. 'But who would have guessed that it would be *General Winter* who would hit us so hard?'[1]

The squad leader looked at Sandkühler and Sturm.

'It isn't just Winter who stopped the advance on Moscow. The supply lines for the fastest moving units haven't been able to cope, for various reasons. I suspect that sabotage has got something to do with it. It was the lack of fuel that halted the armoured units, and the lack of spare parts and replacements for the tanks. Of course the leadership won't admit to this!'

König laboriously tapped out his pipe and filled it with a fresh plug of tobacco. The men standing nearby were deep in thought, perturbed by what König had just implied.

'*Herr Unteroffizier*, why—' began officer candidate Bieler.

König interrupted him, 'You can leave out the "Herr"!'

'*Unteroffizier*, why do you suspect sabotage?'

'I've nothing more to say on the matter!' He plunged his hand into his tunic pocket and brought out a crumpled piece of paper, smoothing it out. 'There's an internal message from the signals unit—it says here:

"On 24 November *Panzer Regiment 20* was attached to *20 Armeekorps*, and prepared itself to renew the attack on Moscow along with *4 Armee* and its neighbours to the left, *Panzerarmee* Hoepner. Here the *19 Panzer Division*, the *Panzer Regiment* from *20 Panzer Division* and *Infanterie Regiment 88* under the command of 15 Division. The attack could not succeed in breaking through due to overwhelming enemy superiority and the attacking units had to withdraw to their start positions on the Narva River. Therefore the attempt to take Moscow at the beginning of December failed".'

Sandkühler refused to give up his optimistic stance, though even his spirits had been dampened since the start of the campaign. 'Our *Führer* will soon make all the right decisions and we will—'

'He may be your *Führer*,' interjected König, 'but he wasn't mine, isn't mine, and never will be mine!'

Bieler looked on, shocked at König's outburst. Sandkühler shook his head and Sturm smiled to himself: he had anticipated just such a reaction from both of them. Now that he had started, however, König was not to be put off.

'I haven't read *Mein Kampf*,' he continued, 'but I know that in it he warned against a war on two fronts—and what have we got now?'

'My father wrote to me in August, that if America joined in the struggle against us, then Germany will lose the war!" chimed in Sturm.

The men in the squad fell silent. They knew from other reports that the pincer movement of Guderian's *2 Armee* at Kalinin in the north and Kaluga in the south had also failed.

One weapon more than any other had been decisive for the Soviets—their new T34 tank. Its wide tracks helped spread its ground weight and allowed it to move over the deepest snow without difficulty, while German tanks stuck fast. A new anti-tank weapon for the infantry just had to come. Until now, infantrymen had made up multiple charges from hand grenades tied together, which gathered power to blow the track off a tank or dislodge the turret from its seating. Another common weapon against tanks was the glass bottle filled with a petrol or phosphor mixture: when the tank was hit, this concoction ran into the air vents and engine compartment, and the vehicle went up in flames. Thus, *Landser* needed only to get near enough to leap onto and off the tank to become an instant hero. There were many such heroes, but many died in these high-risk attempts. The Russians, too, used this weapon, which they nicknamed the 'Molotov cocktail'.

Both sides had another simple, but deadly method of killing each other's tanks—throwing a hand grenade into an open turret hatch.

It was a sombre Christmas Eve, the first in the east. Supplies were once again inadequate, in spite of what the men were assured were strenuous efforts on their behalf.

'We shouldn't complain,' said Sturm. 'We have a warm bunker, some peace and quiet, and not much contact with the enemy.'

Except for the two men on guard duty, König's squad sat around the makeshift oven and stretched their hands out to the fire. Flames licked around the open oven door, the men's faces painted red by their flickering light. Behind them in a corner of the bunker burned two candles mounted on a wooden fencepost.

'And to think I had hoped to spend Christmas at home!' said Heinz Schaller. He was a *Sauerländer*, from the area around Winterberg.

'Around this time we would be getting ready for Matins. I always brought the oil lamps out, I filled them and primed them some hours in advance. Then off we went in a row, me in front, then my wife and little Maria in her arms. It was so quiet, peaceful, devout—the glistening snow, the bells ringing. From the houses all around, all the men, women, and children would emerge….'

The men let their comrade continue with his story as he fondly remembered the religious ceremony. Every one of them could picture his own fiancée, girlfriend, wife, or parents with whom they would have gone to Church services on this holy night. Outside, the storm howled and ice crystals crackled furiously on the window pane. Yet they were all at home, their thoughts reaching back the 1,500 km or so which separated them from their loved ones.

Suddenly the door was flung open and the cold came flooding in. It was *Major* Gröber, the battalion commander, and with him the company commander, *Oberleutnant* Winter. They stooped as they entered the bunker.

'Don't get up men,' said the major to the seated soldiers as the squad leader stood up to make his report. 'I am not Father Christmas, but I have brought you something.'

He took from his pocket some documents and a few small brown paper envelopes. König, Sturm, Sandkühler, and Schaller were presented with the Infantry Assault Badge in Silver, along with its award certificate. Both officers congratulated the men and then shook hands with the others in the bunker before wishing everyone '*Frohe Weihnachten*', and departing in the direction of the machine gun position where the two others were standing guard.

Sandkühler was first to pin on his gleaming decoration, Sturm followed suit, then Haller. König, however, put his award in one of his pockets.

'Bring your glasses over here!' he bellowed to his comrades.

He was probably the only one who had noticed, but *Oberleutnant* Winter had with a nod to the men left a bottle of Brandy behind the bunker door. König poured drinks out for them all and they took a sip, toasting 'a better future, absent friends, the family back home….'

Only König thought to make the toast, 'To a speedy end to this shitty war!' He lifted the bottle up to examine its contents against the light of the candles.

'The rest is for the two on watch, its time to change the guard!' he declared.

It was Sturm and Sandkühler's turn.

14

A Cunning Trap

'Looks as though *Unteroffizier* Übel is going to be out there all night, eh, Heinz?'

Sandkühler lifted the binoculars and checked all around the edge of the wood from which Übel and four others should have appeared.

'This patrol won't achieve much, with the enemy being forewarned!'

'You mean that fire-fight in No Man's Land earlier?'

'Well, of course—it's been getting pretty damned rotten here in the last few days. Unless I am very much mistaken, the Russians have been probing our front lines looking for a weak spot to launch their offensive against, and when they find it—'

Sturm held up his hand and Sandkühler immediately fell silent. They looked to the edge of the wood and heard the snapping of branches as someone moved through the trees. Then came the distinctive sound of Soviet machine pistol fire.

'That's Übel!' said Sandkühler.

The little *Unteroffizier* burst out of the wood and ran zig-zagging towards them. Bullets zipped out of the woods. Sturm pulled back the cocking lever on his machine gun and sent a long burst of fire towards the source. Sturm's bullets passed inches above the Übel's head, who threw himself down into a snow-hole to get out of the line of fire. Swiftly, Sturm depressed the machine gun lower and fired off the rest of the belt of ammunition. In the few seconds it took to fit a fresh belt, the enemy fire grew in intensity and muzzle flashes could be seen among the trees, the enemy bullets slamming into the snow just in front of Sturm's position.

Moldenhauer's machine gun joined in. The bullets whipped into the woods, tearing off branches and ricocheting off in all directions.

Everything went still. Everyone waited for Übel to appear. After the furious fire from the Soviets hard on Übel's heels, no one held out any hopes for the four men who he had taken with him on the patrol.

'No sign of him, Hans. You give covering fire, I'll go take a look!'

Before Sturm could answer, Sandkühler ran off. He made no attempt to crouch or to zig-zag as he ran, but made straight for the point where Übel had last been seen. Only once enemy mortar fire began to land did he show some caution, and run in short dashes until he reached Übel's position.

Mortar shells detonated in front of the German positions. Using a small trench which led to a forward lookout for cover, Sandkühler reappeared with Übel slung over his shoulder. Out of breath, he dropped to the ground after carefully setting down his comrade.

Sturm could see two bullet wounds in the tough *Rheinländer*'s back.

'What has happened Übel?' asked *Unteroffizier* König, who had emerged from the bunker followed by *Oberleutnant* Winter. Both had been awaiting the return of the reconnaissance patrol.

'The Russians took us by surprise. We … we were deep in the forest with the enemy mortar positions just to our front when they suddenly appeared. They came from our left flank and must have spotted us earlier and been keeping tabs on us.' He took a breath, tried to raise himself up, but fell back again. 'They fired, and we returned their fire. Klinck and Loeser must have been killed instantly, Zülke collapsed just as I threw myself beside him. Hüttemann is wounded. I … I was shot in the back. The Russians gave me no chance to go back for him. We must rescue Hüttemann!'

Übel fell unconscious. Loss of blood had severely weakened him, and it was a miracle he had even made it back. As he was being carried back to the bunker, he came to.

'Where exactly is Hüttemann?' asked *Oberleutnant* Winter.

'Behind the point where the thick patch of Alder trees is, and the path towards the enemy bunker branches off. *Herr Oberleutnant*, are you going to bring him back?'

'Of course we will get him, and straight away, before the Russians do. Men! I need three volunteers!'

'Here, *Herr Oberleutnant*,' said Sandkühler, almost before Winter had finished speaking.

'I'll go too,' offered Sturm. Martin Bürger, one of the company runners, was the third. They took machine pistols, hand grenades, and *Zeltbahnen* with them.

'All platoon machine guns train on the edge of the woods. As soon as we've got him we will return, and the Soviets will be sure to follow us. Then you will open fire!' ordered *Oberleutnant* Winter. 'Follow me,' he said, and jumped into the small trench leading to the forward positions.

The men ran on, crouching low. The trench was only a metre deep at most. In the distance, the artillery was at work. The shells flew far over the front line and crashed to the ground somewhere behind them. Sturm followed close behind the *Oberleutnant*. The fire over there grew more and more intense. German artillery responded. This repartee, however, had nothing to do with them.

Yet enemy mortar fire now began to land uncomfortably close by, forcing them to take whatever cover they could in the shallow trench. The *Oberleutnant* crept forward, followed by the men. They felt the cold in their bones. Close beside them, mortars shells crashed to the ground and showered them with snow. The barrage lasted for half an hour, after which they could cross the open stretch. All together, they dashed forward and dived into the cover of the woods. Sturm held his machine pistol ready to fire. Positioning himself behind the company commander, he peered into the darkness.

'Along here! They went this way.'

Sturm felt his heart pound. Why did he volunteer do come along? He wanted to live, to make it through without any serious wounds. Yet he had never taken medical leave when he had the chance. And now here he was, in a combat group that the Russians would certainly be waiting for them. All because the Germans simply would not leave their wounded behind at the mercy of the Soviets.

In front rang out more mortar shots. The rounds flew over them and crashed to the ground by the German positions. They darted forward from tree trunk to tree trunk. If somewhere a branch creaked or snapped, they dropped down together and waited in nervous agitation.

The *Oberleutnant* was first to reach the small clearing with the frozen brook. He threw himself to the ground for cover, and to give covering fire to the men following in case the Russians should attack.

'They are over there, *Herr Oberleutnant*. Just over there, close to the footpath,' whispered Sandkühler.

'Damn it! That looks bad,' thought Sturm out loud. 'The Russians must have already found him and—'

A moaning, barely audible cry startled them. The wounded man whimpered, his spine-chilling groan echoing faintly through the oppressive darkness.

Martin Börger, the company runner, was also a medical orderly. He ran forward as he spotted their injured comrade, who was slowly trying to raise himself.

'No, no, no!' cried the wounded man, raising his arm up to fend off the anticipated blow.

'It's me, Bürger, I'm here to help you!' cried the *Stabsgefreiter*. 'I will help you!'

'Nooo!' howled the wounded German. 'There is a—'

In the same moment that Bürger bent over his injured comrade, a bright red, metre-high flame erupted. A colossal detonation threw him back, and the impact set off three other mines.

Sturm believed that the immense pressure would crush his chest. His ears and head rang. Then he caught a glimpse of where the Russian mortar position must be. Streaks of fire whizzed by him.

Oberleutnant Winter crept slowly forward until he could see what was happening. Sandkühler followed. They saw four metre-high mortar tubes in the snow, and four dark foxholes, from which the lifeless eyes of his comrades gaped.

They crawled back. Despairing, they tried to avoid the machine gun fire which now zipped through the forest. They reached the cover of the trees and threw themselves down into the snow.

'All dead, Hans. The Russians, those bastards—they booby-trapped the wounded man,' yelled Sandkühler, brimming with hatred and repugnance. 'I'll make them pay for this!'

Sturm felt like he was going to throw up. He took deep breaths, only to inhale drafts of cordite from the explosives. Through the haze in his eyes he could make out that the enemy fire had stopped. Then he saw something else.

He raised his machine pistol and fired off the entire magazine. The Russians, who had been slowly working their way behind the Germans, went to ground. Now everyone fired—the *Oberleutnant*, Sandkühler, and Sturm. They fired all their machine pistol ammunition and threw their hand grenades, then crawled 50 m to the side and lay still. The three fitted fresh magazines were inserted into their machine pistols, and they waited for the enemy to advance.

The Russians were about twenty strong. The Germans heard them calling their orders back and forth in subdued voices. The moonlight gleamed against the metal of the enemy weapons, as it filtered fleetingly through the trees. They followed the Germans, and only when they reached the position where the path forked towards the right did they realise the danger—too late.

Three machine pistols rang out. The Soviets didn't stand a chance. Sturm saw Sandkühler leap up. He too sprang up. They ran towards the enemy firing in short bursts, still filled with bile at the booby-trapping of their wounded comrade. Once again, the fury of war had snuffed out two young lives.

Then all three ran back all the way to their own positions. Out of breath and exhausted, Sturm reached his own foxhole. He let himself drop into the dugout. Now that he knew that he was safe once again, the fear of death overwhelmed him once more.

'All dead,' he gasped. 'All dead. These dirty, despicable bastards mined them.'

'And where is Bürger?' asked the squad leader.

'Dead, they are all dead!'

15

The Russians cross Lake Seliger

'Another one, mate!'

Hans Sturm looked at his card. No good, he would probably go bust, and then the pot would be gone. Fourteen now, and still one more card to come—things didn't look promising.

'Here, partner!' Sandkühler gave him a card.

It was a seven. Silently, Sturm laid his cards down and drew the pot over to himself.

'Why can't I have that kind of luck, just once?' said Günther Bieler peevishly.

'New game, new luck. Do you want to try again?'

'Nope, I can't make your stakes!'

'No long speeches, Heinz, just deal the cards!'

Sandkühler obeyed. Sturm's first card was an ace. He grinned and lifted his next card. He laughed out loud and laid both cards face down on the table.

'I'll go fifty.'

He took a fifty-mark note from his wallet and added it to the pot. Sandkühler dealt his own first card. It too was an ace. He silently threw another fifty-mark note into the pot. Sturm raised by another hundred, and Sandkühler followed suit. Then he took his second card. It was a king.

'Damn it. You must have at least two tens, so I'll have to buy another card.' He took another, saw it was an eight, and threw his cards on the table in disgust.

'Damn and blast!' he fumed. 'Show me your cards, pal.'

Laughing, Sturm turned his cards over. First an ace, then a queen. If Sandkühler had only known that Sturm was bluffing, then he would have stopped after he got the king, called, and would have won the 300-mark pot. He was furious. The men laughed with delight at his misfortune. At that very moment, the bunker door opened, allowing a draft of freezing air to enter the bunker.

'The old man!' called Bieler.

Money was quickly stuffed into pockets and the skat cards cleared away. They were already beginning to stand up as *Oberleutnant* Winter entered.

'All right men, carry on,' he said as Sturm approached him.

'How are things with *Unteroffizier* König, *Herr Oberleutnant*?'

'Not as bad as we first thought. You take charge of the squad for the time being, Sturm!'

'Yes, *Herr Oberleutnant*!'

A bullet had landed in König's chest, thankfully missing his heart.

'And any news about Hollerer?'

'That wound won't heal so fast, a bayonet in the lung! But I should be passing on his regards to you. He is being flown out tomorrow morning to Osterode, perhaps they can sort him out there!'

'Anything else, *Herr Oberleutnant*?' asked Sturm, who had heard rumours of another move.

'Tomorrow morning, we move into the sector held by 1 Company.'

'Below the sea-wall?'

'Exactly there, Sturm. Great position, can only be approached from the Front. Assuming the Ivans can't cross over the lake. On the left flank, just at the bend where the small outflow runs to the south, it might just be possible. However, we will be setting up both of 3 Platoon's machine guns to cover that spot just in case.'

'And my leave, *Herr Oberleutnant*?'

'Leave? Just what kind of leaf might you be referring to? I don't think I know the kind of tree you mean,' teased *Oberleutnant* Winter, grinning.[1]

'And I was taken in like a real fool, giving up my cushy billet with the supply section.'

'It won't be much longer, Sturm. As soon as the winter is over and the thaw comes, you'll be one of the first to get leave. When everything turns to mud, no one can move, including the Russians—then, we can let you go home.'

'You have God's ear, *Herr Oberleutnant*!'

'I must get on, men. *Feldwebel* Kionke will let everyone else know about the move. Keep your weapons ready, understood?'

Sturm nodded, but without the customary 'Jawohl, *Herr Oberleutnant*!' He was bitter about his own stupidity and Winter's light-hearted remarks. He looked over at Sandkühler, who was now Number 1 on the machine gun. Everyone was checking their weapons and ammunition. Sturm grumbled about the change in positions over to Lake Seliger. They would now be migrating from reasonably decent positions, and the bunker that they had occupied, to more new tasks and unknown dangers. Always the waiting for the bullet or grenade which would bring death.

Yet somehow none of these fears affected the men as much as the damned cold. Sturm thought of Vogel, crippled by this terrible adversary. If this was to be the only way to get home, then better not at all—yet so it was. It was not the fighting which was the most terrible thing about this country. It was the filth, the temperature, the vermin, and the continuous uncertainty over their fate. This damned lake, for instance—had the Russians broken through during the night to its north or south? This kept Sturm fearful. If they had, then would follow the long trek into captivity, driven by guards through the snow and storms. Whoever tripped and fell into the snow froze solid and never got up again. No, Sturm would never allow himself to be taken prisoner. As he pondered these things, he mechanically checked his Luger and his machine pistol. He would never be taken prisoner, this he swore to himself.

'Bloody cold, damn it,' grumbled Sandkühler.

They lay in their new positions on the southern shore of Lake Seliger, on the left flank of *253 Infanterie Division*. The previous nights had seen unspeakably temperatures. For six days and nights they had waited for the enemy to appear; for six nights the icy winds had cut through their clothing, numbing their senses. Sturm had once almost developed frostbite in his toes. Back in the bunker, he had sat for ages rubbing them before the circulation came back and he knew the danger was over.

'Yes, that ice is thick enough to support the fattest Eskimo on his sledge,' he said. 'And yet the Russians still don't come!'

'No, no. But I bet you they intend to, after the recce results and the evidence of deserters they will have picked up.' Sturm continued. 'Besides, we have heard the sounds of their preparations, especially at night—noises from half tracks, and maybe even tanks!'

'But they can't come here with all that stuff, not over the ice. They wouldn't be that stupid!'

As Feldwebel Kionke approached them, he saw the questioning look in their faces.

'Watch out boys, looks like there's something going on over by 5 Company!'

They could hear the chatter of machine guns and the detonation of hand grenades.

'There you are, you see Hans, over by 5 Company, not here!'

'Just a moment!'

Hans brought his binoculars up to his eyes. He stared out over the lake's open expanse, then passed the binoculars to Kionke. As he looked through them he let out a cry of surprise.

'The Russians! They are coming over the lake. I must warn the other squads. Get your weapons ready!'

Gradually, the shadowy images became clearer. Sandkühler let out a whistle.

'They are out of their minds!' he said. 'They are going virtually arm-in-arm over the ice, just as though they were coming to pay us a social visit.'

Kionke returned.

'We have to stop them as quickly as possible, Hans!'

'No, we must wait until they're only about a 100 m away,' suggested Sturm, 'then we open fire with all five machine guns.'

'And what happens when we have a stoppage—are we supposed to fight them off with our spades?' cried Sandkühler.

'Shut your face,' Sturm barked. 'Set your machine gun to maximum depression. The other machine guns will wait until you fire first.'

Sturm realised that the platoon commander had accepted his suggestion, and had left to advise the other machine gun positions of his plan. The three machine guns of 2 Platoon, which were sited at the edge of the lake, near to the jetty, were ready to fire, as were the two machine guns of 3 Platoon. From out on the lake itself, the machine gun positions were very difficult to see, camouflaged as they were by heavy snowfalls. This was one of Sturm's prime considerations in deciding on his plan. As soon as the machine guns opened fire, the snow would be shaken off and their positions revealed. If the machine guns had opened fire straight away as Kionke suggested, the enemy would have rapidly pinpointed the German positions. With Sturm's plan, the concentrated fire of six heavy machine guns at close range would have a terrific impact on the enemy, before they even had any chance to react. The riflemen, too, would await the fire of the first machine gun before opening up.

Sturm thought out loud.

'The ice is thick enough to support the weight of the Russian half tracks, but they don't trust it, they are frightened that it will give way. The attackers are making their move against this particular promontory to get off the ice as quickly as possible. This gives us our chance!'

The Russians were coming ever nearer, and as all the troops could see by the light of the moon, they were walking fully erect, some even with their arms linked to steady themselves.

'My God,' whispered Sandkühler. 'We must fire now!'

The crazy daredevil was now beginning to lose his nerve, and Sturm realised that Sandkühler was about to fire.

'Get away from that gun,' he yelled at Sandkühler, and shoved him aside.

His words were lost in the drunken cries of the Russians, now only 300 m away, as they began to charge, yelling, 'Urrah, Urrah!'

'Steady now,' Sturm heard *Feldwebel* Kionke say, 'only fire after Sturm's machine gun opens up!'

It was Sturm behind the machine gun now, and he experienced all the action as though it were in an Alpine dreamworld. Many of the attackers slipped and slid drunkenly around on the ice, fell, picked themselves up, and staggered on, firing as they came. Ever and ever closer.

'Fire, fire!' cried Sandkühler desperately.

At this moment, enemy mortar and artillery fire opened up. They shells flew over the Germans' head towards the rear. The Russian assault troops were less than 300 m away.

'*Achtung*, Sturm!' yelled Kionke.

Sturm half-raised himself, and in that moment a rifle butt slammed against the side of his steel helmet. The steel helmet was knocked aside, its chinstrap broken and the butt deflected downwards, hitting his shoulder. Dazed, Sturm saw through a haze of dancing stars *Feldwebel* Kionke grapple with the demented Sandkühler. As his eyes re-focussed themselves, Sturm tried to make out what was in front of him. An endless wave of Russians staggered forward, and they were now almost upon him. His vision had now completely re-focused itself. He heard Kionke shout something. Sturm opened fire, and as soon as he did so two of the other four machine guns joined in. The foremost of the enemy were now only 100 m away.

Machine gun bullets ripped into the attackers and into the ice around their feet. The bullets ricocheted off the hard-packed ice and slammed into the Soviet troops, causing horrendous injuries. The extensive chain of Russians fragmented. The rear of the mass continued with their cries of 'Urrah' and pushed their way forward, driving their front comrades in front further into the hail of deadly German fire. It was a dreadful sight.

Sturm traversed his machine gun from left to right and expended a full second case of ammunition, which Bieler had hurriedly delivered to him. As he already suspected, the Russians wanted first to reach the promontory and then push forward together in this direction. He noted the shattering effect of German fire, but the rearmost of the attackers were beginning to push their way through.

Out on the ice, many dark spots were visible where the dead and wounded lay. The second wave began to take cover behind the bodies of the first wave. Still some Russians came onwards, yelling as they crossed over the see-wall. And then the ice on the lake began to crack asunder, as the German heavy company opened fire and the first mortar bombs fell among the foremost Russian lines. The detonating mortar bombs tossed the Russians aside like rag dolls. They began to retreat. Others, who suddenly lost their will to fight, remained on the German side of the sea-wall, and raised their hands in surrender.

'Move through quickly, quickly,' Feldwebel Kionke said as he waved the prisoners to the rear. At his nod, Görges and Krüger stood up and led the prisoners to the rear. Sturm ceased fire. The last few remaining Russians came forward, almost all of them bloodied and wounded, and some supporting their seriously maimed comrades.

The Germans waited, alert, all through the rest of the night, but no further attacks ensued. Only when the morning light began to grow did the tension ease somewhat. The Germans could see, stretched out before then on the ice, the bodies of hundreds of the enemy. Even if some had survived the German fire, a night out in the open on the frozen lake would have killed them without question. It was an appalling sight, and caused many to wonder what sense there was in all this killing. They found no answer.

Only now, did Sturm begin to feel the pain in his head. He was relieved, and returned to his bunker and removed his steel helmet. His fingers gently probed his head, neck, and shoulder.

'Hans, listen, I—'

Sturm drew himself up. He saw Sandkühler's grimacing features. Spontaneously he grinned, thereby moving his head.

'Absolutely no need to hit so hard, Heinz!'

'I'm sorry, I must have had a screw loose, I don't know what got into me!'

'Never mind, everything's will be fine now!' said Sturm earnestly, hoping the pain between his neck and upper arm would soon fade.

'You know, I didn't mean to hurt you, I only wanted to get behind the machine gun because I was frightened the Russians would overrun our positions.'

He approached his friend and offered his hand saying, 'I must be going crazy!'

'True!' said a voice from the bunker door. *Feldwebel* Kionke entered. He saw the bruise where Sturm had removed his tunic.

'Man, Sandkühler—you were a hair's breadth away from landing yourself right in it, you could easily have ended up on report.'

Sturm shook Sandkühler's hand.

'That's much better, boys!' Kionke mumbled approvingly.

16

January 1942—Retreat

After a few days by Lake Seliger, *253 Infantry Division* was moved down towards the River Volga. By December 1941, the Front stretched from Lake Seliger via Selischarowo, Sokotovo, Lytkino, and Strashjewitschi up to Wyssokaja, and could no longer be held. The pressure imposed by the Soviet 3, 4, and 22 Armies was too strong.

It was a flight which, in the German press and radio broadcasts, was portrayed as a shrewd tactical move and a triumphant withdrawal. In effect, it was the end of German actions under Operation Typhoon.

The *2 Armee*, under Guderian, had struck northwards by Kalinin and southwards by Kaluga in a massive armoured pincer movement designed to encircle Moscow, and was now wrecked. It had already been forced to retreat by mid-December. Units of *9 Armee*, to which Sturm's regiment belonged, were the last to withdraw from the area around Ostaschkow. Last of all were the *Landsern* of *3 Kompanie, Infanterie Regiment 473*.

The enemy were breathing down the Germans' necks, and had in places even managed to get in front of them, occupying villages which lay along the route of the German withdrawal. The Germans were forced to fight their way through in several spots, while communications with other units were often severed by attacks from roaming enemy combat groups.

Sturm's company came to one village which the enemy had set on fire shortly before the Germans arrived. He saw one woman struggling to carry a barrel of grain from her burning house. He ran forward and succeeded, with the woman's help, to manoeuvre the barrel over the threshold of the house. At this point, the balcony above the door collapsed in a flaming heap on Sturm's back. The wreckage was too heavy for Sturm to remove on his own. The woman screamed for help, but before anyone arrived had cleared the wreckage and freed Sturm with her bare hands. The barrel was then rolled clear of the burning house.

Sturm never forgot the sight of that woman, standing there in her badly scorched clothing, shaking her burned hands. Neither did he forget the terrified eyes of her two small children, who sat next to her, whimpering. Russian assault troops had torched their own villages to make the German retreat more difficult. Later, many of these crimes would be blamed on the Germans, and many POWs condemned for it in show trials in 1949.

In one village, Sturm and his comrades came across a disabled truck filled with provisions. There was no alcohol, but plenty of tinned goods of all sizes and types of content. The clerk responsible for this load refused to hand over the contents to the troops without orders from his superiors and stood, pistol ready, to defend his treasure.

The clerk came within a hair's breadth of being shot by the angry soldiers. Sandkühler, however, relieved him of his responsibilities with a sharp right hook to the chin! Why, the soldiers asked themselves, would this idiot be so determined to protect his supplies? They would only be captured by the Russians who followed close behind, anyway! Perhaps he thought he would be treated better by the Russians if he was captured in possession of such a prize.

Even without the attentions of the enemy, the retreat was made very difficult by the wind, the -48-degree temperatures made even worse by the wind chill factor. There was very little chance to rest and no trace of warm rations. The supply section had already withdrawn ahead of them. The roads were in places flanked by snowdrifts up to 2 m deep, which did, however, offer some protection against the wind—though only at the expense of obstructing visibility. Marching into driving snow, the men kept their heads bowed and stumbled along in single file, hoping against hope for a spell of rest sometime soon, somewhere out of the cold, in a stable or hut, and some warm food.

Sturm felt once again the gnawing pain in his intestines. Often he had to drop his trousers to try to evacuate his bowels, but most of the time only passed wind and blood. Sandkühler noticed Sturm bent over with pain. He knew that the charcoal and other tablets supplied by the medic were no longer helping his friend. Only a few days' rest and light food, out of the cold and the wind, could help him get over his bout of dysentery.

'Man, what's up, Hans, can I help?'

'Ach, I have to disappear for a moment.'

'Okay, but don't be too long, they won't wait on you. If you get left behind, you're lost!'

'Yes, yes. It's only a few kilometres up to the next stop.' Sandkühler hesitated a few moments' until Sturm said, 'On you go! You are responsible for the squad now!'

Sandkühler disappeared into the thick snowstorm. Sturm lay his machine pistol behind him. He hadn't even the strength to pull down his trousers, however, and collapsed exhausted to the ground.

You must get up, he said to himself. His head spun. He memory faded, and he had no idea how long he lay there trying to clear his head before he got to his feet. The snowstorm had abated somewhat, but there was no sign of anyone on the road. He set off to follow the company. He winced as he slipped on the icy, rutted surface, falling heavily to the ground. With great effort he raised himself up, wandering further onwards before he had time to gather his thoughts. Why had they left him there? Why had no one come? Where were they all?

'Sandkühler, Kionke!' he cried out.

Each call to his comrades only served to increase his sense of solitude. He was lost! They had given him up. He stood in the middle of the road. Suddenly, his head began to clear. Wasn't this place quite near to the next village, where they had stayed a couple of days during the advance? Hadn't they been friendly towards the local Russians? He had only spoken about it with Sandkühler a few minutes ago. He looked at his watch and was shocked to realise that it hadn't just been a few minutes ago. It was already 17.15 hours, so he must have fallen much further behind the company than he had thought, and they were at the rear of the column. No wonder no one had heard him.

He went back along the route until he found fresh tracks which led off the road. He saw a low hillock off to the right and just behind it a few buildings, almost completely covered in snow. It looked about 400 m away. It was the village of Korowilij.

It seemed like ages until he finally approached the nearest cottage. Once again he fell and was inundated with the thought that this was the end. But once again he fought back and refused to give in. Drawing on his very last reserves, he forced himself onwards. He *had* to get into the village. Perhaps there was another German unit in there. Then in a few days he might be able to join up with his unit again.

As he spotted a thickly wrapped Russian emerge from one of the houses, he began to yell. The old man listened to his calls and footsteps as he crunched through the snow, and waited. He held out both arms and jabbered something Sturm couldn't understand. Now Sturm realised that, as he had approached, his machine pistol was aimed towards the old man, and swiftly lowered it.

'Good friend,' he croaked, 'are there Germans soldiers here?'

'*Njet*, all gone, all away!' said the old man in broken German. His words hit Sturm like a physical blow. His knees gave way.

'Family Wassili Pukorow?' asked Sturm.

The old man nodded. He came to Sturm and took his arm, guiding him on to another house further on. He saw the well and the thick icicles that hung from the eaves. Through a veil of stars and red haze he heard the voices of a woman and a man. Bathed in the warmth of the room, he heard the cries of children, and then everything dissolved into a whirling kaleidoscope of colours as he fainted. When he finally awoke, he found himself lying in a Russian bed. He looked at himself in amazement. Then he saw the man. The old fellow's wrinkled face slowly broke into a smile.

'It is good, in bed. Very good. You lie, sleep, much, long time.'

'How long have I been here?'

The old man shrugged his shoulders.

'Now much better. Only feet bad frost!'

'No, not a cripple!' he cried to himself. He tried to sit up, then fell back exhausted.

'How is it, Grandpa? Feet gone?'

'No, no, feet stay. Maybe pair of toes go!'

The frostbite to his hands and face wasn't too bad, he could tell. His feet were bandaged, he could see that much, as the old man drew back the blanket. He saw he was wearing an old Russian shirt. Maybe the old man had cleaned him up and washed him, if he had messed himself because of the dysentery. His greatcoat and steel helmet hung from the wall, and his other clothing lay over a stool. His machine pistol lay covered up on the floor, but he could see the barrel. In front of the stool stood his boots, the left one split open at the rear.

Why had the Russian given him this life-saving help and not killed him? Was it simple humanity, or his fear of retribution from the Germans, who might have come to search for Sturm? It might also have been the way that Sturm had behaved to the old man's grandchildren. He had given the children gifts of chocolate and built them toys, quickly winning their trust in the few days his unit had been quartered in this village during the advance.

It was two days before Sturm was strong enough to get out of bed. At first, he was a little unsteady on his legs. With two crutches to take the weight off his left foot, he was able to hobble about the room. The children teased him over his limp. With thin soup and light meals, the woman of the house managed to bring his dysentery under control. The pain in his intestines had eased, the diarrhoea slowly faded, and the food remained in his system long enough to help build up his strength.

His host managed to organise a sledge and Panje horse for him. Sturm, once again dressed in his uniform, was loaded into the sledge. He kept his machine pistol out of sight under the blanket on the sledge, and then set off. The woman took the reigns herself.

Within 15 km, Sturm was with his company once more. They were still acting as rearguard. His comrades swarmed round him, Sandkühler dancing for joy, and clapped Sturm on the shoulders. *Feldwebel* Kionke ran over, followed by *Oberleutnant* Winter.

'Man, Sturm, Your name has already been put on the missing in action list.'

'Where have you been? Five days you have been missing!' asked Kionke. 'We were still moving on through the night when we noticed you were missing. Sandkühler had to go forward to see the old man and we had no clue what had happened to you. We just thought you'd had to go behind a bush yet again.'

Sturm briefly explained to them what had occurred. Then Sandkühler and Sturm went over to the old woman and gave her some bread and bottles, which Sandkühler had quickly 'organised'. She wanted no reward for their kind treatment of Sturm; she took for granted that a stranger in need ought to be helped. They put the things in the sledge, nevertheless, and Sturm bade her farewell, waving until she was out of sight.

17

Seli Airfield

The battalion doctor was of the opinion that the degree of frostbite suffered by Sturm to his hands, legs, and most of all to the left foot was serious enough to warrant evacuation home to Germany for hospital treatment, and duly authorised a flight pass.

Sandkühler sought out his comrade in the dressing station. He clapped him on the shoulder and pointed to the flight pass tied to his tunic around the ribbons for the Iron Cross Second Class and East Front Campaign Medal.

'Now you've made it, Hans, you can get away from all this shit—don't forget to look up my parents when you get your recuperation leave!'

Sturm looked at his comrade. They had been close friends ever since their days as raw recruits.

'I hope when we meet again my old bones will be healed. Give my best to the squad!'

'They shook hands. Heinz left without looking back. He wanted to play the tough warrior, and not give away the fact that his eyes were moist with sadness at their separation.

After a journey of an hour or so by sledge, Sturm reached the airfield at Seli. He limped, supported by his crutch, into the dressing station. He wore only his right marching boot, and carried the left one under his arm. After reporting and having himself admitted, he introduced himself briefly to the other wounded. They told him it would be some time before they were likely to get a flight out.

Two days earlier, the enemy fighter planes had shot up two Junkers Ju 52 transport planes. Both had made crash landings, so there were not too many dead, but plenty of bumps, bruises, and broken bones. The next Ju 52s to leave would only depart once fighter escorts had been arranged.

Sturm had been given a slipper. It was for a right foot but would still fit his left. The slipper had in fact come from a comrade who had just lost his right leg. Sturm was soon making himself useful about the ward, helping with the other wounded, many of whom were in much worse shape than he was. Some were blinded or had lost one eye; some had lost an arm or a leg. Sacrificed for the Fatherland! These thoughts passed through Sturm's head as he moved through the various wards in the

Seli dressing station. His nose was assailed by the stench of blood-soaked bandages around the suppurating wounds of his crippled comrades. It was a sad, stupid, despairing sight. When the anguished groans of some of the severely injured finally ceased, it was to the dead, and to some of their living comrades, a blessed relief.

Days went by, during which the airfield and the surrounding terrain came under constant bombardment by the Russians. Soviet combat groups as well as Partisan bands had encircled the Germans and were hitting them hard. Weakly armed units such as supply and transport elements, or hospitals like the one at Seli, made particularly easy targets. The reinforcements sent out around the perimeter could do little to hinder the enemy attacks.

One night, Sturm was awoken by the sounds of explosions and small arms fire. Before he could get to his feet, hand grenades came crashing through the windows of the hospital block and the screams of the wounded filled Sturm's ears. A few days earlier, Sturm had managed to 'organise' a machine-pistol for himself from the medical personnel, and now he wasted no time in grabbing it and hobbling outside, in time to direct a burst of fire at some Russian troops. The fire was returned with vigour, but ducking and weaving, he managed to avoid being hit. The attacking Russians were quickly driven off, all killed, wounded, or captured after a rapidly organised counter-attack by the guards.

Sturm was called to see the chief surgeon.

The surgeon heaped praise on Sturm for his part in driving off the enemy despite his own injuries, and promised him that he would soon be home again. Sturm, however, insisted that there were many with much worse injuries than he who had to be given priority, and requested transport back to his unit until a suitable flight became available. The grateful surgeon was pleased to agree, and provided Sturm with movement papers marked, 'Released to his company at his own request!'

Sturm arranged a lift back to his unit with a supply truck. It was 18 March 1942.

18

Sturm becomes Company Runner

Oberleutnant Winter was astonished when Sturm reported to him.

'Man, Sturm, what are you doing back here? We thought the next we would hear from you would be a letter from home. What's up?'

Sturm gave a brief report on what had happened at Seli, and said that he would be happier waiting for a suitable flight here at his own unit. The company commander retained Sturm on the company staff as a messenger, as he was still unable to wear his left boot.

Oberleutnant Winter had recommended Sturm for the German Cross in Gold. It was a requirement for this award that the nominee already hold the Iron Cross Second and First Classes and had performed multiple further deeds worthy of the Iron Cross First Class.

Sturm had been awarded the Iron Cross First Class in August 1941, and had certainly been involved in enough actions since. The decisive factor, however, was that Sturm, despite being wounded on numerous occasions, had elected to stay with his comrades at the Front when he had had the opportunity to be evacuated. *Oberleutnant* Winter had known Sturm since November 1940 and was able to comment not only on his combat actions, but also his calm and dependable behaviour in any kind of situation.

Stabsgefreiter Alfons Raitler had temporarily taken over command of the squad from Sturm, while Sandkühler had taken over as Number 1 on the machine gun team. The men flew into a rage when Sturm hobbled into the bunker.

'Idiot!' said Sandkühler, who continued after taking a deep breath, 'You are beyond saving!'

The squad had generally felt that although Raitler could not compare with their old squad leader Georg König, as an old sweat he exuded the right air of calmness and experience. He recounted the following tale:

'During our training a *Feldwebel* hammered into us, "In war, a soldier who pauses to think is a dead man, and that's why so many good men die and so many idiots live."

This sort of cynicism is rife in war. What was probably actually meant by the *Feldwebel* was that the good men, who stand firm and fight, become heroes and die. The idiots (who perhaps weren't actually so foolish) keep their heads down—and live.'

Unteroffizier Georg König had been given some home leave from the hospital where he had undergone treatment. Coming home unexpectedly, he had found his wife in bed with another man. He had shot them both, then turned his gun on himself. The men had learnt of this in a letter that one of the wounded men had written from the replacement battalion in Aachen. Sturm was shattered. After Sandkühler, König was his next best friend. He thought long and hard about König's rash actions and came to the conclusion that it was not only the behaviour of his unfaithful wife which had driven König to this act, but his experiences before and during the war.

As a member of the company staff, Sturm noticed the huge difference to service in a front-line combat squad. Of course, he still had to take his turn on guard duties along with the other messengers, medics, *etc.* But the company commander had restricted his night duties to patrolling with the officers.

After the initial retreat of the Germans and the pursuit by the Russians, actions on the Eastern Front became reduced to static, trench warfare just like in the First World War. '*General Winter*' enforced a pause on both combatants. Each side dug themselves in near villages and established bunkers, machine gun nests and foxholes with systems of trenches linking them all together. Slightly further to the rear were the larger bunkers, built using timber and rubble from destroyed buildings. Thus, there were in fact two 'front lines' separated by 2 to 4 km. In between lay open ground, a few bushes, and copses, and both sides were forced to cut down trees in order to give themselves good fields of fire.

Despite his injuries, Sturm joined one of the machine gun teams. His right foot, still clad in a slipper, was bound with a canvas covering tied with the belt from his greatcoat. He drew sketches of the terrain before him, working out ranges, fields of fire, and aiming points, and seeking out conspicuous landmarks, all so that his target acquisition would be so much faster should the enemy attack. These sketch maps were also passed on to the heavy company for zeroing in its mortars and infantry cannon. The maps were in fact required by orders from the regiment—perhaps even from division. In any case, they caused much grumbling, but the men eventually had them all ready.

The terrain continually altered because of the changing seasons. Once barren areas would become overgrown in summer, and new shrubs and bushes would obscure lines of sight. Fresh sketch maps were continually being prepared.

The sector of the Front occupied by *Infanterie Regiment 473* in April 1942 was relatively quiet. The only ones in any real danger were those who moved around in the area between the two lines of defence, either voluntarily or on duty. Sturm remained with the company staff during this period, while his frostbite healed. However, each time a reconnaissance was mounted or an assault group was formed for forward recce to take prisoners, Sturm was among the first to volunteer.

Each recce brought new knowledge. Special maps were made in 1:2,000 scale. On these maps, every bush or copse, every depression or footpath, and every Soviet minefield was marked. Indeed, the Germans made no effort to lift enemy mines. For every known mine lifted or blown up, the enemy would lay another which might remain undetected. It was better to leave them laying there where at least their position was known.

In March and April, a lot of mail arrived from home. Parcels or packages addressed to men who had been killed in action were shared out among their surviving comrades. Packets were also sent by well-wishers, addressed to the 'unknown soldier'. Sturm felt that those who received these packets should at least have the decency to write a letter of thanks. To those who had just lost a husband or son, a letter might in fact re-open painful emotional wounds and not be particularly welcome. However, others would surely be pleased to know that their packets had gone to people who deserved and appreciated them. Sturm told the others that the sender of every packet addressed to the 'unknown soldier' should at least get a letter of thanks, but that the *Landsern* were just to stubborn to bother.

Oberleutnant Winter looked over at Sturm.

'Here then,' he said, 'Have a packet, and when you write back, say hello from me too!'

Everyone in the command post smiled. Sturm looked at the senders details—Monika Binder. It was in the handwriting of a schoolgirl. *Unteroffizier* Willi Reise, who sat next to Sturm, looked at the address and laughed out loud.

'Monika, from Lippstadt, that's the daughter of one of our neighbours, she's only twelve years old. A lovely little girl, but a bit too young for you Hans!'

Nevertheless, Sturm wrote her a letter of thanks. They became penpals and exchanged photos. It would be a very special day for the young lass when 'her' *Gefreiter* with the Iron Cross First Class would also become the first with the *Ritterkreuz*. And when on 17 May 1943 Sturm gave a lecture to the workers of the firm of Heinrich Jungblut, Monika was there, sitting proudly with her parents in the front row, along with the local *Kreisleiter* and Willi Reise, who was home on leave.

'Show me the map again, Alfons.'

Stabsgefreiter Alfons Raitler gave Sturm the map which he had made himself. As so often in the past, he was to escort an assault group to the edge of the forest, where a new enemy mortar position had been set up.

'How far is that from the Russian front line, Alfons?'

'Well, around 2 km,' said Raitler, 'and the Russians have laid mines among the trees in between! There is also a path here, not shown on the map.'

Oberleutnant Winter, who had listened in silence, opened the bunker door.

'Let's get on with it, men!'

'Careful Hans, the Russians will be sitting just behind that row of bushes,' whispered Raitler.

They soon reached the edge of the woods and had penetrated about 200 m when they came across the footpath. The path led towards another clump of bushes. To avoid the guard post for the mortar position they had to make a slight detour and approach the position from the rear.

Sturm released the safety catch on his machine pistol. He noticed Sandkühler and

Raitler crouching over to his side. He beckoned Bieler over to him. As he approached, Sturm pointed towards the bushes. Bieler nodded and crouched down. They had only moved some 30 m further on when they heard the murmur of hushed voices. Metal clinked against metal. Then an order rang out. For several hours, enemy mortar shells had been soaring through the night sky towards the German front line, and four loud impacts followed by four loud 'whoofs' could be heard now.

For a few seconds they lay as if frozen. Then they moved cautiously onwards. The four men reached the edge of a small clearing almost simultaneously, and saw the enemy troops working on their mortars. A couple of them carried fresh mortar shells. All four Germans opened fire at the same time as the crew were about to launch the next salvo. For thirty seconds the clearing was lit by the yellow light of the German muzzle flashes, then all was quiet. Four Russian soldiers who had been on sentry duty came crashing into the clearing, only to be felled by another burst of fire from the German machine pistols.

The Germans ran over to the mortars and Sandkühler carefully placed the 4-kg charge of explosives he had brought. He set the fuse for a twenty-second delay, and they all ran back and took cover in a ditch. With a deafening roar the charge exploded, throwing the four mortars into the air. The patrol had achieved its objective.

Sturm took part in all such combat patrols which were mounted over the next week or so. His experience in many such actions, and his instinct for danger, were a great bonus for the leaders of these patrols. He was considered as a lucky mascot. Sturm also knew the area of No Man's Land like the back of his hand. Along with Sandkühler, he spied on the Russian recce troops as they changed over. They pursued the enemy mine-laying teams and often laid mines themselves in front of the enemy front lines, to improve their chances in future actions.

On one occasion the Russians broke into a forward strong-point of 3 Company on their edge of the wood. They were thrown back by a counter-attack launched by Raitler and Polmeier's squads. With Sandkühler and Bieler, Sturm chased after the withdrawing enemy, throwing hand grenades and firing their machine pistols, making the enemy think they were being pursued by a much more powerful force.

The failure of their mission and the losses they had suffered, along with the probable loss of their commander, threw the Russians into a panic-stricken flight. The survivors ran into one of their own minefields in their rush to get back to their own lines.

Sturm, Sandkühler, and Bieler saw how some of the Russians had been mutilated by the explosions. They then returned to their own lines, sure that the enemy would be back to launch another attack before long.

The Russians made up their losses rapidly with a constant stream of reinforcements, and were determined to take the German strong-point on the edge of the woods, whatever the cost. The area of No Man's Land in front of the German positions was almost completely occupied by the enemy, and several German soldiers were killed or seriously wounded by the Russian snipers.

Oberleutnant Winter was killed by a bullet to the head, and *Leutnant* Friedrich

Zitzer, freshly transferred from the *Kriegsmarine*, took over as temporary company commander.

Sturm organised himself a rifle with telescopic sights. He lay in wait for the Russian snipers who were ensconced in the trees, themselves waiting for an incautious movement from the Germans. The enemy were very difficult to locate and could only be spotted in a moment of carelessness, usually when one sniper arrived to relieve another.

Sturm only shot first if he was sure he would get a successful hit. He didn't just want to hit the enemy—he wanted to kill them. He knew he had succeeded when he saw the body come crashing from the tree. This was Sturm's revenge for the death of *Oberleutnant* Winter, whose batman he had been in France. Winter, then an *Oberfeldwebel*, had chosen Sturm because of his knowledge of French and his ability to 'organise' things. His original batman performed his duties with great enthusiasm, and had been poached by *Feldwebel* Döring, who shared quarters with Winter.

3 and 6 Companies merge

In May 1942, 3 Company had forty-five men, incomplete stores, and no company commander, whereas 6 Company was under the command of *Oberleutnant* Hörstermann and had a *Hauptfeldwebel*, field kitchens, clerks, and around fifty men.

Problematic was *Hauptfeldwebel* Erich Wenner, for instance. In a barracks situation, he would be hard to surpass as *Spiess*; but here at the Front, his manner in treating battle-hardened soldiers was out of place.[1] Wenner felt he had to get front line experience because, deep down, he wanted to be commissioned as an officer. He complained about everything—haircuts, hair not neatly combed, dress regulations, buttons undone, and lots more besides. Buckles had to be polished and boots had to be gleaming. His weapons inspections were a grossly overblown affair, as he checked the oiled bolts of the rifles with a white cloth looking for dirt.

Things took a turn for the worse when Wenner discovered that Sturm and a number of others had no gas masks in their gas mask canisters, among other heinous crimes. Most soldiers used the gas mask canister to carry writing paper, letters, photos, and other personal effects. This should have gone on report, but how would they be able to punish so many offenders? The company commander and battalion commander were in agreement that everyone would be issued with new gasmasks and the case considered closed.

The chasm between the *Hauptfeldwebel* and the messenger grew ever greater. It reached a crisis point when Wenner made it his business to snatch a machine gun from its position, because its crew, busy reading mail from home, had not been paying attention when he approached. The battalion commander couldn't sweep things under the carpet this time. Both gunners would have to be severely punished. Sturm was furious, because he knew that Wenner had tried to swindle his way to an Iron Cross Second Class, which should have been awarded to a man who had fallen in battle. Sturm told the NCO that he would have shot him had he tried to take his machine gun out of his position. He abused Wenner so badly that Hörstermann had him transferred back to his old squad. It was no real consolation for Sturm when he found out that, somehow, Wenner managed to wangle a transfer home on grounds of illness.

Captivity

Stabsgefreiter Raitler was promoted to *Unteroffizier*. Sturm became Number 1 on the machine gun once again, with Sandkühler as his Number 2. The men in the squad were delighted with *Hauptfeldwebel* Wenner, in that it was he who was responsible for Sturm's return.

Ratatatatatatatt, a machine gun stuttered. This burst of fire was followed by the detonation of hand grenades. In a split second, the men were racing out of the bunker. Sturm lunged for his machine pistol, but before he could reach it the bunker door burst open and hand grenades flew in.

The men threw themselves flat. Sandkühler and Sturm flung themselves behind the bedstead on which Sturm had been lying. With an ear-splitting roar, the grenades detonated. Screams rang out through the din, deafening Sturm. He saw that Russian soldiers had run into the bunker, their machine pistols held ready to fire. His own weapon lay on the floor somewhere.

'Hands up!' bawled a voice through the gloom. 'Out here, quickly. If your hands are not up, we shoot!'

Torch light half blinding them, they were driven from the bunker with punches from the enemy troops. They staggered outside: first Sturm, then two wounded comrades, one of them Berg, then Sandkühler. The rest lay dead or seriously wounded in the bunker. With a glance Sturm saw that the Russians were about to 'liberate' his machine gun. What had happened to Raitler and Görges, who had been on watch?

'Come on, move!' shouted the Russian interpreter sharply. He called something to the Russian soldiers furthest away, and they set off immediately towards the edge of the woods. Sturm followed. Thoughts swirled around in his head. What could he do? What chance did he have?

Machine guns and rifles began to fire from the German front-line positions. Tracer fire zipped through the air. Russian mortar shells then began to land in the area between the edge of the forest and the German lines. The group of four POWs were led ever deeper into the woods by two of their Russian captors, while the others covered the retreat.

Again, the Russian at the tail of the column shouted something to those in front. The leader nodded then disappeared into a dugout. The rearmost Russian pushed the

Germans forward, forcing them too to enter. In the flickering glow of a lantern, Sturm saw that Georg and Bieler were only lightly wounded. Sandkühler was unharmed. Sturm couldn't be sure, but he thought that Sandkühler had winked at him.

As another mortar shell detonated nearby, they all ducked. Sturm felt the urge to make a move as he felt the barrel of a Russian machine pistol in the small of his back.

'How are you, Alfons, Günther?' he asked.

Before either could answer, one of the Russians roared out, 'You, not speak!'

Some time passed, during which the sound of small arms could be heard. Hand grenades detonated nearby. The four prisoners listened to the sound of battle. German voices! The sound of a small combat patrol, fighting its way into the forest. If only their comrades would come this way!

'Dawai,' called the Russian.

Both of the wounded raised themselves up, having meantime applied their field dressings to their wounds. Shortly thereafter, they quietly left the dugout and Sturm recognised the direction they were taking. The order was the same. First a Russian, then Sturm, then the two wounded, then Sandkühler, then the other Russian bringing up the rear. If they didn't make a move soon, they would reach the Russian lines.

'At the bend!' Sturm called out, hoping that Sandkühler would understand.

The Russian at the rear called out a threat to Sturm, and he instinctively ducked, expecting a bullet. He moved forward, closer to the lead Russian.

The bend appeared in front of them. Only 100 m or so further on, the forest came to an end. Nearer and nearer they came to the decisive spot. Now they were there. Sturm felt the palm of his hand damp with sweat. Just a couple of metres to go.

By now the rear Russian was out of sight. With a leap, Sturm sprang forward and landed on the back of the Russian soldier and knocked him to the ground. Behind him, the machine pistol of the Russian at the rear began to rattle then suddenly stopped.

Sturm felt the neck muscles of the Russian twitch under the grasp of his hands before he suddenly went limp. The Russian had been bluffing, however, and threw himself up suddenly and reached for his fallen machine pistol. Sturm kicked him in the side then chopped at his neck with the edge of his open fist, hitting the region of the artery. The Russian stopped dead and fell as if pole-axed. Before the war, Sturm had studied Judo for two years. He had been shown this particular punch, but warned not to use it because of its potentially fatal effect.

Sturm leapt forward and grabbed the machine pistol. He whirled around and saw the second Russian raise his weapon ready to fire at Sandkühler's face. Sandkühler, laying on the ground, was trying with all his strength to push the muzzle aside. Sturm wasted no time and let off a well aimed burst of fire at the Russian, who collapsed on top of Sandkühler. Sandkühler pushed the body of the dead Russian aside and took the machine pistol, which was still grasped in his lifeless hands.

Beyond the bend, Russian voices could be heard shouting orders.

'Back,' yelled Sturm.

The two wounded, Bieler and Berg, had thrown themselves to the ground, and now ran off towards the German lines, Berg hobbling a little. Machine gun fire zipped through the bushes and splintered the trees. Sturm saw the shadowy movements of the enemy through the foliage and opened fire. Sandkühler joined in, and the combined fire of the two Germans forced the enemy into cover. Taking their chance, the two ran off after their wounded comrades.

'Don't shoot, don't shoot,' they yelled, as they began to draw fire from their own, German positions.

The firing ceased. They ran across the last 80 m or so of open terrain and threw themselves into a trench. They were once again safe, from out of the mouth of Hell.

Raitler's squad had been severely hit by the attack. Raitler, who had been in the machine gun post, had been severely wounded, and Görges was dead. Of those in the bunker, Sturm and Sandkühler were uninjured because they had taken cover behind the bedstead. Krüger had been so severely wounded that he had later died. Bieler had been wounded in the arm and Berg on the leg by hand grenade shrapnel. Rolf Thiemann and Albert Bottner, who had feigned death, barely had a scratch.

Bieler, as an officer candidate, was promoted to *Gefreiter* and squad leader; Sandkühler was made Number 1 on the machine gun, with Berg as Number 2; and Thiemann and Bottner remained in the squad, which was reinforced with three new men. Sturm was returned to *Oberleutnant* Hörstermann at company.

21

Heightened Alert

The successful Russian penetration into the German lines, and the capture of the machine gun and the bunker of Raitler's squad, resulted in all squads within 6 Company being placed on extreme alert with regards to the edges of the woods in front of their positions. This wasn't difficult during the day, but at night the guard had to be doubled.

In front of the German positions, the pioneers laid mines and additional barbed wire entanglements. The mines were pressure-activated and linked together with trip wires. The three prongs of the detonator made it look like a deadly spider once it had been skillfully camouflaged. The mines threw their deadly load of around 350 small steel balls up to around 1.5 m when detonated.

In addition to those mines laid by the pioneers, Sturm had planted some of his own—though this was strictly forbidden. Occasionally, mines would be detonated by animals or by shrapnel from mortar bursts, and this considerably alarmed the nervous troops, who fired off their weapons though there was no enemy to be seen.

The Russians grew ever stronger and pushed their forward positions to the very edge of the forest opposite the German front lines. They opened up on every movement in the area between the two front lines.

Sturm took it upon himself to crawl out into the minefield and check against his map those mines which had been detonated. He then reported back to the pioneers, who laid replacements.

The pioneers laid new mines and repaired any damage to the trip wires. Their movements were anxiously watched by the soldiers on the front line. The pioneers had no protection against any sudden attack by mortars. Their work had to be carried out both quickly and carefully, and the reports made by Sturm were a great help to them.

Despite all the Germans' attempts at counter-attacks, the enemy continued to extend their hold on the edge of the woods. The possibility of a Soviet attack only served to increase the state of tension which extended all the way up from the troops in the front line to the battalion and regimental staffs.

Individual members of Sturm's squad were still able to move to the rear for a spell of rest and relaxation, but only for a very short period. There they could be de-loused, have a bath, wash out their laundry, get decent rations, and visit the cinema or theatre for a couple of nights in the villages of Bol and Mal Wjasowka. The soldiers knew they were fortunate in being given this relief, and wrote to their families telling them that they were still alive. This was a time when many men put things off, thinking that they would do this or that tomorrow, but the casualty rate was such that for many, tomorrow never came. Many who had no established girlfriend, wife, bride, or fiancé, and whose parents were both dead, thought: if I perish now, I have lost no more than my life—no cock will crow for me!

A soldier from a neighbouring unit had allegedly deliberately injured himself while on a combat patrol. It couldn't be proved, however. He had learnt that his wife at home was pregnant—but not by him. Nevertheless, he loved her, and would be a good father to the child. This news was delivered to Sturm in a letter from *Unteroffizier* Raitler. Raitler was recovering from his wounds and had been told he would be posted to the military school as an instructor.

More sad news trickled down. A member of the battalion had raped and strangled Katja, the daughter of the village elder. In a fit of remorse, the soldier had shot himself the next night.

22

Another Dangerous Task

Oberleutnant Hörstermann came into the company command post. Along with him were the platoon commander *Feldwebel* Kionke and the squad leader *Unteroffizier* Polmeier, who had brought *Gefreiter* Bieler along with him.

'Order from the regiment. We have to capture the strong-point the enemy has established on the edge of the woods!'

'That will be difficult, *Herr Oberleutnant*,' said *Unteroffizier* Risse. 'Three times we've taken it, each time with only slight losses. But this time we are going to need heavy artillery support.'

'We can't have that, the division is using the artillery elsewhere. They have just as bad a headache as us!'

The *Oberleutnant* looked along the row of men, Sturm among them. *Feldwebel* Kionke felt the same way as Risse.

'*Herr Oberleutnant*, we have attacked in the early morning, in the evening, and at night. We have managed to kill plenty of Russians, or drive them out, or take them prisoner; but we have never been able to hold on to the positions, we are just too weak. Every time, the Russians have taken the positions back within a few days. It is senseless!'

'Senseless or not, the regiment has ordered it! The large strong-point directly in front of us is to be taken!'

The men looked at each other in silence. For six months already, they had been defending this sector. For six months, the positions in No Man's Land had constantly changed hands between them and the Russians. Even *Gefreiter* Bieler, who always seemed to support any order from above not just because he was an officer aspirant, had reservations.

'It's easy for those on the regimental staff to give orders when they don't run any personal risks,' he protested. 'Look at what happened to the last three suicide missions, and now another attack, without any heavy weapons in support!'

Oberleutnant Hörstermann raised his eyebrows, but said nothing.

'Nevertheless, we have to try.' Polmeier cleared his throat. 'Perhaps another night attack?'

'No, *Herr Oberleutnant*, this time we must pick a time when the Russians would never expect us!'

'And when would that be, Sturm?'

'Midday, just when they are changing their guard!'

'What?!' cried Polmeier. 'Midday, when we have all that open terrain between us and the objective, and are well within the field of fire of their machine guns?'

'Let Sturm speak, Polmeier!' intervened the *Oberleutnant*, and Polmeier fell silent.

'Tomorrow is 26 August. At midday it will be very hot and the sun will be behind us. That's to our advantage, because the Russians by then will be getting drowsy in the heat—we have already noticed that their attention wanders. The flanks of the strong-point have been strengthened and extra mines laid. I have watched and marked all the positions. Individually, in the course of the forenoon, we must infiltrate into No Man's Land. The Russians have their machine guns in these positions, and here also a light machine gun,' said Sturm, laying out his personal sketch map and indicating the positions.

'Go on, Sturm,' encouraged the company commander, pleased with himself that he had transferred Sturm back to the company staff. The last three attacks had only been possible by heeding suggestions made by Sturm with information from his sketch maps.

'At 11.30 hours, we must be in position at the points I have indicated, in small groups. We will have some cover there. At 12.00, we make our move on the enemy positions.'

'I take your point, Sturm. But the enemy strong-point is occupied in at least platoon strength, and I can only spare two sections for the attack,' said Hörstermann, pointing at Polmeier and Bieler, the section leaders.

'That will have to be enough, *Herr Oberleutnant*. More men would be unable to move unnoticed, in any case. They always have three men in each machine gun position. Hand grenades and the element of surprise will be our main weapons. The main thing is that we must not be spotted. In case we do get spotted by an enemy sniper up in the trees, for instance, and are forced into cover, it might be best if we could have some fire from the heavy company to cover our retreat.'

'Good, Sturm. One more thing—you will have to be ready for the off by early tomorrow morning.'

Both sections lay in readiness in their positions. Polmeier and Bieler accepted that Sturm would take charge and be responsible for whatever happened.

'Everybody clear on what's going to happen, lads? Once you reach your start points for the attack, no unnecessary movement. Don't make your move until I fire a green flare. Each section go after the machine gun nest you've been allocated, quick as you can, right?'

The comrades all nodded.

'Synchronise watches!' he finished. 'It's 03.30 hours!'

In small groups they broke away and moved off. *Gefreiter* Bieler went with the first section along with Sturm and with Berg following. They crouched low as they moved silently through No Man's Land, making their way along the clear path through their minefield. Mist rose silently from the warm soil. Now and again, a 10.5-cm shell from their own artillery flew overhead towards its target in the Russian hinterland, only to be answered by return fire.

Sturm reached the end of the shrub-covered terrain. They lay directly in front of the gully which he had selected as cover for his section.

'Keep your heads down!' he whispered, as the skies grew gradually lighter with the onset of dawn.

After a brief pause, they crept along the gully. The meadow through which they travelled grew ever flatter and more barren. After 80 m or so, they reached a hazel bush and lay in its cover. At one point, a Russian machine gun fired, presumably on one of the other sections moving forward, but it soon ceased again.

'Come on,' said Sturm quietly, 'but keep close together!'

Over the coming hours they moved themselves forward metre by metre. Once, a shot rang out from a Russian sniper in the trees. This was answered by a burst of fire from the German lines. Sturm watched the sniper tumble from his lofty perch. The sun grew hotter and hotter as the morning wore on. At last they reached the small gorse-shrouded depression which was their destination, and crouched down one behind the other among the bushes. The Russian machine gun nest was now only 100 m away from them.

It was 10.30 hours. Sturm felt a ranging thirst. He cautiously unscrewed the top from his canteen, took a swig and put it away again. The cold tea tasted bitter, but did its job. Then Berg belched loudly, a noise that rang out clearly in the stillness of the morning. The three men froze as if paralysed.

At one point, Sturm spotted one of the neighbouring squads. The face of *Unteroffizier* Polmeier appeared momentarily, nodded, and then disappeared into cover again.

'Is everything okay, Hans?' asked Berg.

'Sure, but just keep your head down. So far, everything is going according to plan!'

'This damned waiting!' grumbled Bieler.

'Quiet!' hissed Sturm, as he noticed a Russian appear level with their cover. The enemy had spotted something and pointed in their direction. From the German positions a shot rang out, and the Russian jerked as he fell back into cover. The enemy was now wide awake, and not in the dozy state Sturm had hoped for when he had explained his plan back at the company command post. That was bad, but there was nothing they could do about it now.

It was one minute before twelve. They saw movement in the enemy strong-point, and heard voices. Then, movement at the double. Metal clinked against metal. The minute hand of Sturm's watch reached the hour. He lifted his arm with the flare pistol. He fired then threw the pistol aside and rushed forward. As he ran he unscrewed the primer cap on his stick grenade. To his right, another of the assault groups was also running towards its target, over the last 80 m or so of open ground.

The first burst of fire came from the enemy positions, but by then the Germans were only 50 m away and began to throw their hand grenades. Sturm, too, threw one of his as the enemy machine gun in front of him fired a burst immediately over his head. He threw a second hand grenade, then dropped to the ground.

With the thunderous detonation of the grenade, Berg and Sturm leapt up and threw themselves at the enemy position. Sturm raised his machine pistol and fired off a burst at the occupants of the enemy position. Sturm saw Polmeier stumble as if hit. He called for Bieler, but there was no reply. If Bieler was also wounded or killed, they'd lost both section leaders.

Still more hand grenades detonated and suddenly the enemy machine guns fell silent, while the chatter of smaller calibre weapons prevailed. Russian and German commands and curses, and the cries of the wounded, rang out along the whole length of the strong-point, such that it was difficult to tell which side had the upper hand. Sturm was aware that Bieler, from his own squad, had not jumped into the enemy position with him. Perhaps he had been wounded.

A couple of Red Army soldiers suddenly charged at them, but fell in a hail of fire from the machine pistols of the two Germans. Thirty metres further on, Sturm spotted an enemy mortar. Sturm and Berg both threw hand grenades. The mortar crew were tossed aside by the explosion. One lay dead and another crumpled forward into the dirt. Another Russian returned their fire, but was finished off by a shot from Berg.

The trampling of enemy boots was heard. Berg wanted to pull back, but Sturm saw that it was too late, as the first Russians appeared. As he opened fire, so did the enemy. Berg dropped to his knees, then crawled over towards Sturm.

'Get me back, Hans,' pleaded to his friend.

'Get over here!'

They crawled sideways into the bushes and pushed their way through to a path which led towards the Russian lines. Sturm listened and heard the wild shooting coming from the Russians running to reinforce their strong-point. Berg and Sturm were now effectively trapped between the raging battle and the Russian lines. Escape seemed all but impossible. They would never make it across the open terrain in one piece. The two men forced their way even deeper into the bushes as a further group of Russian reinforcements rushed past.

The attack on the Russian strong-point had only been partly successful and looked to have been costly. The Russians had been forewarned of the German attack, and had been able to mount a rapid counter-attack.

'I can't go any further, Hans!' gasped Berg.

Sturm crept over to him. For the first time he could see that his friend not only had a flesh wound to the left upper thigh, but had also been hit in the chest. He bound the two wounds as best he could with his field dressings, but could do little to the chest wound. Hoisting his comrade over his shoulder, he moved off further towards the Russian lines. As he saw the first of the enemy positions, he stopped, breathless, and laid his wounded comrade gently in the cover of some bushes. He signalled to Berg to keep silent and crept towards a gap in the undergrowth. Instinctively, he drew back as a number of Russians passed, carrying their own dead and wounded on their shelter quarters. Cautiously, he pushed himself backwards a few metres into the bushes. The firing, from both sides, had still not subsided. The sounds of battle faded away only slowly, until Sturm resigned himself to the fact that all of his comrades must be either wounded or dead.

The day began to fade. The last drop of tea from Sturm's canteen passed the parched lips of his now feverish comrade.

'Take me to the Ivans, Hans!' begged Berg. He looked gaunt, and his unshaved stubble made his face look even thinner.

'No, never!'

'Better to get it over with and into captivity quickly, Hans, than die slowly out here!'

'I'll get you back, just wait until it gets dark, Alfons!'

'I have to get out of here. If you don't get me to the Russians right away, I'll cry out.'

'Are you completely insane? You can't do that!' stammered Sturm.

As he looked into the face of his young friend, he could see his eyes glazed with fever and knew that Berg was not in control of himself. Already, he was opening his mouth to cry out.

Sturm's fist shot out and connected with his friends head, knocking him senseless. He lifted his comrade over his shoulder again and set off towards the German lines. With his familiarity with the terrain, Sturm knew that he would come out of the woods around 600 m to the left of the Russian strong-point if he kept on his current course. He wanted to slip between the chain of enemy guard posts and reach one of the positions which linked his own company and its neighbour. The area in front of his own positions was far too open and exposed to try to cross, and the enemy, having dealt with the German attack, would be able to devote all their attentions to Sturm and his load.

By now it was beginning to get quite dark. Berg began to moan again. From somewhere in front came the sound of a twig snapping. Someone was moving about. Sturm could only vaguely make out a shape in the darkness. He hurriedly laid Berg gently on the ground, and moved forwards. The Russian had almost stumbled into Sturm when Sturm struck. The enemy was taken completely by surprise, and the struggle was brief but merciless. It was him or Sturm—one had to die. Sturm took the dead Russian's machine pistol, having had to leave his own behind when he had run out of ammunition, and made his way back to Berg.

He lifted his comrade up again. Speed was now of the essence, and could mean the difference between life and death. He hurried towards the German lines. Two or three times he staggered under the weight of his injured comrade and almost fell. Then Berg began to whimper, sobbing loudly. Machine gun fire began to zip through the air around them. From behind came the stutter of Russian gunfire. Sturm threw himself and his comrade to the ground.

'Don't shoot,' he cried, 'I have a badly wounded man with me!'

'Come on over,' rang out a startled voice.

Berg cried out again as two soldiers clambered out of their foxhole, took him from Sturm's back, and carried him into the German trench where he was gently laid down. The Russian fire had faded away after the gunfire from the German positions ceased.

'Man, where have you come from Sturm?' asked a *Leutnant* from 5 Company.

'Over there, *Herr Leutnant*, from the Russian lines.'

Sturm nodded because in his exhaustion he had difficulty in speaking. He closed his eyes. He had done what he had promised Berg to do, and now the fear, tension, and all other emotions ebbed away. He was safe.

'Here pal, have a drink!'

He took a deep slug of vodka from the bottle offered to him. Another comrade grabbed the bottle from his mouth and offered him a flask of tea. Berg had already been carried off. A last glance and a wave of his hand in thanks, and he was gone.

'Come on, Sturm!' said the Leutnant. 'We must inform *Oberleutnant* Hörstermann of your safe return. He's been waiting for you!'

In the command post, Sturm was greeted heartily. They had already given up on him and Berg. He heard that as well as Berg and himself, four other comrades had made it back safely. From these, two were of 5 Company and had been in one of the assault squads as the Russians made their counter-attack. All of the others were dead, wounded or captured.

Sturm briefly made his report on his and Berg's travails, and described the layout of the enemy positions as best he could. As he finished, the field telephone rang. *Unteroffizier* Risse held the receiver out to Sturm.

'It's the regimental commander, *Herr Oberleutnant*, he wants to speak to Sturm,' said Risse as he looked at the company commander's surprised face. 'The neighbouring company must have passed on the news of Sturm and Berg's safe return when the wounded were sent back.'

'Get on with it then, Sturm!' said Hörstermann.

Sturm repeated his report of the action to the regimental commander, *Oberstleutnant* Schmidt, who interrupted him briefly from time to time with questions about his actions.

Finally, Schmidt said: 'Sturm, in the name of my regiment I want to express to you my appreciation. I'd like to see you tomorrow morning in the regimental command post.'

On the following morning, Oberstleutnant Schmidt once again congratulated Sturm and offered his good wishes.

'Sturm, I have made an immediate recommendation that you be awarded the German Cross in Gold,' he then declared. 'Your brave actions yesterday with the difficult recovery of your wounded comrade, as well as previous actions over this year, are sufficient grounds for the award. In September, I intend to send you, with the rank of *Unteroffizier*, to No. 10 Officer Cadet Course at *Kriegsschule*. Then, by the end of this year, you will be a *Leutnant*!'

Sturm was recommended for the German Cross in Gold on 26 August 1942 for the second time, having already been put forward for the award by his deceased company commander *Oberleutnant* Winter in March. In the event, the award document for the decoration did not arrive until 5 November 1942, by which time Sturm had already received the Knight's Cross of the Iron Cross. He was presented with the German Cross in Gold in a ceremony on 4 January 1943 while in Aachen with the replacement battalion.

23

The *Ritterkreuz*

For the men of *Infanterie Regiment 473*, part of *253 Infanterie Division*, it came as no surprise when the unit was pulled out of the line around Olinin and rushed towards Rzhew, where it was immediately thrown into action. Around mid-August 1942, the enemy had started preparations for a new offensive to neutralize the German positions in a corner of a loop in the course of the River Volga which cut deep into the Russian front line. The Russians would then attempt to penetrate into the rear of the sector held by *9 Armee*, encircle the Germans, and by following up with further attacks from the east relieve the pressure on the Soviet 22 and 41 Armies. The Soviet 39 Army and 11 Cavalry Corps had already been decimated by the Germans.

Three German panzer divisions and two infantry divisions transferring to the southern sector of the Eastern Front had been diverted to this area. In the meantime, *Infanterie Regiment 473* was quickly rushed into the line near Rzhew, arriving in the German bridgehead on the afternoon of 11 September, and placed under the command of *6 Infanterie Division*.

It was the night of 13/14 September 1942.

'Here they come again, *Herr Oberleutnant*!'

Oberleutnant Hörstermann nodded. He peered into the darkness, trying to see something, but nothing could be made out. The barrage of Russian artillery and, in between its salvoes, the howling and roaring of the Katyusha rocket launchers—the infamous 'Stalin Organs'—blazed fiery trails through the night sky, crashing into the German-held positions with a terrifying din, and ripping the landscape asunder.

'Man, Hans, that was aimed right at 3 Platoon. I'll bet *Feldwebel* Kionke has nothing much to smile about now!' called *Unteroffizier* Risse, the *Kompanietruppführer*.

'Why don't they send a runner over to check it out?' asked Sturm.

'What, in this downpour?' ventured Risse with a grimace.

Shellfire erupted and steel fragments zipped through the air. For two days and nights the men of *Infanterie Regiment 473*, attached to *6 Infanterie Division*, had held their positions with little chance of sleep or rest as the enemy bombardment continued unabated.

Sturm's regiment lay in the German bridgehead over the Volga, with 6 Company on the left flank. It was at exactly this spot that the Soviet attack would be aimed. Here

Sturm just moments after the Knight's Cross was hung around his neck, still wearing the blood-speckled tunic he wore in the action which gained him this most prestigious award.

they would attempt to break through and roll up the regiment from the rear. On the northern edge of Rzhew, in the rear of a brickworks that were being used as a first aid dressing station, the men of 6 Company endured their torment as best they could, as salvo after salvo from the enemy artillery and Katyushas thundered overhead.

'Damn it, did you hear that?' asked Risse, as the muted growl of tank engines could be made out faintly in the distance. 'This time they'll really buy it.'

'This stinks, Gunter,' said Sturm, as they heard the machine gun fire from 3 Platoon's positions increase in intensity. The crack of exploding hand grenades could also be made out.

In 3 Platoon's positions, Sandkühler lay with the machine gun which Sturm had passed on to him after he was severely injured in January 1942. Sandkühler had been Sturm's Numer 2, but was now the gunner himself.

Medical orderlies dodged through the shellfire into the foxholes where the wounded lay and brought them back for treatment. The earth was continuously shaken by the detonations of the incoming shells. Amid this gruesome carnage, medics, aided by those who were themselves only lightly wounded, struggled to recover the seriously injured. An order passed down from the regiment prohibited the recovery of wounded during daylight hours. Movement was far too dangerous, instantly bringing down a hail of fire from the enemy. Food and supplies, too, could only be brought up under cover of darkness.

The machine guns of 3 Platoon continued to fire, their noise perforated by the crack of anti-tank guns.

'Quick, Sturm, get over to 3 Platoon's positions and see what's happening, we must know what is going on over there!' called the company commander.

Hans Sturm nodded silently and left the command post, his departure watched by the anxious faces. Ducking low, he dashed off towards the Front. With every metre he progressed, the sounds of battle grew ever louder. Shells crashed into 3 Platoon's positions.

From the right, where the other two platoons lay, machine guns rattled furiously, their targets the Soviet assault troops advancing on the German positions under cover of the artillery fire.

Tracer fire illuminated the scene for a few brief seconds, as Sturm began to pass the lightly wounded who were crawling their way towards the rear. The more seriously injured cried out for help. Sturm promised to fetch some, but first he had to think of his orders.

Sturm finally arrived at 3 Platoon's positions and jumped into the nearest foxhole. 'Where is *Feldwebel* Kionke?' he cried, but the occupants of the foxhole lay dead, crumpled behind their shattered gun. To the left, by the light of the tracers, Sturm could see the advancing Soviets. They had already broken into the platoon positions and were cautiously making their way forward.

Just in front, a machine gun started to chatter. Sturm sensed it must be Sandkühler. A position with a good field of fire, but perilously little cover, it would be dangerously exposed in daylight and was just the kind of spot he would pick.

Sturm finally reached the command post and threw himself in, landing next to *Feldwebel* Kionke, whose left arm had been shattered but was nevertheless preparing a small group of men for a counter-attack.

'The Russians have broken through into our positions, and I have only eight men left fit to fight,' said Kionke, his face smeared with blood and dirt, and contorted with pain.

'Damn it, that's bad," said Sturm, 'Is Sandkühler still in his position?'

'He was still firing a few moments ago, but he seems to have gone quiet,' was the reply.

Despite his orders to return with a situation report, Sturm knew he must stay and help. Sturm worked his way forward towards Sandkühler's position. He could hear the cries of the enemy to his left as behind him another shell exploded. As he threw himself into the shelter of a small crater, shrapnel ripped into the flesh of his right arm. Close to Sandkühler's position, shells were also falling. As Sturm finally threw himself into the dugout, he saw Sandkühler and behind him Löffler, the Number 2. Sandkühler was dead, and Löffler's leg was badly lacerated. Before Sturm could administer any aid, Löffler too slumped forward. Two good comrades, one his best friend, now lay sprawled together in death at the bottom of the dugout.

Fire zipped through the air just past Sturm's head. He thought only briefly of his original mission, as rage and bitterness welled up inside him.

The machine gun was undamaged and Sturm took his place behind it, firing off a burst towards the sound of the advancing enemy, their cries of 'Urrah' growing ever nearer. The belt of ammunition was soon expended. Instinctively, Sturm looked around for some grenades and found some lying, primer caps unscrewed and fuse cords ready to be pulled. Three, four, five grenades went sailing through the air in the direction of the enemy. Sturm used the few seconds' respite gained these gained him to feed a new belt of ammunition into the breech of his machine gun, and quickly opened fire again in the same direction. A hail of bullets from Sturm's MG34 zipped towards the enemy—a risky measure, as Sturm could see that the Russians were taking fire from both sides, and there was a chance that the German soldiers opposite might also be hit by Sturm's fire.

The sound of machine gun fire and the sudden appearance of the deadly grenades could not fail to draw the attention of the enemy to Sturm's position. The Russians, who by now had thought that they had gained the upper hand and successfully neutralised the enemy positions, renewed their attack with vigour. Their 'Urrahs' chilled Sturm's bones to the very marrow.

The leading Russians were now only 50 m from Sturm's positions. He fired again and the light from his tracer shells showed him the enemy was suffering grievous losses, yet still they kept coming. The belt of ammunition rattled its way through the breech, then—a stoppage! Sturm checked it and—a jammed cartridge case! Luckily, the MG34 featured a barrel designed for rapid change over in such an emergency and Sturm, as a skilled machine-gunner, soon had a fresh barrel fitted. Grabbing a case of ammunition, he dashed to another dugout. Shots whizzed past him as he ran.

The Russians were pressing home their attack. Only 30 to 40 m from Sturm's position there appeared a dense wave of brown uniformed figures. The raging fire from Sturm's machine gun cut them down in swathes, but soon his own position was coming under heavy fire. The enemy were determined to eliminate this irksome machine gun nest. They knew that once it was destroyed, the chances for the complete success of their attack would be greatly increased.

With the weight of fire which was landing all around him, Sturm knew it could only be a matter of time before he was hit. Hand grenades began to land around him, but he couldn't afford the time to worry about this—all he could do was keep firing.

Another stoppage! This time it was the extractor claw. He would have to dash back to his old position and fetch the spare which Sandkühler would have carried in his machine-gunner's pouch. On reaching the old position, he could see by Sandkühler's body the haversack with the vital component. Just in time, *Feldwebel* Kionke and two of his men leapt into the dugout to give Sturm covering fire with rifle and machine pistol as he repaired the gun.

Once again Sturm opened fire as the Russians attacked once more, this time supported by three T-34 tanks. One of the tanks was suddenly ripped apart by a direct hit from an anti-tank gun, and a second disabled by the loss of a track. The third retreated. Emboldened at first by their armoured support, the Russians were now a little demoralised and only continued their attack with some hesitation. Still, it already seemed as though the decisive Soviet breakthrough into German positions would succeed and relieve the Russians who had broken into the positions held by 3 Platoon.

The damaged T-34 could not move, but still had full use of its cannon. Suddenly its turret turned and its gun depressed, bringing it to bear directly on Sturm's position. A shell hissed past him, crashing into the ground to his rear. Sturm lost no time in moving to a fresh position and from here, with his MG34, lashed the area all around him with deadly machine gun fire.

The Soviet's were using every possible scrap of cover, including the bodies of their dead comrades. Sturm could see officers crawling along the ground as discreetly as possible, driving their men forward at gunpoint.

It was already beginning to grow light as, with another fresh belt of ammunition laid into the breech, Sturm opened fire yet again, his bullets scything into the attackers. Sturm had no time to ponder the greater meaning of this pitiless struggle, however. Just as he checked his ammunition and made ready his gun to meet the next wave of attackers, a high explosive shell crashed into the earth just behind him. Sturm heard the ear-splitting impact as shrapnel splinters whizzed through the air towards him. He felt a burning pain between the eyes. His shoulder and his hand were also hit. The blast flung him, fast losing consciousness, to the bottom of the dugout.

Loud 'Urrahs' soon brought him back to consciousness. He was in agony and unable to see. Feeling behind him, he located the gun which seemed to be undamaged. He drew the butt to his shoulder, felt for the trigger and aimed at the direction from which the cheers of the attackers seemed to come. Blinded and guided only by his hands, he nevertheless managed to feed another belt of ammunition into the breech and continued his sustained fire at the enemy. They finally broke and ran, as reinforcements finally appeared from the neighbouring companies and the other two platoons of Sturm's own company.

Incredibly, Sturm had almost single-handedly managed to prevent a Russian breakthrough. He had thought only to go to the aid of his best friend, but had become embroiled in a decisive battle. If, in doing so, he had failed in his duty to bring back a situation report to his company, he had nevertheless saved the day.

As *Oberleutnant* Hörstermann, *Feldwebel* Kionke, and the medics recovered the wounded, they came upon a scene of incredible carnage. Sandkühler and Löffler lay dead in the dugout, and all around their positions the crumpled bodies of innumerable enemy.

After the company commander's report reached the regimental commander and the divisional commander of 6 *Infanterie Division*, *General* Großmann, they visited the site of Sturm's action and saw for themselves the significance of his achievement. *Oberstleutnant* Schmidt, the regimental commander, voiced what they had all been thinking.

'This man Sturm! He has prevented an enemy breakthrough, and the encirclement of the entire regiment. This, *Herr General*, is worthy of the highest decoration!'

'He will get it, Schmidt, I guarantee it!' assured the general.

24

Evacuation to Germany

Sturm lay unconscious in *Infanterie Regiment 473*'s first aid post behind the front lines, weakened by the loss of blood and his severe concussion. Brought back to consciousness by a feeling of severe pressure on his face, he could just make out an *Unteroffizier*, whose own arm was bandaged, pressing a wad of cotton wool into the corner of Sturm's left eye, next to the nose, with his thumb.

Sturm discovered later that a sliver of shrapnel had penetrated his eye socket and lodged behind the eye. In vain, the senior medical officer had tried to stop the bleeding. (After the war, Sturm would meet the surgeon, Dr Kiel, once again in Dortmund, where he would practise as an ear, nose, and throat specialist. The doctor well remembered treating the wounded *Gefreiter* who shortly thereafter joined the ranks of the *Ritterkreuzträger*.)

On the transport towards Wjasma, Sturm slept, principally because of the blood loss and the painkillers with which he had been heavily dosed. At the transit stop, he awoke from his fitful sleep on hearing the voices of his comrades and a woman, too. As he later heard, Sturm had in fact lain in the room for two hours without moving. His head was swathed in bandages with only a gap for his nose, and the dressings were soaked with blood. The wound was bleeding again, and the dressing needed changed. From the conversation he overheard in the room, it seemed the others had assumed he had been blinded by his wounds.

'The eyes are hardly damaged. He must be kept still, and quiet!' said the woman, a Red Cross sister.

The voice of the nurse made a deep impression on Sturm—it sounded so much like his mothers. Its confidence and calm penetrated the depths of Sturm's sleep and filled him with hope. He felt as though he were being carried up from the darkness towards the light, and to life. Chains seemed to be falling from him, yet no light came. Frightened, he felt for the bandages over his eyes.

'Are you awake, *Gefreiter* Sturm? Can you hear me?'

Sturm said nothing but nodded his head. The sister sat on his bed and took his hand.

'Speak to me! How do you feel?'

Even under the bandages, Sturm felt his face flush, and close to tears he stammered,

Sturm holds the letter of congratulations
on the award of the Knight's Cross.

'Sister, your voice sounds so much like my mothers, a voice I haven't heard in such a
long time.'

For some time there was silence in the room, then one of the other voice exclaimed
sympathetically, 'Damn it, this is such a shitty war!'

Four days after being wounded, Sturm lay in the eye ward in Field Hospital 2/615
in Smolensk. The bandages over his eyes were the idea of his comrades in Rzhew.
They were still there, in that hell from which he had escaped—but at what cost? Had
he lost an eye, or maybe even both eyes?

He thought of the German Cross in Gold, for which his regimental commander
had recommended him, the course at *Kriegsschule* and the promotion to *Leutnant*
which would have followed. *Oberleutnant* Winter had first recommended him for
the German Cross in March, but now that he was dead, maybe the regiment would
just file away the recommendation and forget it. Now that Sturm's wounds had
taken him out of it all, maybe the second recommendation would be dumped, too.
Of course, Sturm knew nothing about the *Ritterkreuz* at this point.

Sturm soon recovered from his pessimistic mood. The rations were good here. He
had to be spoon-fed with his midday meal by a sister, who helped and encouraged
him with kind words. It was also known around the hospital that the resident doctor
was a highly qualified eye specialist.

The five others with whom he shared a room were all older than Sturm. They all got on well and shared everything they wanted to know about each other. Karl, his neighbour on the left, had a minor eye wound but had lost his right foot. To Sturm's right lay Hermann, who had only one eye and some shrapnel wounds. On the opposite side of the room, next to the window was Bernard's bed. He was blind. In the middle lay Kurt, with an eye inflammation and an abdominal wound. Next to him was Günter, who had lost his right eye and right hand. Sturm was the last to arrive in the room. Karl had introduced himself and all the other comrades so that Sturm could form a mental picture of them all. He was told all about their injuries. In spite of everything, they all retained a sense of humour and were not too depressed. Sturm felt himself slowly grow stronger, but couldn't get up because of the severe concussion. The headaches which had initially been so intense had moderated a little, but the bandages over his eyes were a great source of irritation. With every visit from the doctor, he pressed for a decision on when they could be removed so that he would be able to see again. The doctor wouldn't say, but simply assured him he would soon see again.

Days and nights went by. This world of total darkness made no difference to Sturm. Sleep was almost impossible. Naturally, he had plenty of time to brood. He thought of his comrades in Rzhew, of his father who must be somewhere near Kursk with his bridge-building unit. Sturm also thought of his mother, who he hadn't seen for such a long time. Already her husband and son had been gone a full year, in far off Russia. They must both, however, have received letters from Sturm by now via the field postal service. Sister Irmgard had written them for him.

Sister Irmgard was known to all as 'Irmchen' when she was out of earshot. The men teased her mercilessly, especially about her special care for the 'baby', meaning Sturm. They described her pretty appearance for Sturm, and his minimal chances with her. Well, the bandages would come off soon, he thought to himself, then he would get things off the ground. At the start it was mainly Irmgard who helped him with his midday meal, providing much amusement for the others. Bernhard, the blind guy, said that he was sure that Irmgard had taken a fancy to Sturm. It was he who took Sturm out into the corridor and gave him advice on how to get by when unable to see. Sturm was surprised to see how fast a man's other senses sharpened up when the use of one was taken away.

Nine days after receiving his injuries, Sturm was lying in bed when the others, thinking him asleep, had a conversation that shocked him.

'Do you think Hans will be able to see with both eyes?' a sympathetic voice whispered.

'What do you mean? Of course he can see, the doctor said so—or do you think he only meant to comfort him?'

The others remained quiet. Sturm overheard nothing more said, but the questions he had heard hit him like a blow to the pit of his stomach. The others had no idea of the terror they had instilled in Sturm. He had of course had such thoughts himself, but hearing them spoken aloud was something else. He felt the blood pounding in his head. Were they preparing him for being blind? Ach! Nonsense! After being wounded, he had kept on shooting, he must have seen the enemy...! The memories were very vague and unclear. A chicken will still run around after its head has been cut off, he though to himself. Restlessly he tossed and turned.

The hours until the doctor's next visit passed with agonising slowness. On the following morning, Sister Irmgard noticed his state of agitation and asked him what was wrong. Was he in pain? His comrades were also concerned, but he avoided giving an answer. His breakfast went untouched.

The doctor finally arrived. Standing in front of Sturm's bed he asked, 'Well Sturm, how are you?' He was about to continue when he saw the sister signal to him with her hand.

'*Herr Oberstabsarzt*,' gasped Sturm, 'Will I still be able to see?'

He had asked himself this question over and over throughout the night, and now he had to have an answer or he would go crazy. Silence! Why would the doctor not answer him? Only the whispers of the sister and his comrades could be heard.

At last the doctor answered.

'It was necessary to leave the bandages on your eyes for quite some time because of your injuries and also because of the concussion. I can understand your concern. When we remove the bandages later, you will see again, just like I promised!'

The doctor departed, leaving Sturm brimming with both doubt and hope. His comrades made great efforts to keep his spirits up. Sister Irmgard sat on the bed beside Sturm and holding his hand.

'Hans, you must have faith,' she said. 'They have already set up an X-ray facility in Wjasma. I heard all about it from the *Oberstabsarzt* and *Oberfeldarzt* when they were discussing your head.'

She told him what they had said: The lad has been fortunate. Both eyes are undamaged. The shrapnel has penetrated through the nostril close above the left eye and has lodged in the right eye socket. Its position is accessible so we should be able to remove it later.

Everyone in the room, despite their own injuries, was happy for Sturm, but their constant attempts to cheer him up and keep his mind off his injuries made him suspicious. He tormented himself, thinking that each softly spoken word was about him. He worried only about himself and gave no thought to the problems and pains of his comrades, or of those in the other wards of the hospital. A cold terror continued to grow despite the assurances he was given. Perhaps, after all, he was going to end up a cripple, ever after dependant on others, just like Bernhard. This was an outcome which he feared more than death itself. Better he had fallen in the face of the enemy. Maybe this was the punishment for killing so many Russian soldiers and the misery which his machine gun had caused. Formerly, he only rarely had such morbid thoughts, but now they toyed with him constantly. He wrestled with the overwhelming temptation to rip off the bandages and find out once and for all whether he could still see.

Then, Sister Irmgard stood before his bed.

'Hans, you are to be taken to the examination room!'

Sturm could hardly speak from the amount of tension which had built up inside him. What had the doctor said earlier? 'If we take off your bandages, you will see again.' His eyes flickered nervously behind the dressings as his lips moved speechlessly in prayer. He had not prayed for years.

An orderly had appeared at the door, passing on the message to Sister Irmgard that Sturm was to be brought to the treatment room. His roommates all wished him good luck.

Sister Irmgard led him to the examination room. She said nothing but the tender way in which she took his hand said it all. He heard strange noises around him as medical instruments clinked together, then he heard the soft tones of the Doctors voice. Sturm was sat on a revolving chair and the bandages were slowly and gently unwound. The last few turns were stuck.

Now Sturm's fear welled up once again. The rest of the bandages were softened with a cloth moistened with warm water and carefully loosened. His eyes closed, Sturm felt a comforting warmth, then the bandages were off.

The doctor leaned over Sturm and encouraged him to open his eyes. For days Sturm had waited for this moment, but now he was too scared. He felt as if his eyelids were weighted down. Slowly, he opened the lids just a fraction. He felt his eyes smart and his tear ducts fill with moisture. But what was that? Again, he tried to concentrate and open his lids further. Yes! Through the tears he could see bright sunlight. He was overwhelmed by such a feeling of relief and happiness as he had never felt before. He could see!

One of the sisters gave him a cloth to wipe his eyes, as he slowly opened them again. It would take them a few moments to acclimatize to the light. The single light source in the darkened room was from a number of small bulbs clustered together in the observation lamp. He could make out the doctor, and the sisters standing next to him. Once again tears came to Sturm's eyes, but this time tears of joy and relief as the mental agony of the last few hours melted away like a bad dream.

Gratefully, he shook the hands of the doctor and the sisters. They laughed good-humouredly. This was an experience they had had many times before. For Sturm, this was a gift from fate, or maybe something more.

After asking the doctor's permission, one of the sisters handed Sturm a small mirror. Sturm could see with both eyes, but quickly noticed that something was not quite right with the right eye. The pupil was greatly enlarged, and the iris was drawn up into the right upper corner of the eye socket.

Oberstabsarzt Schüßler place the observation lamp over Sturm's right eye and took a close look. He advised Sturm that the shrapnel had not damaged the eye itself, but had affected the eye muscle. The result was that if he kept his head still and tried to look straight ahead, the left eye would drop out of line slightly. Sturm was given an eye-patch for his right eye and was allowed to make his own way back to his ward. It felt good to be able to move around without a guide. The eye-patch felt strange, but he would just have to get used to it. At least he was now freed from uncertainty and the other, lighter injuries to his left shoulder and left hand had now healed, with only slight scarring.

On the corridor wall leading back to his ward, he passed a row of portrait photos, all men of the *Luftwaffe* with very high decorations. Some had the German Cross in Gold for which Sturm himself had now been recommended. Sturm now saw the award for the first time in these coloured photos, with its large Swastika centre piece. He wondered if he would ever actually get the award. He certainly would not want to wear such a large, conspicuous award, known irreverently to the troops as 'Hitler's Fried Egg', when he went into action on a combat patrol or in an assault group!

Sturm recalled *Hauptfeldwebel* Wenner from 6 Company. While out on a forward patrol, the men had removed all their metal badges and decorations and put them in their pockets. This was a sensible move, as a bright metal object might catch whatever light there was and any reflection might give away their presence. Wenner suggested that this was undermining military morale in the face of the enemy. Sturm attempted to explain that the enemy would shoot first at the one wearing the most decorations. He felt that it was better to be a little cautious, as one was a long time dead. This remark had been too much for the pompous *Hauptfeldwebel*, who put Sturm on report. This went initially before *Oberleutnant* Hörstermann, who was duty bound to pass it on up the line, but Sturm felt sure that the battalion commander, Meurer, and regimental commander, Schmidt, would have thrown it in the waste paper bin!

Sturm's comrades greeted him heartily when he returned to his room, and when Sister Irmgard entered, Sturm went over to her straight away and kissed her in gratitude for all her tender care. Sister Irmgard put her arms around Sturm and returned his kiss.

'Room' was hardly the right terminology for Sturm's ward. It had a high-vaulted roof. Before the Revolution, the hospital had been a monastery. The rations, which were already excellent, got even better. The hospital was to move towards the rear and in view of the coming move distribution of the goods in the ration stores became even more generous. A special perk was the evening nightcap, a kind of bowl filled to the brim with wine, punch, or brandy wine. The previous evening, everyone whose health would allow was permitted two bowls of this heavenly concoction.

Except for the eye, Sturm now felt pretty good. The last injuries to his shoulder had now completely healed. The calendar showed 29 September. Little did he know that this date would be of special significance to him. After the issue of the evening nightcap, Sturm felt drowsy. Through exchanges of tobacco and some persuasion, he had managed to obtain extra rations of the potent brew. He was soon fast asleep. As usual, the radio was playing softly. It disturbed no one, and patients could chose whether to listen or drift off. Most waited, however, for the late night news before turning in. Only then did they find out what was happening outside their own little world here in the hospital. By the time the late news began on the 29th, everyone except Karl was asleep. He had been waiting to tune into the German language broadcasts by the enemy, which came after. This was of course strictly forbidden, but this didn't deter Karl. After each news report came the announcements of the latest *Ritterkreuzträger*. These were two high-ranking officers, and a *Gefreiter* by the name of Hans Sturm!

'The *Führer* has awarded the Knight's Cross of the Iron Cross to Hans Sturm of Dortmund, company runner in an infantry regiment,' sounded the report.

Karl was listening. It had scarcely sunk in that they were referring to the comrade in the next bed, when he leapt up and rushed over to Sturm, shaking him madly to try to awaken him.

'Man, Hans! Are you asleep? Didn't you hear the report? You've been awarded the *Ritterkreuz*. Wake up! Listen!'

Everyone in the room now except Sturm was wide awake, but still the hero of the hour slept. Karl told all the others the news then came back to Sturm. He roughly hauled the blanket off him as all five of his comrades yelled with enthusiasm. Sturm was jerked back and forward until he finally awoke in a foul mood.

'Damn it! What the hell do you want?!'

'We want to congratulate you, Hans. The *Führer* has awarded you the Knight's Cross. It has just been announced on the radio!'

Sturm was still feeling a little drunk and only half awake. He pulled his blanket back over himself, covering his ears. Karl wouldn't have it and shook him again.

'We must get this devil awake and get him to explain why he never told us that there was a prospect of him winning such a high decoration!'

Karl was leaning over Sturm at this point with his mouth right at Sturm's ear when Sturm flicked his hand back to push him away, hitting Karl in his remaining good eye. It was a square hit, and Karl would soon be sporting a fine black eye!

'Ouch!' cried Karl, 'You bloody idiot! Why don't you pay attention? The radio has announced that *Gefreiter* Sturm from Dortmund is a *Ritterkreuzträger*!'

Still tipsy, Sturm thought it was all a practical joke. He apologised to Karl, who was already dabbing at his eye with a damp cloth as the swelling began. In the last few days they had all told each other of the events which had led to their being wounded. Personally, Sturm had only a vague recollection of his last few minutes at Rzhew. It seemed incredible that his actions should bring him such a high decoration, when all he had wanted to do was avenge Sandkühler. No one else in *Infanterie Regiment 473* had the *Ritterkreuz* yet.

In the meantime, some of the others from the bigger ward had wandered in.

'Have you heard about *Gefreiter* Sturm's *Ritterkreuz*?'

'Yes, now tell this idiot. He has slept through everything and didn't hear the report. Now he won't believe that he has won the award!'

Everyone who was able to get up from their beds made their way into the room. A few sisters and the duty doctor came in, too. Everyone wanted to shake Sturm's hand and endless congratulations gushed. Stunned as the reality began to dawn on him, Sturm surrendered himself to his fate. Drawing his knees up, he sat at the top of his bed as friends and comrades crowded round.

The news that a mere *Gefreiter* had won the *Ritterkreuz* spread like wildfire. Despite the lateness of the hour, many of the other patients crammed into the already crowded room. All the beds and spaces in between, even the window ledges, were occupied. Even the corridor outside was soon packed, as everyone struggled to catch a glimpse of their 'hero'. Everyone got especially excited when it was suggested this very special hour ought to be celebrated, and that an extra nightcap would be in order.

Why have I been awarded the *Ritterkreuz*? Sturm asked himself. In March 1942, he had been recommended for the German Cross in Gold. At the end of August, he was recommended once again, this time by the regimental commander. So why a *Ritterkreuz*?

Glasses were being filled. The babble of voices had faded away. Everyone wanted to know what had happened, every detail. What should Sturm tell them? He was only just beginning to take the news in. His attempts to excuse himself from telling his story were swept aside by cheers of encouragement. After a few embarrassed slurps at his drink, he began.

He told them how he had got to know Sandkühler at Herford and of their friendship, which grew right up until the day of his death in the battle at Rzhew. It was just a quirk of fate that he had got the *Ritterkreuz*; he had simply decided to try to help his friend and former Number 2—that was all.

Sturm recounted how had he gone to 3 Platoon's positions on that fateful night because the company commander wanted a situation report to establish enemy strength and German casualties so that he could organise a counter-attack with the other companies. He told them of what ensued: of finding his friend dead and watching Löffler die a few moments later; of the fury and despair which drove him to forget his orders; of the near hopeless battle in which he had sustained his head wounds.

After about half an hour, the senior medical officer, *Oberfeldarzt* Ahrend stood up.

'*Gefreiter* Sturm, you have had much good fortune. We hope it will stay with you for the future also. Enjoy yourself!'

'Sister Märtens! They can have another half hour to chat,' said *Oberstabsarzt* Schüßler as he followed Ahrend to the door. 'Tomorrow is another day!'

The two doctors left the room.

'Goodnight!'

'Goodnight, *Herr Oberfeldarzt*,' came the reply from all.

Sturm continued to answer questions until the lateness of the hour and the drink began to take their effect and many began to fall asleep.

'Men, it's time to call it a day!' With these words Sister Irmgard stood up.

'Our *Ritterkreuzträger* can continue his report tomorrow!' she said looking at Sturm.

'Our *Ritterkreuzträger*?' said Karl. 'Until this afternoon she called you Hans. Are you in with her or not?'

The comrades all grinned and those who were billeted in other rooms began to wander off.

'Irmgard!' called Sturm. 'Stay a moment, please.'

She nodded to Karl, and the orderly and he left the room. The others got into their beds and pulled the blankets up over their ears. Irmgard ruffled Sturm's hair.

'You have to sleep, Hans,' she said, laughing. 'With your head wounds you shouldn't stay up so late!'

Sturm took her hand and kissed it.

'Now that I can see, I know that you are even prettier than they said, even if it is with only one eye.'

'You exaggerate, Hans. Once your head gets better, you will see many other girls, hopefully with both eyes.'

Sturm held her hand tightly.

'My head is spinning from the drink.' He pressed her hand against his forehead. 'There, that's better!'

Irmgard pulled her hand back, then as she straightened up his blanket said, 'Hans, you are a lovely man, but I must tell you that I am engaged!'

'Engaged isn't the same as married Irmgard!'

With a stroke of her hand against Sturm's cheek, she took her leave. As she reached the door, Karl came back and, with an exaggerated bow, said, 'Hans, the golden boy! What luck, to have you in our room, so that we can have such a great party!'

'Wait a moment, I still haven't actually got the award yet!'

'You just wait. Tomorrow it will be in all the papers in black and white. Soon, some bigwig will come and hang the medal round your neck.'

When Sturm didn't answer, he continued.

'Have you any idea what is in store for you? Civic reception in the city from the party—invitations will come rolling in. You will be asked to give lectures. The homeland needs heroes as orators. The enemy always advancing, our 'glorious' retreat—think of Stalingrad. The party bigwigs, those Golden Pheasants, are just not trusted any more to tell the truth when they visit the factories—they actually get booed![1] Everyone knows they talk big but are scared of any personal danger. Now they send proven soldiers in to spout the motto. "The Homeland fights, the Front fights, and we will be victorious!"'

Sturm was already very weary.

'Karl, the only thing a soldier has to do is die,' he answered, yawning. 'That comes to everyone. Who would force me to become a lecturer or some sort of orator, without even knowing if I would be able to do it?'

'You can depend on it, you have shown yourself able to do it, even here in hospital when you told your story. You are not fit for front-line service, so you will have to do your duty somehow. Big demonstrations with flags and bunting, lots of travel, more or less polite audiences in the mines, factories, city halls, village meetings, and, well, just about anywhere where they believe enthusiasm can be whipped up, they will send in an orator.'

'And, the soldier-orator must do all this?' asked Sturm.

'I think so, because you still believe that you serve a good cause,' said Karl grinning.

'For one thing, you won't need to say much to get the ladies going!'

'How so?'

'Well, it's obvious. We are in 1942, it will soon be 1943. If you already have so many glittering decorations on your chest at such a young age, then we must already have won!'

'Tell me Karl, how come you have all the answers? Where do you get your information?'

'From my brother. As a *Feldwebel*, he won the German Cross in Gold and has already been used as a so-called "Front Orator".'

Karl yawned and looked at his watch.

'Oh, the night is almost over. We need some sleep!'

They had been speaking in hushed voices and were the only ones left awake.

'Hans,' came a whisper from the next bed.

'Goodnight,' replied Sturm, with weary eyes. He had removed his eye-patch.

'I just wanted to say,' said Karl, 'They will come to see you, wherever you appear. All will greet you, and you must be polite and thank them. I can already see you surrounded by a circle of pretty girls. They will be all over you, like moths to a flame!'

'I will bear it with my usual self-control, Karl, but for now one moth would be plenty for me!'

'You…! And just in the next room, that lovely Irmgard has already taken you into her heart!'

'Karl, she just helped me make it through until they took off my bandages. Besides, she is already engaged.'

'Ach, I didn't know that—so, goodnight then, Hans!'

'Goodnight, Karl!'

Next morning, Sturm felt a churning in his guts. He would have to visit the toilet. Karl thought it was the excitement of the radio report about the award of the *Ritterkreuz*. Sturm suspected it was too much of the sweetened nightcap he had drunk. His session on the toilet was disturbed by a loud voice.

'Hans! Hans!'

It was Karl, limping along the corridor. 'Where are you hiding?'

Karl found Sturm in the latrine.

'There he is, not letting on!' he grumbled.

'What's up? Is the hospital burning down? Can't you leave me in peace!' growled Sturm.

'What do you mean, 'peace'? We are waiting for you and your explanation. Stick a cork in it—here, take it.' Karl held out a newspaper.

'I have paper, thanks,' Sturm waved him away.

'This isn't arse paper, you idiot. This is the newspaper report of your award.'

Surprised, Sturm reached out and took it. It really was there, in black and white, the text of the brief radio announcement.

. Karl, watching him intently, asked, 'Now, you doubting Thomas, now do you believe it's all real?'

'Where did you get this paper?

'The *Oberstabsarzt* gave it to us. It came with the air mail from Minsk.'

'Take the paper, I'll come straight away.'

The noise of Karl's crutch faded away as he set off down the corridor. For Karl and the others, everything was so simple. They had a *Gefreiter* in their midst who had won the *Ritterkreuz*. They were pleased for him. For Sturm, however, it wasn't quite so clear cut. Such a high decoration was not easy to get. In Rzhew his regiment had been attached to 6 *Infanterie Division*, instead of its own parent division. Subordinated units were usually last in line when it came to promotions, decorations, *etc*. The thought that they had only given him such a high decoration because they thought his wound was worse that it really was gnawed at him. Perhaps they thought he was going to die.

On the way back to his room, he once again passed the row of photographs of the *Luftwaffe Ritterkreuzträger*. Maybe his picture would appear here too—a low-ranking infantryman. He had given up on any thoughts of the German Cross in Gold, that big, precious 'party' award with its huge Swastika.[2]

'Now, take a look at this!' called a voice through the open door of his room. 'Hanging around in total silence looking at the photographs while we are all waiting for him.'

As Sturm passed, Karl patted him on the stomach and said, 'I can hardly wait!'

A friendly crowd had once again gathered in the room, to hear more of his story. Some were faces he recognised from yesterday, others he hadn't seen before. Between Sturm's and Karl's beds, someone had set up a table. Many gifts, large and small, lay there—some from individuals, some from small groups of patients.

'Here is your throne,' said Karl, indicating a pile of blankets at the top of his bed. They didn't give him a chance to look at his gifts. He was only allowed the time for a quick glance at the newspaper reports before they demanded his attention.

'So, comrades…' he began his report, and told them of the days at Welikije Luki and the first minor wound, and of the bullet which had hit his helmet and deflected off. With his final words he opened the drawer of his bedside chest and took the bullet from his haversack.

'Here is the very beast!' he said. 'I found it later on in my rolled up *Zeltbahn*.'

'Hans! You have only had minor hassle with your helmet,' called out Kurt, lying in the next bed. 'A bullet hit mine right in front, penetrated, then ran around the inside between the shell and the liner right above my head and came out at the back!'

Because Kurt sat rubbing the nape of his neck, the others looked on, full of sympathy, wondering what kind of injury had been caused. Kurt then grinned.

'No, dear listeners,' he said slowly, 'not what you think. I wasn't wearing the helmet at the time. It was lying on the ground as a decoy for a Russian sniper and his shot gave him away so he paid for it with his life!'

The others shook their heads at Kurt's macabre joke.

From 13.00 hours to 15.00 hours was the midday rest period. This would have been enforced earlier in the war, but as the hospital was due to close down the staff were no longer so insistent on petty rules.

On the bed beside Sturm sat *Leutnant* Walter Klinger, a young panzer officer. They played chess, having got to know each other at the suggestion of one of the doctors. (Klinger would later win the German Cross in Gold.) They were treated like princes. There was venison with mushrooms, a lovely Rhine wine, a starter, and a sweet course. *Oberfeldarzt* Ahrend had offered Sturm the spare bed in *Leutnant* Klinger's room. This was well meant, but Sturm had declined. He would stay with his own comrades in his old room.

Leutnant Klinger played a good game, and Sturm was soon in a seemingly hopeless position. This second round had reached its climax after Sturm had sacrificed his queen as part of his attack. Klinger had to take the queen, whereupon Sturm was able to checkmate Klinger with his bishop and rook.

'Congratulations, Hans,' said his partner. 'Another game?'

'Certainly,' said Sturm. 'It's the first game on this board that I have won.'

The board was set up again, and the game began. It had been a gift to Sturm from *Unteroffizier* Meier, a cook in the hospital. Yesterday evening he had heard the radio report and come to offer his felicitations. Some words had been exchanged and Meier had asked, casually, if Sturm played chess. Shortly thereafter, he had visited Sturm again and offered him the set. The figures were artistically hand-carved by Meier himself, and must have taken many months to complete. His only condition was that Sturm should keep in touch over the coming years, a modest request in return for so fine a gift.

The board and figures were larger than was customary. The white king and queen wore finely crafted garments. You could recognise knights, artisans, farmers, hunters, and monks among the white pieces. The knights were an amalgamation of Saint Martin, by the insignia on his cape, and Saint George in battle with the dragon. In each pair of rooks, a lookout kept watch from one while the alarm was being blown from the other. Every piece was carved with great delicacy. For the black figures, the king was represented by death, and the queen by Eve with the serpent. The bishops were either Pan, half man and half goat, or the Devil. The knights were a unicorn and a centaur. One rook was a volcano, and the other a mountain. Gnomes and goblins made up the pawns.

The game ended in a draw.

'Thank God!' said Karl. 'Excuse me, *Herr Leutnant*, but we wanted to ask Sturm to continue with his story.'

'Ach, why didn't you say so. Bad enough I haven't heard it from the beginning.' And with that, the *Leutnant* too gave Sturm his full attention.

'Don't worry, Walter,' said Sturm, 'I can tell you the other part another time. But do tell me if I repeat myself!'

'Sturm told them about his father, who had been in Russia since 1941, near Kursk. He was the foreman of a construction unit from a Dortmund firm involved in bridge building, and serving at the front along with engineers, technicians, rivetters, fitters, welders and others. His father had volunteered to replace a younger man with a wife and three young children he was loathe to leave behind.

Sturm told of how his father was a bit of an adventurer, who wanted away from the desk and the drawing board. He was 54 years old, and knew of the danger of partisans, bombs, *etc*. Sturm knew from his letters that he had already been slightly wounded and had received the War Service Cross Second and First Classes. He was a civilian specialist with a rank equivalent to *Oberstleutnant*. He wanted the opportunity to be closer to his son.

'That I would like to see,' Karl said before he could stop himself.

'Perhaps you will have the opportunity sooner than you think,' said Sturm. Turning to the others, he continued, 'Karl has read the last letter from my father. According to it he will be here in Smolensk tomorrow or the day after.'

Sister Irmgard entered the room. Looking round for Sturm, she indicated that he should follow her.

'Hans, you can give your father our—your love, and introduce good Sister Irmgard. He will surely give you his blessing,' said Karl emphasising his words with inappropriate gestures.

'You idiot, you imbecile!' Hermann from the next bed complained. 'Can't you just keep your filthy mouth shut!'

The room rang with laughter as everyone looked towards the sister.

'Oh, sorry Irmchen, I didn't mean anything by it,' said Karl in an attempt to regain face. Irmgard looked over to Sturm but said nothing and left the room blushing.

'Karl, you are impossible!' said Sturm with a dismissive wave of his hand.

'Hallo, Hans,' called Bernhard. 'You should tell us about the airfield in Welikije Luki!'

Because he was blind, he hadn't seen the sister, and hadn't really noticed the embarrassment of the situation. Sturm went on to tell of his experiences over the last fifteen months or so as well as he could remember. Some he had to repeat because some comrade or other hadn't heard part of the story.

It was the early morning on 4 October 1942. The men in the room had washed and breakfasted. The atmosphere was pleasant and the men were happy to have heard all of Sturm's experiences. Unexpectedly, the door opened, and a large man in civilian clothing entered. Everyone in the room fell silent, except for Sturm.

'Father! I knew from your letter that you were coming, but I didn't expect to see you so soon.'

Father and son hadn't seen each other for nearly two years. What do you say to someone when you haven't met for so long?

Then the *Oberfeldarzt* entered with yet another surprise.

'*Gefreiter* Sturm!' he announced. 'An officer has just landed at the airfield. He has brought your *Ritterkreuz*. You must get into your uniform!'

Sturm's father had in fact already met with the officer before coming to the hospital.

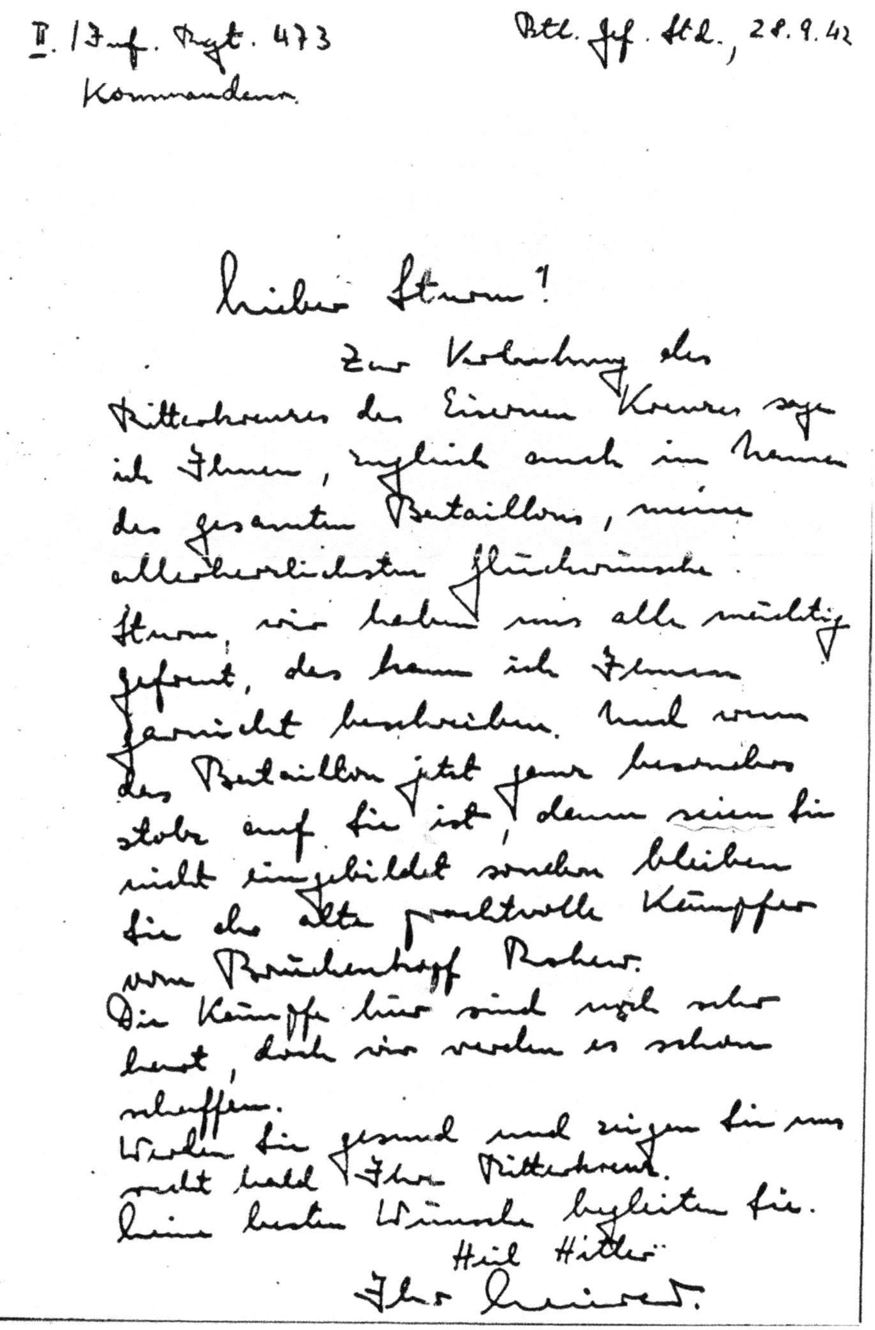

II./Inf. Rgt. 473 Btl. Gef. Std., 28.9.42
Kommandeur

Lieber Sturm!

Zur Verleihung des Ritterkreuzes des Eisernen Kreuzes sage ich Ihnen, zugleich auch im Namen des gesamten Bataillons, meine allerherzlichsten Glückwünsche. Sturm, wir haben uns alle mächtig gefreut, das kann ich Ihnen garnicht beschreiben. Und wenn das Bataillon jetzt ganz besonders stolz auf Sie ist, denn seien Sie nicht eingebildet sondern bleiben Sie der alte prachtvolle Kämpfer vom Brückenkopf Rshew.
Die Kämpfe hier sind wohl sehr hart, doch wir werden es schon schaffen.
Werden Sie gesund und zeigen Sie uns recht bald Ihr Ritterkreuz.
Meine besten Wünsche begleiten Sie.

Heil Hitler
Ihr Meinert.

The original letter of congratulations from Sturm's battalion commander.

Sturm's uniform had only been superficially cleaned. On the collar, the lapels were still flecked with blood. Sturm didn't want to put it on, but at his father's behest he agreed.

The officer bringing the award was *Leutnant* Zitzer, the orderly officer in the regimental staff of *Infanterie Regiment 473*. For a short period he had even been Sturm's platoon commander. Perhaps this was why he had been given the task of delivering the award. Sturm was much happier with this than if he had received the award from some high-ranking officer whom he had never met before.

Leutnant Zitzer was accompanied by the doctors, sisters, and others who were simply curious as to what was happening. Behind Sturm stood his father. After a hearty greeting between the two soldiers, Sturm introduced his father. *Leutnant* Zitzer was taken aback, and said that it was certainly a fortunate turn of events that the father was in Russia to see his son being awarded the *Ritterkreuz*. He took the award from its case and with a few words hung it around Sturm's neck.

'Sturm, it gives me great pleasure, that I can present you with your *Ritterkreuz*, because we have fought in battle side by side, and have experienced and survived much together,' he said in closing.

Zitzer saw how full the room had become, and greeted everyone with a wave of his hand.

'Look at him—he can't see very well, our little brave *Gefreiter*. Many of us thought he would not survive his last serious injuries.'

As well as passing on the good wishes of the regimental and battalion commanders, he gave Sturm good wishes from the company commanders and all his comrades. *Leutnant* Zitzer gave Sturm the award certificate, along with promotion to *Unteroffizier*, and the Wound Badge in Silver. During his conversations with Sturm and his father, many others came into the room to offer their congratulations, and everyone was given a drink to toast the occasion. Just before *Leutnant* Zitzer departed, Sturm learnt from him that the medic, *Unteroffizier* Karl Sippel, had been killed in action. He had been worried that Sturm might bleed to death in the foxhole.

The regiment had issued firm orders that after daybreak, no one was to move about on the front line. Any such movement brought down a hail of fire from the Russians. It made no difference whether those moving were carrying pans of food or were medical orderlies wearing Red Cross armbands—the Russians shot them all. Sippel, who had become friendly with Sturm, had twice made his way to the dressing station with wounded, despite the standing orders. On the first occasion he was with four Russian volunteer auxiliaries, carrying Sturm on a stretcher across to the dressing station. Sturm was unconscious through loss of blood. On the way back to the front line, he was shot and fatally wounded. Sippel had saved the wounded Sturm, and his bravery had cost him his own life.

After all the others had left the room, Sturm finally had the opportunity to talk to his father.

The gravestone of Karl Sippel, who lost his own life in helping to save Sturm's.

Sturm's father (who was also named Hans) told him that on 29 September he had been on leave in Dortmund, when a city official had called to congratulate the parents of Hans Sturm. He brought flowers and gifts along with a letter from the *Oberbürgermeister* of Dortmund, Dr Banike, including a salutation in the name of the people of the city. With great excitement, Sturm's mother and father had listened to the radio report which Sturm himself had slept through. On 30 September, his father had travelled to Berlin to his superior, the KODEIS (*Kommandant der Eisenbahntruppen*) to receive new orders. Naturally, he was given permission to break his journey on the way back to Kursk, to visit his son. Sturm's father had arrived in Smolensk on the night of 3/4 October, and had slept on the station platform because he hadn't wished to inconvenience the hospital by arriving too early. If he had reported to the hospital immediately, of course, the father of the *Ritterkreuzträger* would have been made most welcome! Thus he arrived on the morning of 4 October, just in time to see his son receive the award.

The day passed all too quickly, and just after they took lunch together, it was time

Sturm with his father in the field hospital at Smolensk.

Sturm with some of the nurses who tended him during his recovery.

for Sturm's father to leave. They knew that they would see each other again, but next time, it would be at home.

25

Incident in Brest-Litovsk

In mid-October 1942, Sturm lay in hospital in Brest-Litovsk recovering from his wounds. This was merely a transit point on his way back to Trier in Germany for further treatment and recuperation. One evening, he was awoken by the sound of small arms fire and explosions. He hurriedly dressed and made his way to the main door, where he met one of the staff surgeons, who was about to leave and had his field car waiting. Sturm persuaded the medical officer to take him along and find out what was happening. On the edge of the inner city, they were halted at a roadblock by the *Feldgendarmerie*, but because the car was clearly marked as a medical corps vehicle it was allowed to pass.[1]

Sturm was startled by what he saw. Men from a unit of the SD (*Sicherheitsdienst*, or security police) were clearing the Jewish ghetto. Partisans had attacked and blown up a munitions train a couple of days earlier, causing a number of deaths and many wounded. Two of the partisans had been captured and were found to be Jewish. They belonged to a resistance group and after 'interrogation' were declared to have been supported by the Jews in the ghetto. Now the SD was taking its revenge. In some ways, if what had been alleged was true, Sturm could have understood some form of punitive action being taken—but what was happening here was abhorrent.

One woman, dragged from her bed and only half dressed, was carrying a small child in her arms and leading another by the hand. Both were wailing loudly. Not moving fast enough to satisfy her tormentors, she was being driven forward by the rifle butt of her guard. Now she was crying too. After being hit once again with the rifle butt, the woman and her children fell sprawling at Sturm's feet. In a spontaneous reaction, Sturm leapt forward, and grabbing the rifle from the startled SD guard, smashed the butt against his helmeted head. As the guard collapsed in the gutter, Sturm threw his rifle down beside him. The woman and her children were led off in the direction of her fellow Jews, towards the railway station and an uncertain fate.

Sturm was immediately grabbed by some of the other SD men who were intent on arresting him on the spot. There would not have been much question over what his fate would be after such a crime. The medical officer and the SD unit commander, *an*

Still wearing his eye-patch, a recuperating Sturm visits a display of captured and knocked-out Soviet armoured vehicles.

SS-Untersturmführer, stopped them, however. The surgeon pointed out that Sturm was still suffering from his serious head wounds and motioned to the *Ritterkreuz* around Sturm's neck. Confronted with a genuine war hero, the SD officer relented and allowed Sturm to go unpunished.

On the return journey, the pair had to pass through the *Feldgendarmerie* roadblock once again, and this time their vehicle was carefully searched to ensure that they were not trying to smuggle out escapees.

Reaching the hospital safely, Sturm and the medical officer reported to the chief surgeon. Relieved at their safe return, he was nevertheless aghast at what Sturm had done and shook his head in disbelief, hoping that the SD commander would not report the incident. Coming to the defence of a Jew by assaulting a member of the security police was hardly the sort of behaviour likely to enhance one's standing. Sturm was extremely lucky to have escaped with his life.

This was not the first time, nor would it be the last, that Sturm's gut reaction overruled thoughts of self-preservation where matters of basic principal and humanity were concerned. Sturm had a keenly developed sense of right and wrong and never hesitated to speak out against injustice, whatever the risk to his own safety. From questions he asked officers with whom he spent some time before he was moved nearer home once again, Sturm discovered that news of the incident with the SD had spread. In conversation Sturm learnt more about the SD, the arm of the party most intimately involved in the mass murder of the Jews.

Sturm and fellow patients from the field hospital with nurses in attendance.

Most soldiers, who spent their entire war at the Front, knew little about what was happening to the Jews. Sturm had of course already witnessed some of the treatment meted out to Jews during his school days. And after the assassination of the diplomat vom Rath by a Jew in 1938 in Paris, the Nazis' retribution on *Kristallnacht*, when Jewish businesses, houses and Synagogues were destroyed in an orgy of cruelty, was well known. The brutal treatment of the Jewish woman and her children, however, came as a great shock to Sturm. This was a distressing memory he would never forget.

One of the officers, a *Hauptsturmführer* of the *Waffen-SS*, explained to Sturm the differences between his branch and the SD, even though both services used the same rank insignia. The SS was originally a protection squad, formed in 1925 to provide personal bodyguards for Hitler. Under Himmler it became an elite formation of the Nazi Party in 1929, and it eventually took over the German police and security organisations, including the SD.

The *SS-Verfügungstruppe*, later to become the *Waffen-SS*, was formed in 1934 through a secret order. Before the war, the *SS-VT* had taken part in military operations with the Army on three occasions: the occupation of Austria, the occupation of the Sudetenland, and the occupation of Czechoslovakia. The divisions, corps, and armies of the *Waffen-SS* came under the control of the German High Command of the Army during wartime, and in general had nothing to do with the concentration camps or the SD *Einsatzgruppen* which Sturm had encountered in Brest-Litovsk. The Einsatzgruppen were a branch of the *Sicherheitspolizei* (*SiPo*) and were controlled by the *Sicherheitshauptamt*.[2] Their personnel also wore the deathshead badge of the SS, but were formed into units of around 340 men under the direct command of Himmler for so-called 'actions for the security of service units in partisan infested areas behind the Eastern Front.'

Sturm garnered from this explanation just how multi-faceted the SS really was, and was grateful for this clarification. He could see that it would be a mistake to tar all SS men with the same brush. Many were conscripted, too.

The seven officers and *Unteroffizier* Sturm were nicknamed '*Die Pensche*'. They did almost everything together. *Oberleutnant* Körber asked everyone within earshot if they knew what a *Pensch* was. Naturally, no one knew what it could be. If those they met didn't know, they would make fun of their lack of education and point out that it was the middle syllable of the word '*Lampenschirm*' (lampshade)—a pun over which almost no one laughed.

Sturm had to bear this measure of wit a little longer, as he had yet to travel in the same carriage as the *Oberleutnant* all the way through the Rheinland and into Southern Germany. It was the end of October 1942. The other officers had all left the train at their various destinations. Sturm, however, had to travel to Trier to a special unit dealing with eye injuries. Sturm eventually found himself standing in the corridor of a second-class carriage which was at full capacity. Only officers were allowed to take seats in the compartments. One *Oberstleutnant* had, however, noticed his *Ritterkreuz* and invited him into his compartment. The arm rests were raised so that four instead of three could be seated on each side.

The *Oberstleutnant* asked Sturm his name then introduced him to the other officers, who in turn introduced themselves but without standing up or any such formality. Soon after they had passed Warsaw, some began to take their uniform jackets off, including Sturm and the *Oberstleutnant*. Sturm's eye injury was clearly apparent from the eye-patch he wore, and he was asked how it had come about. Sturm gave them a brief account of his experiences. In Berlin, four of the officers left the carriage and their seats were taken by some of those who had been standing in the corridor. One of them, a *Leutnant* from East Prussia, was on leave and on his way to France. Not long afterwards, he opened his case and brought out sausage, ham, cakes, and alcohol. He shared everything out because he thought that he would not need such things in France, where such items were still plentiful. Some of the others had similar goods in their cases and Sturm himself was able to contribute a bottle of French brandy to the occasion. Small wonder that the atmosphere in the carriage was most congenial.

After the train left Hannover, a *Feldgendarmerie* patrol entered their compartment. A *Hauptmann* checked their papers. He told Sturm that only officers were allowed in the compartments and told him, albeit politely, that he would have to leave, pointing out that there were still officers standing or sitting on their cases in the passageway. *Unteroffizier* Sturm stood up and put on his tunic, fastening the *Ritterkreuz* at his neck. The *Hauptmann* was taken aback, but did not change his decision. The *Oberstleutnant* then explained that he had invited the *Ritterkreuzträger* into the compartment. He stood up, put on his tunic, and motioned to Sturm to take his place while he went out into the corridor. The *Hauptmann* of the *Feldgendarmerie* muttered a few words about this irregular conduct, then saluted respectfully and left the compartment. The journey continued in even better spirits!

PART TWO

Representing the Reich

26

Home at Last

At the beginning of November 1942, the train finally arrived in Trier, a city on the River Mosel which housed a specialist eye hospital. Already the first encounters with people in the station were going exactly as Karl in the neighbouring bed in the ward in Smolensk had predicted. Whether in uniform or in civilian clothing, everyone noticed his *Ritterkreuz* and saluted him. This was a situation which, for a junior rank like *Unteroffizier* Sturm's, would take some getting used to. Even officers saluted him first, if he wasn't quick enough.

From the reporting office at the station he was given directions to the Catholic *Marienkrankenhaus*. He went slowly through the streets looking in shop windows, and found himself standing before the Porta Nigra, the 'Black Gate' of Roman times. For Sturm, who had spent so much time in Russia, the sight of so many people and busy shops was intimidating. Only ten minutes further on from the Porta Nigra lay the hospital. On reporting in, Sturm was escorted to the eye clinic by a sister. In the room to which he was allocated there was only one bed still free. The three other beds were occupied by a *Feldwebel* and two *Unteroffiziere*. After the introductions were made, Sturm had once again to tell his new comrades the full story of his eye injury, the *Ritterkreuz, etc.*

The *Feldwebel*, who had already been in the hospital for two weeks, thought that Sturm was perhaps the first *Ritterkreuzträger* to be seen here in Trier. There had been one *Ritterkreuzträger* from the city, an *Oberleutnant*, but he had been killed in action in the summer. Sturm then had to report to the resident doctor, *Stabsarzt* Dr Kurt Weber, who had already seen Sturm's medical file. After an examination, he said that the prognosis was good for further treatment. He gave Sturm permission to leave the hospital for excursions, but cautioned that his award would attract much attention and that must conduct himself properly in every way.

On the next day, a Saturday, Sturm reported to the senior nurse, Sister Veronika, with the request that he be permitted to leave the hospital to buy some flowers for the altar in the hospital chapel. He went to the market in the city centre and bought some Azaleas to brighten up his room, as well as some flowers for the altar, which would be delivered to the hospital. In a nearby warehouse he bought four flower

Sturm on sick leave and back once again in his home town, pictured here with his proud mother.

vases, and asked for them to be kept aside for him under the counter. On the way back, he passed by a jewellers shop on the right-hand corner of the street which led to the cathedral. There were some items on display which Sturm was interested in. As he opened the door, a bell jangled. Two ladies were in the front shop, both older than Sturm, who was just 21 years old.

He stepped forward shyly and was relieved when the lady behind the counter engaged him in friendly conversation. Sturm showed her the pieces in the window display which had caught his eye. They were made from glass beads strung together. He explained that he would hang them around the vases that he had bought for the hospital room. The lady looked him over from top to toe and laughed. To Sturm's surprise, she said that she would have to ask her father's permission first. Later he realised that this was just an excuse. She had gone into the back room and came back with a tall white haired old man, the jeweller Konstantin Schwarzmann. He cut an impressive figure, and would have been well suited to a general's uniform. The jeweller congratulated Sturm on his high decoration, asked him his name, about his injuries, his home town, and where he was billeted in Trier. After further questioning he presented Sturm with one of his visiting cards.

'*Unteroffizier* Sturm,' he said, 'I would like to invite you to visit me in the *Ostallee*, because I am very interested in learning about your experiences and I can tell you a little about my own work!' He looked over at his daughter, who knew how much he loved to talk with soldiers. 'Come tomorrow around 16.00 hours in the afternoon for coffee!'

Sturm thanked him for the invitation, said goodbye, and left the shop with his goods without having to pay. On the way back to the hospital, his good fortune began to dawn on him. Only one day back home in Germany and he had been invited to the home of one who he would later find out was a jeweller of world renown.

Sister Veronika turned a blind eye to the fact that Sturm had missed his midday meal, maybe because of his token to the altar. Sturm managed to get warmed up leftovers in the kitchen before returning to his room. The others, especially the two *Unteroffiziere* who had been in there three or four days so far and had not yet been allowed to go out, were astonished when Sturm talked of his experiences that day. 'Yes, well, it's all very well if you are a *Ritterkreuzträger*!' said one, and then noticing the *Feldwebel*'s displeasure, quickly added, 'Sorry, Hans, you have earned it!' It was fast becoming clear to Sturm that his *Ritterkreuz* could open many doors.

Konstantin Schwarzmann's house was a villa in the *Ostallee*, built around the turn of the century. It was the jeweller's daughter, Thea, who answered the door and escorted Sturm to her father. During coffee, Sturm had to answer many questions. Then he was shown many articles from newspapers and magazines from all over the world all about chalices, monstrances, crosses, and crucifixes made in his workshops for churches all over the globe.

The old man got quite carried away talking about his work, and it was only after his daughter pointed out to him that he had not yet asked any of what he had intended that he realised he had been talking for so long. He invited Sturm to stay for

Relaxing at home with family and friends.

dinner but Sturm had to politely refuse, as he had arranged to spend the evening with the *Feldwebel* from his room.

'Then come tomorrow for lunch,' was the old man's reply.

Because Sturm was reluctant, saying he had to get permission from the senior nurse, Sister Veronika, the old man replied, laughing: 'Give Sister Veronika my best regards. She will have no objections!'

The evening with *Feldwebel* Herbert Schreiner was quite an experience, especially for him. He wanted to invite Sturm, because they needed ration cards, which they didn't have. However, as Sturm was a *Ritterkreuzträger*, the owner of the pub they chose wouldn't ask them for any money. Three bottles from his special reserve supply of wine also found their way down the throats of the two soldiers.

On Sunday at 12 o'clock, Sturm duly presented himself at the *Ostallee*. A housemaid opened the door and led him into the study, where both daughter and father greeted him warmly. Sturm presented his bouquet of Alpine flowers which he had 'borrowed' from the sister's room.

The magnificent spread in the Schwarzmann house was most impressive, and had been laid out especially for Sturm. The time flew by well into the afternoon, mostly taken up by Sturm answering his host's interrogations. The greatest surprise for Sturm was when other guests arrived, including *Stabsarzt* Dr Weber, who was apparently often a guest of *Herr* Schwarzmann. Then came one of the ladies whom he had encountered the previous day in the shop. She was with her husband Dr Ritter, who, as Sturm later discovered, was a manager from the wine-growing estate 'Maximilian Grünhauser Herrenberg'. Most of the conversation which followed centred on Sturm and his experiences. They were conscious that he might have more of the same in store for him.

In late afternoon, the gathering began to break up. As he left, Dr Ritter said to Sturm: '*Unteroffizier* Sturm! I would like to invite you to our estate. We also have riding horses which you are welcome to use as often as you would like,' and indicating the doctor, he added, 'If it is all right with the *Stabsarzt*, who is already familiar with our estate, and who of course is also invited! My wife would be happy to collect you.'

Dr Weber and Sturm travelled together to the hospital. Weber was born in Trier and, after being wounded during the second month of his tour of duty in Russia, had taken up duties as resident doctor in the eye clinic at the *Marienkrankenhaus*.

'*Unteroffizier* Sturm! Tomorrow at 10.00 hours, come for an examination!' he said. '*Jawohl, Herr Stabsarzt*!'"

The examination revealed that the right eye had improved. The severe double vision had lessened and the severe sensitivity to light was much less painful when the eye-patch was removed. The sliver of shrapnel, however, remained in the eye socket.

'Sturm! On Monday you must come to the University Clinic at Heidelberg. There, we will be able to check and see whether it is possible to remove the shrapnel.'

'*Herr Stabsarzt*! Will you be removing the sliver of shrapnel yourself?'

'That's something I cannot say.'

Because Sturm looked so troubled and uncertain, the doctor placed his hand on Sturm's shoulder and said: 'The professors in Heidelberg have much better equipment and a much bigger brain than I have. The doctors there will make every effort on your behalf and give you the best advice, but in the end it is you who must decide!'

The rest of the week went by very quickly. Sturm was, so to speak, shown off. There were visits to wine tastings in Trittenheim, Saarburg, and with the Trier Residents Association, and further visits to *Herr* Schwarzmann, who was also well known as a regional writer in the Mosel area. At the weekend Sturm and Dr Weber were the guests of the Ritters on the wine estate. The trip around the vineyards took up the entire morning and ended with a visit to the stables. There were four fine horses, which the men took the opportunity to ride. This short trek, at midday, was a grand experience for Sturm. He knew that with his 'dice-beakers' (Army boots) and uniform trousers he didn't look very stylish, but was told that he looked quite the part as a horseman. Before his military service began, Sturm had only once sat on a horse, but in Russia during his time as a company messenger he had often practised on the Russian Panje horses, and was only once thrown off, when his horse jumped a hurdle. Here, on a first-class steed at walking speed, it was more of a sight-seeing trip than a riding lesson. Dr Weber and Sturm discussed the opportunity of coming again.

In the evening, the two drank a bottle of fine wine in the *Stabarzt*'s room, which they had brought from the vineyard. After the wine tasting, Sturm had been given two cases of it, from which his comrades in the ward were able to sample as much as they liked. The conversation between Sturm and the doctor was relaxed and comradely, and after the second bottle of wine, they reverted to the informal '*Du*' when referring to each other. A while later, Sturm asked what he should do if the specialist in the Heidelberg clinic recommended an operation.

'Hans, you must listen carefully to what he says and then make the decision for yourself, perhaps after sleeping on it first.'

'I want to know what you think though, Kurt. What would you decide?'

The eye doctor, who was still relatively young himself and certainly a specialist in his own right with up-to-date knowledge of the latest procedures, was reluctant to answer. He looked at Hans, who waited anxiously for his reply, then raised his glass and took a drink.

'I would go for an operation to remove the sliver of shrapnel as soon as possible. There is still the possibility that the left eye could be endangered. The shrapnel could possibly become encapsulated. The eye muscle would slowly regain its original position, and the momentary double vision would fade. The iris itself would contract and the sensitivity to light would therefore fade.'

Both were silent for a while. Then Sturm thanked him. After the third bottle of wine was finished, he took leave of his friend with a firm handshake.

Sturm went to the Heidelberg clinic and was examined from head to toe. If he agreed to the removal of the shrapnel, they would have to remove the eye from its socket. After the removal of the shrapnel it would be replaced and would regain its function. Complications were unlikely, but possible. Once returned to Trier, he wrote a letter to the University Clinic in the presence of Dr Weber, asking to go ahead with the operation and thanking the staff for the preparatory examination. To Sturm, it was obvious that his special attention and treatment in the University Clinic had largely to do with his *Ritterkreuz*.

In the second week of November, Sturm was visited by Sister Margot from the field hospital in Smolensk. She brought with her a number of photos from his time in there, and also of the other seven officers who were his companions. Unfortunately, she was only able to stay over in Trier for one night.

The following week he was able to visit his mother and Edith, the spoiled youngest daughter of a clothing manufacturer in Dortmund. The Sturm and Roth families were well known to each other, as the wives had both been at the same school. The meeting of mother and son was very emotional. With Edith it was different; she smothered him with kisses, as if they were almost engaged. Sturm could only fend off her attentions with extreme care, and made compliments to her so as not to offend. She had never shown any interest in him before he became a soldier. Sturm thought that it was surely the *Ritterkreuz* which attracted her now. In a later meeting with Sturm in Dortmund her father had said: 'Hans, I am happy that you two didn't get together. I wouldn't want to see you two married.' His mother wasn't interested in the *Ritterkreuz* or any of the other decorations, but showed concern over the patch over his eye. Sturm had to remove the patch over his right eye to prove to her that he could still see with both of them. The double vision was still severe, however, and prevented his seeing too clearly.

Sturm's mother and Edith spent three days in Trier. He had booked them into a good, bargain hotel, to the great displeasure of *Fräulein* Roth, who thought it too common! The jeweller, *Herr* Schwarzmann, once again invited Sturm and his guests. The lively conversation between him and his daughter, and Sturm and his mother was spoiled by Edith, who constantly tried to dominate the conversation in a pushy, inflated, and self-centred manner. The farewell from the jeweller and his daughter ended with the promise that they would keep in touch. Sturm said he would write to them. It was the quiet manner of this highly intelligent man, almost fifty years his senior, which in these first few weeks back in the *Vaterland* made the war in Russia and all its cruelties seem so very far away.

Sturm took his mother and Edith to the station. His mother he would see again soon when he got leave, but he wasn't so sure about Edith! Two days later, he left the hospital and travelled to Aachen to the replacement battalion of *Infanterie Regiment 473*. On his arrival he was pressed by all his comrades for a full report on his recuperation leave. His friend, *Stabsarzt* Dr Weber, promised him that he would let him know as soon as he heard any news on the condition of his eyes.

Return to Dortmund

Sturm remained in Aachen only briefly before taking his regular leave. He left on the first available train to Dortmund. Only once did he have to change trains, and he finally arrived at his house in the late evening. It was the beginning of December 1942.

A long welcome home party was held, with his friends and relations. The only disappointment was that Sturm's father couldn't be there. His last letter had come from the area around Stalingrad and left them profoundly unsettled, declaring that Stalingrad 'would become a graveyard for Hitler's army!' This slogan was announced regularly by loudspeaker by the Soviets all around the front lines.

Sturm visited the *Oberbürgermeister*, Dr Banike, who had promised him two boxes at the state theatre if he ever wanted to visit. Sturm later heard that the Dortmunder *Oberleutnant* Helmut Schnatz and *Oberfeldwebel* Friedrich Vogelsang, who had also been awarded the *Ritterkreuz* in September 1942, had been given a grand reception, with many gifts. The fact that he was not a party member perhaps played some part in his being given a less elaborate welcome. In contrast, the reception from *Kreisleiter* Knoop was a modest affair, very personal and sociable.[1] Among other gifts, he presented Sturm with the Golden *Hitlerjugend* Badge. He had been in the *Jungvolk* just before the Nazis came to power in 1933, but a month later had left and in 1937 had discharged himself for various reasons. He was therefore not a party member.

The newspaper captions read: '*Ritterkreuz* winner Hans Sturm, who had previously served in the *Hitlerjugend* […]'. In the paper was a photograph of *Oberleutnant* Knoop taking his leave from the *Ritterkreuz* winners *Oberleutnant* Cordes and *Unteroffizier* Sturm as he left to return to the Eastern Front. Knoop, Cordes, and Sturm had all served in the same sector and in close proximity to each other: Knoop with the panzers, Cordes with the *Luftwaffe*, and Sturm with the infantry.

Sturm and his mother had a peaceful, pleasant few days together. She spoiled him during the day, and in the evening he visited local bars with his friends. Sturm was astonished by how many people wanted to be his friend and bask in his glory. In the *Fürstenhof*, an orchestra played 'Rosamunde' especially for Sturm. Thereafter, each time Sturm entered, and the band leader spotted him, he would stand, lift his baton, and the band would strike up the same piece. Almost everyone there, mostly soldiers on leave, would join in and sing heartily.

Service as a Lecturer

In the third week of December, Sturm received a letter from the command of *Wehrkreis VI* in Münster. He was to be offered a short spell of leave, ending on 28 December, after which he would be employed as a speaker to factory workers, public meetings, and that sort of thing. Sturm was astonished at the invitation. His neighbour in the hospital in Smolensk, Karl, had been correct in his warnings. Sturm wrote out two A4 pages, with details of his military career, his service in various units, promotions, wounds, decorations, *etc*. At the end of his letter, he declared his willingness to take up these duties but asked if they would consider, in view of his need to recuperate from his eye injuries, delaying his appointment until the end of January. Sturm finished his letter and put a stamp on the envelope. In the evening he went off into town to have a drink with some friends, the letter still lying on his desk. Returning later, quite merry with the effects of the alcohol, he decided he should write a much longer letter, in case his meagre two-page effort made him look too stupid to write more. He made himself a pot of strong coffee, and after a couple of cups his head felt a little clearer.

His new letter filled eight pages of neatly typed A4 paper. After posting it he lay in his bed, hoping all the more that they would agree to the postponement. This was, however, not to be, and Sturm received orders to report to *Ersatz Bataillon 473* in Aachen on 3 January 1943.

On 4 January, there was a great surprise awaiting Sturm, as the commander of the recuperation company to which he was attached handed him a small black case containing the German Cross in Gold. The case had been damaged on its way to him. Sturm couldn't understand why the award had taken so long. The recommendation had first been made by his company commander *Oberleutnant* Winter, and then by his regimental commander *Oberst* Schmidt. On that same day, Sturm visited the eye surgeon and was prescribed an opaque lens for his glasses, which he would have to wear for some weeks. This, his friend the eye surgeon in Trier advised him, augured well for the further improvement of his eye. In the evening, Sturm received instructions to report to the Hotel Excelsior in Cologne on the next day. A great reception was planned and in the course of the day, he would meet thirty other speakers ranking from *Unteroffizier* to *Oberleutnant*. There were two other *Ritterkreuzträger*, one a *Leutnant* and the other an *Oberleutnant*. For every speaker who was a front-line soldier, there was one from the party and one from the administration of the city in which the speaker would make his first address.

The theme was 'Front and Homeland'. Also present were the *Oberbürgermeister*, the *Kreisleiter*, the senior district military officer from Cologne, Roeder von Diersberg, and from Düsseldorf, *Generalmajor* Lorenz. Up for discussion were the combat actions of the Front speakers; fulfilling duties on the home front; and Germany and Adolf Hitler in general. Front-line soldiers convivially socialised with representatives of the party and the armed forces.

One week later, an article appeared in the *Kölner Illustrierte*: 'Köln receives its guests—Artists and Soldiers visit the City on the Rhine'. The photo depicted the sculptor Arno Brekker, *Gauleiter* Josef Grohe, and *Kreisleiter* Alfons Schaller at Brekker's Exhibition; another photo showed the actor Hilde Krahl and Paul Hubschmid in *Kabal und Liebe*; and in yet another there was Sturm, standing in front of a huge piece of machinery talking with three workers. In a fourth photo, Sturm sat in the foyer of the Hotel Excelsior with soldiers and party members, including the district foreman from Bonn, Peter Bruckner. In the late evening Sturm travelled to Bonn, where he was to stay in the Königshof Hotel, near the *Stadtpark* and the university.

29

A Busy Week in Bonn

In the morning, Sturm met with the *Kreisleiter*. The usual battery of questions and answers followed. Before his departure, the *Kreisleiter* offered Sturm the choice of either a painting or a book to commemorate his visit. Sturm chose the book, and asked whether he might have one in which he could log details of the firms and businesses he visited, and the speeches he made. Sturm had received a list from the command of *Wehrkreis VI* in Münster, from Prof. Dr Gierlich, the *Oberstleutnant* responsible for military speeches and lectures in Gau Köln and Aachen. It detailed six speeches to be made in Bonn in the first week, followed by fourteen in Düren the next.

Sturm was presented with a beautifully bound, grey pigskin-covered volume. Sturm then had an idea—instead of simply logging his visits, he would ask those he met to make a short entry in the book. He asked the *Kreisleiter* to make the first of many. Sturm soon needed a second volume, which was gifted by the *Oberburgermeister* of Düsseldorf, Hermann Freitag. These entries went on up until the end of the war, the last being made on 14 April 1945. Soldiers, party members (including two *Gauleiter*), over fifteen generals, directors, factory managers, school principals, workers, women from all walks of life, Hitler youths, and BDM (*Bund Deutscher Mädel*, or 'League of German Girls') girls were immortalised in these books. One of the latter was Hilde Neerfeld, who was to become Sturm's wife.

The first speech Sturm made was at the Hans Miesen company, which fitted out ambulances. A special display followed in which, within just sixteen minutes, a fully functioning temporary hospital unit was erected from prefabricated sections carried in four trailered trucks. In the evening, the director of the factory had reserved a table at the Hotel Dreesen. Sturm met the owners, Fritz and Georg Dreesen. Fritz, the elder of the two, was a holder of the 'Blood Order' and the Gold Party Badge.[1] He had taken part in the 1923 march to the *Feldherrnhalle* in Munich and was a personal friend of Hitler's. Sturm was allowed to stay in a special suite of their hotel, which was reserved for Hitler's personal use. The Dreesens, who were on friendly terms with Miesen, joined them at their table along with Kreisobmann Bruckner, who escorted Sturm around all his speeches in the Bonn area. There were also some men from the factory and the factory foreman.

During their conversations, Sturm asked Fritz Dreesen why he didn't wear his gold Party Badge. After a pause, he replied: 'Perhaps I'll tell you about it another time— after all, you still have a full week here yet.'

Sturm didn't know what to make of the use of the familiar '*Du*', or his quartering in this first-class hotel, and looked at the smiling faces of the others round the table with bewilderment. For the whole week he was to occupy a suite of rooms identical to those reserved specially for the *Führer*.

The second speech was on the following morning in the light metal works in Bonn-Beuel on the other side of the Rhine. There were many flags, garlands, and flowers giving the event a very festive air. A brief introduction and a song from the works choir preceded Sturm's speech. Sturm had also been given a guided tour of the factory beforehand, and afterwards a meal in the works canteen.

The afternoons were free and party member Bruckner showed Sturm the sights of Bonn. This process was repeated most days, with afternoons left free for sightseeing. Once, Sturm wanted to go to a rather downmarket cafe which featured a band and where there was dancing. Bruckner wasn't too keen, and certainly refused to go in uniform. Sturm insisted, however, and Bruckner eventually grudgingly agreed after Sturm said he would be sure to salute any high-ranking party members he saw.

As Sturm had expected, the place was very busy, with many soldiers and their wives or girlfriends in attendance. Sturm spotted a table just in front of the band

Sturm during one of his lectures at an engineering works. The flag in the background is that of the *Deutsche Arbeitsfront*, the official trade union of the Third Reich.

and made a beeline for it with Bruckner. All those present seemed to be just in the right mood to have a good time. The good atmosphere was made even better by the popular hit songs played by the band. Things reached a climax when Sturm was invited to conduct the band in a rendition of his favourite tune, 'Rosamunde'. Bruckner later admitted that he too had enjoyed himself, but just hoped that their photos would not be in the next day's papers, as a reporter had been in attendance and had been snapping away at the camera. As it turned out, only one photo was published, showing Sturm conducting the band.

The third speech was with the firm of Soenneken. Originally a manufacturer of fountain pens, the firm now made bullet cartridges and other military wares.

Sturm's fourth speech was given in lecture hall No. 10 at the University for Agricultural Studies. On this occasion, there was a bit of a panic when it was discovered that Sturm's original ten-page report—which he always carried with him and used as a form of aide memoir—had gone missing. Bruckner had taken it upon himself always to make sure that the report was placed on the lectern before Sturm began his speech. Now it could not be found and Bruckner just stood there, open mouthed, waving his hands about and nervously running his fingers through his hair, worrying about the blame which would be laid at his door if things went awry. Without his report to use as a prompt, Sturm would now have to speak off the cuff. After Sturm's very first speech, Bruckner had said, 'Your speech was excellent, but I think some of the audience might not have understood everything because you spoke so fast.' Now, Sturm spoke much more slowly, as though weighing every word before speaking. He concealed his nerves well, and used hand gestures for emphasis. His talk about the Front, which used to take about thirty to forty-five minutes, now lasted much longer. Sturm found himself sweating with excitement at making his first speech without any notes.

The State Farmers' Leader (*Landesbauernführer*), *Freiherr* Elz von Rübenach, thanked Sturm for his interesting and informative talk. He invited Sturm and the others in Sturm's company to a wine tasting. Also in attendance were Generals von Diersberg and Lorenz, who Sturm had already got to know in Cologne. They all sat around a large round table, with the generals either side of Sturm. The whole evening was a memorable experience for the young infantryman.

More memorable still was Sturm's fifth speech, which took place in the famous Beethoven Halls—at that time not yet damaged by the bombing—in front of the assembled city administration. His brief speech was followed by a concert by the best known military band in Germany. It was intended as a 'filler' for the interval, but when he finished his speech and the audience began to applaud, the noise filled the entire structure of the wooden hall, amplified by the superb acoustics. This was such a thrill that it made the hairs on the back of Sturm's neck stand on end.

The sixth speech was in Rheinbach, just south of Bonn. It was Sturm's first open public address. Unfortunately, Bruckner's car wouldn't start. It was Sunday morning and no assistance was available. It took both men some time to get the car moving and when they finally arrived at the venue, they were very late and filthy. Sturm wanted to go immediately into the hall from whence a loud hubbub could be heard. The *Ortsgruppenleiter*, however, would have none of it and insisted that first they must clean up and have some refreshments. Sturm ignored him and went straight into the hall, where he was met by a storm of applause. It was festively decorated and filled to capacity, with many standing in the aisles. The audience was mixed—men, women, young girls and boys, many of them in uniform. There were also quite a number of soldiers present, several with bandaged injuries. Sturm spoke for almost an hour and a half, taking time to answer questions. As on previous occasions, he had spoken only of his own personal experiences, and had introduced no political propaganda to his speech. He no longer needed the ten pages of prepared notes and, as Bruckner had confirmed, now spoke in public like a natural. On his last morning, just after breakfast, Fritz Dreesen came and sat down beside him. After a brief general conversation about nothing in particular, he finally broached the subject of why he did not wear his Gold Party Badge.

'A number of us, perhaps ten, retired from the party last year in protest at a massive fraud, which had been discovered in the highest financial and Government circles. The guilty ones were not punished like any ordinary citizen would have been. On the grounds of the effects on both internal and external politics if it had become known, any thought of punishment was swept under the carpet. The files on the incident were quietly lost in the cellars!'

30

Armed Forces Day

Armed Forces Day fell on a Sunday, and was celebrated lavishly throughout the whole of Germany. All military barracks held an open day, in which every visitor could observe how soldiers lived and inspect the latest weapons and equipment. The recuperation company of *Ersatz Batallion 473* had had a brainwave. It had invited a small carnival show along, with carousels and stalls and prizes of all types for adults and children alike. All the proceeds from this day went into a single pot, and were contributed to the war effort. The company commander had organised some tame riding of horses and ponies. During an excursion, Sturm had spotted a donkey ride at a local beer garden and had borrowed it for the day. By early morning business was brisk, and almost all of the barracks was busy with visitors.

Sturm had to go into Aachen at midday to act as the auctioneer at a sale on the *Elisenbrunnen*. It had already been advertised for some weeks in the display window of a WMF (*Württemberger Metallwaren Fabrik*) shop near the state theatre. There were many lots to be auctioned. Soldiers from Sturm's company had built, carved, and painted souvenir items, and there were paintings and valuable books too, including two antique bibles which had been donated. On display was a life-size oil painting of Sturm based on a photo which had been taken just after the award of the *Ritterkreuz*. The painting was not for sale, but merely there to help publicise the fact that this highly decorated *Gefreiter* would be there to lead the auction. The painting had been done by an artist called Schopen from Bonn and gifted to Sturm. It was not so much the *Ritterkreuz* and other decorations which made the painting so impressive, neither was it the blood-stained, crumpled uniform he wore, but the fact that the artist had not covered his injured eye with the eye-patch, the exposed injury lending the young soldier's face a most striking appearance. The artist had not been fit for front-line service and right up until the end of the war, was posted to the replacement depot in Aachen. His striking portrait turned this little known young man into something of a local celebrity, the oil painting for all to see in the shop window making him look like a wild dog.

The auction began at 11 a.m. Sturm was assisted by *Oberfeldwebel* 'Bubi' Hörstgen, who wore the German Cross in Gold, and other soldiers from the unit. As was

Sturm as an *Unteroffizier*. On his right breast pocket is the sunburst star badge of the German Cross in Gold.

customary, bidding began at the reserve price. From a pack of cigarettes to a bottle of wine, from bottles of brandy to framed portraits—all went 'under the hammer'. One particular oil painting drew special interest. Also inspired by a photograph, it depicted an Alpine chalet and had attracted the attention of two young girls at the front of the crowd. Bidding against them was a man who Sturm thought looked like a wealthy butcher, and another who looked like a Privy Councillor in his black bowler hat. The bidding quickly reached 400 RM. At 600 RM, the 'Privy Councillor' dropped out, the crowd having already made it clear that their sympathies lay with the girls, drowning out his bids with yells every time he tried to increase his offer. This left only the butcher in competition. One of the girls then left. Sturm surmised she was going to fetch more money so they could continue their bidding. Hörsken had pointed this out to Sturm, who decided to take a short break for a drink of water, to allow the girls more time. Eventually, the butcher also withdrew, perhaps out of kindness, or perhaps in an attempt to appease the crowd. The final price of the painting was 800 RM—a tidy sum. As the girls handed over the money, the crowd broke into loud applause.

The remaining lots were quickly sold and the soldiers went to work cleaning up the square, while the cashier checked the takings. Hörsken and Sturm then discreetly made their way back from Elisenbrunn to Kaiserbrunn, where they caught a tramcar to the barracks. Both were hot and tired. The turmoil at the barracks drew hardly a glance from them as they made their way into the canteen and had a cold glass of beer each. Sturm was only thirsty, not hungry, so didn't bother partaking of the well filled cooking pot in the kitchen, but made his way to the room he shared with Hörstgen and lay resting on his bed. Hörstgen went out again shortly afterwards.

As a bearer of the German Cross in Gold, Hörstgen had certainly proven himself a brave soldier. Sturm had also observed that he was attentive in the role of husband. If his wife paid him a visit, he would be kindness personified. As soon as his wife left to make her way home, however, he would wave goodbye and then be off to call on his current girlfriend, often a married woman with a husband at the Front. The marital status of his partners made no difference to him, so long as they were willing. When Sturm questioned him, he simply said: 'That's life. This is war, and everything might end tomorrow, for me, and for these girls too!' After a year's training and Labour Corps service, Hörstgen had volunteered for the military and was a career soldier as opposed to a conscript.

Sturm was awoken by a noise. The aroma of freshly brewed coffee wafted through the room.

'Get me a cup of coffee, Bubi,' said Sturm, sitting up drowsily.

'If you want coffee and a piece of cake, go down and get some yourself. They are all wondering where you are down there!'

Shortly afterwards, Sturm and Hörsken went off through the fair towards the bandstand and square, where the soldiers often met to pass the time. Everyone was surprised at how many visitors were still around. Going into the canteen, they found a table where there was a free seat. Sturm sat down, and Hörstgen went across to the bar and reaching behind it 'acquired' one of the barstools, brushing off protests from the *Unteroffizier* barman with a laugh and a wave. The two had scarcely sat down when Hörstgen pointed out two girls who were just entering the canteen. They were the girls who had bought the oil painting. Hörstgen wanted to go over to them, but Sturm held him back and went over himself. As he led the two girls back to the table he found that his comrade had 'arranged' two more seats for the girls. The girls introduced themselves, and Silvia Hoppmann explained why she had wanted the oil painting so badly.

'We had actually been there, in the village in the painting, as children. I wanted the painting as a gift for my father as it is his birthday today.'

'That was a generous present!' said Hörstgen.

At that moment, *Hauptfeldwebel* Raschinski appeared.

'I see you are in good company boys,' he said, 'but remember you were invited to my 10th anniversary celebration!' With a nod towards the girls, he added: 'You are of course invited too!'

They assembled in a small side room, the *Hauptfeldwebel* and his wife, the company commander and his wife, Sturm, Hörstgen, and the girls. After about an hour, *Fräulein* Hoppmann asked if she could telephone her father, as she would have to excuse herself for being late. Sturm took her to the company office and waited while she made her telephone call. After a brief conversation with her father, the two returned to the others. *Fräulein* Hoppmann said to the *Hauptfeldwebel*: 'I must go home, we have guests and they are waiting for me. Thank you very much for the invitation to your party!'

The girls took their leave and were escorted by Hörstgen and Sturm. Hörstgen had linked arms with Silvia's friend Heidi and suggested that they escort the girls to the Kaiserbrunn. They went along the main street towards Eliesenbrunn. Around half way on the left there stood a large building, one of the big department stores. They went over to the corner and stood beside four large display windows. Silvia stood beside the entrance and shouted. After a brief pause came a reply.

'Silvia, is that you? I'm coming!'

'That's my father', said Silvia.

Sturm took his leave of the young ladies, with Hörstgen following only hesitantly. Both had reached the corner when Hörstgen clapped him on the shoulder.

'Man, Hans, you've done all right. Do you know who she is? She is the daughter of Hoppmann, owner of the biggest department store in Aachen.'

Then he added with a moan, 'And we haven't made a date to see them again!'

It was rapidly growing darker as the two stood there. Sturm could only just make out the great size of the building, with two stories above the ground floor.

31

The Invitation

Just then, a voice rang out.

'Hey, come here, both of you!'

The two went back, somewhat surprised, and were met by Hoppmann and his daughter.

'Now, come with me! You can't just carry off my daughter on my birthday, and then just simply leave her standing here!'

As they reached the living quarters, *Herr* Hoppmann saw that his second wife had everything in hand. (Silvia's mother had been dead for many years). There were four couples present, including Heidi's parents, and all had already eaten from the sumptuous buffet. The two girls, Hörstgen, and Sturm had also eaten their fill at the *Hauptfeldwebel*'s celebration. The atmosphere became all the more friendly when Hörstgen and Sturm, after a brief discussion with the lady of the house, offered to act out a playet which they had often presented at evenings in the mess and which had always been well received there. The two were provided with all the clothes and props they required, and played the parts of an elderly lady and gentleman meeting again for the first time after a fifty-year separation. There was a fine, silver-gripped walking stick and a monocle for the gent, and a silver purse and pair of Lorgnettes for the lady.

The two entered from opposite ends of the room. It was a moving scene, both touching and cheerful, and when finished was greeted with cheers by the small audience. It was by then getting very late, and the two soldiers had to leave. Earlier, they had arranged a date with the two girls for the following evening. One of the guest couples who were going in their direction gave Sturm and Hörstgen a lift back to the barracks.

On Thursday (four days later), Sturm was going to take a trip into Aachen by tramcar. On the other side of the street was a small delivery van. The driver got out and called his name. It was Silvia Hoppmann. Sturm immediately crossed over to her.

'Are you going into town? Get in and I'll give you a lift. I have a delivery to make first, then we can go into town together.'

Sturm obeyed. He was glad to be out of the wind, and the slushy snow which was beginning to fall. He looked at the pretty girl, with her shoulder-length, auburn hair. In her leather jacket she certainly looked less ladylike than in the pretty dress she had worn last Sunday. On her hair and face glistened drops of melting snow. When she looked at him with her dark brown eyes, Sturm had to admit to himself that he was quite taken with this one.

The van stopped at a soap works and they got out. *Fräulein* Hoppmann went into the building. Some lads then appeared and began unloading the van. As far as Sturm could see, there were underclothes and other garments, towels, cloth, *etc.* Packets with soap, washing powder, and other such items were then loaded back in. Then Sturm was alone in the van. This kind of bartering was inevitable in wartime; supplies of all sorts of commodities had become scarce. It was 1943, and all sorts of goods changed hands—clothing, porcelain, petrol, dairy produce. The black market was thriving, while the economy suffered.

Sturm got into the driver's seat and turned the van around, pulling up to the entrance. Just as he was about to get out and move back into the passenger's seat, Silvia reappeared. She got into the passenger seat and said, 'Now we can go into Aachen!'

Sturm sat hesitantly back down into the driver's seat. He had a driver's licence of course, but because of his military service, hadn't had the occasion to drive since October 1940. The weather was still as bad as before, snow covering the streets which were by now criss-crossed with tyre marks. Despite Sturm driving with great care, there was an accident. At a right-hand bend, the front wheel hit the cobbled pavement. The van swerved to the left, skidded across the slushy street, and narrowly missing a tree ran into a ditch, though fortunately didn't turn over.

Sturm and some of the cargo were thrown from the van, and he was hit on his left temple. His glasses lay behind him on the embankment. As he came to, his first thoughts were for his companion. She lay slumped in the driver's seat with her head against the windscreen. Sturm went over to the van as fast as he could. *Fräulein* Hoppmann tried to raise her head and Sturm could see that her forehead was bloody. On her right temple, just below the hairline, was a 10-cm gash. Her right leg hung out of the van and on the knee was a bloody wound. As Sturm tried to carefully lift her from the van, she fell back into the seat. Clutching Sturm's hand, she said in an agonising voice, 'Hans, I was driving the van!'

For Sturm, this was the least of their concerns. The insurance company could sort all that out. Worried about the strong smell of petrol, presumably from the leaking fuel tank, rather than wait for a doctor, he lifted and laid her on the embankment a few paces away, making her as comfortable as he could.

Just past the bend was a guest house, from which ran two men. One, the owner, knew *Fräulein* Hoppmann and ran back to phone for a doctor and to let her father know there had been an accident. The younger man brought a cushion and some blankets to cover the now unconscious girl. When the owner of the guest house returned, he waved away other drivers who had slowed down out of curiosity. The ambulance was soon racing up towards them. The doctor and his assistants busied themselves with the injured girl, whose father arrived a few minutes later. He saw that his daughter was being well looked after and turned to talk to Sturm, who explained the circumstances of the accident. He also said that he had been at the wheel, though Silvia seemed anxious to claim otherwise.

'That's not important. What matters is that Silvia has no internal injuries—will you come to the hospital?'

Herr Hoppmann thanked the guest house owner and his son for their speedy assistance. They promised to deal with the breakdown wagon and the van's cargo. With blue lights flashing and sirens wailing, the ambulance sped off again. *Herr* Hoppmann and Sturm followed close behind.

The hospital examination revealed that Silvia had no internal injuries. The wound in her head would need stitches, but a slight alteration to her hairstyle would ensure that any small scar would be concealed. She had mild concussion, which was already clearing. Worse was the leg wound. It wasn't broken, but the cuts and severe bruising would be slow to heal. After treatment in the operating theatre, Silvia was soon back in her hospital room. She was still a little shaken, but was already asking to see herself in a mirror. Her face, still speckled with blood, didn't please her at all. They had put her hair up so that they could bandage her forehead. Sticking out of the bandages, her locks made her look like a feather duster.

After the first shock, a smile appeared on her face. She had been quick to regain her sense of humour. She asked Sturm to let her hair down and then wanted to shake her head to free it, but couldn't because of her concussion. As the father took his leave, Sturm held her hand and said: 'Silvia, I couldn't help the accident. I'm so sorry!'

'There was nothing you could do about it. We were just unlucky. It certainly brought us closer, yes?' With a laugh and pursing her lips, she said, 'I think I deserve a kiss!'

Sturm was more than happy to oblige. The duty sister, unnoticed by them both, stood at the doorway having seen and heard all. Happily for the young couple, she quietly closed the door and left them alone.

Sturm visited Silvia in hospital as often as he could, even bringing Hörstgen along sometimes. Heidi had quickly seen off the skirt-chaser and broken off their friendship. Perhaps Silvia had passed on some of the stories of Hörstgen's womanising told to her by Sturm. Sturm didn't feel guilty about this indiscretion, however—even friendship has its limits.

32

A Tragic Event

During a speech he was giving to the staff of the firm of Xox, a well known biscuitier in Kleve, Sturm had made mention of his squad leader, *Unteroffizier* van der Kerkhoff, when he noticed that a Red Cross sister sitting in the front row looked rather upset. She cried uncontrollably and had to be led away by a colleague. Sturm had been describing the actions of 29 July 1941 for which he later received the Iron Cross Second Class. The squad leader, who had been standing right beside him, had been hit in the head by a bullet and killed outright. His body had lain for almost four weeks in No Man's Land before it could be retrieved by a burial squad and laid to rest. Sturm took a short pause before continuing his report.

After the conclusion of his speech, he went into the administrative office. There sat the Red Cross sister. Somewhat calmer now, she explained that she was *Unteroffizier* van der Kerkhoff's sister. The unit commander had of course written to her about her brother's death, but not in such gruesome detail. Sturm expressed his condolences, and apologised for describing her brother's death in such depth, but explained that he had been told to make his reports about war and all its cruelties in this forthright manner.

This experience, and an exchange of correspondence with his father in August/September 1941, made Sturm decide on a change to his speech-making. In his letters, Sturm's father had written about those who fulfilled their duty on the home front. Sturm could see that the burden carried by those at home was growing more and more unbearable, especially for the women whose husbands, fathers, sons, and brothers were fighting and dying at the Front. Living part of their lives in dank air-raid shelters with their children in their arms, mothers also had to do their bit, working on the railways, in hospitals, or in factories making weapons and equipment. When their men-folk came home on leave, they made every effort to put a brave face on things and pretend that all was well, wanting to spare them any more anxiety when they returned to the Front. All this, only to receive a telegram advising them that their man had 'fallen for *Führer* and Fatherland'.

Another factor in deciding Sturm to change his reporting style some 100 or so speeches into his lecturing tour was an experience in Gelsenkirchen. The wife of a bank director, who worked in a factory while her husband was serving at the Front as a high-ranking officer, had written to the local paper asking the *Kresleiter* just what the wives of all the top dignitaries were doing to help the war effort. The *Kreisleiter* had answered via the newspaper, listing examples from all over Germany of wives of party members, company directors, and officers who had volunteered to work. The *Ortsgruppenleiter* of the city in which the lady lived retorted that the *Kreisleiter* should have given examples from Gelsenkirchen, as that was after all what the lady had asked about. Sturm had therefore discussed with the lady in question, as well as the *Kreisleiter* and *Ortsgruppenleiter*, what form his new speeches should take.

Sturm's speeches about women's assistance to the war effort had up to then encompassed a full and frank description of life at the Front, for instance for nurses in occupied areas, and were always well received and deemed appropriate for talks given in factories and at public meetings. Henceforth, he would tone down the more brutal episodes of his stories to spare the audience's sensibilities, particularly those of mothers and wives. Speeches given in the factories were brief, and were tailored for the type of business, the composition of his audience, and its size. At youth gatherings and in schools, his speeches were delivered in another style, more suitable to the ages of his audience. His experiences in combat, his decorations, *etc.*, were covered only briefly and only if called for in order to answer questions. Things went well on the whole, but there were sometimes less successful occasions, such as at the Xox firm in Kleve.

Silvia's and Sturm's parents got to know each other. At the end of April, Sturm took Silvia to meet his parents in Dortmund. Silvia's injuries had healed well and she was eagerly looking forward to the trip. Sturm's father had also returned home, having now spent more months in Russia than his son. He had been in the Stalingrad area in January 1943, and had been wounded and decorated. He was indeed fortunate to have been flown out of the enclave before its collapse. He had already arranged travel passes to the rear, in the area around Woronesch and Woroschilowgrad, for his men.

Sturm's parents, who had been told about how Silvia and Hans had got to know each other and about the auto accident, took this long-haired bundle of energy into their hearts straight away. The Sturm family home, with its modest four bedrooms, proved unfamiliar surroundings for Silvia. She, the daughter of a rich store owner, was accustomed to a very large house. It was the style in which she took to her new surroundings so naturally, as well as her physical attractiveness, which endeared her to everyone. *Herr* Sturm was filled with enthusiasm for the young couple and showed it at every opportunity. A formal engagement was planned for Whitsun 1943. Back in Aachen, Silvia's father gave his blessing and insisted on a celebration in Aachen.

Sturm had had little opportunity to attend the State Engineering School in Aachen. He had a lot of work to catch up on with his studies, and put in a lot of effort in order to reach the required level. The time until Whitsun thus went by very fast.

For the celebration of the engagement, Sturm's mother and father travelled to Aachen. Only the nearest relatives attended, but it was decided that the wedding, also to be in Aachen, would be a big affair. This was Silvia's father's wish, as he had decided also to marry his sweetheart, who had already been living as the lady of his house and with the family for many years.

After a speech on 28 April in the *Magnetfabrik-Bonn*, Sturm made an embarrassing blunder. After asking the factory foreman to make an entry in his book, Sturm asked the managing director of the Wessel Werk AG, Konsul Wessel, to also make an entry. He wrote: 'To the *Ritterkreuzträger* and *Unteroffizier* Sturm, we thank you for an interesting lecture; to Sturm the man, for your visit, which must not be the last. Hoping to meeting again soon, in war and in peacetime. Bonn 28 IV 43, Wessel.' (It was common for dignitaries or others of high rank to sign with their surnames only). In this case, the name of the factory, the name of the location, and the name of the owner were all the same. Not thinking clearly, Sturm asked him to sign with his title. He added three crosses at the bottom of the page and continued in the overleaf, 'The *Ritterkreuzträger* does not think my name is good enough. I am, however, manager of the Wessel Werk AG Bonn.' He returned the book to Sturm and asked, 'Well, will you tear out these pages?' Sturm, reading the supplement to the entry, turned a bright shade of red and shook his head. The page remains in the book to this day.

By June, Sturm was serving as a squad leader at the troop training grounds at Elsenborn. He was involved in the training of snipers in the use of telescopic sight for sharp-shooting at long ranges. One night, Aachen came under attack by a massed wave of enemy bombers. All of the soldiers at the training grounds were put on full alert and quickly made ready for action. They could hear the bombs exploding as the air raid sirens wailed. Flares dropped by the enemy pathfinders illuminated the skies over Aachen, as the searchlights sought out targets for the flak gunners.

Sturm's squad was sent to assist at the Kaiserbrunn. Other groups were allocated areas throughout the city. Halfway from the barracks into town, the men had to disembark from their trucks and proceed on foot, the roads having been rendered impassable by bomb craters and debris from damaged buildings. Many houses were on fire and civilians were frantically trying to save what they could of their belongings. Others merely stood by, stunned and tearful in the streets.

At the Kaiserbrunn, fire-fighters and emergency rescue crews were in action. Sturm and his men were able to proceed along the *Kaiserstra⊠e*, the main business thoroughfare which led to the Elisienbrunn. It was still night, but the flames from the burning houses illuminated a terrifying scene. The wounded were helped or carried away along with the dead. Sturm and his men gave help wherever it was most needed. Vehicles were still unable to progress along the streets, despite the efforts of the emergency crews to clear away the obstructing debris.

Sturm and his men eventually arrived at Hoppmann's store. Bombs and incendiaries had totally destroyed the building. It must have gone up like a huge torch. All of the floors had collapsed, as had some of the walls. Radiators and refrigeration units hung dangling from their connecting pipes. On the concrete floor under which lay the cellars and the air raid shelter was a layer of smouldering ash and debris. Sturm went along to the next street, to the door to the living quarters. It was obstructed by rubble, but this made no difference, as the house behind it was burned out and totally destroyed. Both buildings shared a communal cellar area, with only a firewall, designed to keep out flames but to be easy to break through in an emergency, dividing it into two. The emergency exit had been rendered useless by a bomb which had detonated right next to it.

The next building along the street didn't have an emergency exit. It was a large butcher's shop, which had its cold storage room through the wall from the Hoppmann's cellar. The shop owner had refused to allow an exit to be cut through the wall, even when Hoppmann had agreed to meet the cost. Sturm knew of this from the tour he had been given of the Hoppmann property, including the cellars and air raid shelter.

A woman approached Sturm from the opposite side of the street. Her face blackened from smoke, she carried the body of her little dog which had been killed in the raid.

'*Unteroffizier* Sturm,' she said, 'The Hoppmanns must have stayed at the house last night. Just before the first early warning alarm and then the main air raid warning, I saw a light on, even though there is a blackout!'

Sturm was shocked. He knew that, what with the increase in danger from enemy night bombing attacks, the Hoppmanns often stayed at another house they owned just outside the Aachen city limits. It was possible, however, that the Hoppmanns had been caught out by the raid when visiting their property.

Attempts to penetrate into the cellars were almost hopeless. Hopes of finding anyone still alive were slight. Using pickaxes and crowbars to remove debris, Sturm and his men knocked down a wall which had been built in front of the cellar windows to protect them from bomb blasts, and wrenched out the window frames, already cracked by the pressure waves of the detonations. A fierce wave of heat emanated from the cellar. The railing in front of the cellar next to the air raid shelter was removed and, despite warnings from the leader of the rescue crew, Sturm prepared to enter. Wrapping his hands and face in cloth and leaving only his eyes exposed, he tied a safety rope under his arms and climbed into the cellar. His progress was halted, however, by the sheer intensity of the heat. With eyes closed, he stumbled back in the direction of the cellar window and was carefully lifted out by his comrades.

Later that afternoon, he discovered that, using heavy equipment, rescue crews had been able to break through the wall of the house and clear a way through some of the debris. Two squads working in shifts throughout the night also managed to punch holes through the concrete floor of the store, to allow the searing hot air from the cellar to escape. The rescue squads were permitted to continue, and Sturm firmly believed—because he had assured by their leaders—that there was a chance that any of the Hoppmann family might still be in the shelter. Hoppmann was also, of course, a distinguished citizen who had done much for the city. The fact that *Fräulein* Hoppmann was engaged to a *Ritterkreuzträger* probably also increased the willingness to continue the attempts to gain access to the shelter. The *Kreisleiter*, the local police president, and the local military district commander among others had all sent their congratulations to the couple on their engagement.

Sturm and his squad were eventually transported back to the barracks, but despite his absolute exhaustion, he was unable to sleep. On the following day, the rescue squad finally penetrated into the air raid shelter, and Sturm was there with them. He found the body of his fiancée lying on a cot, covered with a blanket. She was uninjured and looked just as if she was asleep. The bodies of Hoppmann's second wife and another woman he did not recognize were also there. Sturm thought that they might well find the bodies of the lady's husband and his intended father-in-law when they broke through the firewall which divided this cellar from that of the house next door. The wall was breached, but smouldering rubble hindered their progress into the adjacent shelter. All of the inhabitants were dead, and from the looks on their faces had agonisingly suffocated to death. The flesh on the corpses' faces, arms, and hands looked as if it had been cooked.

Despite the suffocating heat, Sturm sat with the body of his fiancée until it could be carefully removed from the cellar. The funeral of the Hoppmann family was attended by many friends, representatives of the state and the party, and the local business community. Many relatives, however, now lived in the USA and because of the war were unable to attend the funeral.

Sturm was relieved that his attendance at training and other duties had resulted in him missing the dreadful bombing raid on Aachen. He had seen so many corpses in his young life, and had become somewhat hardened to it all. Nevertheless, the loss of his Silvia and her father, as well as other acquaintances, affected him deeply for several weeks.

Sturm attempted to volunteer for a return to the Front in order to get away from Aachen and its unhappy memories, but failed at the first hurdle on the insistence of commander of Military District IV in Münster, *Oberstleutnant* Prof. Dr Gierlich. Even a plea made in person was rejected. It was felt that Sturm should not interrupt his training at engineering school. Sturm suspected that a plot had been hatched by the *Oberstleutnant* and his own battalion commander to prevent him from returning to the Front, although Sturm himself felt fit enough for combat duty again. His eye injury was now much better, and only mild headaches and double vision still affected him. At first, he had worn an eye patch, then spectacles with an opaque lens for his right eye to correct the double vision. Now, he wore ordinary glasses. He had asked the advice of the chief eye specialist and was told to try to look straight ahead if possible and turn his whole head if need be, rather than just move his eyes when looking to the side. This worked well and he now only suffered from slight double vision and dizziness if he looked up or down too quickly, an effect which would last throughout the rest of his life.

Further lecturing visits to factories, public meetings, and schools followed, this time in Dortmund, Ahlen, Bielefeld, Herford, Bad Oeynausen, Minden, Salzkotten, Paderborn, and Lippstadt.

33

Leave in San Remo

One day, Sturm happened to overhear a remark passed between *Obergerfreiter* Alfred Rademacher and *Hauptfeldwebel* Toot Daams in the battalion office.

'It's a shame we have this chance to send a soldier to San Remo on leave when there is no one available!'

'Did I hear you right?' asked Sturm. 'Leave in San Remo—I'm available!'

'Keep calm, Hans,' replied the *Hauptfeldwebel*, 'We can't let you go. For one thing, you have your studies, and for another, Münster wouldn't approve because they might need you!'

'The Engineer School is on holiday just now, and as far as Münster is concerned, I can arrange things quickly enough. Just give them a call, Otto!'

'I can only contact Münster with permission of the battalion commander and he isn't available today,' said Daams.

'You go and call him yourself then, Hans,' said the *Obergefreiter*.

'Alfred, what would we do without you!' said Sturm, lifting the receiver and speaking to the operator. 'Wehrkreis IV, Münster!'

'*Unteroffizier* Sturm, here. I would like to speak to *Oberstleutnant* Gierlich!'

'One moment please, I'll connect you,' came the reply.

'Gierlich here!'

'*Unteroffizier* Sturm. *Herr Oberstleutnant*, I have a request. The Replacement Battalion 473 in Aachen has been offered a vacancy by Berlin for a soldier to be permitted three weeks' leave in San Remo at the beginning of August:'

There was a short pause.

'Of course you can go Sturm! After your personal tragic loss, a break would do you good.'

'Would you confirm that please, *Herr Oberstleutnant*? I'll give you our *Hauptfeldwebel*.'

Daams took the handset and Gierlich gave his confirmation. He had scarcely put down the receiver when the *Obergefreiter* let out a cheer.

'Hurrah! Now we have our candidate. You are going to be the guest of our beloved *Führer*!'

Villa Zirio in San Remo.

The *Hauptfeldwebel* shot Rademacher a furious glance.

'No, really,' he swiftly continued, 'I just mean that it is a great honour to be his guest. We'll have to get all the paperwork sorted out.'

The *Hauptfeldwebel* reached over and, lifting up two sheets of paper, began to prepare Sturm's travel orders for the commanding officer's signature.

Alfred Rademacher was genuinely exited at his friend's trip to San Remo.

'Hans, you know that we have a florist's business in Bochum? Well, we get lots of flowers from a firm in San Remo. I will give you a letter to take to our business contacts there. They will certainly look after you.'

Sturm then went off and brought back a couple of bottles of wine and a bottle of cognac, and he and his two friends spent a pleasant evening celebrating his good fortune.

Everything then began to move quickly. On 28 July Sturm travelled to Dortmund, and on 29 July celebrated his 23rd birthday at home. Later that same day, he had to set off for Munich. In the meantime, Sturm had learnt that he would spend his leave at the Villa Zirio in San Remo. The villa was the personal property of Adolf

Hitler, gifted to him by a German who had married into a rich Italian family but had fallen in battle. He wondered who else would be put forward by their units for this special honour. Would they be high-ranking officers or, like him, soldiers who had been decorated in battle?

On the early morning of 30 July, he arrived in Munich and made his way to the rendez-vous point at the Hotel Europa. He booked into his room and had a shower, but was too excited to lie down and rest. Going down to the reception area, he made himself known to the others who were to be his companions on the trip to San Remo. Sturm was surprised to find only one officer present. This was *Hauptmann* Schulthus, who was to be in charge of the group. The others consisted of one *Oberfeldwebel*, some *Unteroffiziere*, some *Obergefreiter* and *Gefreiter*, and one private, who had been a motor-cycle despatch rider and had lost both his legs in the Battle of France. Everyone signed Sturm's book, including a party Official who wore the political rather than military uniform.

The Iron Cross First Class was the highest decoration worn by any of the others. Sturm was the only one with the German Cross and *Ritterkreuz*. The Hauptmann then told them that from the day of their arrival in San Remo, they must wear civilian clothes only, because of the delicate political situation in Italy. The groups had already been informed of this by their own units.

Sturm's new companions came from every corner of the Reich. Out of thirty-six possible units, thirty-two were represented here. Four units which had been invited to do so had failed to nominate anyone. If Sturm hadn't been in the battalion office and overheard that conversation, there would be no one from *Ersatz Battalion 473*, either!

The *Hauptmann* wished everyone an enjoyable day in Munich, but warned them to report promptly at 0800 the next day to get the places that had been reserved for them on the train. The train would be sure to leave without them if they were late! The crowd split up into small groups and went off to see the sights in Munich. Sturm explained that there was an acquaintance from his boyhood whom he wanted to visit. His last contact had been a letter just after he had been awarded the *Ritterkreuz*.

Sturm arrived at his friend's house, and despite ringing the bell several times got no response. A neighbour out tending his garden explained that the Trilling family would not be back from their holidays for another fourteen days. Sturm was annoyed with himself that he hadn't telephoned first. If he had realised that his friend wasn't here, he could have gone off and spent the day with his comrades. The neighbour beckoned Sturm over, and opened the small gate connecting the gardens of the two houses. He was impressed by Sturm's high decoration and wanted to learn more. He knew Sturm's name because his neighbour had proudly told him about his friend and had shown him photos and newspaper cuttings. So, Sturm's visit wouldn't be a complete waste of time after all! He suggested that the two should have a beer together. Sturm politely declined and returned to his hotel room, had a light snack, and caught a few hours' sleep.

34

The Premiere of 'Baron von Münchhausen'

In the late afternoon of 30 July, Sturm sat by himself in the almost deserted dining room. None of his companions were anywhere to be seen. He looked at the cinema ads in the newspaper and quickly spotted one that particularly took his fancy. It was the new UFA film directed by Erich Kästner, 'Baron von Münchhausen', with Hans Albers in the lead role. A large photo showed him in the role of the Baron, mounted on a canonball flying into the Turkish encampment.

Sturm asked the head waiter, 'Where is the cinema? I'd like to see this film!'

With a laugh, the waiter answered: 'This is the film's premiere. It has been sold out for months!'

Sturm asked him for directions anyway, deciding that the exercise in walking over there would do him good. Outside the 'UFA Palace', many people were milling around. They had all collected their tickets from the box-office and were ready to spend this fine summer evening at the cinema. At the door stood two pretty young women who checked their tickets as they entered. To the one on the right, Sturm asked if there was any chance of seeing the film, and explained that he was only in Munich for one night and must depart for San Remo in the morning as a guest of the *Führer* at the Villa Zirio. The other attendant clearly overheard the conversation. Despite Sturm's uniform and the *Ritterkreuz* at his neck, she did not at first believe him. All that was missing was a gesture of her forefinger to her temple to suggest he was mad. One of three gentlemen who stood in the foyer beside a large stairway saw what was happening. He came closer and asked what the disturbance was about. Sturm explained that he wanted to see the film but couldn't get a ticket.

'Then come with me, *Unteroffizier*!'

Sturm, laughing, waved his hand to the two attendants. Once again, his *Ritterkreuz* was serving him well. The gentleman led him towards his two companions, one of whom was an *Oberst*. Sturm saluted and learnt during the introductions that the gentleman who had spoken to him was the manager of this cinema and the other gentleman in civilian clothes was the director of all UFA cinemas.

A gong rang to signal the patrons to take their seats. The four made their way up the stairway and into the centre box. Sturm sat in the middle, in a comfortable chair.

On one side was the *Oberst* and his wife, and on the other the UFA manager and director. Sturm though to himself, 'If only that head waiter could see me now!'

The film was everything that they had said of it. Hans Albers played the role of the much loved figure in his own inimitable fashion. Münchhausen would relate tales of his 'wondrous journeys over sea and land, campaigns and exciting adventures' in the company of trusted friends and acquaintances, normally after the evening meal, in front of a roaring fire, with his Meerschaum pipe in hand and a steaming bowl of punch behind him. All of the audience were thrilled and applauded the film for several minutes after its end.[1] The *Oberst* gave Sturm a lift back to his hotel, where he sank into his bed, content.

Over breakfast the next day, Sturm's astonished companions listened intently as he recalled his experiences of the previous evening until *Hauptmann* Schulthus reminded them that time was short and they had a train to catch. The group assembled punctually on the platform at 08.00 hours with all their baggage. Clerks counted off the numbers and, once it was established that all were present, they boarded the first-class carriage which had been prepared for them. All the compartments had plenty of space, as only four men had been allocated to each. The atmosphere was very convivial. The *Hauptmann* took his place in a compartment with the platoon commanders as the train rumbled on via Innsbruck to Milan, where there was a brief halt while the carriages were coupled to a new locomotive. Then they travelled on to Genoa. The restaurant car provided coffee, tea, juice, water, and wine. The *Hauptmann* had warned them against taking any strong drinks, as they would have to drive to the villa once they arrived in San Remo, so the bottles of spirits they had all brought with them had to stay in their suitcases.

Unteroffizier Sturm was allocated a seat in a compartment with three *Obergefrieter*. He had noticed that, since the Brenner Pass, the trains had been checked by patrols from the *Feldgendarmerie* at every station on the Austro-Italian border. These controls must have been related to the tense political situation in Italy. Trains were being shot at by partisans and, especially in the south of the country, some had even been blown up.

Benito Mussolini had until the beginning of 1943 held the reigns of power tightly in his hands, despite the failure of his military adventures in North Africa, Albania, and Greece. Yet the continuing decline in the fortunes of war for Italy would soon put an end to the mythology of Mussolini as the great dictator. He could only countenance victory; defeats made him depressed and disorientated. On his arrest he wrote, 'Within a few years, all memories of me will be erased!' Sturm, who was well versed in the political and military relationships of the North–South axis between Germany and Italy, explained the situation to his three comrades. They were comrades in other senses too, as all four were experienced combat infantrymen, which gave them much to talk about.

The journey from Genoa via Savona and Alassio towards San Remo was interesting as well as spectacular. On their left lay the Ligurian Sea, and on the right the blooming landscape and awesome mountains. The best time to holiday on the *Riviera di Ponente*, west of Genoa, and the *Riviera di Levante*, east of Genoa, was in May. Now, in July and August, the heat was oppressive. In the well ventilated compartments, however, nothing could spoil the good atmosphere and holiday spirit.

In the late afternoon, the train arrived in San Remo. They were all glad to disembark from the train and stretch their legs as the *Hauptmann* and an *Oberfeldwebel* went off to report their arrival. Small groups of Italian soldiers stood on the platform, providing a special guard for the compartment with the German soldiers. All were still in uniform and Sturm was smartly saluted by an Italian officer. Sturm could not rid himself of the impression, however, that the Italian soldiers and civilians' sympathy for the German visitors were rather strained.

35

Guest of the *Führer*

Two military buses transported the group to the Villa Zirio, where a single guard stood at the entrance. As they drove on, however, Sturm spotted a machine gun position in the shade of a tree, and behind it another guard post. The villa itself could be seen behind a row of palms and large cactus plants. It was an impressive building. Scarcely were the soldiers disembarked when porters arrived to carry their baggage into the reception hall. Rooms were quickly allocated. The villa had twelve single and twelve double rooms. Eight of the singles and twelve of the doubles were allocated to them. Some didn't want single rooms, preferring to share with a comrade, so four of them remained free. Sturm was allocated a single room on the second floor with a view over the harbour. Here he would stay, from 1 to 18 August. The villa itself was old, but the facilities were very modern.

By the first mealtime, the soldiers were already expressing astonishment over the rich offering of foodstuffs, ranging from starters to sweet courses whose names they could scarcely pronounce, let along recognize. Five waiters dressed in formal black with white shirts and ties served the meals to the soldiers, who still wore uniform. All sorts of drinks, including beers and strong wines, were easily available.

After they had all eaten, their time was their own. *Hauptmann* Schulthus made all present aware that no one should make a fuss about the great luxury with which they were being treated. They would later realise that in fact there were almost as many staff as guests at the villa, if one counted the gardener and instructors for the sports facilities such as the swimming baths, sauna, gymnasium, tennis courts, *etc.*, among them.

The house manageress, *Frau* Rosella Langwich-Scharer, who had welcomed her guests at evening mealtime on the first day, wrote in Sturm's book: 'As House Manageress of the Villa Zirio in San Remo, I wish *Ritterkreuzträger Unteroffizier* Hans Sturm, who has come to our house for a rest period, all good luck and great success in the future. San Remo, August 1943.'

Sturm spent the evening in the company of his three infantry comrades, polishing off a bottle of brandy he had in his room. The following morning, he awoke with a dreadful hangover to loud bangs on his door. It was Walter Rohrmann, one of the *Obergefreiten*.

Sturm relaxes at an ornamental fountain at Villa Zirio.

'Hurry up now, little fellow, or you'll miss breakfast. We have all already eaten!'

After a cold shower and a shave, Sturm was about to put on his uniform when he noticed that Walter was in civvies, wearing black trousers and a polo shirt. The breakfast was so lavish that Sturm thought it could have fed a reinforced infantry squad. Sturm, still suffering somewhat from the excesses of the previous evening, took only a roll spread with butter, marmalade, and honey. Walter held back to take another cup of coffee with Sturm and the two were the last to leave the room.

Walter decided to go swimming, while Sturm made up his mind to go and visit Alfred Rademacher's business contact in San Remo and with him the letter he had promised to deliver. Given directions by the house manageress, Sturm slowly passed the other villas. It was getting very hot indeed, so he was forced to keep to the shade of the trees wherever possible. Along the harbour promenade, he came to the Yacht basin. Sturm knew from the house manageress that both sailing yachts and a motor yacht were available to hire. He made a booking for the following day with the boat owner, who had already been told of the German soldier's arrival by *Frau* Langwich-Scharer.

In the commercial quarter, near the railway line, Sturm found the florist business. Having introduced himself, he was warmly welcomed by Piero Bertoldo. On reading the letter, he exclaimed: '*Ritterkreuzträger*! Why are you not in uniform?' Sturm explained how he had come to be on the trip after overhearing the conversation between Rademacher and the *Hauptfeldwebel*, and that they were advised to wear civilian clothes for the duration of their visit.

'Well, yes, some people here are a little anxious about the way the war is going, but I don't believe there would be any direct danger for anyone on leave.' After a short silence, he added: 'I haven't seen my friend and business partner for some years. Before the war, I was often in Germany, especially in Bochum. How is he?'

'Because of his war injuries, he is desk-bound now, and is just sitting out the end of the war and hoping for a favourable outcome, for him and his family,' Sturm said. 'His father takes care of the business, as you will know.'

'Yes, I know, but this letter is so brief, he hardly tells me anything in it!'

The time passed by so swiftly that Sturm feared he would miss his evening meal at Villa Zirio. Sturm wanted to be on his way, but Bertoldo held out his hand to stop him.

'So, you would leave so soon, when I am still so curious to know more!'

He left the terrace and returned a few moments later with his wife, a pretty Italian lady in her prime. After introducing him and telling his wife that they would have a guest for afternoon coffee, Bertoldo telephoned Villa Zirio and explained the situation to the house manageress. Sturm thanked them for their hospitality with two signed photos of himself in uniform wearing his *Ritterkreuz*.

Back at Villa Zirio, Sturm took a refreshing shower and swam a few lengths in the swimming pool. Feeling refreshed, he was ready for an evening in the company of his comrades. As the evening wore on, many took their nightcaps back to drink in their own rooms. The 'hard core', of which Sturm was one, took themselves off to the skittle alley where they had great fun. At midnight, however, the *Hauptmann* ordered them to bed, as the noise they were making was likely to disturb the others.

Next morning, Sturm met the *Hauptmann* on the tennis court and was well beaten. Sturm hoped to get his revenge in the evening, when they had arranged a game of chess, and indeed was the better player. After the midday meal, Sturm went off to the yacht basin, where the boat owner had a small sailing yacht all ready and waiting for him. The owner was born in Spain, and invited Sturm to call him by his first name, Alfonso. He spoke, like almost everyone here, reasonable, if broken German. Sturm was able to show Alfonso quite quickly that he was an experienced sailor, thanks to his training and qualifications with the *Marine-Hitlerjugend*. This led to arrangements being made for them to go out again the next morning on a bigger vessel. That being the case, Sturm decided it would be a good idea to bring four of his comrades along for the trip.

In planning the third day of his leave, Sturm had no problem in finding four comrades willing to come along. There were three infantrymen, plus *Oberfeldwebel* Kesefroge from the *Luftwaffe*. The house manageress provided them with abundant food for the trip. The boat owner welcomed them all and allowed Sturm to take command. The boat was a 470 Jolly Boat with around 25 sq m of sail, including the foresail. Sturm had never captained such a boat, especially as he had been only a junior rank in the *Marine-Hitlerjugend*.

The freshening wind promised a good trip. They turned the boat into the wind, then half into the wind, and then ran before the wind. That manoeuvre complete,

Relaxing with some of the staff from Villa Zirio.

they tacked back and forth against it. It was good sailing weather and the cloud cover let the sun through quite often, so all of them got a good sun tan. Everyone enjoyed the day, and Sturm gave the boat owner a generous tip upon their return. He had smuggled a considerable sum of hard currency into Italy with him. It was just as well their special carriage had not been checked by customs. If they had found Sturm with all that money, it might have had serious consequences for him.

The fourth day of the trip was taken up with mini-golf, swimming, tennis, and lounging around. In the evening, they played cards or other games such as billiards. Occasionally, the seating order at mealtimes was changed to ensure that the men got to know each other and no cliques would form. The place settings were usually decided by the *Hauptmann* in consultation with the manageress.

On the fifth day, Sturm met up with Piero Bartoldo after breakfast. Bertoldo had had an idea. He gave Sturm a considerable sum in *lira*, which he wanted to exchange for *Reichsmarke* for his trip to Germany just before Christmas. The arrangement required a great deal of mutual trust, but Sturm agreed without hesitation, having gained a very favourable impression of Piero, who had used the friendly and familiar '*Du*' with Sturm from the start. The two drew up a document in which the sum and its equivalent in the different currencies were set out, with a codicil that, in the case of either being killed, the next of kin would honour the agreement. After both had signed, they drank a large bottle of wine together. Sturm was certain that the agreement favored him rather than Piero. When he asked why Piero didn't wait until just before his trip or even until he arrived in Germany to exchange his currency, he simply said, 'You can put the money to good use during your leave here,' and with a laugh added, 'You get the money as a gift from me here in Italy, and give it back to me in Germany.' Then they worked out their plans for this and the next day. Firstly, they went into the city and bought some lightweight white summer clothing for Sturm, washing materials, shoes, *etc*. Sturm came back dressed like a new man. On returning to Villa Zirio, he was naturally bombarded with questions. He explained, partly telling the truth, that a friend had lent him the money, but didn't go into any further detail.

Sturm changed before the midday meal and found himself a shady place to sit out of the fierce rays of the sun. The heat at midday was almost unbearable. Some of his comrades sat at the air conditioning vents around the villa just to try to keep cool. His three infantry comrades continued to question him, circling him like moths around a flame. He explained who his patron was and provided them with small amounts of *lira* for which they paid him in *Reichsmarke*.

In the evening, he took a walk along the promenade with the Bertoldos and visited some local bars. The pair had willingly taken up Sturm's invitation to join him, saying that the opportunity to hear of all of his experiences was well worth the cost.

Sturm's sixth day was dedicated to doing nothing. Some went swimming, to the Bull Fight, or played table tennis after supper. The holidaymakers were no longer surprised by any of the facilities on offer at the villa. The bedrooms were well furnished, with baths en suite, and all modern conveniences. The dining room and other public rooms were all also well fitted out. Yet in most cases, their eyes were still bigger than their stomachs, though at midday, only light meals were served— puddings, stuffed eggs, Waldorf salad, and various desserts.

A special surprise awaited Sturm on day seven. The Bartoldos had been invited to join an Italian lady, whom Sturm later discovered was extremely wealthy, for her birthday party, and had decided to ask him along. In the forenoon, Sturm and some comrades went down to the shore. Bertoldo had told him of a bay in which, although swimming was forbidden, there were tremendous breakers which made a great challenge for strong swimmers. The group took no notice of the warning signs and rushed into the foaming rollers dashing onto the rocky coast. The swimmers yelled in delight as they were picked up by the waves, reached the crests, and were then swept down into the troughs and rolled in towards the shore. Swimming was barely effective; it was more a case of battling against the force of the waves which rolled them in towards the shore then swept them back out with incredible strength. On the edge of the promenade, bystanders watched those insolent enough to pit their own feeble strength against the force of nature. Some called out warnings.

Sturm noticed one comrade trying vainly to reach the jetty and let himself be carried by a wave in that direction. Before Sturm's powerful strokes could carry him over to his friend, a wave had rolled over him and dragged him down. His head re-emerged and a desperate cry for help came from his mouth. Sturm grabbed for his hair and saw that the water around him was stained with blood. With the help of another comrade they brought the injured man to the shore. The three collapsed, exhausted by their efforts, their feet still in the water as the rolling waves snapped at them. A sharp-edged underwater rock had inflicted serious gashes on their comrade's legs and stomach. On the promenade, two men ran to assist them. One helped guide an approaching ambulance to the spot. The injured man was carefully lifted onto a bunk in the ambulance. Using bandages and plasters from a medicine box, Sturm was able to administer first aid himself. The injured man said nothing, but just sat grimacing. After a short journey they arrived at a first aid post where a doctor declared that the damage was not as serious as had been first thought. After a tetanus shot and some more bandaging, the wounded German was allowed to return to Villa Zirio. The others at the villa were astonished to see one of their friends return in such a state, and demanded to know what had happened. Sturm already blamed himself for suggesting they go swimming where the activity was specifically forbidden, and the *Hauptmann* left him in no doubt that he too placed the blame firmly on Sturm's shoulders. Everyone was made to promise that there would be no further incidents of this type, but the resulting costs were met by the villa management without question.

In the afternoon, Sturm had time to recover from the shock of today's incident. Of swimming, he had had a bellyfull. With his three infantry comrades, he took a walk up the hill to the rear of the villa. There, in a garden restaurant with a beautiful view over San Remo, the harbour, and the sea, they rested and let the tensions of the day ease away.

The birthday party in the evening should have been a small, private affair, or so Piero had thought. On his advice, Sturm wore black trousers, a white shirt, black tie, and white jacket. In his new clothes, he felt like a shop window dummy. Also at Piero's request, he had pinned a miniature clasp showing all his decorations on his lapel. Sturm was introduced to the lady whose party it was, to her daughter, and to most of the rest of the guests. The men wore black or white suits, while the extravagant dresses worn by the ladies were, Sturm could tell, certainly not off the peg and were designed to show off their figures to best advantage. As far as the expensive looking jewellery they wore was concerned, Sturm felt sure it was all the real thing.

San Remo had before the war boasted the biggest gaming table in Italy, perhaps in all Europe. It had been closed since 1939, however. With the scope for socializing thus curtailed, those of the social elite took every opportunity to dress up in their finery, especially the women. Sturm was impressed at the sheer scale of the event and the costs which must have been incurred. The flower arrangements alone—for which his companions, the Batoldos, had been responsible—must have cost a fortune.

Soon, Sturm was engaged in conversation by other guests. Most could speak a little French or English, so conversations were not too difficult. Sturm soon realised that they had taken him to be a German officer and were surprised to hear he was a mere *Unteroffizier*. He explained to them that he was a guest of the *Führer* at the Villa Zirio, and the significance of the military decorations displayed in miniature on his lapel. He was asked about his experiences in Russia, but found conversation a little difficult in anything other than German. His school-level French and English were not up to the task of a proper conversation. Then, an interpreter arrived. It was the attractive daughter of their hostess. She suggested that Sturm might not like to be the centre of attention like this, and that perhaps they should find somewhere quieter where they could talk.

Sturm found himself in the reception hall from which a huge staircase led to the upper floor. Taking their drinks with them, he and the hostess's daughter moved into the study, which featured a large, heavy, writing desk and many bookshelves. The woman introduced herself.

'My name is Vermiglia, but call me Vermi please, Hans!'

Sturm was surprised, but willingly kissed the lips which were offered to him. Their glasses clinked and her eyes sparkled like the diamonds in her necklace. Her plunging neckline also got more than a casual glance from Sturm. Vermi spoke an almost accent-free German, and she explained that she had studied German in Berlin for two years before the war. The conversation was interrupted by an invitation to take their places at the table in the reception hall. Vermi arranged it so that Sturm would sit next to her. Around eighty guests took their places at three long tables. The hostess sat at the centre of the top table, flanked by her friends and relatives. She cast a kindly smile towards her daughter, sitting next to the young German, then welcomed all her guests, thanking them for their good wishes and gifts. She toasted her friends and hoped they would enjoy the rest of the evening.

It was a great party. Sturm saw the Bertoldos smiling broadly at him and his pretty companion. Before departing, Sturm had thanked the hostess for allowing him to take part in such a wonderful birthday celebration. Taking his leave, he kissed her hand, not an uncommon gesture in such high circles. He also made an arrangement to take Vermi sailing next morning, an invitation which she readily accepted. Shortly before midnight, the Bertoldos brought him back to the Villa Zirio. Sturm thanked them for the evening and bade them goodnight. His friend Bertoldo had known exactly what he was doing when he arranged the currency deal and the purchase of the new clothes for Sturm, having always intended to invite him to this party. Tired but very happy, Sturm took his night-cap to his room and dreamed of the palms, the sea, and pretty girls.

The eighth day was the best of the entire trip. Vermi and Sturm met at the jetty. The young Italian girl looked entirely different to how she had appeared last night. Dressed sportingly, she walked along swinging her handbag, a pair of fashionable sunglasses shielding her eyes. Alfonso, who had already made the small sailing boat ready, whistled in surprise and admiration as Vermi approached. He already knew her from previous sailing events in which she and her circle of young friends had taken part.

Thick clouds scudded across the sky. A squally south-westerly wind called for extreme concentration on leaving the harbour. Sturm soon realised that his companion was also a better than he. They crossed a wave against the wind and then slackened sail, and allowed themselves to run before the wind to get back towards the coast. They repeated this manoeuvre several times. Sailing farther out, they struck the mainsail and tied the rudder fast.

Vermi and Sturm now made themselves comfortable and opened the picnic hamper provided by the staff at the villa. They lay back and relaxed. Both enjoyed the peace and quiet, while Sturm took the opportunity to look over this lovely young Italian as she lay beside him. She was a little older than he was and certainly not inexperienced with men. In comparison, he was still rather naïve, he thought to himself. Her dark, tanned skin glistened as if oiled, and her long black hair lay spread around her head. Her nose was beautifully formed and her unpainted lips puckered up. She must have been aware that Sturm was looking at her! Slowly raising her eyelids, she looked at him with her pitch black eyes and laid her hand on his arm. Sturm was only too happy to oblige with a kiss, when a sharp, strengthening wind and the extent to which they had neared the coast meant that such distractions would have to wait. Sturm would have to man the tiller as she set the mainsail.

After returning to the jetty without incident, Sturm escorted Vermiglia back to her villa. As fortune would have it, her parents were not at home. The servants brought them refreshments and a light snack and then, with a wave from Vermi, took their leave.

The bathroom was very large and most comfortably appointed, with two showers and a sunken bathtub which looked as if it could accommodate at least four people. After showering, the two climbed into the warm water to which Vermi had added plenty of bath oils and salts. Her voluptuous body, which Sturm had already taken great care to examine during their boat trip, was partly obscured by the amount of steam created by the showers.

With a laugh, she moved over to him, stroked his head with her slim hands, and kissed him tenderly. In the late afternoon, Vermiglia's mother returned and they all took supper together. The look that passed between the two women made it clear that the mother realised what had happened, and Sturm began to feel like some sort of play-thing. It occurred to him that the women had accrued their experience and wealth much like the great gaming houses of San Remo—with their doors open, as the men from the outside world brought their money to the city. Sturm took his leave of mother and daughter after promising to come back again next week. Vermiglia, who escorted Sturm to the door, took him in her arms and kissed him and at once all suspicions and unpleasant thoughts were blown away.

On the ninth day, a special programme had been organised for all thirty-two of the guests. After a generous breakfast, they would be taken on a coach trip to Monaco. They would visit the country's sights, as well as Monte Carlo and La Condamine. In the evening, a visit had been arranged to one of the casinos. Monaco represented the richest 2 sq km of land on the planet.

The soldiers eagerly got onto the bus which was ready to depart. A travel guide greeted them all in faultless German and wished them a pleasant journey. Sturm, sitting at the front of the bus with *Hauptmann* Schulthus, could speak to the guide in between her commentaries over the loudspeakers. She was a good-looking student who had taken a job with the tour firm during her summer break. On the journey from Ventimiglia to Monaco, the young Italian guide, who had introduced herself as Vittoria, gave them a brief history of Monaco. The first settlement in the area had been in the fifth century BC under the patronage of Grimaldi, a true nobleman. During Napoleon's time the French had annexed Monaco, and since 1918 it had been a protectorate, with its own customs. The reigning prince at this time was Rainer II Grimaldi.

In Monaco the group partook of a meal together. Afterwards, they visited the castle and the cathedral. It was not easy to monitor one large group with so many members, so the *Hauptmann* had split the numbers down into four small groups and made one person in each group responsible for keeping in contact with the others. The tourist trade was the main source of revenue in Monaco, together with perfume, fancy foodstuffs, and confectionery. After seeing the sights, the group had their evening meal in Monaco. It was in a local restaurant, recommended by the villa manageress. The meal and drinks had all been pre-arranged for them and, due to wartime rationing shortages, all the required victuals had been provided by Villa Zirio. The highlight of the trip was a visit to a casino. Once again, the Germans split into four smaller groups, and agreed to meet up again at 22.00 hours at the exit.

With comrades from the *Luftwaffe* and *Waffen-SS*.

The German soldiers mingled with the gamblers, and particularly in the two gaming halls, which were filled with 'one-armed bandits' as well as small Baccarat tables. The tour guide, the *Hauptmann*, and Sturm all went into the third hall, where the betting was without upper limit. They identified themselves and were signed in as guests, the *Hauptmann* carrying a letter of introduction from the manageress of the Villa Zirio. The roulette table seemed to be the most popular. Sturm had deliberately brought only a small amount of money with him to avoid temptation, and contented himself with watching the other gamblers. They were a mixed bunch—men and women young and old, pale and swarthy, Latin types. All watched with fascination as the ball rolled round the roulette wheel. The betting was brisk, as the piles of chips stacked up on certain numbers testified. Some took winning and losing without batting an eyelid, their fixed expressions betraying neither pleasure nor disappointment. Others could not prevent their joy at winning, or their dejection at losing, from being patently obvious. One woman in particular seemed extremely agitated, as she nervously toyed with her handkerchief as a considerable pile of chips was gathered up and swept away by the croupier. The gentleman behind her laid a reassuring hand on her shoulder. He encouraged her to play on as she placed her last three remaining chips on number seven. '*Rien ne va plus*!' called the croupier, and spun the wheel. The ball rolled around the wheel and clattered in and out of a few compartments before settling in number seven. Gasps of exitement were heard all around. The woman could hardly believe her good luck, then, squealing with joy, she scooped up her winnings with both hands. Throwing one chip back, she said, 'For the Banker!' The croupier thanked her with a nod of his head and a polite 'Merci'. Then the game moved on.

The fortunate winner had scarcely left her seat when it was taken by another, keen to try their luck. A security man appeared before the happy couple with a small bag in which to put their chips. The pair left the roulette table and from the look on the lady's face Sturm assumed that the outcome of their evening had been most satisfactory.

Vittoria, like all the others present, had watched all the exciting. From the look on her face as she made her way towards Sturm, he assumed that she too had had some good luck. Both followed the *Hauptmann*, who had signalled to Sturm that it was time to leave. Gathering at the exit, the group compared their fortunes. Inevitably, there were several losers for every winner.

The return trip was made in high spirits. The bus driver had bought bargain-priced drinks, and soon the bus was ringing with soldiers' songs. This lasted all the way back to the Villa Zirio. On arriving back, they all thanked the tour guide and the driver for such a nice trip, the *Hauptmann* tipping the driver generously on the recommendation of the manageress.

Vittoria lived only a few houses along from the villa, and asked Sturm if he wanted to spend a little time with her—he did! So, for Sturm the day had a very enjoyable ending. After sharing breakfast with Vittoria, he took his leave and returned to Villa

Zirio, happy that he would soon see her again. Sturm had arranged a sailing trip with his infantry comrades that day, but had to put up with a stream of patronising and suggestive remarks about his success with the ladies.

On the next day, Sturm had arranged to pick up Vermiglia and her rich mother. On his arrival at their villa he was met by the butler, who explained that she had taken up an invitation to sail over to Naples with some friends in their motor-yacht. The Butler had been asked to pass on their hope that he would enjoy the rest of his leave and their best wishes for the future. He gave Sturm a hamper filled with cakes and sweets, as well as an envelope. It was a letter from Vermiglia. She wished him good fortune and hoped that he would survive the war safely, and that they might meet again some time in the future.

The rest of Sturm's leave passed uneventfully enough. Sturm met with the Bertoldos several times and went out with Vittoria twice. The two got on well, but it was clear to Sturm that they would only ever be just good friends. With Bertoldo's help, Sturm had acquired some fine silver jewellery, earrings, necklaces, bangles, and the like, which he gave to Vittoria as a parting gift.

The remaining days went by all too quickly, Sturm to a great extent just lazing around, or making the most of the sporting facilities, both in and on the water. Two letters which had arrived from Germany gave the group plenty of grounds for discussion. One was a letter from *Führerhauptquartier*. In it Hitler expressed his hope that the soldiers would return refreshed, with renewed strength and determination to fight on for the German fatherland until the war's conclusion. The discussion of this call to arms which followed would not have pleased those at the *Führerhauptquartier*. *Hauptmann* Schulthus tactfully left the men on their own, not wanting to hear what was being said! The second letter was from a friend of *Oberfeldwebel* Keesfroge of the *Luftwaffe*. An attached article from a newspaper told of the promotion of *General* Adolf Galland. Galland was promoted *Generalmajor* on 19 December 1942, making him the youngest *General* in the German armed forces. Born in Westerholt on 19 March 1912, he had joined the *Luftwaffe* in 1930. During the war he flew 705 missions (including 280 missions during the Spanish Civil War). He had scored 104 victories in the West. On 28 January 1942, he was awarded the *Ritterkreuz mit Eichenlaub, Schwertern und Brillanten* ('with Oak Leaves, Swords and Diamonds'), and he also possessed the Spanish Cross in Gold with Diamonds and the Pilot Observer Badge with Diamonds. In the articles was a copy of a report from a British newspaper, mentioning that an opponent of Galland's, the British fighter pilot Bob Stanford Tuck, had been shot down on 28 January 1942 by an anti-aircraft gun (Keesfroge's friend was a member of the gun crew) over St Omer in France. On hearing of this, Galland had invited him to his base, where he was offered dinner in the officers' mess. Before Tuck was taken off to a POW camp, the *Luftwaffe* fighter pilots presented him with a bottle of quality Scotch whisky. This chivalrous treatment was considered very noteworthy in the British press.

As an infantryman, Sturm had experienced and survived many dangerous

Unteroffiziere des Heeres
mit dem Ritterkreuz

S a m m e l b i l d e r

Unteroffizier Hans Sturm,

geb. am 29. 7. 1920 in Dortmur ' /GauWest-
falen-Süd), erhielt das Rit erkr uz am 26. 9.
1942 als Gefreiter in einer In eterie-Kom-
panie. Als Kompaniemelder brachte er aus
selbständigem Entschluß bei schweren Kämp-
fen im Raum von Rshew ein Maschinen-
gewehr in Stellung, dessen Bedienung aus-
gefallen war, und wehrte trotz Verwundung
und stärksten Feindbeschuß durch sein gut-
liegendes Feuer den bolschewistischen An-
griff erfolgreich ab.

Foto: OKH/Archiv

Ein Sammelalbum zum Einkleben der Bilder ist
bei der Annahmestelle für Unteroffizierbewerber
des Heeres erhältlich

Boys of future generations would collect picture postcards of pop stars or footballers; so did the young lads in those days avidly collect picture postcards of war heroes. This is the official collector's card showing Hans Sturm.

situations. An infantryman's war was a completely different affair to that fought by a fighter pilot. To the infantry, it was not always implicit that there was a need to actually kill the enemy. It was often enough to render him unfit to fight or to capture him. This in fact has often been a factor in the design of modern weapons. When an enemy soldier is killed outright, he is immediately removed from the equation. A wounded enemy soldier, however, requires medical assistance and evacuation, and doctors and other support arms to treat and help him recover. A wounded man is thus a much greater drain on enemy resources. Yet a captured enemy soldier may be interrogated for intelligence, and may be put to work, so actually killing the enemy might not always be the most effective course of action in the long term, either. To Sturm, it seemed that fighter pilots, whatever their nationality, singled out and hunted down their opponent, aiming to destroy him in single combat, man to man. It was often a matter of dumb luck when an enemy pilot was able to bale out. Sturm pictured fighter pilots, on hearing the alarm, dashing from the officers' mess and jumping into their planes. After a brief and hopefully successful sortie, they would land again and celebrate their victory in the mess with some fine Scotch whisky. It was a romanticised view, of course, but one commonly held by the 'stubble hoppers' of the infantry. Sturm had often wondered about fighter pilots, especially those *Ritterkreuz*-winning aces whose photographs he had seen in the corridor of the hospital in Smolensk. Galland was one of them. For Sturm, an infantryman still of humble rank, thoughts of winning such a distinguished award were beyond his wildest dreams. Sturm's comrades, too, wondered why he held the fighter aces in such awe, when he had already won the German Cross in Gold and the *Ritterkreuz* as a mere *Gefreiter*. All agreed, however, that Galland was indeed an exceptional soldier. At this point Sturm could have no idea that he would soon have a personal and unpleasant encounter with the fighter ace.

The three Italian guards at Villa Zirio certainly had an easy life. They were well fed and worked easy in eight-hour shifts. Sturm had noticed on more than one occasion the laxness of the guard at the gate—cigarette in his mouth, cap pushed back on his head, slouched back and reading a newspaper, his machine pistol on the ground beside him.

Two days before the end of their leave, all hell broke loose. A group of Italians broke into the villa's store room. The guard patrolling the grounds heard nothing, being busy at the other end of the villa. Nevertheless he bumped into two of the intruders as they tried to make good their escape, and arrested them. They had at first ignored his warning shouts, but after he had fired a burst from his machine pistol over their heads, they dropped their loot and gave themselves up.

The sound of gunfire alerted all the visitors, the management, and the staff. Shortly afterwards, a Jeep appeared from the nearby Italian military post and, after briefly questioning the intruders, took them into custody. The Germans discussed the incident among themselves, but few wanted to admit that after this break away from the Front, the sudden sound of gunfire had made them very jumpy. After one or two glasses of wine to settle their nerves, they all went back to their rooms.

On the morning of the last day, Sturm said his goodbyes to the Bertoldos and promised to keep in touch, and to pass on greetings to their business contacts in Bochum, especially Alfred Rademacher from the battalion office. At midday, Sturm went out on a last sailing trip with Alfonso, the boat owner. His thoughts, however, were on Vittoria and Vermi. In the evening, a farewell party was thrown at Villa Zirio. The good atmosphere was heightened by the announcement that they were to be the very last group of soldiers to spend their special leave as guests of the *Führer* here at Villa Zirio. Everyone present contributed an entry to Sturm's book. Unbeknownst to him, however, Sturm would indeed see Villa Zirio again, but this time in 1944, as a front-line soldier once again.

On 19 August 1943, the long return trip to Germany and an uncertain future began. Most of the group, after a brief stop with their respective replacement battalions, would travel on to rejoin their units at the Front. In Munich there was only a brief halt to change trains. Here, the men said their goodbyes and promised to keep in touch. Sturm in particular wanted to remain in contact with the infantry friends he had made.

36

The Konstantin Mine

Back in Dortmund, Sturm could make a stop for only two days. His superiors had already made arrangements for him to deliver several more speeches during the remainder of his summer break from engineering school. This time, Sturm's travels took him to two coal mines, known as 'Konstantin' and 'Friedrich'. There was a major inspection on at 'Konstantin' on the day of Sturm's visit. The press, mining officials, assessors, business managers, the *Kreisleiter*, district propaganda official, some civic dignitaries from Bochum, and the works foreman, *Herr* Mawick, were all present. All the visitors were issued with protective clothing and the journalists took their first photos. Using an express elevator, they were soon 900 m below the surface, where they were shown numerous tunnels and galleries, including the coal face where they chatted to some of the miners. The foreman explained the various safety measures and methods of ensuring that there was sufficient oxygen for the men to breathe. He showed his visitors the various methods of working the coal, dependant on the height and width of the gallery, and explained how the empty spaces in the areas where all the coal had been extracted were filled in with rubble to keep the area stable. By then the visitors had had a lungfull of coal dust and began making their way back to the elevator.

Herr Mawick asked Sturm if he would like to see something else of interest. Sturm could not see the grins of anticipation on the faces of the others standing behind him.

The foreman led Sturm into a small tunnel which led off to the side for a way before sloping steeply downwards. The roof was rather low, forcing both men to stoop, and before long they had to resort to crawling along on their hands and knees and eventually on their bellies. The roof was so low by this point that each time Sturm tried to raise his head to look forward, his helmet would bump off the tunnel roof. All he could see were the soles of the foreman's boots, illuminated by the lamp on his helmet. Crawling headfirst down the steep slope, Sturm could feel the blood rushing to his head. Growing somewhat claustrophobic, he was soon sweating heavily. He reassured himself that if the somewhat chubby foreman could make it through without getting stuck, then he must be able to as well.

At last the nightmare was over, and they emerged into a roomier chamber. Sturm tried to act *blasé* about the trip, and with a miserable attempt at a grin asked the foreman what it was he wanted to show him that was of interest. Mawick explained that the narrow tunnel they had just passed through was used as an emergency exit and to provide ventilation. The express elevator soon had them back on the surface where they were met by the grinning, blackened faces of the others. It transpired that the special 'inspection' of the narrow tunnel had been arranged for Sturm beforehand, and that all the others were in on it.

One of the others approached him, and Sturm suddenly recognised who it was— Alfred Meyer, *Gauleiter* and *Reichsstatthalter*, *Oberpräsident* of the Province of Westphalia. Due to his busy schedule, he had not been able to participate in the inspection and had only just arrived. He wanted to meet the young *Ritterkreuzträger*. Sturm was somewhat taken aback when the *Gauleiter* clapped both hands over his shoulders and said, 'Now, *Unteroffizier* Sturm, tell us what you thought of your little expedition!' Looking the *Gauleiter* in the eye, after a brief hesitation and a glance at the others Sturm responded: '*Herr Gauleiter*, I would rather creep through an enemy position knowing a machine gun might open up on me at any moment, than go through that torture again—I am soaked in sweat from head to toe!' Everyone laughed and took up the glasses of schnapps which had been laid out for them. As they toasted each other, Sturm looked sternly over at the foreman and wagged an admonishing finger at him. Still covered in coal dust, the group helped themselves to the wide assortment of refreshing drinks and cold beers which had been laid on. After that practical joke, fresh air and cold beer were just what was needed.

Because most of them wanted to drink a toast with Sturm, they all ended up having several more glasses of wine before the *Oberbergrat* offered his guests the chance to clean up and listen to the speech Sturm was scheduled to give. Sturm cleaned his face, but on looking in the mirror saw that his eyes were still black with coal dust. He took up the sponge and a hand towel again, as well as some renol—a special cleanser intended to remove grime from the hands. The alcohol Sturm had drunk was probably responsible for his carelessness in using the renol. Looking in the mirror, he could see that the coal dust was gone, but that his face was now bright red and beginning to burn as the tender skin reacted to the strong detergent. No one had told him that it was best to rub on a little grease to loosen up the dirt then use ordinary soap and water.

The others were already present and waiting when Sturm arrived to give his speech. They could hardly fail to notice his bright red face. The manager told Sturm that if he could bear some pain for a few seconds, he had something which would help. Imagining that he meant some soothing ointment, in his distress, Sturm nodded his agreement. Even though the others expressed their sympathy for Sturm's predicament, he could see that most of them were quite amused. Only Mawick, the foreman, seemed genuinely concerned. What the manager in fact produced was a small bottle of *Eau de Cologne*. Pouring a measure into Sturm's outstretched hands he said, 'Now, close your eyes tight and rub this on your face!' Sturm did as he was told and immediately felt a burning agony, as though his face was going to burst. It seemed to last an age, but in fact it was only a few moments before the pain began to subside. Slowly, Sturm opened his eyes and saw the amused expressions on the faces of the others. Wiping his eyes with a towel and drinking a glass of water hastily handed to him, Sturm began his speech. He knew the audience were not expecting a lengthy discourse and was thankful to be able to keep it brief. On its conclusion he was applauded, and thanked by the manager of the mine.

After the evening meal provided at the mine, a party which was set to last well into the night was thrown. At about 22.00 hours, Mawick said to Sturm, 'I'm going to have to leave. It's my wife's birthday and we will have a house full of guests by now!' Sturm didn't hesitate, and to Mawick's astonishment said, 'Well if you'll invite me along, we'll leave together.'

The party was in full swing by now, and having quaffed generous amonts of alcohol the *Kreisleiter* and the others were in a generous mood. The two were excused because of *Frau* Mawick's birthday. On arriving at Mawick's house, they were welcomed by thehis wife, Erna, and the other guests. The celebrations lasted well into the early hours of the morning and, although Sturm could hold his drink well and was still on his feet, he was relieved to be able to accept the invitation made to him to stay the night.

After a bath, a hearty breakfast, and some very strong coffee, Sturm took his leave, giving the Mawicks a signed photograph with a dedication as a souvenir and token of friendship. A young friend of the Mawicks gave Sturm a lift back into Dortmund.

On the following day, Sturm travelled to Bochum to visit the 'Friedrich' mine. The district foreman escorted him to the mine where, at the end of the morning shift, he would address the miners. Sturm and his escort travelled by tramcar to the terminus, from where it was only a short walk to the mine. Met by the manager, they were taken to the area set aside for the speech. There were about twenty rows of seats, but only the first row was occupied—by the foremen, various officials, engineers, and mine safety personnel. Of the miners themselves there was nothing to be seen, but certainly plenty to be heard. From the area behind the rows of seats, Sturm could hear the rattling of chains accompanied by yells, curses, and shrill whistles. Sturm could not understand what was going on so the manager explained.

'Most of the workers here are malcontents who refuse to support the regime or the party, or criminals sent to work here as punishment.'

He shrugged his shoulders and added, 'We have turned off the water to the showers so that they can't get washed up unless they come and listen to your speech!'

Sturm came down from the swastika-bedecked lectern and went over to the source of all the commotion.

'Damn it! What's up with you all? Speak your mind, I won't bite you!' he entreated them.

He could see the miners, their faces and hands black with coal dust. The whites of their eyes stood out on their grimy faces as they turned towards Sturm. Their mouths opened to yell in protest once again, then they noticed the *Ritterkreuz* at Sturm's neck and hesitated. Sturm went over to the nearest miner, clamping his hands on his shoulders and giving him a gentle shake.

'Look,' he said. 'I know it's disgusting that they switched off the water to force you to come and listen to me, but I promise you I personally had nothing to do with this!'

The noise by now had completely subsided. One miner called out, 'We thought you were another of these party big shots they send to speak to us!'

Sturm drew himself erect and said: 'Who ever wants to listen, come forward. I promise I'll keep it short so you can get all get off home!'

Few came forward, most preferring to stand in the background. After a quarter of an hour, Sturm finished his speech and took his leave, refusing a meal offered to him by the manager of the mine and accepting only a glass of water. On the way back to the tram terminus, Sturm complained to the district foreman over not being informed that the miners were dissidents. As the two stood waiting for the tram to arrive, miners began to appear, one by one at first, then in small groups. Some of the men he had just spoken to, going off home now that their shift was over. The miners stood off to one side until one, an older grey-haired man, approached Sturm nervously and asked if he would tell them a little about his experiences at the Front and especially how he came to win the *Ritterkreuz*. Sturm agreed and told them of his experiences in that dreadful battle; of losing his best friend; and of how the medic who brought him back for treatment lost his own life because of his concern for Sturm. The miners listened attentively, as did the conductor of the tramcar, which had by then arrived at the terminus. Then, it was time to go. The small crowd broke up and made their way to their homes.

On his return to Aachen, Sturm reported to his battalion commander and found him with an *Oberleutnant* by the name of Pütz. Pütz was the current careers advisor to young men who wished to enlist in the Army as potential NCO or officer candidates. He had been carrying out these duties while recovering from wounds received at the Front. Now that he was recovered, he was due to return to his unit and it fell to Sturm to take over his duties. Sturm would be working alongside *Unteroffizier* Walter Marx and *Obergefreiter* Wolfgang Kottnick. Marx had lost his left arm but was still classified as fit for garrison service and was able to return to his home in Aachen each evening. Kottnick had suffered a lung wound but was on the mend and would eventually be classified as fit and return to his unit at the Front. Both knew Sturm already, not just by sight, but because their respective tasks had often brought them into contact with each other.

Sturm required no special introduction to his new duties. During his lectures in schools he had often talked about his experiences at the front, and about the infantry as 'Queen of all the Arms', with the result that many of his listeners decided on the infantry for their careers. *Unteroffizier* Sturm, with his *Ritterkreuz*, German Cross, and other decorations was an enticing example for those thinking of joining this particular branch of the services. He also made use of publicity material such as books and photos. This material came from Münster and was brought over on a weekly basis by two soldiers who would make the most of the opportunity to stay overnight and enjoy themselves.

Sturm's area of responsibility was from the area between Aachen and Düren, the Eifel region up to Schleiden and Monschau, and westwards towards Eupen, Malmedy and St Vith. In all of the schools in this area there would be willing recruits for a career as a regular soldier. These schools included the *Wehrertüchtigungs-Läger* (*WE Läger*, 'Military Preparatory Schools' or camps) and the *Ordensburg Vogelsang*, a *Napola* (*Nationalpolitische-Führungsanstalt*), and a *Kinderlandverschickungslager* (a camp for children evacuated from cities prone to bombing raids). *Oberstleutnant* Gierlich at the command headquarters of Military District VI in Münster was also responsible for this entire area, and had known Sturm since early that year.

Sturm drove the two in *Oberleutnant* Pütz's field car to the *Wehrertüchtingungslager VI* at Buhlert, in the Monschau area, this being the camp for Westphalia. The young lads there were only too keen to show the visiting *Ritterkreuzträger* all they had learnt, and listened excitedly to Sturm's speech. Afterwards he was warmly thanked by the camp commander, Diekamp, for his visit. Some of the boys came forward to ask for application papers to take home to their parents. On the return journey, Pütz admitted to Sturm that he thought the young *Ritterkreuzträger* far more suited to the job than he.

In the evening, they ate at the Hotel Horchen in Monschau, where Sturm got to know the hostess, *Frau* Horchen. She would later come to his defence in his conflict with *General* Galland.

On the following day, Pütz went off on leave, after which he would rejoin his unit at the Front. More school visits followed including several to schools in the Eupen area, where he was escorted by the *Hitlerjugend Bannführer* for Eupen, Heinz Engel.

After two recruiting drives in Düren and Schleiden, Sturm arrived at around 14.00 hours one afternoon at the Kern guesthouse in Schleiden. The guesthouse had been recommended to him for its fine foods and, because it was a popular place, for holding parties and all sorts of celebrations. Guests came from Aachen, Düren, Köln, Bonn, and all over the Eifel region. He hoped he would still be in time for lunch and as he took a seat at a table. A waiter appeared and asked what he wanted. When Sturm said he would like something to eat, the waiter replied that, regrettably, the kitchen was already closed but he would have a word with the chef and see what could be arranged. A moment later, the owner, *Herr* Albert Kern appeared and welcomed Sturm to the hotel, saying that he could offer him a nice veal cutlet if that would suffice. Sturm readily agreed and enjoyed a glass of cold beer as he waited. A few minutes later, *Herr* Kern reappeared with the food and a nice bottle of red wine—there would be no charge, Sturm was to be his guest! Impressed by *Herr* Kern's benevolence, Sturm asked him to take a seat and join him in a glass of wine. He thanked his host for his kindness and hospitality and presented him with two signed photographs as a souvenir. Kern asked Sturm if he would do him a special favor, and give these photos personally to his invalid son. They went upstairs to the Kern's private quarters and entered the child's room. Rolf was an unfortunate 12 year old with terminal Leukaemia. His eyes sparkled at the sight of the *Ritterkreuzträger*, who, having introduced himself, presented the boy with the signed photos. *Herr* Kern produced an album in which there were already several photos and letters from various *Ritterkreuzträgern*. Sturm, however, was the first to visit in person. He promised to visit again whenever time permitted. When Sturm offered Rolf his hand to shake before taking his leave, the boy would only reluctantly release it. *Herr* Kern wrote in Sturm's book: 'Much admired Mr Sturm, your visit today has been a great honour, and you will always have a home here in our house. Affectionately yours, Albert Kern.' Rolf died and was buried just two weeks later. As he stood and watched the small coffin being lowered into the ground, Sturm could not stop emotion from welling up inside him. Thereafter, each time he visited the Kern guesthouse, he noticed that the staff and family, especially *Herr* Kern, treated him just like one of the family.

Autumn was coming on fast, and the deciduous trees in the beautiful Eifel forests changed from green to brown, red, and yellow. Through arrangements made by *Herr* Kern, Sturm went on a hunt with some *Jäger* he had befriended. The bellowing of the stags echoed through the dense forests, swathed in mist in the early mornings. The rising sun would soon burn back the mist, however, and the clear blue skies promised another beautiful day. Stags clashed their antlers together, or bellowed out their challenges, probably to some other young male, making his challenge to the 'King' of the forest. Sturm was offered a shot at one particularly fine specimen, but declined the chance to shoot such a magnificent beast.

Sturm lingered for some time at the *Ordensburg Vogelsang*. He had obtained a projector and some films which he reluctantly showed. They purported to show the life of the infantry in combat, but were chimerical and manipulative in their depiction, full of acts of great heroism and the message of undoubted Germanic superiority over other races and ethnicities. To the leadership of these *Napola* schools, these films were like manna from heaven. The convinced National Socialists attending these schools already considered themselves as the master race, and such films merely only served to support their twisted ideals. In the discussions which followed these screenings, Sturm made them firmly aware that, in the real world, war for an infantryman was something cruel and pitiless. The conditions under which the infantry fought were terrible. They had to live on whatever they could carry with them, their packs being left behind with the supply columns (unlike the motorised and *Waffen-SS* units). Then there were the dreadful wet seasons with the horrendous mud and cold of the Russian winter of 194–42. There was rarely the chance of warm food. The three-day ration packs, which were the usual provision then, were normally used up on the first day, except for the bread, which had to be carried next to their bodies to keep it from freezing solid. They also lacked warm winter clothing, perhaps because of supply problems, or sabotage. For the divisions in the central sector of the Eastern Front, however, the fight against the enemy was not always the most difficult challenge. Rather, it was the battle against the all-pervading damp, the terrible cold, the lice, and the despair of knowing that you would not come out of the terrible 'cauldron' between Olenin and Rshew alive. The infantry grumbled, but of course carried on and did their very best. There were some units in the infantry which were well equipped, for example the SS units. They were used as a kind of fire brigade, rushed from one sector to another wherever the danger seemed thegreatest, and throwing back the enemy, often with severe losses. Sturm brought up the example of the SS unit 'Fegelein', supported by an 8.8-cm flak unit which had rescued his own company from a particularly desperate situation. The Russians had inflicted grievous losses on the company, the battalion commander being so seriously wounded that he later died. Pinned down in an area perilously short of cover, had the SS troops not rescued them, their only choice would have been to either freeze to death or go into Soviet captivity. After the battle, both units withdrew to lick their wounds. The infantry certainly didn't envy the SS troops, who risked all in ruthless battle only to be left in the shit, rushing back and forward along the Front to try to fool the enemy into believing the German forces were stronger than they really were.

The boys, and also their instructors, who had been so excited by the film, were given food for thought by Sturm's open and honest descriptions of infantry fighting on the Russian Front in winter. Several of the lads came forward and declared their interest in taking up a career as a regular NCO or officer, nevertheless. On 18 October 1942, it was decreed that all infantry regiments be renamed grenadier regiments, with the result that they would be better armed and equipped, also partially motorised.

37

A Confrontation with
General Adolf Galland

One evening in October 1943, Sturm arrived back in Monschau at around 21.00 hours. He went straight to the Hotel Horchen dining room. As he went to his usual seat at the table reserved for regulars, he found it occupied by *Generalmajor* Adolf Galland, accompanied by a woman who it would later transpire was his 'girlfriend'. Sturm stood smartly to attention and reported, '*Unteroffizier* Sturm, *Herr General*!'

Sturm gestured to indicate his wish to sit down. A curt glance and a nod was the only response. The general was very busy with his girlfriend and Sturm got the impression he was a little drunk. Sturm took his seat and a few moments later the owner's wife, *Frau* Horchen, arrived and sat down beside them at the table after giving Sturm's order to her husband. Sturm had now been on friendly terms with the owners for some time.

Two more of the regular guests arrived and took their places at the table, a farmer and a local craftsman. The latter was much impressed to find himself sitting at the table with two *Ritterkreuzträger*, one of them a general and with Oakleaves, Swords, and Diamonds, no less! He must have noticed, however, that the two did not speak to each other at all. Sturm ate his trout, which despite the strained atmosphere at the table tasted wonderful. The farmer had brought some wine and they toasted each other and engaged in friendly conversation, taking no further notice of the general and his companion.

Galland, who perhaps in turn felt that the others at the table were deliberately ignoring him, directly several very frostily glances at them. Sturm was unused to this sort of behavior, but as a mere *Unteroffizier*, did not feel it his place to try to enter into conversation with Galland, a man he greatly admired. His rudeness to the other guests at the table came as a great surprise to Sturm. Sturm's duties had brought him into contact with many highly ranked dignitaries, both civil and military, and they had never behaved with such airs and graces.

The waiter had already brought Galland a couple of Carafes of wine, and these had been swiftly emptied. His brandy glass, too, had been refilled a couple of times. Galland's girlfriend asked Sturm to excuse his behaviour, as she attempted to calm the general down and tried to persuade him to retire for the evening. This

Adolf Galland, a superb fighter pilot with a
prickly personality, as Sturm was to discover.

seemed to anger Galland even more. He turned and barked rudely at Sturm, 'It is the
Unteroffizier who should be leaving the table!'

The owner's wife, who could see the effect that the general's behavior was having
on the other guests , retorted, '*Herr General, Unteroffizier* Sturm has long been a
welcome guest at our table, and he may stay as long as he wishes!'

Galland was visibly infuriated by *Frau* Horchen's intervention. Sturm, who
was about to answer the general's remark, was restrained by the others. Galland's
companion once again apologised for his behaviour, and finally succeeded in getting
him to stand up and leave the table. As he stood, however, he stumbled against a
chair, and Sturm stretched out a hand to steady him, only for his hand to be brusquely
brushed aside. Sturm dejectedly returned to his seat. On the next morning, Galland
and his friend left the hotel early, before the other guests had arisen. Sturm was
greatly disappointed not to have been able to talk to the general before he left, and
not to have been able to have put this unpleasant incident behind them.

As well as giving careers advice to the local youths, on 13 October 1943 Sturm
gave a speech to a mass rally at the town hall in Malmedy. The place was full to
bursting, with every seat taken and people standing in the aisles. After the speech,
Sturm had the opportunity to make many new acquaintances, many of whom made

entries into his book. Looking back at some of these entries, Sturm later reflected that some of them, especially the ardent young National Socialists among them, should have been filling in the gaps at the Front. There was the *Kreisleiter*, Maal, then the *Kreisorganisationsleiter*, *Kreishauptamtsleiter*, *Kreissachbearbeiter*, *Schriftleiter*, *Kreishauptstellenleiter*, *Bahninspekteur*, *Amtsgerichtsrat*, *Bannstreifendienstfü hrer*, *Partei-Stellenleiter*, *Kreiskassenleiter*, *Oberamtsrichter*, *Führer* of *SS-Sturm 10/58*, the deputy *Bannführer*, *SS-Unterscharführer*, the *Obersturmbannführer* of *SA-Standarte 174*, the *Ortsgruppenleiter*, *Kreiskassenwalter*, two *Oberleutnante*, a *Zellenleiter*, *Ortsgruppenkassenleiter*, *Kreisamtstellenleiter*, *Stammführer* of III/674, *Oberstadtdirektor*, the *Bürgermeister*, *Rektor*, *SA Sturmführer*, *Oberinspekteur*, and many others.... So many people to fill in the plethora of posts which fuelled the beaurocratic machinery of the Third Reich. How many of them could have been made themselves useful, serving their country at the Front?

38

Visit to the Mountain Troops at Garmisch-Partenkirchen

Through his unit, Sturm had made contact with the NSDAP/*Hitlerjugend* High Mountain Military Preparatory Camp of the Reichsjugendführung at Garmisch-Partenkirchen. Subsequently, an invitation arrived from this camp for twenty boys to visit. With some effort, Sturm had managed to assemble a group of volunteers after getting permission from their parents, school teachers, and headmasters (because this 'holiday' was to take place during term time). On 22 October they arrived in Munich. They stayed overnight in a youth hostel, where the little group was received with great ceremony. Sturm had used his influence with the local political leadership and been given permission to mobilise help from a women's group, *Hitlerjugend*, and *BDM* girls, and these had organised the accommodation, rations, and much else besides for Sturm and the twenty young boys, all between the ages of 15 and 16.

On the following day, they went sightseeing in Munich. In the evening they went to see a film about the *Freikorps* leader Ferdinand von Schill in the fight against Napoleon. (Schill had fallen during the street battles in Stralsund, eleven officers tried under military law and shot, and 550 Husars were carried off to serve as galley-slaves on French ships.)

On the third day, they travelled to Garmisch, where for one week the boys were accommodated at the barracks of the 1 *Gebirgsjäger Ersatz Bataillon 98* in Garmisch-Partenkirchen. When it came to accommodation, meals, and 'pay parade', the *Hauptmann* and bataillon commander, Rusterer, treated the boys just like young soldiers, but dressed in civilian attire. The young lads were allowed to visit the training area up in the mountains after they had been kitted out with special equipment. Their high spirits knew no limits, as the *Gebirgsjäger* made every effort to show the boys all their weapons and equipment and answer every question.[1]

The bataillon commander had, as a special treat for the young lads, arranged a combined daylight and night-time training exercise. The *Gebirgsjäger*, of course, used only blank ammunition, but the crack of gunfire and cannons made it an exciting spectacle, as they climbed over obstacles moving up and down on their ropes. In October, it grew dark quite early, so the muzzle flashes and tracer bullets made an impressive sight. 'Wounded' were recovered and treated by medics. Accommodation

A portrait shot of Sturm taken in
Aachen in 1943.

on this and the following night was at the WE camp at Kreuzeck. Just staying in
barracks was in of itself considered a privilege by the young lads. Together with the
exciting training exercise and the opportunity to meet other boys from the WE camp,
this was a great experience for them. These mountaineers made great efforts to
make their visitors from the Rhineland welcome, and to show them all that they had
learnt without any show of arrogance. The evening ended with a sing-song around a
blazing campfire.

39

Reunion with Heidi

Heidi was the daughter of Sepp Staller, the manager of the Railwayman's Hostel in Garmisch-Partenkirchen. Railwaymen could sleep overnight there while waiting for their train, or during long stop-overs. Sturm had first met his friend Sepp in 1937, when he asked him for information. Sturm had been with his girlfriend Ursel at the time. Both were invited to coffee by the friendly gentleman. At his home, they made the acquaintance of his wife and his then 12-year-old daughter Heidi.

In those days, Heidi had already been an experienced ski instructor and gave them good advice on where the best slopes were to be found. Sturm was invited by Sepp to spend his winter holidays in Garmisch, where he could stay in the Railwayman's Hostel. No better offer could have been made to a poor student, and Sturm willingly took it up. He had since spent his winter holidays in Garmisch in 1938, 1939, and 1940. He was accommodated and fed for free, the only costs being the few small gifts he gave Staller as a token of his appreciation. Sepp treated the young Sturm like the son he had never had. Heidi kept in touch with Sturm by letter during the war years. She saw her soldier become an *Unteroffizier* with many decorations. Now, as an 18 year old, she finally met him again. This was a good enough cause for a great party with all the family.

Sturm had briefly said hello when he arrived in Garmisch, but later excused himself from an evening with his band of young lads and spent a happy evening with his friend Heidi. The last evening of the trip to Garmisch was a very special experience for the boys, and for Sturm and for Heidi too. The then world-famous singer Erna Sack, known as the 'German Nightingale', gave a special concert. The concert hall was overflowing. Most of the audience were soldiers away from their units recovering from wounds. Heidi sat between Sturm and *Hauptmann* Rusterer in the front row.

The first half of the performance went down exceptionally well and at the interval the applause was tremendous. *Hauptmann* Rusterer turned to Sturm and said in jest: 'Take no notice. They see the singer often. They are assuming the performance is especially for you!'

Sturm looked at the other two in disbelief. Getting up from his seat, he headed for the dressing room, intent on obtaining a signed photo of the star of the show. His way was barred by a member of the *Feldgendarmerie*, who Sturm eventually persuaded to let him past. After knocking and hearing a 'Come in', Sturm entered the dressing room. It was quite dark, the room illuminated solely by the small light bulbs around the dressing table mirror. As the singer turned around, she said: 'Ah, it's my little *Unteroffizier!*'

Still surprised, Sturm formally introduced himself: '*Unteroffizier* Sturm, madam. I wanted to ask you for a signed photograph!'

Frau Sack offered him her hand, Sturm stood there as if frozen, as the singer approached. On stage she had looked so young and radiant. Now, close up, Sturm could see she was much older and wore very heavy make up. She, noticing his bemusement, said with a kindly laugh: 'I know what you are looking at. This is necessary, especially around the eyes, for working on stage—otherwise, those at the back of the auditorium can scarcely make out the detail of one's face.'

Sturm apologised for his ungentlemanly reaction. In response to a gesture from her husband, who Sturm had not at first noticed in the darkened room, the singer lifted a photo—not one of those with a facsimile signature already printed on it—and personally signed it with a special dedication to Sturm. With profuse thanks Sturm took his leave of the dressing room and returned to his seat to tell the others of his experience. The concert continued, and after a couple of encores the singer received a standing ovation.

Hauptmann Rusterer departed for the *Gebirgsjäger* barracks having said goodbye to his young friends inside the hall, while Heidi and Hans went off to a nearby hotel where they had booked a table for dinner. In the large dining room, just about every table was occupied. The two ordered a refreshing drink and some ice cream.

A few moments later, *Frau* Sack and her husband entered the room. They took their places at a table full of couples, mostly dignitaries from the city and their companions. Sturm's position offered him a good view of the other table without having to appear too nosey. Shortly thereafter, *Herr* Sack got up from his seat, came over, and invited Sturm and Heidi to join them.

The others at the table, Sturm discovered, were the *Bürgermeister*, the *Kreisleiter*, and the senior district military officer, all with their wives. Sturm was by now quite accustomed to such situations, and happily accepted the invitation and joined in the conversation. Heidi, however, was shy and somewhat overawed at the company in which she found herself; she remained quiet and reserved despite attempts to bring her into the conversation. This unexpected ending to the evening was all a little too much for her. Only when the subject turned to winter sports could she take part with some enthusiasm. *Frau* Sack made her a gift of a small pocket handkerchief and a bottle of perfume. After a little while, Sturm excused them from the table and took Heidi home. He had to get back to barracks before it got too late, as he had a long journey ahead of him in the morning.

Sturm and his twenty young lads were given a hearty send off on their return trip next day. *Hauptmann* Rusterer and some of his troops, particularly those who had been looking after the boys, came along, as well as a contingent of officers and boys from the WE camp. The return journey was uneventful, with only a brief stopover in Munich. The time flew by as the boys talked excitedly about their experiences. Many photos had been taken during the visit, and copies would certainly be circulated, giving everyone involved and those boys back home who were unable to make the trip much to talk about over the coming months.

40

Revision

Sturm had much to do to catch up on his studies at the State Engineering School in Aachen. He often had to swot well into the night, but was fortunately able to call on the willing help of his classmates, who showed him their notes and essays on lectures he had missed. Several of them visited him regularly at his accommodation block, where they grilled him to ensure he had understood the notes on lectures he had missed. These sessions were particularly helpful on the theoretical side. On the bright side, Sturm had already proven himself an excellent draftsman during his earlier studies at the *Oberrealschule* and the *Maschinenbauschule* in Dortmund.

These study periods often developed into social events. Sturm was often given small gifts as tokens of appreciation for his speeches, including food, drink, and occasionally an envelope with extra food coupons, as contributions towards his studies. Sturm was only too happy to share his good fortune with his comrades, and on these occasions, *Unteroffizier* Marx and Gisela Körber would produce a fine cold buffet. (*Obergefreiter* Kottnik had already been returned to the Front at this stage.)

During the many trips he had to undertake in the course of his duties, Sturm had got to know a young conductress on the railway. On one trip to Münster, he had had difficulty finding a seat in the packed carriage. A pretty young girl, she had come past and invited him to sit in the compartment reserved for the guards and conductors. Sturm grew to know her in their conversations in this compartment. Lilo Hartwig was 20 years old, and had decided to take work on the railway after taking her *Abitur*. Her father was the station manager in Hamm, Westphalia. The guard himself said little and took no part in the conversation, contenting himself with sitting there, eating bread and drinking from a bottle. Before closing the door when he left the compartment, however, he turned, nodded, and gave Sturm a meaningful wink.

Lilo admitted that she had spotted the conspicuous, highly decorated young *Unteroffizier* on the platform before he boarded the train in Aachen as he stood speaking to one of the *Feldgendarmerie*. Before he left the train in Münster, he arranged a date with her in Aachen, where the train would often be delayed for a few hours while the locomotive was changed. They met here many times and once, stayed overnight together. Anyone seeing her in her uniform would hardly be able

A fine shot of *Unteroffizier* Sturm before his promotion and assignment to the *Kriegsschule*.

to guess at what a shapely body was concealed within. Lilo was an overwhelmingly beautiful girl. Sturm carried a photo of her in a stylish, strapless dress in his wallet. Her face, framed in shoulder-length bronze hair looked like the portrait of a young film star.

One day, a call came to Sturm's office. It was Lilo, and she sounded very upset. Her voice broke with sobbing. She wanted, if it was possible, to meet with him in Dortmund. She couldn't say more over the phone. Sturm met her at the station and wanted to take her back to his house. She declined and burst into tears once again, only beginning to calm down when Sturm gently took her arm and led her into the station restaurant. There, Lilo explained her distress. She had gone to an engagement party of one of her friends in Hamburg. The fiancée of her friend was an *SS-Obersturmführer* who had also invited some of his comrades along. Some were with their own partners, but one was alone, and had immediately fallen for Lilo. It was no wonder—she was such a beautiful girl. The relaxed atmosphere and copious amounts of alcohol they drank had led to their inevitable conclusion. In the morning, Lilo had awoken to find herself in the guest room of the large villa, in bed with the

SS officer. Shocked and deeply ashamed, she had fled the villa without speaking to a soul. It was a flight rather than a departure, Lilo wishing to expunge the memories of the event from her mind as quickly as possible. Soon afterwards, an express letter from the *SS-Obersturmführer* had arrived, in which he asked to see her again as soon as possible. Lilo showed the letter to Sturm.

The officer, Rolf Schmitt, spoke of his great regret for his behaviour that night. In his defence, he blamed the amount of alcohol. Sturm read on. The *SS-Obersturmführer* also asked her to go to a doctor as soon as possible. He explained that his own unit doctor had diagnosed that he had venereal disease, and he was worried that he might have infected her. He had also written two subsequent letters, which Lilo had not opened. She gave these, too, to Sturm, so he could read them and advise her.

In the meantime, Lilo had visited her doctor and was being treated for VD. The doctor had explained that with men the symptoms manifested themselves quite rapidly, with an intense inflammation, but that recognition of the disease in women took longer. The treatment would not, however, be difficult, as the disease had been spotted in its early stages. Sturm was conscious that he himself might have been infected in turn, if their own, intimate relationship continued. It was terrifying how quickly this so-called 'cavalier's disease' could spread. The source of the infection had to be traced back by the doctors as quickly as possible.

It was clear to Lilo that her relationship with Sturm had taken a knock. Sturm opened both letters and read on. The officer's loving words showed how genuinely smitten by Lilo he was. He again asked for a meeting, because he was to return to the Front, this time in Russia. Previously he had served in France, where he had picked up the infection. The young girl listened quietly, deep in thought. Sturm knew how much she liked him, and how she had wanted them to grow closer. But how could they, now? With a smile, she asked Sturm if he would contact Schmitt on her behalf.

That was easier said than done however. Schmitt had since joined his unit in Russia. Eventually, through the intervention of *Oberstleutnant* Gierlich as the district military command in Münster, it was possible to arrange a brief spell of leave for Schmitt. Lilo and Schmitt were engaged at a celebration in his parent's house. Sturm was unable to attend, as he had himself by then returned to the Front. The two were married at Christmas 1944, but again, duty prevented Sturm from attending.

41

Sturm volunteers for front-line service

Sturm travelled around Aachen and the Eifel area Sturm in his own vehicle. Trains or buses between town and village were far too time-consuming. Also, he had to take with him much additional equipment—namely film projectors and recruiting material. By then, an album entitled '*Unteroffiziere* of the Army with the *Ritterkreuz*' had been published, with all the accompanying photos. Collector's photo No. 11 showed *Unteroffizier* Sturm, with a short explanatory text on the *verso*.

Sturm often visited the *Ordensburg Vogelsang* and various schools in the area. *Hauptmann* Traut, the deputy commander at *Vogelsang*, wrote in Sturm's book: 'So long as the German *Wehrmacht* has soldiers like Hans Sturm, we need not be anxious about the future of the German people and of the Reich!'

Such complimentary entries only served to remind Sturm of how far-removed he was from the war and his comrades, who were still fighting, dying, or suffering dreadful wounds. It no longer satisfied him to be told how important his duties as a speaker and recruitment NCO were. For Sturm, the end of his engineering studies was a moment of great significance, these having been one reason he was denied permission to return to active duty. Constant reminders of the death of his fiancée also reinforced his determination to leave the city. A chance occurrence brought an opportunity to do so much sooner than he might have expected.

Whenever Sturm was sent to Düren, Köln, Münster, or the Ruhr area, he went by rail. That way, he got to know many of the *Feldgendarmerie* on duty at the stations. As a *Ritterkreuzträger*, he always received sympathetic treatment from these often unpopular soldiers. At the beginning of December 1943, Aachen suffered many air raid warnings during which everyone who was in the station had to go immediately to the air raid shelters. Fear bordering on panic often led to the crowds to shove and push past to get into the shelter. As Sturm entered the shelter from the cold outside, his glasses misted up. Someone shoved him from behind and he tripped over a suitcase which was in his way. In stumbling he bumped into someone standing just in front of him.

'Now then, slowly young man!' they grumbled.

'What are you complaining about? If this is your case, you should have moved it out of the way!'

Sturm in his official duty vehicle.

As he spoke, Sturm wiped the lenses of his spectacles, and recognised that he was talking to an officer—and a full colonel at that! He saluted immediately and shuffled the small suitcase to the side.

'Thank you, *Unteroffizier* Sturm!' said the *Oberst*, who Sturm did not recognise. Seeing the bemused look on the young Sturm's face, the Oberst went on.

'Don't be so surprised. You've been here in Aachen a year now and have become well-known as a bit of a character. I know more about you than you might guess, including the loss of your fiancée. I heard about that from my wife. She is a friend of the Hoppmann family and knows Silvia's mother well!'

Sturm listened in surprise as the *Oberst* continued. He was reporting for duty in Berlin. Sturm promised to get him a window seat for the full journey, a promise which the expression on the *Oberst*'s face suggested he didn't think Sturm could deliver. The conversation was interrupted by the all-clear. Sturm grabbed the *Oberst*'s suitcase and ran as quickly as he could up to the platform, which was already beginning to fill up as soldiers and civilians emerged from the shelter. As the train rolled slowly into the station, the passengers pushed forwards, intent on securing a good seat as quickly as possible. At one of the windows and on the footsteps of some of the doors stood armed *Feldgendarmerie* troops. To the one at the window Sturm held up two fingers. The *Feldgendarm* nodded. Sturm was confident that two seats would be held for him. He then went to seek out the *Oberst*, who was smaller than he, and who regarded him doubtfully over the tops of his gold-rimmed, half-moon glasses.

'You promised to arrange two windows seats and yet you are back already?'

'Connections, *Herr Oberst*. One must have connections. It makes everything in life so much easier!'

The station platform had emptied fast, apart from a few latecomers and those bidding a fond farewell to their loved ones. Sturm took the cases and went over to a carriage with a first-class compartment. Behind him followed the *Oberst*, mumbling, 'I like the boy's style!'

As promised, the two window seats were waiting for them. The *Feldgendarm* stood guard at the door of the compartment. Sturm thanked him and swore to pay a social visit to him and his comrades at the first opportunity.

In conversation with *Oberst* Rohr, Sturm learnt that his regiment was in action in Italy. Sturm told him of how he had tried to get away from his post in Aachen, but in vain. The *Oberst* suggested that he should join his regiment in Italy. He suggested that Sturm give it some thought. If he agreed, a transfer to Italy could be arranged. The *Oberst* gave him his personal card and suggested that Sturm visit his wife, who would pass on a message from Sturm should he decide to accept. Sturm doubted whether the *Oberst* would have the influence to arrange his transfer. *Oberstleutnant* Gierlich at the military district command would certainly not agree to it. *Oberst* Rohr retorted that he was a very determined man, and could also make his voice heard in the right places!

Two days later, Sturm visited *Frau* Rohr, taking with him a large bouquet of flowers. She had been expecting his visit and entertained him with fresh coffee and cakes. This very pleasant, delicate old lady very much looked the part in this large house, fitted with what appeared to be very expensive furnishings. The quality of the decor spoke volumes for her good taste. Sturm began to wonder where the conversation was leading. The old lady was treating him as well as if he were her own son. She told Sturm that she was utterly against him seeking a return to the Front; that both as a soldier and in his private life, he had sacrificed enough in this war, and there was no need to go back to the fight in Italy with her husband. His regiment was in the south of Italy. Fortunately, it was now pulling back, having suffered heavy losses in men and material, but there was no telling when it might be sent forward again. Sturm was impressed with her well-meaning advice. *Frau* Rohr also spoke of the Hoppmann family, and showed Sturm photographs of their two families together, including one in which his Silvia, still a young child, could be seen. She understood why he wanted to leave Aachen—but to what end? With no great pleasure, she agreed to pass on Sturm's decision to her husband, saying: 'My prayers will go with you, *Unteroffizier* Sturm.' She showed Sturm photos of her two sons. One, a young *Leutnant* had already been killed in France. The older son had been severely injured as a tank commander in Russia. He was an *Oberleutnant*, and had been blinded in both eyes and terribly burned. He was now in a special ward at the Aachen University Clinic, with little chance of surviving.

'I visited him only this morning and left the ward with my dearest wish that the Lord God release him from his suffering,' she explained, her voice full of emotion. 'Please may He grant that you, my dear young man, survive this war in one piece. You have, even with your eyes and other injuries, had very good fortune. Think of your parents. You are their only child!' she continued.

Sturm thanked the old lady for her kindly words, as she wiped the tears from her eyes.

42

Sturm meets his future wife

In the second week of December 1943, the chief medical officer of *Ersatz Bataillon 473* sent Sturm to the *Marienhospital* in Wesel, Niederrhein, where a friend of his would perform an examination of his eye injuries. The results were promising. The shrapnel splinter in his right eye socket still caused painful headaches, sometimes exacerbated by the weather conditions, but otherwise was no great problem. The eye itself had returned to almost normal function. Only sudden glances upwards or downwards sometimes triggered slight double vision. The pupil was slightly enlarged and sensitive to light.

That evening, Sturm went into the city to have a light meal and visit the cinema. The city grew dark very early these days, due to the blackout because of enemy bombing. Other than going to the cinema, there was not much else to do. In the row to his front and to the left sat two young girls, one brunette and one blonde. They cast furtive glances in his direction, probably because of his *Ritterkreuz*.

As the film came to an end, Sturm noticed the two young girls heading for the stairs leading to the exit. One dropped a purse from her handbag and several food rationing coupons spilled out onto the floor. Sturm held out his arm to prevent those behind him from trampling over her stuff. The girls thanked him. They were going off to have a coffee and invited the *Unteroffizier* to join them. As they chatted to each other, Sturm explained that he was only on a short visit due to his attendance at the hospital. He had taken a fancy to the blonde girl.

At the next junction, by the Berlin Gate, they split up. Sturm had to go on straight ahead. The brunette, whose name was Maria Torberg, had to go left towards the main street, and the blonde, Hilde Neerfeld, to the right. Sturm knew that there was a guesthouse just a little way off in the direction she was heading in, as he had called in there for a meal earlier that day. Saying that he wanted to go for a beer, Sturm offered to walk a little way with her. The brunette nodded knowingly and excused herself with a smile.

Two blocks further on, *Fräulein* Neerfeld and Sturm stood before a shop selling children's wares as darkness began to fall. She explained that she had left her bicycle here. Now she had to collect it and cycle back home to her farmhouse in Brünen, 9

Sturm's own personal favourite photo, taken just after meeting his future wife, Hilde.

km from Wesel. The moonlight revealed the impish delight on her face at Sturm's look of surprise.

'It would have been better for you to walk my friend Maria home. She lives here in Wesel and has a lovely little house.'

Sturm was glad that she couldn't read his thoughts! To change the subject and avoid further embarrassment, he looked up at the window above them, from which bright light shone and the sound of numerous voices could be heard.

'What's going on up there?' he asked.

'It's the Wehlings, they're celebrating a family reunion.'

'Yes, that will do for me, since our meeting has ended so quickly,' he said provocatively. 'If you are going off back to Brünen on your bicycle, I'll ask if there is room for me upstairs!'

'No, you can't do that. I hardly know you!' came the shocked reply.

'That doesn't matter. That lot above won't bite me, and they'll know me better if we meet again in the morning.'

Then he rang the doorbell, but heard nothing over the noise from above. After another ring of the bell, a light came on in the vestibule. A young boy opened the door. He look at the strange soldier in surprise then noticed the young blonde, who he knew well, as he had often visited the Neerfeld's farm on school holidays.

'You're crazy! They will throw you out!'

Sturm ignored Hilde's protests, and with a grin greeted the young lad, finding out that his name, too, was Hans. Then he walked past the girl and went straight on up the wooden stairs.

As he reached the door to the flat, warm air engulfed him. His glasses misted up. Before he could take them off and clear them, he was greeted by a loud male voice.

'Hallo! Now, who have we here? Where have you come from?'

The stranger, still with his glasses in his hands, now recognised the uniform of another *Unteroffizier* and the *Ritterkreuz* at the open collar of Sturm's greatcoat.

'Man, you're dressed up to the nines!'

Sturm was welcomed into the living room. Little Hans and Hilde stood talking outside and then went off into the kitchen.

'Look, see who I've got!' said the other soldier, ushering Sturm into the room.

Sturm gave his name and was introduced to the other guests. It turned out that *Frau* Hanni Wehling was the owner of the shop. Her husband was an official, his brother had his own business, and the other brother was the head of the finance department in Wesel. The Unteroffizier who had greeted Sturm was the red-haired Willi Rohlow. He was a career soldier, and wore the Iron Cross First Class among other decorations. His wife was the sister of Hanni Wehling. The husband of the younger sister Tilli had been listed as missing in the Battle of Stalingrad.

Because Sturm at this time didn't really drink strong spirits, he took only a small glass of wine. The happy atmosphere which had previously been enjoyed was to some extent interrupted by this new arrival as so many of the other guests wanted to talk to him and hear of the exploits of such a highly decorated soldier. Sturm was kept busy by the other guests, but his mind was constantly on Hilde, who still hadn't come into the living room but remained in the kitchen. He excused himself from those around him, wanting to apologize to the lady of the house for gate-crashing the party. She accepted his apologies gracefully, and went to bring in Hilde, her light blonde hair framing a face red with embarrassment. Not seeing her reproachful glance, Sturm went straight to her, clasped both her arms and apologised profusely for his impudent behaviour. He held her fast as if frightened she would pull away, looked at her imploringly, but with laughter in his eyes. It was love at 'second' sight, at least for him.

As it later transpired, Hilde felt the same. At first she had been hesitant, worried in case he was simply another skirt-chaser. The two took their leave of the jolly family celebration. As a small token of thanks, Sturm decided to send round a bouquet of flowers on the following day. Sturm helped to carry the bicycle down to the street and they arranged to meet again the next day.

He used a trip to the dentist in Wesel as an excuse for going into the town, and asked her to keep quiet about their encounter for the time being. His attempt to take her arm failed and she swung herself up onto her bicycle and cycled off. Slowly, Sturm walked back to the hospital. His thoughts were on the farmer's daughter, but also on Maria Torberg, who had shown interest in him too. Little could he guess then that she would die in an air raid in early 1944.

Frau Wehling thanked Sturm for the flowers and young Hans, just 12 years old, was given a signed portrait photo. When he mentioned that he would be seeing Hilde again, the young lad said to him in earnest: '*Unteroffizier* Sturm, I can understand why you have fallen for her. Don't disappoint her, don't play with her. I know her well, she is a fine girl, from a good family!'

Sturm thanked the lad for his advice, to which he did indeed give much thought. He intended to go the farmhouse soon. His days in Wesel were limited, and he may have to return to Aachen as soon as the following week.

The following day, his blonde angel met him outside the dentist's. Hilde had declined to visit him at the hospital where he had his own room, so the two went to the nearest cafe to get to know each other. Sturm suggested they visit her parents' house. He could borrow a bicycle from *Frau* Wehling, as she had already agreed to this. Surprised at this unexpected development, Hilde at first declined. But Sturm held her hand and pled so convincingly that she eventually gave in.

First of all they went to visit a photographer, who took a snapshot of them which Sturm would carry next to his heart. The photographer had greeted him warmly. It had been he who had escorted Sturm to some of his first speeches in Bonn. This was one of Sturm's most prized photos.

43

The Visit

They went by bicycle to Brünen. The farmhouse lay about 2 km from the centre of the village and was reached by a twisting path over the fields. Eventually they reached the farmhouse, from the chimneys of which smoke was slowly drifting, suggesting a warm welcome. Their journey ended at its rear. Both were happy to get out of the cold and biting wind and pushed their bicycles into the long threshing room. To their right, the cows stood alongside each other. The beasts emitted their own warmth and peculiar smell. Right behind them were the pig styes.

Sturm, who rarely showed any inhibition, was tense at the thought of meeting Hilde's family. Through a stall door they entered the front part of the house. They took their gloves off and lay down their hats and coats and rubbed their cold hands. They could hear voices coming from the kitchen off to the left. There, sat in an easy chair, was the farmer Heinrich Neerfeld. His wife Emma stood at the hearth stirring a huge pot of soup. The smell of the soup seemed to fill the room. At the table sat Hilde's sister Elfriede, two years older that Hilde at 21, and her younger brother Heinrich, known as Heini, just 15. Hilde introduced her friend, Hans Sturm. They said 'Hello' to everyone, and Sturm received a warm handshake from the father. He was welcomed like a member of the family and shown to his seat at the table, facing the farmer. The beef soup with meatballs tasted wonderful. The meat was eaten with gherkins and mustard. The main course consisted of roast, potatoes, and vegetables, and was followed by pudding with fresh fruit. Such was their Sunday dinner in the fourth year of the war!

After Lunch, Sturm had a long chat with the farmer. The others round the table listened intently as Sturm learnt that *Herr* Neerfeld had served as a lancer in the First World War, with the *Jäger zu Pferd*.[1] He had been seriously injured by a rifle bullet which had struck him in the left cheek and smashed his upper jaw. After this chat, Sturm was given a tour, visiting all the animals in their stalls, starting with the cows—all of which had pet names—then the cattle, pigs, hens, and hunting dogs in their kennels. Cats ran around shiftily, suspicious of the newcomer. The main farmhouse had two annexes and at the side, a shed for the farm machinery. Set a little off was a small bakehouse in which there some bread was always being prepared.

The fields and pastures around the farmhouse looked bleak and bare at this time of year. The farmhouse had been in the family's possession since the turn of the century. Hilde's great grandfather had married into this property, having come from Neerfeldshof, a farm in the same neighbourhood—though the nearest neighbour was some 800 m away.

From the living area, the door at the front of the house led into a garden. This was used only on special occasions, such as weddings, funerals, and baptisms. Here the family photographs would be taken, and Sturm had the opportunity to look at some of these: heavily bearded men with their wives, children, and grandchildren, as well as happy couples themselves, all in the dress of the period. Oil paintings of earlier ancestors hung in the farmhouse.

Facing south from the garden, around 500 m away, one could see a forest which stretched off into the distance, almost all the way to Damm and Schermbeck. Sturm promised Hilde that he would return again, in the early spring of the New Year at the latest, to see the landscape in its full splendor. In December it got dark quite early. Sturm took his leave of this friendly family who had all made a lasting impression on him. Their home, with all its traditions, made Sturm feel even closer to Hilde. Sturm, born and raised in a big city, knew that he could only find a suitable trade or profession in a large town. If he and Hilde were married, they would have to move to the city, perhaps even into an apartment block. This would be a major change of lifestyle for her. Here, she lived freely, on her own family soil.

The Neerfelds were a large family, the type which typified what was considered 'the best of German stock'. Father Neerfeld had three step sisters. His wife, Hilde's mother, had twelve, all from one mother. All together, they could almost populate an entire village! They were, however, widely scattered. The men were farmers and artisans, both employees and employers, while the women were much prized by their husbands for their healthy savings and considerable dowry. Sturm had never had the chance to meet all of Hilde's family, but in the course of conversations with other members heard all about their progress, marriages, deaths, and births. At a wedding or funeral, rarely fewer than 150 family members would turn up.

After taking his leave from Hilde and making arrangements to meet next day when she would visit him at the hospital, Sturm cycled back to his quarters, his thoughts on the events of that memorable day. On the next day, 20 December 1943, Sturm had three meetings to attend: one was with *Kreisleiter* Kentrat of Wesel, one with *Bürgermeister* Burgner, and finally one with *Landrat* Raim. All made their own personal contributions to Sturm's book. The latter wrote:

To *Ritterkreuzträger* Sturm, I wish that he stands the tests of life equally well as a civilian as he has done at the front, and may the same lucky stars light his way. With the 'right stuff' inside him, he will be master of his life. I wish him also soldier's good fortune. Heil Hitler!

Raim
Landrat, Wesel

The *Landrat*, whom Sturm had already met on his first day at the hospital in Wesel, chatted to Sturm on a whole range of matters, including hunting, which he was passionate about. Sturm explained that, even in his youth, he had accompanied his neighbours on several hunts. Sometimes it had been quite an effort for him, as such a young lad, to get up so early and climb up into the hills. Later, he would serve as a beater and witness the beast being brought back to the track by the successful hunter and the horn being sounded to signal that the hunt over! After too much celebrating on the return journey, Sturm's neighbour had caused a road accident. He subsequently paid for Sturm to learn to drive so that Sturm could get him and two other hunters to a meeting in Sauerland and then back home in one piece.

The *Landrat*, who had listened with interest, asked Sturm his opinion on conservation, and the breeding and rearing of wildlife. Impressed with Sturm's obvious love of nature, the *Landrat* had Sturm complete an application form for a hunting permit and duly handed over the authorised document. Sturm was fully aware of the high honour this represented.

On 21 December Sturm was released from hospital. His meeting with Hilde was brief—too brief for the young couple. Hilde's parting question to Sturm on the platform of the railway station was a heartfelt plea for reassurance.

'Will you write to me? Will we see each other again?'

After a long and tender kiss, Sturm responded firmly, 'I will write to you and we *will* see each other again, you can be sure of it!'

Sturm stayed only one day in Aachen, where he carried out some minor duty appointments. *Unteroffizier* Walter Marx had the post of Careers Advisor for Officers and NCOs well in hand. Sturm had no time to visit any schools, but he did manage to distribute some recruiting material.

From 23 December onwards, Sturm was given a weeks leave in Dortmund. He went twice to the theatre with his mother. Two seats were always available for him, and should he need them he had only to ask. In the same theatre box, he had gotten to know the liquor manufacturer Christian Peters and his wife. He had visited the distillery and been given some bottles of strong liqueur. He went with his friend, the *Ritterkreuzträger* Udo Cordes, on 27 December. Peters mused in Sturm's book:

Alcohol, I'm pleased to say, is good for many ailments. Yet it punishes me terribly when I use it without due care and consideration!

In the evening Cordes and Sturm went to the reunion of former friends from the *Oberrealschule* with two bottles of the strong liquor. The reunion was always held on the third day of Christmas, and had been founded by Dr Jäde. All former students, and later also the students from the lower school, made every effort not to miss these reunions. Dr Jäde continued to keep in touch with Sturm even after he had returned to the Front, sending him a newsletter in which all important matters were covered. There, he could learn about those who had got married, had birthdays, been wounded or killed, or received decorations. Of twenty-three students of the combined Classes A and B, only fourteen were still alive: almost one third having been killed, taken prisoner, or were missing in action. Cordes was from Class A and Sturm from Class B. Also in Class B were Hans Kortmann of the Kortmann Furniture House and Willi Wilms of the Wilms brickworks. Both were bigger and older than Sturm and first after two 'laps of honour' (repeat years) had come into Sturm's class. Included in the thirty members were also four teachers: Dr Jäde, Dr Richter, Dr Althoff (who Sturm knew from his boyhood as the teacher lived only three houses along from him), and Dr Göbel (who lived in the house directly behind Sturm's).

Sturm got on very well with Dr Jäde, who taught Natural Sciences. Jäde had invited Sturm to join a newly formed club, the *Sternfreunde*. Here he lectured with great clarity on astronomy, and very soon all the students could draw up a star chart of the northern hemisphere. Sturm remembered a holiday in Garmisch-Partenkirchen. One night, he could not sleep, and dressed himself in warm clothing and went out on to the terrace. The house lay under the highest peak in the area. It had snowed all day long, but still the skies were clear and the stars easy to see. At this altitude, around 2,800 m above sea level, and without the lights of a city, the stars seemed ever so near. Sturm saw the Milky Way, thought of the hundreds of millions of stars, and considered that this was all only one galaxy among millions. It was difficult to believe that only here, on this tiny planet, was there intelligent life.

This meeting was a particularly successful one, not only for the former students, but also for the 'old gentlemen'. For Cordes and Sturm, it was their second meeting since December 1942. They knew each other not just from their schooldays, but also from their time in the *Jungvolk* and the *Marine-Hitlerjugend*. After leaving school, Cordes had volunteered for the *Luftwaffe* and had become a career soldier. He wrote in Sturm's book:

> Whomsoever loves life, who is kissed by sin, gives their heart to the ladies all without fear, then if death greets us, that is a flyer's lot. In commemoration of drunken nights in Dortmund from 23 to 29 December 1943. Your drinking companion, Udo Cordes *Oberleutnant* and *Ritterkreuzträger*!

Sturm and Cordes could not know that they would spend four years in captivity together in a Soviet prison camp after the German surrender in 1945. Cordes was allowed to return home in 1949, even though the Russians knew of his military exploits. Sturm was held for a further 4½ years, after one of his own 'good Comrades' sought to curry favour with the Soviets by denouncing Sturm for his previous patriotic lectures in support of the German war effort. In the week after Christmas, Sturm had a promise to keep to a friend of his father, Hans Roth, in between his military duties. Roth's business made equipment for the *Wehrmacht* and Sturm had already received two fine uniforms and a greatcoat from them. The Dortmund newspaper *Tremonia* featured an article on the following day, showing

Sturm with two seamstresses. 'One of our Dortmund *Ritterkreuzträger*, *Unteroffizier* Hans Sturm, after a few introductory words from the *Gefolgschaftsführer* Roth, spoke of his experiences in the East,' began an explanatory report on his appearance at the factory. It continued,

> With breathless attention the audience listened to his concise description of a simple fighting soldier who had surpassed himself in battle. A *Wehrmacht* like ours is no small thing to have, said Sturm in closing, and we need the help of all of you

Sturm had given this speech without being asked to do so by the military authorities, as a simple favour to a friend.

Sturm spent 30 December with his parents. It was a peaceful evening, spent in reflection under the Christmas tree. Foremost in his mind was Hilde Neerfeld, as he described to his parents his friendly reception at the farmhouse in great detail. Sturm's mother and father were particularly happy that he seemed to have overcome the grievous loss of his fiancée, Silvia. Sturm spoke at length with his father about the war, the dreadful losses, and Germany's almost certain defeat. They were silent for a while, drinking their brandy wine and looking at the flickering candlelight. On evenings such as these, Sturm's father would often play the violin, an instrument which he had more or less mastered after considerable practise. His mother, on the other hand, was an accomplished piano player, and remained so until she died at the age of 94. In an attempt to lighten the mood, Sturm's mother played some Christmas songs, but the men were not inclined to sing along. Yet his mother was on edge, too, like so many other women. Both men in her family were at war, and her husband had now been away in Russia longer even than her soldier son. The evening passed too quickly, and in the morning it was time for Sturm to return to Aachen.

44

New Year 1943

On New Year's Eve, Sturm met up with some friends at the Hotel Horchen. There were sixteen people, including six married couples, plus of course the hotel owner and his wife. Some men were in uniform. The time slipped by, and it was nearly midnight when Horchen had a bright idea.

'We should take some bottles with us and go over to Carlchen Müller.'

The others looked over in surprise as he added, 'But we won't go along the road, we'll go over the mountain!'

Free-flowing alcohol filled them with bravado, and no one contradicted the plan. No one gave a thought to the heavy snow which lay on the ground, even though the road had been cleared and it would only have taken half an hour to reach their destination the sensible way. On the mountain side the snow lay about half a metre deep. The hotel owner and some of the others stomped determinedly through the snow; then came the women, and then Sturm who escorted the owner's wife at the end. Torchlight eerily lit the footpath and the heavily laiden trees occasionally lost their covering of snow as the merrymakers passed, startling them and giving rise to embarrassed laughter.

The jovial atmosphere took a knock when one of the women slipped, skidded sideways, and landed under a fallen branch, hurting herself. Laughing, she was helped up to her feet by her husband, but gave a gasp of pain and slumped down again. Perhaps she had sprained her ankle, or even broken it. Sturm hurried on down to their destination and returned with a litter. A doctor was called and arrived soon afterwards with an ambulance which took the unfortunate woman and her husband off to hospital. The doctor had bound the injured ankle, but only an X-ray would reveal if the bone was broken.

The rest of the party continued on their way and were met at Karl Müller's house with punch and mulled wine. They gratefully dried their damp clothes in front of the open fireplace. Some women had taken their shoes off for the journey, as they really weren't suitable for walking through the snow. *Herr* Müller accepted the bottles the guests had brought with them and, amused, served them bottles from the very best of his own stock. If Sturm was annoyed at the pointless and dangerous trek across the countryside, he kept it to himself so as not to spoil the occasion.

It was the early hours of the morning when the party finally broke up and the guests returned to the hotel, this time along the road, singing merrily as they went.

On 14 January 1944, Sturm gave a speech at the Army NCO School in Düren. Oberst D. R. Wüst left the following approbation in his book:

For you excellent speech at the Düren Army NCO School, I give you my grateful thanks. You have, through your concise and exacting detail in describing the detailed work of the infantryman, ensured that the *Unteroffiziere* candidates here benefit from these personal front experiences, and realise the urgency and necessity to learn well from their training.

If Sturm was in Düren, he took riding lessons whenever possible, now as in the past. The riding instructor was *Rittmeister* A. D. Werner Knobloch, who called Sturm a 'bloody beginner'. It was of little interest to him that Sturm already had some riding experience, or that during his time in Russia as a company messenger he had often used a Russian Panje horse. Sturm still had to begin by grooming the horse and cleaning out the stables like a novice. Only then was he allowed to sit on the animal and take it over some basic jumps and obstacles.

At midnight on 14 January, Sturm was at the military district command in Düren. The commander, *Oberst* Streibel wrote in his book,

Mutual trust guarantees the comradeship between officers and men. This is a pre-requisite for the fighting spirit of the troops. In commemoration of your military recruitment duties at the district command.

The book was also signed by the divisional commander *Generalmajor* Gruner who, in peacetime, was the senior military officer in Düren.

At his hotel, Sturm had got to know three other gentlemen. They met once a week when time allowed to play skat. Sturm had happened to be watching them play when one of the number, a Dr Blun, had been called away to a serious automobile accident. The other two gents invited Sturm to sit in for him until Blun return. He gladly agreed, as he hadn't had the chance to play skat for ages. When Dr Blun did reappear, Sturm stayed in the game. After some time, they gave up playing cards, and drank a few glasses of wine. Dr Blun drank a little too much and it was necessary for Sturm and one of the others to make sure he got home safely. They were met by Dr Blun's wife and his 16-year-old son. The wife made some strong coffee, which didn't do much to wake up this homecomer. The son asked Sturm for a signed photo and he was happy to oblige, after the youngster explained to him that he heard him speak at an open public meeting. Dr Blun invited Sturm to a family celebration on 20 January. In commemoration of the happy event, they all made entries in Sturm's book.

It was an unfortunate coincidence that the young Klaus Blun would become a fellow inmate with Sturm at the Soviet labour camp in Tqibuli. Sturm recognised him and helped him wherever possible. The other captured comrades in their cell gave him what they could spare, too. The youth, on his way to becoming a man, was always hungry. In thanks, Klaus kept the room neat and clean for them, helped with the washing and delousing of clothes, sewed on buttons, and mended torn socks. One evening, Sturm came back to their room after work and noticed an elaborate leather writing case he had been given by a comrade was missing. The fellow inmates, all officers, were helpless. Because nothing else was missing, there was no question of telling the Russians. They asked Klaus whether he had taken it, but he denied being able to commit such a terrible offence. Some time later, Klaus was spotted trying to sell Sturm's writing case to a trader in a Russian market. Friends of Sturm's reported the incident, but Klaus once again denied the theft. Sturm didn't want him punished so let the matter rest, but he insisted that Klaus should never enter their lodgings again. The young man, by then fully grown, and taller and of heavier build than Sturm, henceforth avoided all contact with them and any of the other German prisoners. Shame and self-reproach drove him to despair. He was often seen approaching the fence of the camp, a forbidden zone, tensing himself for the feel of the Soviet guards' bullets. He gradually grew thinner and weaker, his meagre rations now unsupplemented by gifts of extra food from his comrades, and eventually took ill. Never fully recovering, he died in hospital before he could be released. Sturm attended the burial ceremony at the cemetery. When, in September 1946, Sturm was allowed to write home for the first time, his first card was to Hilde at her home in Brünen. His second went to his parents, who knew nothing of his fate other than that he had gone missing in action. His third card, obtained in trade with fellow prisoners, went to the parents of Klaus Blun.

PART THREE

Götterdämmerung

45

A Fresh Chapter

Time went by quickly and a message arrived at the Hotel Horchen instructing Sturm to return to Aachen. There, in the offices of *Infanterie Ersatz Bataillon 473*, were two letters waiting for him. The first was from *Oberstleutnant* Gierlich in Münster. It released Sturm from his duties in giving patriotic speeches and as a recruiter, and thanked him for his efforts in both areas. It also wished him well for his return to active service in Italy. Sturm had in fact almost put all thoughts of *Oberst* Rohr out of his mind. Now his transfer had been rushed through. The second letter announced his transfer, without delay, to *Grenadier Ersatz Bataillon 88* in Fulda, prior to which a ten-day spell of leave had been authorised. Some of this time would have to be allocated to completing his studies, and an arrangement was made with the engineering school to speed up the completion of his course. Taking into account his voluntary return to combat, he was allowed to sit his final examination early, and after a short test was pronounced as a qualified engineer with a rating of 'very good'. Thereafter, Sturm had to say his goodbyes to his comrades and acquaintances. His friend *Unteroffizier* Walter Marx got a new boss in the person of an elderly *Leutnant* who was unfit for front-line service due to war wounds. Sturm also paid a brief visit to *Frau* Rohr, who asked Sturm to pass on her greetings to her husband and wished him well for the future. She advised him not to take the *Oberst* too seriously. He gave the appearance of being stern, but in reality was very kind-hearted. Travelling through the afternoon and into the evening, Sturm arrived at Hilde's farm. The whole Neerfeld family, not least his Hilde, regretted that he could not stay longer and would soon be in danger again. His promise to write often was only a small consolation.

From Brünen he went on a short leave to Garmisch-Partenkirchen. There, he reported to the *Gebirgsjäger* barracks, where he was given quarters. The battalion commander, *Hauptmann* Rusterer, gave him *Feldwebel* Johann Ott as a guide for his trip up into the mountains. The days went all too quickly. One evening was spent in a visit to Heidi, whereupon he was introduced to her boyfriend, a skiing instructor and student from Munich—a nice lad, Sturm thought. Both vowed that their meeting had been 'love at first sight'. Sturm was delighted for them.

On the following day, Sturm and *Feldwebel* Ott went off on the rack-railway. They wanted to travel via Höllentalhütte and the Waxenstein to Grainau. A dreadful accident prevented them from completing their journey, however, and brought the hitherto pleasant trip to an unpleasant conclusion.

A group of young lads from a WE camp on the way to the Knorrhütte had been buried alive by an avalanche. There had been twelve of them, moving upwards through snow a full metre deep when the avalanche had swept down from the higher level and buried some of them. A rescue mission swung into action as soon as the alarm was raised. *Feldwebel* Ott and Sturm joined in with the rescue team and, using snow shovels and sounding poles, tried to locate and administer first aid to the injured. Some of the boys were able to dig themselves free, or could be helped from the snow. For others, the rescue party came too late. A snow shower developed into a severe storm, hampering the rescue efforts as visibility was drastically reduced. *Gebirgsjäger* and another rescue column arrived on the scene, but the efforts had to be called off due to the weather. The bodies of the leader of the group and one of the boys were only found several days later. In the late afternoon, Sturm and Otto returned to Garmisch Partenkirchen. These events had left them in a sombre frame of mind.

Sturm said his goodbyes to Heidi and her parents and returned to Dortmund, where he could only spend one night. His parents, to whom he had already explained his posting to Italy, were none too happy, and even his father chastised him for wanting to return to combat duties. The evening was peaceful nevertheless, his mother sewing while he and his father played cards over a few glasses of toddy.

In Fulda, Sturm only spent a few hours with *Grenadier Ersatz Regiment 88*, while his travel papers were made ready. *Oberst* Rohr had exerted some influence at the military district headquarters in Münster and Aachen, and especially at the unit base in Fulda, so that any further delay in setting off was out of the question. Sturm was fortunate in getting a window seat, facing the direction of travel, in the train to Munich. In the event, however, he didn't see much anyway, sleeping through most of the journey. In Munich there was a three-hour delay while he waited for a connection, so he paid a visit to the Hotel Europa for a meal, where he was recognised by the chef and several of the staff from his stop-off on his way to San Remo the previous year.

The next stage of the journey, to Mailand, went without hitch. Once there, however, there was a considerable delay. Sturm sat on his luggage in the waiting room of the station. Suddenly, a *Feldwebel* of the *Feldgendarmerie* entered, picked up one of Sturm's bags, and told him to follow. A little surprised and somewhat apprehensive, he followed the *Feldwebel* into the duty room. There he was greeted warmly by the other military policemen. They had spotted him in the waiting room looking rather lost and alone, and clearly unable to leave his baggage unattended. The *Feldwebel* explained that he would have at least four hours to wait, as the engine had been severely damaged in an attack by partisans. He asked to see Sturm's travel orders, and left the room. Sturm wondered what was going on, but the *Feldwebel* soon returned and handed them back. Sturm glanced over them and was astonished to see that he had made entries explaining that Sturm had been delayed due to a bombing raid in Munich, and consequential damage to the track. The signature was unreadable, but the stamp of the powerful *Feldgendarmerie* was clearly legible. At first, Sturm was angry at this falsification of his papers, but when he realised that they were only trying to be kind and give him a little more time before reaching the front where death could come quickly enough, he decided that this deviation from the truth was perhaps not so bad. He wondered what *Oberst* Rohr would make of it, though! He then happily joined an *ad hoc* party organised by the *Feldgendarmerie* and two other soldiers in transit to Italy—even some Italian girls joined in, and a wild night ensued.

Without regrets Sturm continued on his journey to Genoa the next day. At the reporting station he learnt that his unit was no longer in combat, but due to heavy losses had been pulled back. Now it lay in Genoa and on the coast adjacent to France. Sturm was pleased not to be going straight into a combat situation, but to be stationed on the western Italian riviera was a real surprise. Having spent his leave in this area only the year before, he could hardly have guessed that he would return here so soon. The regimental staff were based in Pontedecimo, a small village north of Genoa. He wondered which duties he would be given when he joined his unit.

After a telephone conversation with the regimental staff, a driver came and picked him up. *Oberleutnant* Rehbein, the commander of the staff company, greeted the highly decorated NCO in a very friendly manner. He checked his marching orders with the entries made by the *Feldgendarmerie* explaining the late arrival. He thought that Sturm had had an adventurous journey, but didn't want to know any more. His expression was enough to tell Sturm that he wasn't remotely taken in by the explanation on his papers!

On reporting to *Oberst* Rohr, Sturm found his reception rather brusque. His new commander greeted him with a terse 'It's about time you got here!' Still, Sturm managed to pass on greetings from the *Oberst*'s wife before being dismissed. On his first meeting with Rohr in the air raid shelter at Aachen Station, and the subsequent journey to Berlin, Sturm had formed an impression of him as a fatherly figure, with his soft-spoken voice and gold-rimmed glasses. Here in the field, Sturm hadn't exactly expected

Sturm in Italy with his new company.

to be greeted with a hug, but neither had he anticipated such a sharp dismissal. Sturm then recalled *Frau* Rohr's cautioning—that her husband sometimes seemed harsh, but that inside he was good-natured. Sturm subsequently heard this from other officers in the regiment. *Oberst* Rohr's bark was much worse than his bite!

The regimental HQ was in a villa near a gorge which opened out to the sea, giving a view of Genoa. On his arrival, Sturm still held the rank of *Unteroffizier*. Shortly afterwards, he was promoted to *Fahnenjunkerfeldwebel*. As OIII on the regimental staff of *Infanterie Regiment 871*, he was appointed Officer in Charge of Defensive Constructions. The necessary maps were provided at a briefing with *Oberleutnant* Rehbein, with whom he quickly established a good working relationship. *Infanterie Regiment 871*, of *356 Infanterie Division*, had been withdrawn from the front line in severe need of a period of rest and refitting. Replacements were drafted in to build up its strength again. Its task was now that of securing its area of responsibility and building new defence lines in the area around Genoa and along the coast to the west, via Savona and Albenga, and eventually from Alassio and San Remo to Ventimiglia, next to the French border.

For Sturm, his new duties were a tremendous change when compared to his former service as an infantryman. He had to visit every sector and compile a register of defensive positions, strengths in men, weapons, equipment, *etc*. In his weekly report to the regimental commander, he had to paint a broad picture of the situation, restricting himself to the essential facts. His area of responsibility also encompasseed airstrips and radio stations, as well as Italian police posts. In alarm situations, his unit was responsible for co-ordinating and concentrating various elements, and getting them ready for action. A further important task was to visit all bridges and roads and check their suitability for heavy traffic movements and their load-bearing capacity, and preparations for demolition, from the coast right into the hinterland. His engineering training helped, and he had a technical advisor, *Leutnant* Marker, the commander of the *Pioniere* platoon. When Sturm reported to the regimental staff, he took with him two skilled cartographers who prepared detailed maps for use in his presentation.

After the day's duties were done, Sturm played cards most evenings. *Doppelkopf* was a regular feature, a game for four players which used forty cards. Sturm enjoyed playing cards; though this particular game was new to him, he picked it up quickly. He had learnt to play card games at a very early age, when his father and his friend needed a third man for a round of skat. It was in this context that Sturm saw another side to *Oberst* Rohr, who *Leutnant* Marker and the others thought the toughest commander in the whole *Armeekorps*. When playing cards with his men, he relaxed considerably, and came across as remarkably benevolent. When Sturm escorted *Oberst* Rohr on inspection trips, the fierce martinet was once again supplanted by a man who opened up about his personal life—his wife, his son who was killed in France, and of his other son, now blinded and mortally wounded. He once moaned that, despite his length of service and experience, he had not been promoted to *Generalmajor*. Sturm was a good listener, though he often wondered at the frankness with which his commander spoke. Still, he expected that everyone had the right to let off steam from time to time.

46

Partisans

The Italian riviera was a beautiful place, but life there was made uncomfortable by the presence of partisans. Even regimental HQ suffered from their attentions.

Sturm often used a heavy motorcycle on his duty trips and when acting as a courier to division. On one occasion, a shot rang out as he was driving along alone. The bullet just clipped the shoulder of his leather jacket. A second shot rang out and a rifle bullet hit the rear tyre of his motorbike. Sturm lost control as the bike slewed sideways across the street and he flung himself off into the scant protection of a roadside ditch. He didn't know from which direction the shot had come, and having no chance of gaining better cover or escaping, elected to play dead.

Two partisans emerged and slid down the slope on the opposite side of the road, making their way towards him. They spoke briefly and then one remained behind to give his comrade cover. Normally, Sturm would have been armed with a machine pistol and could have made short work of these two. On this day, however, he had only his pistol. Sturm lay on his belly, the pistol in his hand concealed by his body. The strain was almost unbearable as he heard the partisan approach him. Would he pump a few shots into the apparently lifeless German just to make sure? The Italian strolled over, apparently convinced there was no danger—he didn't realize he was dealing with a hard-bitten veteran of the Russian Front, however. Sturm rolled over in a flash and raised his pistol, firing off two rapid shots. The first hit the nearest partisan full in the face. He fell back, dead before he hit the ground. The second shot hit the other Partisan in the chest. As he raised his machine pistol to loose off a burst at him, Sturm's third shot knocked him off his feet. The burst of fire from his machine pistol zipped harmlessly over Sturm's head.

Sturm had escaped the ambush with nothing more than some minor grazes and bruising down his left side. Only his forearm and shoulder ached somewhat. The back of his left hand had been cut as it was scraped across a jagged stone when he fell from his bike, and a few drops of blood smeared his hand. Sturm mused that this minor scrape would count officially as a wound received in action, while the first rifle shot—which came so close to ending his life—would not even be recorded. Sturm was about 3 km from the next village, where the regiment had located one of its companies. A march to this next unit was spared him, however, when a motorcycle combination and a light truck appeared, slowing down as they arrived on the scene.

The *Landser* got out, greeted the *Ritterkreuzträger* as they took in the sight of the two dead partisans sightlessly staring up into the sky, faces contracted in pain. The bodies were loaded into the truck and Sturm got in too, giving the soldiers a brief report of the action. They looked at him in wonder and heartily congratulated him on his success. It was not the first time that his journeys had been threatened with such danger. Once, while travelling with *Oberst* Rohr, their car had been the victim of a concealed roadside bomb. The driver was killed and the co-driver wounded, but Sturm and Rohr got off with little more than a fright. Sturm looked at the bodies of the two Italians. They were typically good-looking lads. But partisans were not a problem specific to Italians: there were also Spaniards, Serbs, Russians, and even a few German deserters among them. Sturm often asked himself what drove the latter group to such actions. He thought back to Russia, where the partisans were considered heroes, yet were often hated by the locals because of the reprisals that their actions provoked and their plunder of the local supplies. Sturm believed that many of them were idealists; he would not classify them as 'bandits', unlike the authorities.

On hearing his report, *Oberst* Rohr insisted that from now on he use a car with a driver and a two-man escort. They were to be armed with machine pistols and a machine gun. Sometimes, they did indeed have to defend themselves vigorously, and on one occasion one man was wounded and the vehicle destroyed by fire. *Leutnant* Merker, who had often escorted Sturm on his trips, was lightly wounded in an action with his pioneers. The regimental commander ordered that Sturm, if only for a short time, take over as platoon commander. To Sturm, it seemed they were asking too much of him, a junior ranked infantryman, to carry out the tasks of an officer of the pioneers. It was an almost impossible task. *Oberleutnant* Rehbein put his six section leaders at his disposal. They knew Sturm of course, having encountered him in the course of his duties. These *Unteroffizere* were all, like Sturm, long-serving soldiers. The oldest, Paul Mohr, had eight years' service and wore, among his other combat decorations, four tank destruction strips on his left arm.[1] He was a bulky, strong man and without doubt a good fighter, but he did have his faults. He drank readily and too often, and had been twice demoted because of his binging sprees. Had he not drunk so much, he would have made *Oberfeldwebel* long since.

Sturm's success in his encounter with the partisans was celebrated with his friends in a small tavern in town. One of the others warned Sturm about Paul and his unpredictability once he'd had a few too many. He showed him two scars on his left calf, flesh wounds caused by shots fired off by Mohr in a drunken stupor. Paul had been saved from severe punishment by *Leutnant* Merkel, who reported the incident as a genuine accident. Paul had gotten off with a severe warning. He had been so drunk he hadn't realised the potential consequences of his actions. As the celebration reached its peak, it was decided that a break for some food would be advisable.

Sturm found himself in the kitchen with the *Unteroffizier* who had warned him about Mohr. The two had decided to help the small, plump Italian owner prepare some food. The two were startled when a shot rang out.

'That'll be Paul!' said the *Unteroffizier*. 'Be careful if you go up against him,' he added, as the two made their way in the direction of the shot.

As they hurried along the corridor towards the dining room, they spotted Mohr in the first room, pistol in hand. He had shot a small canary in a cage hung from the wall. The landlady cried out in anguish over the loss of her beloved pet, and Sturm could only calm her with great effort and the promise to pay for any damage and a new bird. She was the least of their problems, however, as Sturm turned to face the drunken *Unteroffizier* who stood grinning at them challengingly. Everyone was anxious to see how the new platoon commander would handle the situation. Paul was full to the brim with alcohol.

Sturm went over and clapped him on the shoulder, saying: 'That was a good shot Paul, but it's a pity about the poor bird. Anyone could have hit that target though!'

Not having got the reprimand he had expected, he looked bewildered.

'What? Are you suggesting a competition?' he asked in amazement.

'Why not?' was Sturm's response, much to the others' surprise.

Sturm walked over towards Paul gesturing for him to hand over the pistol. He pointed to a lamp next door in the second room across the corridor. The lamp was strung with a shade made from small wooden beads. In the centre was a bulb, as small as a hen's egg.

'We'll shoot at that,' said Sturm, ignoring the landlady's jabbering protests.

Paul Mohr looked quizzically at Sturm then shrugged his shoulders as if to say, 'OK, but on your head be it!'

'You have the first shot!' he said, and handed the pistol over to Sturm.

Unseen by most of the rest of the company, Sturm ejected the magazine from the pistol. It now only had the one single round in its chamber. He handed the pistol back to Paul.

'No,' he replied, 'I made the challenge, so you get first shot!'

The fat *Unteroffizier* looked at the pistol, then at Sturm. Looking round at the others he shrugged his shoulders again. Why was he giving him the pistol back? And why was he challenging him to shoot? Slowly, Mohr tried his best to stand straight and take aim, only barely succeeding in his drunken daze. The pistol roared and the beads on the lampshade only fluttered slightly from the pressure wave of the bullet as it sped past to bury itself in the wall behind the lamp.

Paul turned round and gave the pistol back to Sturm.

'That's hardly a fair competition. I'm too drunk. Now you don't even need to fire. It would be a shame to smash the pretty lamp!'

Sturm stuck the pistol back in its holster, which hung with its belt from a hook on the wall. Everyone was pleased and relieved that this potential disaster had been defused so diplomatically. Sturm had avoided having to pull rank on his drunken comrade, knowing any disciplinary action would surely have resulted in the severest penalties for Mohr and would no doubt have damaged the good relations he had established with the others in the platoon. Laughing, the rest of the comrades clapped both men on the shoulder and led them back to the party. The previously cheerful atmosphere was quickly restored and the wine flowed again until, as the night wore on, Sturm eventually called a timely halt to the festivities.

Unfortunately, there were still repercussions to come over that night's events. The rabbits which had formed the basis of their meal had been bought from an Italian civilian. The skins had been removed before they had been bought, and the *Unteroffizier* who had bought them wasn't even totally convinced they were actually rabbits. It would not have been the first time that a skinned cat had been offered as a substitute! The problem was that the rabbits had in fact been stolen and the skins, rather than being buried, had been carelessly thrown over the thief's garden wall into a bush. Two scavenging dogs had found the skins and been seen by passers-by fighting over them. The Italian was soon discovered and arrested. The situation was aggravated by the fact that the rabbits had belonged to the sister at a nearby hospital who, now full of righteous indignation, demanded the severest punishment for the thief. The thief tried to put the blame on the Germans, insisting he had stolen them under orders from an *Unteroffizier* in the pioneer platoon. The Italian police and *Oberleutnant* Rehbein, as commander of the regimental staff company, were forced to deal with the case formally. After long and somewhat embarrassing interrogations over this 'serious crime', the police satisfied themselves that the Italian was the sole culprit and that the *Unteroffizier* had known nothing of where the rabbit had come from. The Italian was punished—how and where Sturm neither knew nor cared. He was just happy that there had been no ramifications for himself as the person responsible for the party or the *Unteroffizier* in question. The men were all given a stern warning by *Oberleutnant* Rehbein about being careful in future when buying anything from strangers.

The period during which he served with the pioneers was a valuable experience for Sturm, though he would admit in truth to being little more than an observer, watching and learning as they went about their tasks. Sturm developed a firm friendship with Mohr, who became his second in command as deputy platoon commander. Eventually, *Leutnant* Merker took control of the platoon again having recovered from his wounds, and Sturm returned to his primary task as officer in charge of construction of new defensive positions (which *Oberleutnant* Rehbein had carried out in his absence). A small celebration was held to honour Sturm's return—this time, without further incidents!

Sturm's most significant experience in anti-partisan warfare came in May 1944. A few squads from the pioneer platoon—the bulk of the platoon, in fact—were given a special task in the area further along the coast. The men were to act as supplementary reinforcements for the escort troops travelling with a large weapons and munitions convoy. On a winding road snaking through a steep gorge—along which Sturm had already travelled many times—partisans had prepared an ambush. Their spies had obviously tipped them off about the contents of the convoy and the strength of its escorts. The attack, when it came, caught the Germans completely by surprise and gave them little opportunity to defend themselves. In a classic ambush, both the lead and tail vehicles were taken out first in a furious hail of fire. The whole column was soon a raging inferno as the Germans desperately sought cover. Several were killed or wounded in the first moments of the attack through gunfire and grenade shrapnel. The officer in command of the column, a *Hauptmann*, was among those killed. *Leutnant* Berger, the pioneer platoon commander, was severely wounded. Of the four *Unteroffiziere* present, two were dead and one badly injured. Only Paul Mohr had so far escaped without a scratch.

Oberst Rohr was informed of the attack by radio and immediately ordered Sturm to lead a small relief force using two armoured cars from the regiment's recce unit. On arriving at the scene, Sturm's unit immediately opened fire at the partisans' suspected positions on the hillside opposite. The lead armoured car, in which Sturm travelled, raced to the middle of the column. Sturm recognised Mohr, who appeared to be gathering his remaining combat-worthy troops to launch a counter-attack. As Sturm dismounted from his vehicle, Mohr looked around at the destruction surrounding him with a bitter smile on his face. Under cover of heavy machine gun fire from the armoured cars, Mohr gave Sturm a brief report on the situation. Sturm took command and led the counter-attack, his experience in close combat on the Russian Front paying dividends against the much less experienced enemy, who were eventually driven off after a furious fight. They were greater in number than had been suspected and fought bravely, but were no match for the Germans once reinforcements under the command of a highly experienced 'Front Fighter' arrived.[2]

Unteroffizier Mohr and his men, still in a raging fury at the destruction of their convoy and the death of so many of their comrades, were in no mood to show mercy to the partisans who had been captured. Sturm had to intervene to prevent them being shot on the spot, an intervention to which Mohr took great exception as he roundly cursed the partisans, the war, and the God who allowed such killing.

Later, after calming down back in their quarters, Mohr grudgingly admitted that, had their roles been reversed, he too might have become a partisan to fight what he saw as his country's enemies. He later did in fact get his long overdue promotion to *Oberfeldwebel*, and took command of the pioneer platoon.

In addition to those killed in the initial ambush, one more was killed and three wounded during the counter-attack. In total, eight died and twenty were wounded in the partisan attack. The enemy suffered only three dead and seven wounded. What was even more disturbing to Sturm was that he later learnt that in a nearby village two men had been arrested after being denounced by their own neighbours. They were alleged to have been involved either in the ambush itself, or in its preparation, and were shot without further ado. No real effort was made to establish whether the allegations made against them were true. Sturm was disgusted at this summary justice. Rumours were already spreading of such actions, and would do little to improve relations with the Italian population.

In regimental orders and in the unit *War Diary*, *Fahnenjunker Oberfeldwebel* Sturm was praised for his actions in driving off the partisans on that day, as well as for numerous other actions in the preceding months. He was awarded the Anti-Partisan Badge, but in protest at the brutal executions of the two suspects refused point blank to wear it.[3] This was taken very badly by *Oberst* Rohr and the other officers on the regimental staff. He was told in no uncertain terms that his behavior was an insult to the military leadership who had instituted the award, as well as to comrades who had been killed or wounded in this incident. The previously excellent relationship between Sturm and *Oberst* Rohr now became decidedly frosty, and only relaxed somewhat when the *Oberst* heard that he had finally gained his belated promotion to *Generalmajor*. He had to move to Berlin to take up his new duties, but before he left made an entry in Sturm's book.

> For your service with the staff of *Infanterie Regiment 871*, my thanks. For your future, I wish you a soldier's good fortune. Best wishes and a safe homecoming, Rohr, *Generalmajor* and regimental commander.

Snapshot taken in Italy in May 1944.

After Rohr's entry came dedications or autographs from many other officers and NCOs of the regimental staff. Paul Mohr, his right hand heavily bandaged, simply made three large X's with his left hand. He had been wounded in further attacks by partisans since, but had refused recuperation leave. The last entry was by the Italian Piero Perzoli, owner of the villa in which the Regimental Staff was quartered.

On the orders of the regimental commander, Sturm was transferred to *Ersatz Unit 88* in Fulda, from where he would be sent to the *Kriegsschule* at Hagenau. Regrettably, he was unable fulfill his wish to visit the Villa Zirio in San Remo before his departure, even for just one day, to say goodbye to all his friends there. The memories of his visit there the previous year were still vivid. A proper visit would probably have been possible had he remained, and had his unit been pulled back to the rear area around Savona, Albenga, Imperia, and San Remo. This had at one point seemed a distinct possibility. Luck was on Sturm's side once again, however. On reaching the *Ersatz* unit, he learnt that two battalions of the regiment, along with the regimental staff, had been moved up to the front line just after his departure and suffered heavy losses. *Oberleutnant* Rehbein and *Oberfeldwebel* Paul Mohr were among the first to be killed.

47

An Unexpected Meeting

Before reporting to *Ersatz Bataillon 88* in Fulda, five soldiers from *Grenadier Regiment 871*, including Sturm, were given a special task. They were to contact *Hitlerjugend Bann 761* in Melsingen near Kassel, the sponsoring unit of the regiment. Their first move was to report to the *Generalkommando* in Kassel. There, *Leutnant* Thelen, *Unteroffizier* Wagner, *Obergefreiter* Sczensny, *Gefreiter* Löffert, and Sturm met with the *Hauptmann* who was the liaison officer with the *Hitlerjugend* unit. He in turn had been ordered to bring the five to *Oberst im Generalstab* Schiffer. In conversations with the *Oberst*, Sturm learnt that the commanding general of the area was *General* Schellert! Sturm could hardly conceal his delight that he would have the chance to meet with his old divisional commander from *253 Infanterie Division* once again. Everyone listened intently as Sturm described how as a simple machine-gunner and later *Gefreiter*, his battalion commander had awarded him the Iron Cross Second Class and then loaned him his own Iron Cross First Class, won during the Battle of France, until his recommendation that Sturm be granted the award was approved by Schellert!

Another time, he told his listeners, Sturm had been insolent with three officers who had shown up at the Front dressed in fine winter clothing, while the exhausted troops shivered in the same summer uniforms they had worn when the German armies had first swarmed into Russia in July 1941. These swaggering gentlemen in their fur coats and felt boots had been taken by Sturm for rear echelon types who came to the Front for a sniff around from time to time. The officers had full beards, fur hats, and upturned collars. In addition, they wore no rank insignia. Sturm explained how he had been shocked to discover he had been mouthing off at his divisional commander. There had been no consequences for Sturm, as the kindly Schellert forgave his insolence and appreciated the reasons for his bitter outburst. This incident, too, had become the talk of the division and led to Sturm being known as a bit of a 'wild dog'. He gave his listeners other examples of his wartime experiences, some which showed him in a negative and others in a positive light, all leading up to the award of the German Cross and *Ritterkreuz* of the Iron Cross. Sturm was anxious to discover whether the *General* would recognize him.

The five soldiers were eventually brought before the *General*, who were each introduced by name by his *Adjutant*. From a few paces back, Schellert looked thoughtfully at the men, then addressed them wishing them well for their meeting with *Hitlerjugend Bann 761*. Then he spoke directly to Sturm.

'*Feldwebel* Sturm, you are a *Ritterkreuzträger* and have the *Deutsches Kreuz in Gold*. When did you earn them?'

'Two years ago, *Herr General*.'

'With what rank?'

'As a *Gefreiter*, *Herr General*!'

'You were on the Eastern Front? In which sector?'

'Middle sector, *Herr General*, around Olinin, then in Rzhew, *Herr General*!'

'My *253 Division* was there too!'

'I know, *Herr General*!'

'What division were you with when you earned your *Ritterkreuz*?'

'With *6 Infanterie Division*, *Herr General*, for actions around Rzhew on the night of 13 to 14 September!'

Sturm hoped the *General* would not be too displeased at this protracted way of bringing him up to speed. Sturm had served with *253 Infanterie Division* commanded by the then *Generalleutnant* Schellert, but his regiment had been temporarily attached to *6 Infanterie Division*, where he received the *Ritterkreuz* in arrangement with 253. Everyone waiting for the *General*'s reaction.

'Sturm, what was the number of your regiment?'

'*Infanterie Regiment 473*, *Herr General*!'

All eyes were on the big officer, who pulled himself totally erect, his expression changing as he walked slowly forward towards Sturm and embraced him.

'Our Hans Sturm, *Man*,' he said, taking a step back. '*Man*, you were always one for surprises, but this....'

The *General*'s face was filled with emotion, and his voice beginning to break. Sturm felt his eyes well up with tears. The others stood watching, some of them, too, feeling lumps form in their throats, clearing their throats and trying to disguise their feeling with sympathetic laughter. A flood of questions and answers followed as the *General* brought himself up to date on Sturm's career. Schellert then made the following entry in Sturm's book:

To my surprise and great pleasure I met with you here in Kassel, my dear Sturm. In our old *253 Division* you became the first *Gefreiter* to win the *Ritterkreuz*. Just as I and the entire division were proud of you then, so am I still proud of you today.

Schellert,
General der Infanterie and Deputy Commanding General X Army Corps, Kassel 11 May 1944.

On 12 May, *Leutnant* Thelen took his group to a reception at the army reporting office in Melsungen, and on 13 May the group attended a wreath-laying ceremony at the local war memorial on the Heiligenberg. The delegation was led by the *Kreisleiter* of the NSDAP, Dr Schmitt. In attendance were also the deputy *Gauleiter*, the Commissioner for State Defence, and the Health Leader Dr H. Reinhardt, as well as some *Hitlerjugend* and BDM members from the district.

In the days which followed, the five soldiers took part in numerous *Hitlerjugend* and BDM events and presentations, helping to cement the friendly relations between the regiment and the youth organisations. The final event in this period was a grand reception on 17 May in the hall of the Berghof guest house. Sturm had already agreed to a request from the others to give a speech and this was received with enthusiasm and applause. Afterwards, the *Bürgermeister* of Melsungen and other civic dignitaries made entries in Sturm's book. On 18 May, the team took their leave of their young comrades of *Hitlerjugend Bann 761*. Now they would take a well deserved spell of home leave.

Sturm spent one day at home in Dortmund, but his real pleasure lay in visiting the Brünen farmhouse in Niederrhein. He had kept up correspondence with his beloved Hilde, but was anxious to see her in person once again. Sturm was particularly keen that Hilde should meet his own parents. Sturm's parents were also keen to get to know Hilde. They had already seen photos and the excited way in which Hans would speak of her. This attractive girl resembled the figure portrayed in so much National Socialist propaganda—posters, books, and films—as the ideal image of German womanhood, the perfect Nordic wife and mother. Hilde was scarcely aware of all this. She was simply a happy Rhineland girl who had tamed this stubborn young mule of a Westphalian. The invitation to Sturm's parents to visit the Neerfeld farm was readily accepted. Sturm himself could not go, as he first had to report to *Ersatz Bataillon 88* in Fulda before going on to the *Kriegsschule* at Hagenau. There, he acted temporarily as a recruiting sergeant.

There were two *Kriegsschulen* in Hagenau, in the *Elsaß* region. In mid-June 1944, Sturm was ordered to report to *Kriegsschule II*, commanded by *Oberstleutnant* Hack. His company commander was *Hauptmann* Ernst Conrad, and his squad leader *Leutnant* Brundt. *Kriegsschule I* was commanded by *Generalleutnant* Regener, who in fact held overall responsibility for both schools. *Fahnenjunker Feldwebel* Sturm was the only *Ritterkreuzträger* at the school during this period, and was appointed the spokesman for both schools. This meant that he was required to report to *Generalleutnant* Regener each Monday at midday with any requests from the officer candidates for improvements or with complaints about food, for example. Sturm could never have suspected that these meetings, which also gave him the opportunity for personal conversations with the *General*, would be his salvation when he found himself in a very serious predicament.

48

Kriegsschule

Service at the *Kriegsschule* followed a predetermined course: tactical instructions, weapons training, and sports. The recruits were kept busy throughout the day. The time spent together at the end of the day's duties, as well as in training during the day, consolidated comradeship between the trainees. So-called 'free time' had to be used for what were considered suitable activities, such as group discussion or writing up theses. For private conversations and letter-writing to relatives, there was very little time. Yet Sturm always made time to answer questions from his roommates about his experiences, even if he did have to keep his reports brief. In the tactics lessons, Sturm was easily able to come up with correct answers and suggestions, principally due to his own, extensive combat experience and sixth sense for unusual circumstances. These exercises were carried out on scale models of the terrain in the 'sand-box' or out in the field. One had to justify one's answers and suggestions in order to get a good mark from the trainer. Sturm had experienced and survived many incidents where there was no time for planning, and decisions had to be made instantly.

The dislike of National Socialism held by men like Hans Sturm was obvious to all. They sought no active part in the opposition, but they certainly did not count themselves in the ranks of the '*Sieg-Heil* screamers'. At the Front and in his lectures and meetings up to the end of the war, Sturm had met people who had doubts about National Socialism and the *Führer*. One such man was even prepared to sacrifice himself—the *Ritterkreuzträger Freiherr* Axel von dem Bussche-Streithorst. Sturm heard all about it in a conversation with a senior officer. In 1943, during a display of new uniform designs to Hitler and Göring, von dem Bussche-Streithorst had the task of describing the relevant features of the new uniforms. He had been prepared to throw himself at Hitler with explosives strapped to his body and detonate them when fate intervened. The review of the new uniforms had to be cancelled after they were destroyed during an allied bombing raid the day before the intended review. Von dem Bussche remained a conspirator in the opposition to Hitler, however. On 7 March 1944, he was awarded the *Ritterkreuz* as a *Hauptmann* in command of *1 Kompanie, Grenadier Regiment 9*, and in June of that year was promoted to

Portrait photo of Sturm as a
Fahnenjunker-Oberfeldwebel taken at the
Hagenau *Kriegsschule*.

Major. Sturm actually got to know this officer personally in the latter months of the war. He heard from him in person why he wore his *Ritterkreuz* to the bitter end: 'Because it would be seen as evidence, that I can distinguish between Treason and High Treason.'[1]

Then there was also Fritz Dreesen, who had been at Hitler's side during the Munich Putsch of 8/9 November 1923 when Hitler and *General* Ludendorf marched on the *Feldherrnhalle* in the abortive attempt to overthrow the regime. Dreesen had been awarded the Gold Party Badge but discarded it when he left the Party in disgust at the Nazi's corruption and political machinations.

On the evening of 21 July 1944, Sturm sat with four other Fahnenjunker discussing preparations for training exercises the next day. Sturm was in command, with one of the others as his deputy and the others to act as umpires. During the day they had all toured the exercise area on bikes to check everything one last time. The exercise involved the inspectorate in company strength using a pincer movement to repulse an enemy force which had broken into their area. The enemy would be destroyed, the counter-attack regaining the lost territory. Having completed their preparations, the five men permitted themselves a few glasses of wine, and all were in congenial mood.

Not surprisingly, the topic of conversation turned to the attempt on Hitler's life the previous day, and one *Unteroffizier*, known for his devotion to Hitler and National

Sturm's status as an officer cadet is shown by the bars of braid across the base of his NCO shoulder straps.

Socialism, became quite fervent in his condemnation of the conspirators. Sturm listened to the conversation without taking part himself. It was clear to all that the failed attempt would have grave consequences for *Graf* Schulenburg and all the others in the resistance. Sturm in his many and widespread travels had himself seen the clear conflicts of loyalty which raged among the German people. Most patriotic Germans, conservative Christians, and those from a Prussian military background admired or at least tacitly supported Hitler. But Nazism, which was once greeted by the majority of Germans as their country's greatest hope for the future, was now coming to an end, and many recognised their own share of guilt. Sturm personally felt that an end to the terror was preferable to terror without end, and interrupted the conversation with the fateful words: 'Perhaps it would be best if the war could be ended today.'

The fanatical *Fahnenjunker* leapt to his feet.

'Hans! This sort of sentiment, coming from a *Fahnenjunker* at military school, must be reported. It is tantamount to suggesting that the attempt on the *Führer* should have succeeded!'

Sturm quickly realised that he had spoken too freely about the political situation in front of those who, until that moment, he felt had been 'pals'. *Unteroffizier* Adolf Müller was already on his way to the door as the others tried to hold him back. He was treated to abuse for threatening to report a remark made in private among friends. Müller refused to be distracted from his intent, however, and made to leave the room. As he reached the door, he turned and looked reproachfully at the angry Sturm. Perhaps he had given a moment's thoughts to the possible repurcussions.

'Will you apologize, and explain that you really didn't mean it?'

Sturm stared at him, not saying a word and shook his head. Müller left and the others immediately reproached Sturm for refusing the chance to recant. Most, however, believed that Müller would cool down after sleeping on it that evening. This was not to be, however. Despite the lateness of the hour, Müller went looking for the squad leader, *Leutnant* Brundt, and when unable to find him, went directly to the company commander *Hauptmann* Conrad. Conrad was most displeased at Müller's hand-written report and immediately tried to calm him down, suggesting he think it over. Sturm could be demoted, lose all his decorations, and be sent to a punishment battalion. Müller, however, demanded that his report be forwarded up the chain of command.

On the following morning, *Hauptmann* Conrad was obliged to pass on Müller's report to *Oberstleutnant* Hack. Hack was deeply troubled, as he had grown to like Sturm. Neither could know at this time that they would in fact spend four years together in captivity in the same Soviet labour camp after the end of the war. Hack was furious and disappointed. As a *Fahnenjunker*, and a *Ritterkreuzträger*—Sturm was expected to be an example to the others. Hack was an extremely smart officer, a military man from tip to toe and a fine combat soldier, who wore the German Cross in Gold like Sturm. *Fahnenjunker* Sturm and the three others were individually interviewed by Hack and made to submit formal statements. Sturm stuck to his opinion, and denied that his statement could be interpreted as implying he was as bad as those who conspired to assassinate Hitler. An inquiry was convened with Hack and *Unteroffizier* Müller as the prosecutors and with *Hauptmann* Kersten, chief of the camp inspectorate, and *Leutnant* Koehler as his defence team. Sturm's defence had been selected by *Generalleutnant* Regener from the staff of *Kriegsschule I* after the report of the incident reached him. From 22 to 27 July, Sturm was suspended from duty and held under a kind of house arrest, restricted to his quarters and only allowed to speak to his defence team. They went to great pains to contact as many prominent personalities as possible to give good character references for Sturm.

First came Fritz Dreesen who, along with his brother Georg, owned the Hotel Rheinterrasse Dreesen, a popular stop on excursion trips in the area. Dreesen immediately pronounced himself ready to speak on Sturm's behalf. He would make an important witness. *Oberstleutnant* Prof. Dr Gierlich from *Generalkommando VI* in Münster, and *General* Schellert with *Generalkommando X* in Kassel were also prepared to speak for Sturm. The defence team also spoke with many dignitaries from the Party who had got to know Sturm and were familiar with his opinions. As a front-line soldier who had travelled so widely in his duties on leave from the Front, Sturm probably had a better overview of Germany's precarious position than most. Most soldiers, like much of the civil population, were unaware of just how totalistic and inhumane the persecution of the Jews had become. In Brest-Litowsk, however, Sturm had witnessed the brutal deportation of the Jews with his own eyes.

The prosecution tried to portray Sturm as sympathetic to the Jews. Party officials in Dortmund had presented them with suitably incriminating 'information' about Sturm's past. His voluntarily leaving the *Hitlerjugend* in 1937 was brought up, as was the fact that his father had already handed back his Party membership book as early as 1935. It was also revealed that he had struck a Party official, requiring his victim to need hospital treatment, though when the circumstances of the Party member's insults against the military were explained, this matter was quietly dropped. But most decisive of all were the reports from his commanding officers relating to his duties in giving patriotic speeches, his voluntary return to combat service—putting his life in danger on numerous occasions when he could easily have sat out the remainder of the war in a safe home front posting—and not least the proof of his personal gallantry in the numerous combat decorations he had won.

Generalleutnant Regener, head of the combined *Kriegsschulen*, interpreted Sturm's statements thus: 'perhaps it would be best if the war was ended today.' He suggested that *Fahnenjunkerfeldwebel* Sturm had used an unfortunate choice of words with a bad timing, but only to say what all reasonable men must feel—that this terrible war must soon end. The *Generalleutnant* was not prepared to transmit the report further up the chain of command, even though this was his duty.

A brief discussion ensued between the defence and prosecution, and *Oberstleutnant* Hack and *Unteroffizier* Müller left the room briefly. When they returned they agreed that they would not insist on the report being pursued further, much to the delight of the defence.

Hilde and Sturm's mother wanted to visit him on 29 July to wish him a happy birthday. They wanted to see him and had to wait in the guard room. A *Feldwebel* Sturm was brought in, but not the correct one. It was Anton Sturm, a trainer on another course. He knew of the difficulties being experienced by the *Fahnenjunker* with the same name.[2]

Fahnenjunker Sturm participated in the exercise he had helped to prepare on 29 July, but fortunately *Unteroffizier* Müller was transferred to another inspectorate. His task as umpire was taken over by another *Fahnenjunker*. The training was met with fulsome praise by *Oberstleutnant* Hack, chief of the inspectorate, *Hauptmann* Conrad, and the squad leader *Leutnant* Brundt, for all who had taken part. Only in the evening did Sturm finally manage to meet with his mother and Hilde. They were shocked at his strained appearance. During the preceding days he had been subjected to interrogations and accusations deep into the night, and this had all left its mark on him. He said nothing to them of the precarious position he had found himself in, mostly through his own incautious statement.

Hilde and his mother remained the entire week in Hagenau, though they were only able to meet briefly in the evening for short periods after his duties were over. Hilde returned again to visit Hans for another week, but this time alone. Even if

Sturm's mother sits with his company commander (wearing the peaked cap) during her visit to Hagenau during a sports event.

they could only meet briefly in the evenings, the two thought it well worthwhile. Sturm managed to get more free time by undertaking to arrange a social evening for the officer candidates that week. Together, he and Hilde visited the brewery in Schweighausen where a room was kept free for such occasions and drinks could be supplied. The evening meal was to be goulash with noodles. The starter and sweet courses were provided by members of the local Ladies' Guild, while girls of the BDM undertook to decorate the room. Many devoted much time and energy in their efforts to help.

It was a grand evening, with much additional drink supplied from various sources. All the *Fahnenjunker* and their guests were delighted with the outcome, and *Leutnant* Brundt said a few words of thanks for everyone's efforts to make the evening a success. On the following day, he made an entry in Sturm's book.

> Your obedience shall be your distinguishing feature. Your orders in themselves shall be obedient! (Nietzsche)

August 1944
Leutnant und *Abteilungsführer*

The *Kreisleite*, also in attendance as a guest, wrote:

To *Ritterkreuzträger Feldwebel* Sturm, in commemoration of our meetings in Barbarossa's old town Hagenau!

16 August 1944
Hannes
Kreisleiter

Leutnant Koehler, who had assisted in Sturm's defence, contributed a quotation from Hölderlin, then finished: 'In commemoration of a fine day in your time at military school, with best wishes for further success after the war.'

Meanwhile, the war on the East and West Fronts was fought with great determination. The Russians had continued to push further westwards and the Germans were forced back into their 'fortresses', while the Allies had landed in Normandy on 6 June 1944 with overwhelming might in men and material. Bomber squadrons dropped their lethal loads around the mouth of the River Rhône. Around two months later, the next assault followed—the major landing on 15 August 1944 south-west of Freus, 100 km from Marseilles. The attack was well prepared. Thousands of bombs, heavy-calibre artillery shells from warships offshore, and support attacks from the French resistance had caused great breaches in the front of *19 Armee*, led by *General der Infanterie* Weise. Because of the attrition suffered by the German forces due to the fighting in Normandy, *19 Armee* was reduced to seven (mostly static) divisions. Crucially, there were no panzer divisions. The most heavily defended area of occupation was between Marseille and Toulon—the rest of the coast was only lightly defended. Six American and four French divisions which formed the US 7 Army under General Patch were available for the attack. The allied landings were a complete success. The Americans had learnt from former experiences and altered their strategy accordingly. They avoided their normal tendency in spending too much time and effort consolidating their bridgehead and thus allowing the German forces time to reorganise and stiffen their resistance, and instead pushed forward inland almost uninterruptedly into the rear of the German front line. The American divisions pushed remorselessly forward towards Marseilles and Toulon in a pincer movement intended to trap the weakened Germans as they pulled back northwards through the Rhônetal. The eventual allied goal was Grenoble.

These offensive movements, because they had not been expected, met with little serious German opposition. The dam had been broken and fate took its course, as the invaders flooded into the hinterland. It quickly became obvious that the Germans were fated to be trapped in yet another pocket. By 27 August, the Americans had already reached Avignon and Arles in the lower Rhônetal and had taken 24,000 German prisoners. The Americans' success left the Germans with only one option—retreat northwards as fast as possible. As commander in chief of the German armed forces, Hitler accepted the futility of the German attempts to hold the area, let alone drive back the invaders, and authorised the withdrawal of *19 Armee* and the *Armeegruppe* to which it belonged back to the upper Marne, the Saone, and ultimately to the Swiss border. Far too late, the *11 Panzer Division* was allocated to *19 Armee* as its sole fully motorised formation. It had single task: to cover the retreat.

Because the bulk of the German defensive forces were occupied in the scramble to halt the US forces, by the end of August they had been reduced to fighting only limited small-scale actions. Fighting in divisional-sized formation was no longer possible, as the German forces no longer had sufficient manpower or weapons. The bulk of the weak German rearguard and individual *Kampfgruppen* were now utterly exhausted and fighting under great strain. Incredibly, at this stage it was decided to commit the trainees and staff from the *Kriegsschulen* at Metz and Hagenau to battle. Continual artillery bombardments supported by the US Airforce and the French maquisards, and now a surprise breakthrough by the American ground troops, decimated the German units and saw their fitness for combat ebb away from day to day.

One crisis followed another. The German defensive capabilities lessened, as the few experienced German units remaining found themselves no longer able to cope with the pressure of the American advance. The *11 Panzer Division* covered the retreat of *19 Armee* through 450 km of hard-fought rearguard actions. It was solely thanks to the efforts of this lone armoured unit that *19 Armee* avoided being fully encircled and destroyed. With the arrival of long awaited reinforcements, *19 Armee* was finally able to establish solid defence lines in front of Belfort and deny the Americans the opportunity to swing right along the Swiss border and into the underbelly of the Reich.

That the Germans eventually succeeded in halting the American advance did little to reassure Sturm, who could see the way the war was going. Meanwhile, so heartened by this campaign was General Eisenhower that he declared: 'The end of the war is near. It will be brought to a conclusion in record time!'

338 Infanterie Division now lay in positions behind the Doubs River. Its opponents were the men of the US 3 Infantry Division which was pushing into the German positions with its armoured spearheads. The Americans discovered a ford 1.5 m deep, passable for armoured vehicles and shallow enough for the infantry to wade through, and in a night action crossed the Doubs under cover of darkness. Apart from a 5-cm anti-tank gun, the German battalion opposing them had no heavy weapons. Even that sole anti-tank gun was forbidden to open fire in case it gave its position away to the attackers prematurely. That, and the fact that there was in any case very little ammunition available—every shot had to be made to count.

The German armies were awash with rumours of new 'wonder weapons', such as missiles, planes that could fly faster than the speed of sound, and tanks which were vastly superior to anything in the American or Soviet arsenals. Such gossip was encouraged so as to invigorate morale. Thousands of gullible German soldiers clutched at these stories like straws.

The cursed rearward slog didn't suit the *Landser* who had enjoyed the 'easy life' in France during the occupation. They had never experienced the physical and mental torment of the Russian Front, the veterans of which were accustomed to living their lives 'in the shit' and simply did so again now. Yet Sturm had had more than enough of this already!

In France, the German command still clung to the idea that by shortening the Front it would still be possible to hold back the enemy. *19 Armee*'s trek through Burgundy was even more disastrous: it was decimated by continuous attacks from enemy artillery, fighter-bombers, and the dreaded 'Jabos'.[3] The Americans took no unnecessary risks: they called in artillery and air support and threw in masses of material at the enemy before committing their troops, thus keeping human losses to an acceptable level. The Germans would need five times as many men and machines as they had to stand any chance of retreat with minimal losses. The only real reason that the retreat of *19 Armee* had not turned into a total and absolute catastrophe was the Americans' tendency to be over-cautious in their advance, often losing out on opportunities to carve up and encircle retreating German units.

Because the situation was altering daily—indeed, often hourly—and only very little news reached Hagenau, *General* Regener had ordered up some large wall maps so that he could mark the various unit displacements and keep track of the course of the campaign. There were countless situation briefs with *Oberstleutnant* Hack and the course leaders, as well as the section heads.

Recruits undergoing live ammunition training. Barely visible, they are lying in a circle around the site of the explosion. This training was intended to familiarise them with close proximity to shell fire.

From *Führer* Headquarters orders arrived for the *Kriegsschulen* to move into a state of readiness. On receipt of a codeword, each *Kriegsschule* had to be equipped and ready to march within twelve hours, with sufficient ammunition and infantry companies, but without heavy weapons other than the standard 8-cm mortars and heavy machine guns. *Generalfeldmarschall* Keitel had already ordered the *Kriegsschule* Metz into action. They had been given the task of forming defensive positions on the Vosges Mountains on the banks of the Rhine. Enemy bombing raids were launched against the positions, but often simply dropped their loads at random, causing great danger to the civil populace in the region. There were scarcely any anti-aircraft guns to oppose the enemy, as these had all been sent to critical areas in Italy, Northern France, and most of all the Eastern Front. For the men of *Kriegsschule* Metz, the action began on the next day. They were rapidly transported to the Doubs Front near Besançon and thrown into the line. There they were left to hold it because *338 Infanterie Division* had had to wait on the retreating *159 Infanterie Division* and part of a *Luftwaffe* field corps. These *Luftwaffe* soldiers had little or no infantry experience, with the exception of the *Fallschirmjäger*, who were now being used in an infantry role as there were no longer sufficient planes or fuel for them in even limited airborne operations. Using *Luftwaffe* personnel (ranging from bomber pilots to ground crews) in ground operations was a grave misjudgement, and the same was true of the deployment of *Kriegsschulen* personnel. Though borne of necessity, this policy was severely flawed in that most of these men had almost completed their courses and would soon have been returned to their units, where they might have done some good. Instead, within just two days, *Kriegsschule* Metz had lost almost half its strength in men killed, wounded, or taken prisoner. A decisive factor in the extent of German losses at Doubs was the commanding officer of the 1 French Armoured Division, *Général* du Vigier. On meeting strong German resistance he sent a radio message directly to the VI US Corps, which was intercepted by the Germans. It said,

> Forward units of 1 French Armoured Division on the road to Dole near Hill 999 hit by surprise German artillery fire. Panic. Heavy losses. Immediate support from the heavy Corps Artillery essential otherwise the advance will stop. Signed Du Vigier.

General Truscott, commander of VI US Corps, lost no time. At least forty-two heavy artillery pieces, mostly on self-propelled carriages, were thrown into action. The hellish barrage destroyed not only the German artillery, but was the signal for a renewed allied attack towards Pontarlier, facilitating the breakthrough towards Besançon. The *19 Armee* had thrown a number of Russian Cossacks into the line near Pontarlier. Up until then they had fought well, but as the front began to disintegrate they fled. 5 Cossack Company had only two German officers, both of whom were killed almost as soon as the artillery barrage began. The Russians officers lost their nerve. Into this breach were thrown the men of *Kriegsschule* Metz,

Sturm's recruits march off on a training exercise.

and only at the price of terrible losses were they able to hold the line for a short while until relieved by *338 Infanterie Division*. A special decoration in the form of a sleeveband bearing the inscription 'Metz 1944' was created in recognition of the achievements of these troops.

In the meantime, the codeword '*Gneisenau*' had been received in Hagenau. On the double the infantry companies were formed up and ready for action. The serious losses suffered by the personnel from the *Kriegsschule* Metz, however, resulted in the mobilisation orders for *Kriegsschule* Hagenau being cancelled at the last minute. Sturm and his comrades were happy enough that the *Führerhauptquartier* had rescinded this command, but a subsequent order required the disbandment of the *Kriegsschule* Hagenau and the return of all trainees to their units. This meant that premature promotions were rushed through where the progress of individual soldiers allowed and many advanced to *Fahnenjunker*. Roughly one third of trainees were to be further promoted to *Leutnant* within two months, their combat achievements on various fronts having already demonstrated that they merited their commissions. The majority would gain their commissions after they had proven themselves further on return to their units.

49

Leutnant Sturm

On his departure from the *Kriegsschule* Hagenau, *Leutnant* Sturm thanked *General* Regener, his course chief, *Hauptmann* Conrad, and his section leader, *Leutnant* Brundt. Sturm would meet *General* Regener again on the Oder-Neisse Front, unbeknownst to him. He would also spend the first four years of his captivity in the same prison camp as *Hauptmann* Conrad in the southern Caucasus. Sturm expressed his gratitude to the officers for the good reports he had received and for including him in the group of soldiers given advanced promotion to *Leutnant*.[1] The mood of the closing down party at the beginning of September was somewhat spoiled, partly by the fact that not all the trainees had been promoted, but also by thoughts of the great losses suffered by their comrades at the *Kriegsschule* Metz.

Sturm returned to *Infanterie Ersatz Bataillon 88* in Fulda a 'freshly baked' *Leutnant*. On that same day he was granted two days leave to visit his parents in Dortmund. He was warmly greeted by his mother and father and Hilde, whom his parents had informed about her boyfriend's unexpected leave. Time was short, so he could only visit a few friends and relatives, all of whom warmly congratulated him on his promotion.

Back in Fulda, he was attached to the recruit-training company set up in a woodland area remote from the barracks, where there was little danger of attack from allied bombers. Here, the recruits would get as realistic a training as possible, away from the 'luxuries' of barrack life. The three platoons of the company were commanded by one *Oberfeldwebel* and two *Feldwebel* respectively. Sturm at first did not interfere, but merely observed. He quickly formed a very poor impression of their techniques, however.

The young recruits were mostly 18-year-old boys and Sturm could see that the majority had already adopted the same attitude as some of the 'professional' corporals he had known, who, having reached the furthest rank that they could, and with no future to their career, became cynical and obdurate. One *Feldwebel* stood watching with obvious delight as an *Unteroffizier* in his platoon repeatedly had his recruits crawl fully laden through muddy puddles. The recruits were covered from head to toe in filthy muck, as were their weapons. This special form of training was, Sturm felt,

Sturm as a freshly commissioned *Leutnant*.
Residual eye problems still meant that Sturm
was occasionally obliged to wear eyeglasses.

completely out of place in the fifth year of the war. These young men had little time
to train and were still far too green. Admittedly, they had already had their basic
weapons training, including the use of the machine gun, but Sturm was shocked to
discover that none had yet been selected specifically as machine-gunners, an absolute
must for any infantry or grenadier squad.

Sturm tried to persuade the *Feldwebel* and *Unteroffizier* to adopt better training
methods. Both were decorated soldiers who should have known better. Nothing
improved, however, and Sturm was forced to speak to the company commander
about their behaviour. Both being classified as fit for action, they were immediately
transferred to the Italian Front. The company commander himself had received one
particular wound which was not healing as well as had been hoped, and he was forced
to return to hospital for treatment. Sturm was promoted to temporary company
commander, while a *Feldwebel* who had just returned to duty after recuperating
from wounds was given command of the 'problem' platoon.

Sturm ordered the *Hauptfeldwebel* to erect a large canvas tent, as big as could be
kept efficiently heated, so that the men could get together in the late afternoons and
evenings after training to socialise and entertain themselves. The *Hauptfeldwebel*
could hardly believe the orders, but Sturm explained that he wanted to build a good,
comradely rapport between the trainees and the NCOs to encourage them in their
training. On the following morning, the groups assembled as usual, the squad seniors
reporting to the squad leaders, who in turn reported to the platoon commanders,

who themselves reported to the *Hauptfeldwebel*. All were present and correct except for those on sick parade. The *Hauptfeldwebel* ordered 'Attention!' and reported the numbers present to *Leutnant* Sturm.

'Good morning, men!'

'Good morning, *Herr Leutnant*!' roared the assembled recruits.

Sturm thanked them and ordered them to stand at ease. After a few opening words, he instructed the men to be ready for the field in fifteen minutes—fully kitted out, armed, and wearing their steel helmets. Before the time was up the company had reassembled. A few recruits looked a bit slovenly, but after a few moments straightening belts, doing up buttons, and setting their helmets straight, the group was ready to move.

'Company ready, *Herr Leutnant*!' reported the *Oberfeldwebel*.

'Company, right turn!' ordered Sturm, and moved to the head of the column before adding, 'Forward March!'

Marching off with a *Ritterkreuzträger* in the lead was certainly a new experience for the group. Beside the platoon commanders marched the squad leaders, and behind them came the three machine-gunners, their weapons over their left shoulders. Then came the recruits, with the tallest bringing up the rear, carrying their ammunition boxes and weapons. Sturm led the company out from the training area into the town, past the cathedral and the barracks and again up into the wooded area. The marching troops drew quite a bit of attention in the town. The weather began to worsen—into '*Sauwetter*', as the Germans say. A cold snap had turned the dampness in the air to snow at higher levels. The flakes were large but damp and melted as they hit the ground. Higher up, however, the snow began to cover the ground like a thick white blanket. For the recruits, this was a long, unfamiliar march.

At last they came to a wide open plain. Sturm watched the men, and was sure he could read their minds. What the hell is going on with this new commander, they were surely thinking. Then, Sturm let the cat out of the bag. The reason they had been brought up into the snow covered hills was to have a snowball fight! A free-for-all, with himself and the instructors included. On his order of 'Fire at Will', the men could let fly; they could continue to do so until he gave the order 'Cease Fire'. The men were astonished, but set to work with a will, preparing their ammunition; there was no shortage of snow to make up the missiles.

The game was great fun for all, and no effort was spared to make sure the commander and all the instructors were well battered with snowballs. Sturm brought the fun to an end before things got too out of hand and formed the men up again for the march back through town. They took the shortest route to their tented accommodation, where they dried off and cleaned themselves and their weapons. After changing into dry drill uniforms they had a hot meal, and then met in the big communal tent which Sturm had ordered erected.

Sturm gave a lecture on the combat tasks of an infantry company, known since the end of 1942 as 'grenadiers' and now much better equipped (with anti-tank weapons and assault rifles, for instance). Soon his men would be going off to the Front. It was essential that Numbers 1, 2, and 3 on the machine gun teams be selected and given specialised training—in setting up positions, working out fields of fire, rapid position changes, changing barrels, and unblocking stoppages, all under extreme conditions (usually much of this training was carried out with the recruit blindfolded). Afterwards, Sturm led the men in a sing-song, starting with the old soldiers' favourite, '*Wenn die Soldaten durch die Stadt marschieren, öffnen die Mädchen die Fenster und die Türen*'.[2] Many other songs were sung besides, and the men got better with practise. The chorus ran, '*Ei warum, ei darum, ei warum, ei darum, ei blos wegen dem Schinderassa, Schinderassa*'. The beat was perfect for marching men to keep time. Sturm was well aware from his own recruit days of how valuable good marching songs were for morale, too. He had even composed some lyrics of his own to an existing tune, and soon had the men singing along to this one too: first 3 Platoon, then 1 and 2 Platoons joined in. The atmosphere became elated, more so when the *Hauptfeldwebel* arrived with a huge cauldron of hot sweet tea laced with strong rum, after which the men's time was their own. The new Company Commander could content himself that he had made a good impression on his men, and that training and morale would change for the better after this most enjoyable day.

One of Sturm's favourite portrait shots.

50

Return to Barracks

The evening after rthe snowfight, Sturm had a semi-official chat with the battalion commander. They drank a bottle of port wine which Sturm had brought along, and the conversation eventually turned to the recruits and their training. Sturm wanted them to have at least two weeks' training in the barracks. The complacency he had witnessed in some of them when he first arrived would, he felt, be put right by a brief period of training in a real military environment and on proper training grounds. Without this, they would end up as little better than cannon fodder.

The battalion commander was far from convinced. The move out of the barracks had taken place because the barracks themselves were no longer considered a safe training environment due to allied air raids. Sturm eventually persuaded him, however, and he agreed to approach *Generalkommando X* in Kassel for permission to return to barracks. At this time, Sturm could hardly guess that his recruits would have an important role to play in the aftermath of one such bombing raid. Permission was quickly given, with personal greetings to Sturm from *General* Schellert.

The order to return to barracks came as a pleasant surprise for all members of the company. As company commander, he attributed little value to the previous drill training the men had received, which he had once experienced himself. His own priorities were for weapons training with machine gun and rifle both in the shooting gallery at traditional target rings and on the open range against realistic dummies. It did not take Sturm long to select the best marksmen as Numbers 1, 2, and 3 for his machine gun teams. Snipers were also chosen. The recruits' enthusiasm for their duties grew in leaps and bounds.

The company march from the barracks out to the training area was a great experience for all. In this the fifth year of the war, the citizens of Fulda had lost much of their initial zeal for the military, but the keen young recruits, singing as they went, attracted quite a crowd had formed. Their determination seemed to sparkle in their eyes, while at their head marched the young *Leutnant*, the *Ritterkreuz* at his throat. Onlookers must have uneasily wondered what would become of these young men. All hope of life in peacetime and freedom would be cruelly obliterated for many of them.

At the end of September 1944, Sturm wanted to buy a new pair of boots. He went to the the the ebert shop in *Mittelstraße*, where he had purchased shoes on previous occasions.[1] The manageress, *Frau* Ebert, welcomed him, this time as an officer. She called an assistant who had just finished showing a previous customer to the door. This young, particularly pretty girl sat at Sturm's feet as he tried on a pair of *Rieker* boots. She wore an engagement ring and, in conversation with Sturm, explained that her fiancé was an *Oberleutnant* in the panzers and, like Sturm, wore the German Cross in Gold.

Sturm pronounced himself satisfied with the boots. The transaction, however, was interrupted by the loud howling of air raid sirens. The early warning signal was followed rapidly by the full alarm. The anti-aircraft cannon had already opened fire on the high-flying bombers rapidly approaching in this unusual daylight raid. *Frau* Ebert closed the main door of the shop and escorted a customer who had two young children with her in the direction of the air-raid shelter, beckoning for the assistant and Sturm to follow her. Sturm hesitated, because he was much too curious and wanted to see whether there really was any danger. His doubts were swept aside when, before he could even move from the main shop area, the bombs started falling. There was a huge detonation, the shop window burst, and splinters of razor-sharp glass flew. Sturm, who had raised his arms to protect his head, was hit and thrown across the room to land among the overturned seats and shelving. From out in the street he could hear wailing and crying. Sturm stood up and brushed off the splinters of glass and debris. Looking down at his feet, he noticed that he had his old boot on his left foot and a new one on his right. He moved to the door but could not open it because of all the broken glass and debris, so he exited the shop through one of the shattered windows, the glass cracking and breaking under his booted feet. It was probably only a minor raid, maybe even a case of bombers returning from a raid on another target unloading what they had left.

It seemed to have been principally the houses off down a small side-street which led from *Mittelstraße* to *Kanalstraße* which had been hit. Four houses were burning, having been hit by incendiary bombs. Rescue and rubble-clearing columns were already on the scene. Sturm noticed that some men on the other side of the street were pointing to the building he had just left. He looked up and saw that the curtains at one window were ablaze. Clambering back through the shop window as *Frau* Ebert emerged from the shelter, he asked her to reassure the people still in there, then to follow him upstairs, where there appeared to be a fire.

Upstairs, Sturm discovered a large shelf with fire fighting equipment on it. There were also some fire buckets filled with sand. He grabbed a fire extinguisher and moved towards a door from under which smoke was streaming. He could feel the intense heat on his approach. Inside, the whole room was ablaze, from the carpets on the wooden floor up to the wooden ceiling. The flames grew even stronger, fanned by the fresh air coming in through the door Sturm had opened. *Frau* Egert appeared behind him and clasped her hand over her mouth to stifle a cry of shock. She realised

An off-duty moment with his fiancée and pet dog.

the seriousness of the situation and ran back down, reappearing a few seconds later dragging a fire hose.

Sturm soaked his head and uniform with water to give himself some degree of protection from the heat, then turned the hose on the fire. The seat of the fire appeared to be a sofa into which was lodged an incendiary bomb. The hose was not powerful enough to put out the flames, so Sturm used the sand buckets to suffocate them, while *Frau* Ebert took over the hose. She suggested heaving the sofa and with it the incendiary bomb out of the window, just in case the flames were only smoldering and not properly extinguished. Sturm smashed the window frame with a fire axe after checking that no one was in the street directly below. In a combined effort, they then heaved the sofa out into the street. The initially overwhelming heat and smoke had eased, and the two set to extinguishing a few remaining flames. Only now did they notice the burns on their own hair, faces, hands, and clothing.

The siren gave the all clear. Frau Ebert hugged Sturm in gratitude for his help, then hurried below. The danger seemed to have passed, and Sturm also went downstairs. The customer with the two children had emerged from the shelter and *Frau* Ebert took them into her own living quarters where, apart from a broken window and smashed vase of value, there appeared to be no damage. *Frau* Ebert tended to her minor burns and wanted to treat Sturm too, but he declined her offer and went out into the street.

Emerging, he could see that other houses had suffered, but in most cases the fires had been extinguished successfully by the occupants themselves. Sturm realised he was still wearing two odd boots when the leader of one of the rescue squads ran up to him.

'*Herr Leutnant*! Perhaps you can help us. The house at the end of the side-street has been seriously damaged. We managed to get all the people out of the air-raid shelter except one old couple, the owners of the house. They refuse to leave the shelter. We must get them out, because there's an unexploded bomb in the house nextdoor.'

As Sturm followed, the other explained: 'The man is an old soldier and has been decorated in both World Wars. This time around he lost an arm and a leg in Russia. His wife is very sick. Both know that the house and everything in it is beyond saving. They have lost all their will to live!'

They clambered over the rubble and debris into the shelter. The couple, sheltering under a blanket, sat on a bench hugging each other. An emergency lamp illuminated the scene. They had their eyes closed. The man who had summoned Sturm to help was an old neighbour who had known them since boyhood. He turned to Sturm.

'*Herr Leutnant*,' he said, 'if this good old soldier is spoken to by you, a *Ritterkreuzträger*, maybe he will listen and we can get them both away from the danger zone.'

Sturm clapped his arm comfortingly around the old man's shoulder, shook him gently, and asked where he had fought and lost his limbs. The man opened his eyes and stared at the young officer. He tried to shake the two from their despair and persuade them to leave the cellar, and indeed seemed to be having some success in getting through to the old man. Then, just as he was speaking, there was an enormous explosion. The unexploded bomb nextdoor had detonated. The whole house shook and rubble began to fall from the ceiling. All four instinctively ducked and shut their eyes against the whirling dust. The exit from the cellar was blocked, as was the emergency passage through to nextdoor's cellar. Both Sturm and the squad leader set about trying to dig their way out, Sturm with his bare hands and the other with a shovel. The air was thick. The old couple remained sitting on the bench as the husband tried to calm his tearful wife. Help was coming from the outside, but it would take at least a quarter of an hour before they would be able to dig them out. At last the rescue crews broke through, but instantly Sturm noticed the smell of gas. The mains must have been ruptured. They were still in great danger.

The hole was rapidly made big enough for a man to get through. Sturm went directly to the old couple and offered the old man his help, which this time was accepted without hesitation. Two rescuers outside helped him from the cellar, too. Sturm and the rescue squad leader next helped the old lady.

Then all four were out in the fresh air. The neighbors came and took away the sobbing couple, who gave Sturm a grateful nod and grasped his hand firmly. Sturm looked at the huge crater made by the bomb and thanked the men of the rescue column. Fortunately, there had been no deaths as a result of the bombing raid, only injuries.

Sturm peered along the street towards the shoe shop and saw *Frau* Ebert there beckoning to him. She invited him into the living quarters, but first he wanted to gather together the other halves of the odd pair of boots he wore. At last he could clean off some of the dust and dirt that covered him. His uniform had suffered somewhat with scorch marks, but overall the damage was not so bad. The Roth outfitters in Dortmund, owned by old friends of Sturm's family, had in any case promised him a new uniform and greatcoat on his promotion to *Leutnant*. Sturm put his old boots back on and carried the new pair, packaged and wrapped up, under his arm on the walk back to barracks. *Frau* Ebert had insisted he accept them as a gift and categorically refused payment. She told her husband all about the bombing raid and the young *Leutnant's* assistance.

Herr Ebert, an *Obermaat* serving in a naval command post in central Germany, wanted to meet Sturm. The meeting with him and his commanding officer *Kapitänleutnant* Fries took place two days later in Bad Hersfeld. Three other sailors were also present, and Sturm took part in a drinking session in which, on finishing proposing a toast, the 'Kaleu' fell through a glass table and smashed it. Sturm wondered all the while what a naval station might be doing so far inland!

Returning to barracks, Sturm told his *Bataillon Kommandeur* about the bombing raid. The minor injuries to his hands, neck, and face were hardly worth bothering about, but if he had wanted to so, he could have had them recorded as wounds received in action against the enemy!

Shortly afterwards, Sturm was invited to the *Ordensburg* at Sonthofen for an introductory chat with the staff there.[2] It was intended that he be posted there as an instructor for the leadership trainees. After discussing the matter with his superiors, Sturm asked the school command staff to pardon him for refusing their offer, which he had to decline, having so recently taken command of the recruit company.

The announcement that he would join his company at the Front was received with delight by his men. Since he had taken over, their training had gone like clockwork. Sturm's leadership style had made him a very popular officer. Sturm's plans were altered, however, by a telegram which arrived from Dortmund on 6 October 1944. It read: 'Hans, come immediately. Your father has been buried in the rubble. Hilde.'

Hans left for home on the morning of the 7th, fraught with worry throughout the journey. He could think only of his father, and the possibility that he might still be alive, buried under the ruins of his house....

As a bridging engineer, Hans Sturm had returned from Russia to serve with a construction unit of the *Organisation Todt*. His main task was to repair bridges which had been damaged in allied bombing raids in the Ruhr. His tasks involved much travel, and he was often able to make an overnight stop at his own home in Dortmund. 'Wheels must turn for Victory!' This exhortation, which had begun to appear in huge posters by the roadsides and in railway stations from 1942 onwards, emphasised the strategic importance of rail in the National Socialists' war plan. Naturally, this made the railway a major target for the Allies, and as an important rail centre, Dortmund was subjected to a panoply of raids—hundreds of minor ones, over 100 'bigger' raids, and eight of what were classified 'major' raids. The city was reduced to little more than a sea of rubble by March 1945. The fifth major raid on Dortmund, flown by the RAF on the evening of 6 October 1944, was particularly devastating. Over 1,200 Germans were killed, as over 170,000 bombs comprising 1,700 tonnes of explosives rained on them. The main railway station was particularly badly hit. Many passengers travelling during the evening rush hour were trapped by the bombing. One train from Hamm was set ablaze as it pulled into the station. Passengers on another train from Holzwickede only made it into cover because the train driver ignored red halt signals and took his train into the station and a modicum of shelter. Many were unable to reach the relative safety of the railway tunnels amid the panic—many civilians being trampled or crushed to death in the frenzy. Others were killed by the explosions and hail of shrapnel as they stood on the open platforms, exposed.

Sturm arrived on the afternoon of 7 October after some delay and learnt that the rescue columns had already saved many. 'The heavens, all the way to the horizon, were painted red and black by the smoke and flames,' recounted one surviving rescue worker to Sturm. Sturm could make out nothing but a sea of charred beams, twisted girders, and mountains of stone and rubble scattered around the city. Another eyewitness to the raid who walked with Sturm from the station recalled that this

Sturm in a portrait taken after
commissioning.

whole quarter was littered with corpses. Among the dead was an officer with the
Ritterkreuz.

As Sturm made his way into town, he had to travel along the centre of the road
to make his way through the rubble, making room for ambulances and trucks
carting away rubble to pass. Eventually he reached *Jägerstraße*. The church
fronting *Bornstraße* was destroyed and the houses of Dr Isbruch and the building
contractor Gröwinghof severely damaged by bomb blast and fire. The next house
was Sturm's home, No. 21. Neighbours and onlookers stood in front of the house.
Ortsgruppenleiter Halsband spotted Sturm approaching and beckoned him over,
clapping his arm around Sturm's shoulders as he expressed his sympathy for
Sturm's loss.

Sturm looked at the house. Along with the home of the electrician *Herr* Köchling
nextdoor, only the outer walls were still intact. Both houses had had their interiors
ripped out by high explosive bombs and razed right down to the foundations. The
wooden floorboards and ceilings had merely fuelled the flames. Twisted drainpipes
and guttering hung in the air, shaped almost like question marks, asking 'Why?'

Sturm's birthplace after its destruction in an allied bombing raid.

Sturm asked for information about his mother and was told that she had been taken in by some old friends, the Hofstetter family, who lived not far away on the *Bornstraße*. This family owned a food processing factory which had also been badly damaged in the bombing. Sturm could see that the rescue workers were toiling without the aid of heavy equipment; all they had were pick axes, shovels, wheelbarrows, and their own hands. They had yet to establish for certain that the father of the local *Ritterkreuzträger* had indeed been killed in the raid—so far, he could only be posted as missing.

A second column, this time from the *Organisation Todt*, relieved the first. Sturm was of course anxious for a definitive verdict on his father, but could not help but think of the previous evening's raid and how many others might also be trapped and might yet have a better chance of survival if these columns were sent elsewhere. Still in denial about his father really being buried under all this rubble, Sturm asked Halsband, who was toiling away in full uniform (complete with swastika armband and bedecked with awards), who might be able to give him as full a report as possible over the incident. Halsband referred him to the warden of the air raid shelter under the station on *Gronaustraße*. There the warden, *Herr* Wilde, expressed his sympathies to Sturm and described what had happened:

> The air raid alarm came at midday on 5 October, the full warning coming almost immediately after the preliminary alarm. Everyone in the neighborhood hurried to the shelter and your mother, *Frau* Sturm, was one of the last to arrive. I saw her turn and speak to someone as she left your house, and this person stayed behind.
>
> Before your mother could reach the shelter, bombs were already falling. She was thrown to the ground and lost her purse. I ran over and picked it up for her then helped her into the shelter. More bombs fell and some landed in the *Bahndamm* and blocked the entrance and exit to the shelter.

After a short pause for a sip of water from a flask, he continued.

> Your mother was very excitable and couldn't be calmed down, she was so worried about your father who had stayed in the house and wouldn't come to the shelter. After the all-clear we eventually got out through the exit at the other end of the *Bahndamm* and stood looking at the ruins all around us.

Ortsgruppenleiter Halsband took over.

'The fire brigade and rescue operations began almost immediately,' he said, 'but had to be halted on the evening of 6 October because of a further heavy air raid.'

Sturm thanked both men, who continued with their digging in the attempt to find at least one identifiable body part so that Sturm's father could be officially registered as dead. He hurried off to the house of the Hofstetter family, and there met his mother and Hilde. They embraced, in tears, and Hilde explained that on the following day she and Sturm's mother would travel to her parents' home. There, in the Neerfeld farmhouse 2 miles away from the nearest village and far away from this destruction, Sturm's mother could begin to come to terms with the loss of both her husband and her home. Almost miraculously, from the wreckage in the street outside Sturm's home a couch cover, only slightly soiled, and a framed photograph of his parents were recovered totally undamaged. The photo was taken on 2 October 1940, the day before Sturm's enlistment. The cover and photograph must have been thrown from the collapsing house by the blast. The glass had been smashed by the myriad of small stones sent flying by the explosion, but the photo itself was untouched.

Sturm travelled to Brünen, where *Frau* Sturm was warmly welcomed by Hilde's parents, sister, and brother. His mother could not have guessed then that this would become her home for the next nine years, which her son was destined to spend in Soviet captivity. Satisfied that she was in good hands, Sturm returned to Dortmund. There, the digging continued.

The way to the cellar of Sturm's house had been cleared but nothing was found. The cellar was not damaged because its roof was the concrete floor of the bathroom. The only things recovered were jars of jam, some bottles, some coal, and a trunk full of items of clothing which were sent on to Büren. Sturm asked himself repeatedly why his father had unexpectedly returned home to stay the night and had then refused to accompany his wife to the air raid shelter—he would never find the answers. If he had been in the main part of the house when the bomb landed, he would probably have been blown to pieces, and any remains found would be beyond recognition. *Ortsgruppenleiter* Halsband promised that every effort possible would be made to find identifiable remains.

After almost two weeks, Sturm returned to Fulda. His company had been allocated a new commander, and in Sturm's absence had been rushed off to the Front. Sturm was greatly disappointed: he had taken pains to form a close bond with his men and win their respect and admiration. He could only hope that their new company commander, an officer he didn't know, would command the same degree of respect and loyalty.

51

General Unruhe

The battalion commander gave Sturm a letter, wherein he was requested to report to a board of enquiry headed by *General* Unruhe. *General* Unruhe was also known as the *KV-General* (*Kriegsverwendungsfähig*, or fit for front-line service) because he controlled all the offices, depots, and administrations in the home front for soldiersfit for front-line service who might have escaped their duties. Soldiers truly unfit for front-line service were put into their posts to release these men for active service.

General Unruhe and *Oberleutnant* Wirbel knew Sturm by reputation. Sturm knew that he was fit to fight and had no fears about doing so, and thus no apprehensions about meeting the general. He had to report to the board at the main command headquarters of *Wehrkreis X* in Kassel, where it had its offices. Firstly, he had to undergo some superficial checks with an *Oberstabsarzt*—Sturm felt these were unnecessary. Then he had to report to *General* Unruhe, who, to Sturm's surprise, greeted him warmly.

'Sturm, you would fit right in in my little commission here—*Unruhe*, *Wirbel*, *Sturm*!' he laughed, despite his reputedly stern personality. (These names literally mean 'turbulence', 'whirlpool', and 'storm' in German!)

Sturm permitted himself to laugh along with the *General*, but still couldn't imagine what they wanted with him. The *Adjutant*, *Oberleutnant* Wirbel, handed Sturm's Soldbuch back to him open. Sturm looked and was aghast to see an entry certifying him as unfit for front-line service due to a blood disorder.

'You will be posted as a special operations officer to the leadership staff of the *Volkssturm*,' *Oberleutnant* Wirbel explained. 'There you will serve as a section head at the troop training grounds at Gräfenwöhr.'

Both officers looked attentively at Sturm, awaiting his reaction, but before he could reply, the *General* motioned him to silence with a gesture of his hand.

'At Gräfenwöhr you will train *Volkssturm* company and battalion commanders in their duties,' the *Oberleutnant* continued.

Visibly bewildered, Sturm looked at the *General*, who nodded his permission for Sturm to speak.

'*Herr General*! Please excuse my objections, but I can't agree to this. In my opinion I am completely healthy, and I want to lead the recruit company I trained—at the Front.

General Walter von Unruhe, who led the board of inquiry into accusations against Sturm. (*Joseph Charita*)

Only the death of my father in a bombing raid on Dortmund prevented me from leaving with my men. My company was already on its way when I got back to Fulda!'

The *General*, who had been leaning back in his chair, straightened up and declared with a stern look: '*Leutnant* Sturm, you will follow your orders whether you like it or not!'

After his meeting with Unruhe, Sturm reported to *General* Schellert, his former divisional commander.

'If they have sought you out, a mere young *Leutnant*, for this job, you should take it as a great compliment on your actions in Russia, your success as an orator, your service in Italy, your advanced promotion to *Leutnant*, and the way in which you led the recruit company!' he explained. 'You have proven in many instances that you have a skill for leading men and great persuasive abilities. In our new job, this will be very useful as you will meet with people who will be older than yourself and often of higher rank.'

By now, Sturm could no longer restrain himself.

'*Herr General*, I beg your pardon for interrupting so disrespectfully, but I cannot believe that setting up combat units with *Volkssturm* men is the right way to produce a positive turn to this war!' he burst out. 'These men will be dragged away from their families and thrown into action, and in many cases will hardly be of much help to combat units, whether they are volunteers or not. How can I achieve anything with them?'

General Schellert had politely listened to the young officer without interrupting. Now he stood up, laid both his hands on Sturm's shoulders, and looking him firmly in the eye said: 'You will do the best you can!'

Sturm was given three days leave from *Ersatz Bataillon 88* in Fulda. Two of these he spent in Dortmund. The digging had had to be interrupted for one week when an unexploded bomb was encountered in the garden of a neighbouring house. This had to be defused and moved to safety.

Sturm was present when, on 21 October 1944, the remains of his father were found. All that was recovered was his right arm, identifiable because of his wedding ring. This was sufficient for the authorities to at last complete the formalities and declare him dead. Halsband promised to cut through the formal red tape and allow a burial to take place as soon as possible.

On 22 October, Sturm went to Wesel. He was determined to wait no longer, and to ask Hilde to marry him so that they could celebrate their betrothal before he returned to his duties. He thought of his former fiancée, Silvia. He had recovered from his grief over her death with time, and the war had besides hardened him. In Wesel he went to a goldsmith's to buy a ring. He too had a small hand and knew that he and Hilde both had the same ring size. The jeweller welcomed the young officer and asked what he wanted. Sturm explained that he wanted to get engaged. A conversation developed in which he recounted his experiences over recent weeks. The jeweller expressed his sympathy over the death of his father and the destruction wrought by the air raid. He was able to recall the photos of *Unteroffizier* Sturm which had appeared in the *Weseler Zeitung* in December 1943, and laid a pair of gold engagement rings before Sturm for his appraisal. They had been ordered by a previous customer and never collected. The rings were both of the same size and fit. Sturm asked how he should pay, but the goldsmith waved him off.

'Come by and visit sometime with your fiancée if time allows,' he said. 'I'd like to meet her.'

Sturm had brought several jars of jam and bottles along with him and wasn't too keen on having to carry them the 9 km to Brünen. Neither was he keen on travelling by bus—too much hassle, and in any case there would still be a 2-km walk from the bus stop to the farm. He went to the district command post and asked whether they could transport him to Brünen with his luggage—being a *Ritterkreuzträger* he could, after all, afford to ask for such luxuries! He was not disappointed.

At the farm, his arrival was awaited with some excitement. Most importantly, he reported to them that his father's remains had been found, though he thought it best not to tell them at this point that they consisted of one arm. Such things could be talked about much later. *Ortsgruppenleiter* Halsband himself would escort the remains to Brünen for burial. Sturm knew that on the night of 22 October, his last evening there, there would be only very little time for he and Hilde to be alone together. He told her about Grafenwöhr and his new duties and Hilde hugged him, happy to hear that he was not to return to the Front as she had feared. As they embraced, Sturm asked Hilde if she would be his wife. Hilde had in fact been anticipating this for some time, and the bond between them was sealed by a particularly affectionate kiss. They put on the rings and went back into the living room to announce their betrothal.

A small party was held. There was so little time—Hans would depart early in the morning, and the night was far too short. Exactly nine months later, on 21 July 1945, their son was born. Sturm would by then have been a prisoner of the Soviets for three months; he did not meet his son for almost eight years.

Back in Fulda, Sturm visited the Ebert family. Herr Ebert made an entry in Sturm's book dated 27 October 1944:

My dear Sturm,
Please know that despite the heavy blows you have suffered, once victory is won, the sun will shine in gratitude to you. Wishing you a soldier's good fortune,
Yours always,
Franz Ebert

The old couple whom he had helped to rescue from their cellar were now in a retirement home and he paid them a visit, too. Both had regained their will to live. The old, severely disabled soldier thanked Sturm with a firm handshake. His wife went to kiss Sturm's hand, but Sturm instead gave her a warm hug.

Sturm's new duties at Gräfenwöhr started at the beginning of December 1944, when he took over the responsibility for the marksmanship training of recruits. Letters from Hilde kept him informed of developments at home and he learnt that his father's remains had been buried alongside those of his paternal grandmother. All the necessary forms and documents, like family birth certificates and certificates of ancestry, had to be made ready for his forthcoming marriage. All were sent to the Army Personnel Department in Berlin, where, to Sturm's great annoyance, permission for leave to get married was not granted. The reason cited was that it would interfere with his duties at Grafenwöhr and it was suggested that a proxy ceremony be held. (This was often carried out at the bride's home.) Angry beyond measure, Sturm wrote an incandescent letter to the authorities, threatening that, if permission was not given, he would travel to Brünen anyway and find a local priest to marry them in a simple civil ceremony. A *Major* at the Army Personnel Office could only offer modest hope that a few days' Christmas leave might be arranged. Sturm's obstinacy in refusing the proxy ceremony would reap grave repercussions for Hilde. She would eventually lose much of the maintenance allowance which were her due as an officer's wife, and which would have otherwise increased after the birth of their son—all that was lost, as they unable to marry until Sturm's release from Soviet captivity over eight years later.

The last entry in Sturm's book before leaving Fulda was made by the *Kreisleiter*.

My dear Leutnant Sturm!
I am very pleased to have got to know you, such a brave soldier here in a district which already has thirteen *Ritterkreuzträger*.
Please consider this 1,200-year-old city your second home.
Karl Ehrer
Kreisleiter

52

Volkssturm

Sturm's area of responsibility within the *Volkssturm* was *Mark Brandenburg*.[1] His first task was in the area near Frankfurt-on-Oder, where he was responsible for organising, supplying, equipping, and training *Volkssturm* units from all over the Reich. Sturm's personal papers were signed by *Gauleiter* Sturz of *Mark Brandenburg* and by *SS-Obergruppenführer* Gottlob Berger, which certainly opened all sorts of doors for him.[2] He was empowered to call upon assistance from party leaders, police officials, and even the *Hitlerjugend*, and so had more than enough assistance in his duties.

Some special groups, each led by an experienced officer with two or three sergeants or staff sergeants, gave brief weapons training in the assault rifle, anti-tank weapons, and mines. Weapons and equipment came mostly from captured enemy supplies. Once they were more or less trained and prepared, these *Volkssturm* units were assigned to the area east of Frankfurt, along the Schwerin–Meseritz–Zullichau line. Most, in Sturm's view, were worthy enough chaps, however, it would be a senseless, almost criminal sacrifice to send these men into battle—especially since the enemy had already encroached onto German soil on both Fronts. Once, while present at a drinking session in the Nazi Party headquarters in Berlin-Brandenburg, Sturm openly spoke his mind on the senseless waste of thousands of good family men in places where they didn't belong. Present at Sturm's outburst were *Gauleiter* Stürz and other party 'big-wigs', including Hitler's personal secretary and head of the party chancellery, *Reichsleiter* Martin Bormann. Bormann made it clear to Sturm that he and his defeatist talk were unwelcome. Such remarks were unsavoury, and an influencial character such as Bormann could well have had Sturm's head. Indeed, Sturm often wondered how he got away with it—perhaps because, at the end of the day, he was a good soldier who would always do his duty, no matter what he thought the outcome might be.

Volkssturm units could in fact be of little or no help to the front-line combat units. Single men and small groups were therefore posted in the rear areas to help establish defensive positions. Sturm's combat experiences on the Oder–Neiße Front began in the middle of March 1945. Sturm was based in Cottbus, from where he directed the supplies for his *Volkssturm* men. At his disposal were four trucks with trailers, which on the return journey to carry refugees away from the danger areas. Sturm

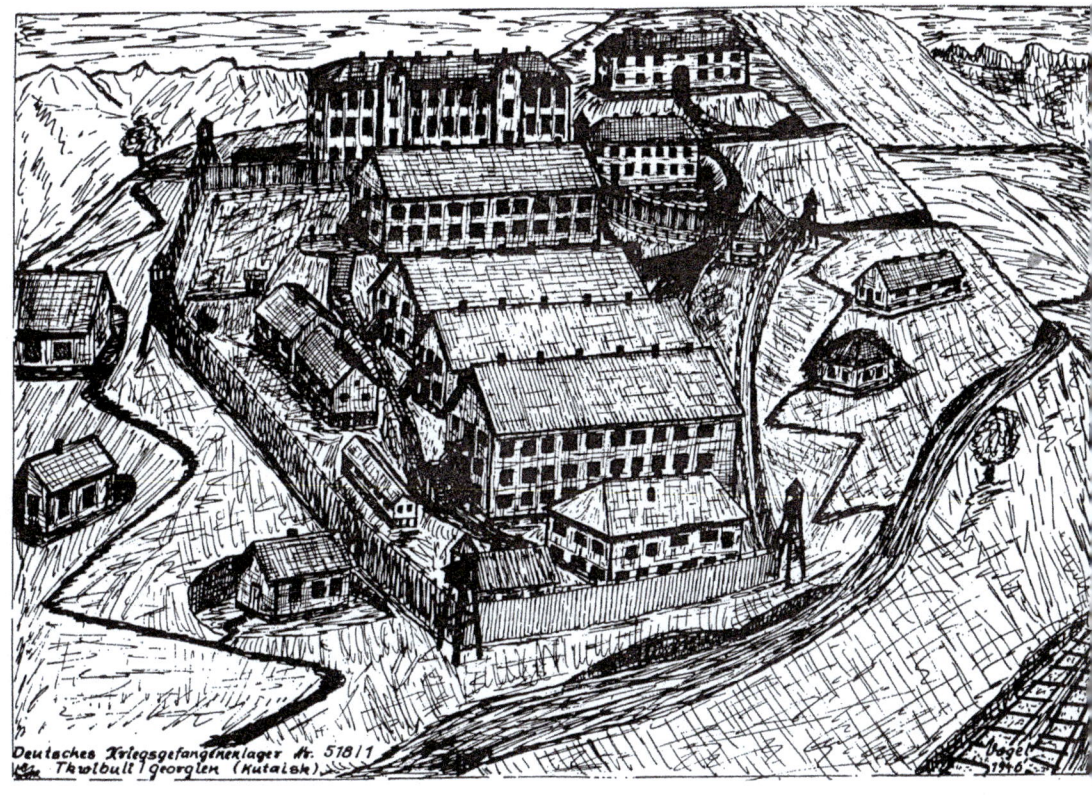

Deutsches Kriegsgefangenenlager Nr. 518/1
Tkwibuli Georgien (Kutaisk)

An etching of the prison camp in Georgia in which Sturm was incarcerated.

travelled all over the front and rear areas. He was shocked at the cruelty visited on the civilian population by the avenging Russians. The treatment of women and young girls was particularly harrowing. However, he had heard it reported that one Russian officer had personally shot two of his own men for acting in such a bestial manner, so perhaps not all Russians were so bad.

Sturm regularly found himself in contact with the enemy. Once, when returning to Cottbus in his staff car, he saw soldiers dashing across the road ahead of him. A bit unusual for a training exercise, he thought. Suddenly, a *Feldwebel* sprang into the road in front of the car, his hand raised, clasping a machine pistol. He yanked the door open and dragged Sturm out into the cover of a ditch, just as a hail of bullets slammed into his car, igniting the petrol tank and setting the vehicle ablaze.

The Russians had broken through and there had been no time to organise a counter-attack. Sturm found himself standing in for the seriously wounded company commander of the men who had intercepted him, and soon found himself back in the thick of the fighting, as the Russians were slowly pushed back.

On 21 April 1945, Sturm was on the road from Cottbus to Forst when he encountered a group of *Hitlerjugend* boys commanded by their *Bannführer*, Erich Schmidt, with whom Sturm was friendly.

'Hans, there has been a tank alarm. The Russians have attacked with Stalin tanks and are heading along the highway, pushing towards Berlin.'

'Erich, just what do you think you, can do about it?' asked Sturm.

The boys' faces were smeared and dirty, and dwarfed by their steel helmets. They didn't look very dangerous, to be sure, but they seemed determined enough. There were but nine of them, all on bicycles. They had adequate weapons—*Panzerfaust* anti-tank projectiles—and had had some degree of training. Still, there was a big difference between training and engaging a real enemy.

'Erich, if it's all right with you, I will take command,' said Sturm, and saw the enthusiasm for his suggestion in his friends eyes.

Sturm took his assault rifle from the car and, at a nod from the *Bannführer*, one of the youths gave Sturm his bike. With Sturm in the lead, the group set off through the wooded area around Forst and got through it without mishap. Soon they came to the autobahn, along which the Russians were said to be attacking, and dismounted from their bikes. Sturm ordered them to make ready, and prepare their *Panzerfäuste*. Sturm took the two projectiles which were tied to his bike. Sturm was extremely conscious of the need to set a good example to these impressionable young lads.

'Form up,' he ordered, as the youths closed up for action.

'Erich, you take the right flank.'

They emerged from the wood and drew nearer to the *Autobahn*. They could hear in the distance the coarse growl of tank engines. As they looked along the road, however, they were disappointed to see that the tanks had already passed and only a few support vehicles were still around.

'*So*,' whispered the *Bannführer*. 'Shit, Hans, we can still catch up with them.'

From the distance they heard the vicious crack of the 150-mm guns carried by the Stalin tanks. Sturm could easily guess what had happened. The Russians had met with opposition and stopped to take care of it. In response came the bark of a couple of 88-mm guns from German Tiger tanks. As they neared the scene, Sturm could see the burning husk of a Tiger; nearby, three of the leading enemy tanks also lay in flames.

'Leave your bikes and follow me,' said Sturm.

In the cover afforded by the bushes along the side of the road, Sturm's group approached the enemy in single file. They saw two of the steel colossi, their gigantic turrets rotated to the side, guns belching flame. None of the Russians had sensed the danger to their rear.

'Man, now they are just scrap,' whispered one of the boys enthusiastically, while another began to sob quietly.

'First three *Panzerfäuste*, make ready!' ordered Sturm. 'When I give the signal, fire. Erich, you take the front of the tank, I'll take the middle, and you, my lad, take the rear!'

The rest of the group crept back into cover. Sturm adjusted his sights and crept forward a little. He rested the tube of the *Panzerfaust* on his shoulder and with a glance from the corner of his eye, he saw the other two following suit.

'Now!' he called, and opened fire.

The three projectiles instantly sped towards the Stalin tank in front of them. They bored their way through the steel plate and after the ear-splitting detonations, the tank burst into flames.

'The next one!' called Sturm.

Twenty seconds later, another three projectiles sped towards the next Stalin, and although only two found their target, it was more than enough to finish off the enemy tank. By now, however, the Russians in the support vehicles had spotted the danger that lurked at the forest edge. They sprang from their vehicles, firing as they ran. The boys dashed for their bikes as Sturm fired a burst from his assault rifle at the charging Russians to cover their retreat. As Sturm reached the spot where the bikes had been left, he found the boys had waited—no one wanted to leave until they knew he was safe.

'This way!' called the *Bannführer*.

They sped off along the forest track on their bikes, the angry shots of their pursuers ringing out behind them. Their bikes allowed them to get quickly out of range, and the entire group escaped without a single loss.

On another occasion, Sturm was travelling from Berlin to Frankfurt-on-Oder via Cottbus, Forst, Peitz, and Guben, and on to the Oder–Neiße line. In March and April, *Generalfeldmarschall* Schörner had issued orders that all unnecessary vehicular traffic not directly related to military actions cease, in order to conserve precious fuel supplies. The *Feldgendarmerie* halted all vehicles to check the drivers' papers, and anyone found carrying out non-essential journeys was ejected from the road. Subsequently, their wheels would be removed to prevent any future unauthorised journeys. Even vehicles stored away in garages had their wheels removed to prevent their use. After a meeting with the commander of a *Volkssturm* unit and his men, Sturm had his own vehicle commandeered by the *Feldgendarmerie*. Sturm's car had been brand new. It was a beautiful sports car with immaculate paintwork and shiny chrome, though Sturm had reluctantly had to spray the entire vehicle in matt field grey paint.

The *Volkssturm* commander had given Sturm a lift into Cottbus, where a senior military staff headquarters was located in a large hotel. All military units in the south of *Mark Brandenburg*, including the *Feldgendarmerie* who had commandeered his vehicle, were answerable to this command post. On entering the main reception hall, Sturm found many officers, including senior ranks from the general staff, sitting or standing around in small groups awaiting an audience with the appropriate senior commanders. Sturm, a mere *Leutnant*, was too insignificant to attract any notice. Encountering a *Hauptmann* of the *Feldgendarmerie*, Sturm showed him his papers and explained that his need for a vehicle was essential for the fulfilment of his duties. He pointed out that his papers had been authorised by *SS-Obergruppenführer* Gotlob Berger of the *SS-Hauptamt* in Berlin-Grünewald. The *Hauptmann* agreed to look into matters and left Sturm to wait.

Sturm was beginning to get the feeling that he had been fobbed off, and when the *Hauptmann* came back, Sturm loudly berated him for failing to help. Speaking in such an aggressive tone in such august surroundings was a major faux pas: the *Feldgendarmerie* officer summoned two of his men to have Sturm escorted from the building. When Sturm showed no sign of leaving, the *Feldgendarme* grabbed him by the shoulder. For Sturm, this was too much. He pulled his pistol from its holster and warned the *Hauptmann* and his men to back off.

At that very moment, *Generalfeldmarschall* Schörner and his staff entered the hall. Sturm quickly holstered his pistol, but it was too late—the *Generalfeldmarschall* had seen. The *Hauptmann* saluted Schörner and explained that the *Leutnant* was demanding a replacement for his vehicle. *Generalfeldmarschall* Schörner looked at Sturm for a moment, then rounded on the military police officer.

'I know this Leutnant,' he snapped. 'Sort things out, *Hauptmann*!'

In the event, Sturm didn't get a new car—but he did receive a fine motorbike, and was once again on good terms with the *Feldgendarmerie*! Sturm had once met *Generalfeldmarschall* Schörner, by accident, when visiting the *Großdeutschland* unit in Cottbus. Now, he showed Schörner his pass, which among other things allowed him to make use of any telephone facilities at all military units, party headquarters, airfields, railway stations—anything that would facilitate maintaining contact with Berlin. Schörner listened as Sturm explained his duties with the *Volkssturm* and assured him that he would be given every assistance.

53

The End

By spring 1945, the once mighty Third Reich was being battered on all sides by the overwhelmingly superior numerical strength of the Allies. Great tracts of land on both Eastern and Western Fronts were already in their hands. The war in Europe was now in its final stages. Yet the leadership of the Reich remained uncompromising and insisted on the fight being continued. Even Berlin, the capital, was a front-line city, every row of streets and every block of houses to be defended to the last. It played host to a bloody and senseless struggle.

In January 1945, the Red Army was pressing home its last great offensive of the war along the entire Eastern Front. The German high command knew that, ultimately, the enemy offensive could not be halted. All the major cities in the eastern provinces of Germany were declared fortresses from which any form of retreat would not be countenanced. Berlin was to be one such fortress. The defensive positions on the outskirts of the city stretched from the *Tiefensee* and the *Havelsee* to Erkner. Behind this were erected the so-called 'defence rings', the final layer of which ran along the *Ringbahn*. In the meantime, the Red Army was opening the second phase of its offensive, aimed directly at Berlin. Two Soviet army groups broke through the Oder bridgehead near Küstrin on 16 April. After heavy fighting and huge losses on both sides, the German defences along the Oder were overrun and 9 *Armee* routed.

The 9 Armee, commanded by *General der Infanterie* Busse, had stood alone with its few meagre *Korps* and battle-weary *Divisionen* against eight whole Russian armies. The enemy units were at full strength in terms of weapons, vehicles, ammunition, and above all manpower. In addition, the Red Air Force had complete control of the sky. Within just five days of the breakthrough at the Oder bridgehead, the spearhead tank units of both the main Russian army groups, commanded by Marshalls Zhukov and Koniev, had reached the southern and eastern outskirts of the city.

Hitler had appointed *Generaloberst* Heinrici to command 'Fortress Berlin', but on 22 April took over direct control of the defence of the city himself. This was the situation in which the *Reichspropagandaminister*, Josef Goebbels, issued his daily bulletins, informing the populace that Berlin would be 'defended to the last'.

On 19 April, the German military strength in Berlin stood at around 40,000 men, including many *Volkssturm* units and armed *Hitlerjugend* boys, all without any chance of the yearned for 'turning point' in their fortunes. There was a reserve and replacement battalion east of Friedrichshain, a workshop battalion east of the *Tegelersee*, and a *Volkssturm* battalion on the western edge of Gatow Airport. They could expect to hold up the advance of the Russians for only a few days at best, although the *Volkssturm* battalion did have the advantage of fire support from 8.8-cm guns mounted in the flak towers of the massive Zoo Bunker. The remnants of *9 Armee* tried desperately to break out to the west. Only *LVI Panzerkorps*, under *General der Artillerie* Weidling, remained relatively intact and cohesive. On 23 April, Weidling was ordered to the *Führerbunker*, where he was appointed to command the defence of Berlin.

During the night of 23/24 April, Sturm made his way towards Berlin on his motorbike. Fortress Cottbus, according to reports, had fallen on 23 April, and Sturm was one of the last to escape before the city fell. Under cover of darkness, torrential rain, and strong winds, he had slipped unnoticed past the Soviet guards. By the time they had spotted him and opened fire, it was too late.

Sturm's journey westwards took him past the fish farm at Peitz. In the atrocious weather the rear wheel of his bike slid in the muddy ground and his bike ended up slipping down the embankment into one of the ponds. Sturm was forced to seek help from one of the nearby houses. The two men to whom he spoke made out that they could not understand him. They were from a former West-Slovakian ethnic group which had settled between the Elbe, Oder, and Saale Rivers in the eighth and ninth centuries. They no longer wished to consider themselves German as the Red Army rapidly approached. Sturm was forced to demand their assistance at pistol point, whereupon they suddenly found themselves able to understand him after all. With a civilian leather jacket and cap over his uniform, he would have at least some chance, in this filthy weather, of not being instantly recognised as German.

Only on reaching the outskirts of the city of Berlin did Sturm finally meet any German units, and Sturm found himself in the midst of a titanic traffic jam, making its way slowly into the city. Suddenly, a tracked vehicle in front of him went into reverse. Sturm had no chance of avoiding it, as the track ran over his front wheel. Sturm lay under the bike, and only the rapid intervention of a *Feldgendarm* who stopped the traffic saved him from serious injury or death. In the event he suffered only bad bruising.

The *Hauptmann* in charge of the column appeared and began to slate Sturm, as though the accident had been his fault for not paying attention. Sturm opened his leather jacket and took out his Ausweis, signed by *SS-Obergruppenführer* Gottlob Berger and *Gauleiter* Stürz. This, together with the sight of the *Ritterkreuz* produced a marked change of attitude on the part of the *Hauptmann*, who immediately made his own jeep available to take Sturm to the *SS-Hauptamt* at Berlin-Grünewald. There, Sturm found that all of the senior officers had fled southwards in the direction of Czechoslovakia, leaving only an NCO and a few men behind to destroy any important papers. Any feeling of accountability to the *Volkssturm* leadership evaporated: they had abandoned Sturm and the men for whom he was responsible to save their own skins. Sturm took the opportunity to avail himself of a camouflaged combat jacket, but refused the offer of large sums of money which was being removed from a safe and burned to prevent it being looted by the Russians. All valuables met the same fate.

Sturm then made his way to the villa of Grafen von der Goltz, which was situated in the exclusive Wansee area. He had often stayed there overnight as the Graf had offered to keep some rooms available should his duties ever require him to stay in Berlin.[1] The villa and its neighbourhood were badly damaged, but still fit for occupation. Bombed-out Berliners were everywhere. In one room, Sturm found *Oberleutnant* Heinz Müller, a company commander responsible for four 10.5-cm guns covering the Glienicke Bridge and the bridge at the Wansee Station. Sturm decided to join this group. He was wearing civilian clothes at this point.

'Sturm, you had better put your uniform back on,' Müller warned him. 'The *Feldgendarmerie* might shoot you as a deserter, or you could be hanged by the Russians as a suspected spy.'

During this period, flying courts martial scourged the streets. Anyone found without correct papers would likely be tried and sentenced to death, and within minutes hung from the nearest streetlight. Civilians had also been hung for showing white bedsheets at their windows as a sign of surrender, thinking the Russians closer than they actually were.

After being introduced to the rest of the group, it was decided that Sturm should take charge. The group included some elderly *Volkssturm* men and some *Hitlerjugend* who had become separated from their units and had no rations. Not knowing to whom they should report, they too had joined Müller's group. There was only very little ammunition for the 10.5-cm guns and, in any case, they could only be fired with express permission from the *Kampfgruppe* commander, *Oberst* Meier. Meier was in fact in no position to carry out any kind of effective action with the mixed rabble of troops at his disposal.

The final phase of the Battle of Berlin started on 25 April at 05.30 hours, with an hour-long artillery barrage from every one of the available Soviet batteries, arranged in rings around the city. After this onslaught, the enemy began probing the German defences to ascertain how strong the resistance might still be. The battle grew in ferocity. Each row of streets, each block of houses, each ruin, and each individual cellar were bitterly contested.

General Weidling had located the *18* and *20 Panzergrenadier* Divisions in the Grünewald and Potsdam sectors. If they were weakened enough by heavy losses, the enemy could take the entire area of the Schäferberg and the *Volkspark* of Klein Glienicke. Müller and Sturm decided to attempt a breakout towards Potsdam with their little group, and spiked their 10.5-cm guns. The dash over the Glienicke Bridge would be rendered more difficult as it had been weakened by mines. The desperate attempt to break out over Babelsberg and towards Potsdam was halted by the enormous strength of the opposing Russians. Sturm and his comrades no longer fought for the freedom of Greater Germany, but for sheer, naked survival.

The attempted counterattack to relieve Berlin by *General* Wenck's army, on which all hopes of a breakout rested, were of no comfort to Sturm and his comrades. Wenck's *12 Armee* only made slight progress around Postdam, where the Russians were weakest, but soon foundered. The counterattack which was to have been launched by *11 Panzerarmee* in the north and on which Hitler had pinned his last remaining hopes had not even begun. The commander, *SS-Obergruppenführer* Felix Steiner, had realised from the start that such an attack would be completely senseless and had no intention of sacrificing his remaining men in such a futile gesture.

The battle in which Sturm had participated in these last days of April 1945 often degenerated into hand-to-hand combat, more dangerous and savage than he had experienced in the whole fourteen months he had spent on the Eastern Front in 1941–42. Sturm was wounded twice more. On April 29, he was hit behind the left shin, shrapnel tearing into his leg through his boot, and on 1 May he received a flesh wound on the rear of his neck.

'Sturm, you have been lucky again, the shrapnel didn't hit the bone, and the bullet that hit your neck passed cleanly through,' declared the *Kampfgruppe* commander, *Oberst* Meier. 'You have now qualified for the Gold Wound Badge.'

Sturm had already won more than his fair share of awards and at this stage had ceased to care about decorations. The commander, in view of the hopeless situation, authorised his men to attempt their own breakout, either individually or in small groups. Sturm recommended to Müller that the two of them, with at most two other men, should attempt a breakout. With his infantry combat experience, Sturm was confident that a small group could make it through. Müller, however, had been through a lot with his men, and would not leave any of them behind. In fact, there were by now only around twenty still fit to fight, and most of them had been wounded in some way or other. There was also an elderly *Volkssturm* man from Hamburg, and a *Hitlerjugend* boy from Frankfurt-on-Oder. With such a group, Sturm knew there was no real chance of breaking out. Together with elements of *18* and *20 Panzergrenadier* Divisions, they nevertheless succeeded in crossing over the bridge at the Wansee Station. The heavy weapons available to these troops helped the surprise attack to succeed. They intended to fight their way free to the south, but powerful enemy counter-attacks soon saw the force being fragmented. As the ever dwindling group made their way through a wooded area, they came across a roadway controlled by the Russians. In pairs, they dashed across. Sturm was the last to go, and as he ran he heard fire coming from ahead of him. These were, however, only warning shots fired by some Russians who had spotted them.

As he reached the edge of the small wood, Sturm saw a row of enemy armoured personnel carriers. Sturm had thrown himself into the cover of a drainage ditch. To the left and right behind him lay *Oberleutnant* Müller and the *Hitlerjugend* boy. An enemy half-track began to approach them.

'So this is how it ends,' thought Sturm to himself.

'Sturm, don't fire,' cut Müller's voice through the quiet of the morning, 'or none of us will survive.'

Sturm hesitated a few seconds. The idea of surrendering to the Soviets and allowing himself to be taken prisoner was completely contrary to his nature. Yet if he didn't, the Russians would fire and the others would all be killed. He surely could not rob them of a chance to survive. A young Russian started towards Sturm, his machine pistol loosely held in the crook of one arm, calmly beckoning Sturm forward with the other hand. In despair Sturm stood up, his assault rifle at the ready. In 1942 he had spent a couple of hours as a prisoner of the Russians, and it wasn't an experience he was prepared to repeat.

'Sturm, give up your weapon,' Müller entreated him, once again.

Grudgingly, Sturm lay the weapon down on the ground before him. The Russian came up to him.

'*Carascho, woinja kaput, scoro damoi.*'[2]

Clapping his hand on Sturm's shoulder, he relieved him of his pistol. *Oberleutnant* Müller and the others were standing a little way off, having surrendered their weapons, and held their hands aloft. Strangely, the enemy were making no attempt to search them for valuables or loot any of their possessions. Russians were notorious for this practise. The Russian who had spoken to him now noticed the *Ritterkreuz* visible at the neck of the camouflaged jacket.

'*Nix gut, politruk böse,*' he said.[3]

Sturm removed the *Ritterkreuz* and unpinned all of his other decorations. He gave them to the Russian thinking he would take them as souvenirs, then he walked over to join the others. Sturm had by now noticed that the group of Russians who had captured them were in fact officer cadets, which probably went some way towards explaining their disciplined behaviour. He was worried, however, that all of his awards had imparted the impression that he was some sort of Nazi fanatic. The others also feared for Sturm and positioned themselves in front of him to shield him from the Russians. Still, Sturm was brought before a group of officers with an interpreter. The senior Russian, a colonel, held Sturm's decorations in his hand. The Russian who had taken them from Sturm had obviously handed them over.

Hans Sturm was asked if the decorations were his as the colonel held them out, offering them back. Sturm, suspecting a trap, remained obstinately silent. Had he taken them, he expected that he would have been beaten or kicked and then dragged off and shot. The interpreter angrily grabbed Sturm's arm and held out his hand into which the colonel placed his awards. He pinned the German Cross in Gold onto one pocket and the Iron Cross First Class, Wound Badge, and Infantry Assault Badge on to the other. The Russian officers waited until he had once again hung the *Ritterkreuz* around his neck and then, to the astonishment of Sturm and his comrades, the Russian colonel saluted him. Sturm smartly returned the salute and, somewhat dazed, was allowed to return to his comrades. Clearly, these were Russians who appreciated combat gallantry and were willing to show respect for a defeated foe who had fought bravely.

Sturm and Müller spent four years in captivity together. Müller managed to make his way home in 1949 and became a successful hotelier. Sturm, on the other hand, would not gain his freedom until October 1953.

54

Soviet Captivity

The prisoners were first sent to a collection camp near Berlin, where convoys were formed for the long trek to the Soviet Union. Sturm's last commanding officers persuaded him to lead a company composed of trained technicians and those with specialist skills. Sturm led his comrades on the long march towards Hoyerswerda, where the men were absorbed into a huge holding camp. The prisoners were forced to take whatever jobs they could to make life that bit more bearable. For instance, Sturm's former *Oberst* became a cook in the camp kitchens. Around 2,000 officers were held in this camp.

Everything of value that Sturm owned had been looted, except for his uniform and a few possessions he was able to conceal. Sturm became the 'fixer' for his group of comrades, 'arranging' everything they might need from a shaving brush upwards. Sturm managed to scrounge enough food so that he and his comrades did not go hungry.

The 2,000 officers were held separately from lower ranks, while the influx of enlisted men was constant. Eventually, the officers were loaded into cattle trucks and transported by train through Germany into the Soviet Union. There were forty-five to fifty men per carriage, packed so tightly that only a few could lie down and rest at a time. The German prisoners were allowed to get out of the rail cars and stretch their legs three times during the journey: once in Brest-Litowsk, once in Rostow on the Black Sea, and finally once in Baku on the Caspian Sea. Each time they were thoroughly searched. They were also de-loused and had their heads shaved. The only ones allowed to leave the railcars were the dead, whose bodies were laid next to the railway lines. Those who carried on had mixed thoughts about their fallen comrades. At least they were spared whatever horrors might lie ahead, and now there was a little bit more space. This was a terrible journey. The Germans got the distinct feeling that the Russians didn't know what to do with them. The doors were only ever opened rarely, when the train stopped. Otherwise, the only fresh air to be had was at the four viewing slats at the barred windows. The prisoners drew straws to see who would have the privilege of standing next to these windows. They were forced to urinate through a hole in the floor, 'watering' the railway tracks. The only facility for defecating was a foul smelling bucket in one corner.

After Baku, the prisoners arrived in Tribuli, a small village near Kuteisk in the southern Caucasus. They were in luck! The countryside and climate could not be more pleasant. The prison camp was on the south slope of a hillside at about 500 m's elevation. The village was surrounded by the Caucasus Mountains, which rose to about 1,800 m in a semi-circular ring some 3 to 4 miles distant.

Of the first batch of 2,000 'officer' prisoners, only 30 per cent were in reality of this class. The remainder were police officials, fire brigade personnel, and members of government who had joined the officer group in the hope of gaining better treatment. And what a privilege it was—being transported to Russia with no hope of return in sight. Had they remained in Germany, their prospects would have been much better, as many others in such positions who stayed there ended up back in their old jobs, simply working for a new master.

At Tribuli Camp, there were already around 650 enlisted prisoners assembled, all from Germany. They were good men and formed the core of the prison inmates. They had been promised that when the officer prisoners arrived, the enlisted men could go home. Those who survived were not in fact released until 1949 at the earliest, and some not until 1955.

Everyone had to work regardless of rank, including the nine generals held in the camp. The generals and those who were unfit were permitted to work within the camp's confines, whereas most of the fitter men were put to use in the local coal mines and factories. This was work for which they actually received payment, albeit meagre, and this allowed them to buy extra rations. There was also a demand for skilled men such as carpenters and bricklayers to work on reconstruction duties. Sturm worked for two months as a mechanic, four months as a foreman-mechanic, and 3½ years as supervisor of the entire specialist group serving in the electro-mechanical workshops, the main repair centre for two nearby coal mines. There was also a smelting plant to make cast iron.

There were about 100 Russians, Georgians, and Armenians, plus the same number of German prisoners in the work force. In the engineering shop, the Germans worked alongside not only Russians, but one fully qualified engineer with a university degree and one practical engineer. Both were from Germany and selected Sturm, with his engineering background, right from the start to work with them. It was an opportunity that Sturm was glad of, and within six months his skills had made him popular with both the camp commander and the camp as a whole. The man Sturm replaced had been beaten to death and the cause of his demise recorded as 'pneumonia'.

Bartering, black market deals, and the meagre prison pay received had enabled Sturm to build up a supply of roubles. For their upkeep alone, the prisoners had to pay 400 roubles, and the camp commander took 30-per-cent cut of any money that was left over. The maximum anyone was allowed to keep was 150 roubles. Any excess over this amount had to be handed over for 'safe-keeping', which basically meant that it was unlikely to ever be seen again. During the Russian currency revaluation in

1947, Sturm was allocated a mere 100 roubles from the considerable sum which he had handed over.

Sturm's experiences should not, however, be considered typical, especially since he had avoided being sent to one of the hellish camps in the frozen wastes of Siberia. He had been very fortunate in possessing the technical skills that the Russians needed so desperately during post-war reconstruction and thanks to which he was, in comparison to many prisoners elsewhere, very well treated. The mine workers, for example, who did the most dangerous and difficult work under dreadful conditions, were allocated no pay until after their second year in captivity. Only the shift leaders received remuneration, though most of them shared it out with their less fortunate comrades. There were huge disparities between the 'earners' who worked in mines and factories and those who worked within the camp itself and were paid nothing.

All prisoners had to fulfill 100 per cent of their work quota in order to receive full rations. Their 18 oz of bread were cut to 14 oz if they failed to meet their quota. The rations also included three helpings of watery cauliflower soup per day, seldom with any meat in it except for maggots and dead flies. Sometimes there were very small pieces of fish, half the size stipulated for prisoner rations. The fish smelled like rotting meat and the stink assailed the men's nostrils as they approached the kitchens. There was, for most men, just a little too much food for them to actually starve to death, but too little to maintain health. Around 20 to 25 per cent of the prisoners died in the first year of captivity, mostly the older and infirm officers with whom Sturm had been transported to the camp. Some of the elderly survived, however. One *Oberleutnant* named Burger was 25 years older than Sturm. Sturm had known him since about 1943, when he had worked in Duisburg in a construction unit alongside Sturm's uncle, *Hauptmann* Friedrich von Keitz. Of the seven other officers from the same unit who were transported along with Sturm in 1945, only Burger survived. Of the others, three died on the long trek eastwards, and three in the camp. Sturm did his best to help his older comrade wherever possible, and Burger's family treated Sturm like his saviour. The old man survived his captivity and eventually died in 1980.

Burger had at one point lost the will to live. His nerves were shot and he was physically run down. He refused to eat what little food was available, and his clothes were soiled and crawling with lice. He had forgotten all about his home and family. Sturm helped him with contributions of cash and other things. Even though he was old enough to be his father, Sturm gave him a stern telling-off, took his clothes, and had him washed and his things deloused. He was force-fed with easily digestible food which he tried to spit back out. Sturm had some of his other friends watch the old man night and day, afraid he would try to commit suicide by drowning himself in the cesspool or throwing himself at the fence where the guards would shoot him without hesitation. These sorts of things had already happened on several occasions. Burger eventually recovered, and Sturm pasted back together a photo of his family that the older man had torn up in a fit of depression. After a few long chats, he took it back and kept it as a momento of what he had endured in that camp and a tribute to Sturm. It was eventually hung in his flat in Düsseldorf after his return home. Sturm was invited to visit Burger at his there in 1954, where he met his wife and family.

In the beginning, work could only be carried out with crude hand tools. For instance, sheet metal and steel stock were cut with a hammer and cold chisel. Welding could only be done with an arc-welder, for which the prisoners fashioned their own handmade electrodes. Sturm had them fabricate a few basic instruments to make life easier for both the prisoners and the Russians, such as a simple press, a drill, a die press, and a rolling mill. The bonus money Sturm's skills occasionally afforded him was shared out among his fellow inmates, including those restricted to camp and thus unable to earn. The camp workers did manage to earn a few roubles here and there for jobs outside, such as washing and mending clothes, darning socks, or knitting gloves and hats, or occasionally through craft work such as painting, whittling, and leatherwork.

There were many jobs which could only be carried out because of the availability of the German labour. For instance, a 25-m pylon had to be built to provide cable access to a new valley for the mining operation. If they had had to be constructed in the nearest metropol and transported to the site, the costs would have been exponential. To make space for the operation, a barracks had to be demolished and cleared. Sturm came up with a few ideas which were successfully implemented, even though the camp commander was less than enthusiastic and gave Sturm's plans little support. Sturm was, after all, a trained construction engineer.

Most of the Russians in the area were there as some form of punishment. Sturm's foreman mechanic was being punished for being fraternisation with the Germans. The man at first treated Sturm like a son, but another German instigated a quarrel between Sturm and the mechanic and it was eighteen months before the two were on speaking terms again.

Sturm spent a total of six years in Georgia. Four were spent in Tkibuli and two in Tiflis, the Georgian capital. The Russians erected a steel mill in a desert, with nothing but the River Kura, sand, and turtles to populate it. There was no iron ore, no coal, and no wood. By normal standards, this could never have been considered an economically viable proposition. Yet a whole city was established around the steel mill, all the materials for which had to be transported in at great cost.

At Sturm's second camp, he worked as a mechanic in a timber yard which featured a gigantic saw mill. Here, Sturm deliberately kept a low profile, hoping not to be noticed or considered too useful because a number of prisoners had been released from this site and allowed to return home. Sturm hoped that by keeping his head down he might be included in such a release, but had no such luck.

During a particularly rough, four-hour-long interrogation, Sturm learnt why he was being detained while others were being allowed to go home. Sturm tried to defend himself and ended up with two broken ribs and a dislocated shoulder. It turned out that a 'friend' at camp had denounced him, saying that he had given many talks during the war aimed at keeping up morale and helping the war effort. Many other comrades in the camp knew of Sturm's duties as a speaker, but only this one spoke to the Russians. Fortunately for him, he was released and allowed to return home (probably as a reward for denouncing Sturm) just two days before the other prisoners learnt of his treachery. Had they found out sooner, it is unlikely that he would have got home in one piece.

In December 1949, Sturm spent three weeks in solitary confinement in a cell just 1 m by 1.5 m. Because of his dislocated shoulder and broken ribs, he had difficulty moving around and keeping warm in the freezing cold. The Russians were hoping he would die of pneumonia. Only several days later were Sturm's shoulder and ribs tended to. One of his guards, an old Georgian who hated the Russians, took pity on him and put a strong bandage around his ribcage. He allowed Sturm out of his freezing cell into the heated corridor and permitted his friends to bring him extra food. Sturm had a few good friends in other cells to keep watch so that the other Russians guards would not catch them unawares. This old Georgian didn't just help Sturm, but other German prisoners too, at first for no reward. After a while he began to accept gifts of a few roubles from the Germans and sent it home to his family, making a tidy sum. Sturm sincerely hoped he was able to enjoy his money; he was no longer around when Sturm eventually got out of solitary.

Interrogations were always harrowing. They would sometimes be conducted formally and other times in quite a friendly manner. They could just as well be accompanied by gifts of sugar-coated bread as by severe beatings. Sturm was sometimes taken into an overheated room and made to stand there, wilting in his heavily padded winter clothing. Then, under a barrage of sarcastic remarks about being too warm, his outer clothing was removed and he was made to stand outside on the balcony in the freezing cold for the amusement of his guards. After considerable time had lapsed they would let him back inside and ply him with hot tea and vodka, apologising for having 'forgotten' that he was still outside.

A junior lieutenant and three other officers tried to extort information and confessions for spurious crimes from Sturm with a combination of kind words, severe beatings, and ominous threats. They accused him of being a Nazi propagandist—a matter of interpretation in view of Sturm's duties as a speaker. They insisted that if he was allowed to return home, he would repeat his crimes and fight against the Soviet Union. Contrary to their insistences, however, Sturm was not a professional officer, but simply a commissioned reservist who would have reverted to his civilian trade after the war.

In Tiflis, Sturm was sentenced to twenty-five years' imprisonment for stealing three sleds of hay from civilians during the war. This was nonsense, of course—why would he have need of hay in the first place? His name was entered into a record of war criminals. Sturm refused to sign any confessions but was still sentenced.

Around 20,000 other German officers were similarly sentenced to long terms of imprisonment for invented crimes. This sentencing was only handed down after Sturm had already been in captivity for five years, and these five years were not taken into account. The sentences were so ridiculous that some of the Germans had difficulty taking them seriously.

Shortly afterwards, Sturm was made foreman in the saw mill. The sheer size of this place may be reflected in the fact that it boasted eight power-driven main saws, capable of swallowing entire forests! There were also ovens, dryers, planers, and many other machines to further process wood, rail tracks and storage areas, too. This was a gigantic operation.

One major problem was the amount of sawdust and wood chips from the main saws. Sometimes this was collected by hand and carted off on a sort of wooden stretcher, then put into carts and pushed manually to a dump—a dismal task which necessitated shutting down the main saws. Sturm gave instructions for a sort of conveyor belt to be made from cable, wooden plates, and brackets and the problem was solved. Equally frustrating was that rare and precious woods were often marked down as plain construction-grade timber. The Russians had so much of it that it made no difference to them that such a precious natural resource was being wasted.

Sturm spent his last 2½ years in captivity at Stalino in the Ukraine. He was fortunate to have only spent time in three camps during his 8½ years. More often than not, other prisoners fared much, much worse. At this third camp, Sturm led a construction crew. As a labourer, he moved sand, cement, gypsum, and rock by wheelbarrow and shovel. The tasks got bigger and bigger, and the fifteen-man squad

22. September 1946.

Meine Lieben!
Seid ohne Sorgen,
mir geht's gut
bin gesund
hoffe dasselbe
besonders dem Kleinen
Grüsse an alle
baldiges Wiedersehen
in alter Frische
    Euer   Hansi

The first card Sturm was permitted to write to his fiancée, and the first indication she was to receive that he had survived the Battle of Berlin. Only a fixed number of words were permitted.

grew to thirty, forty, then fifty men. Soon, they were a crew of 100 men, including crane operators, mechanics, welders, carpenters, and scaffolders. Sturm and his comrades erected hospitals and NKVD buildings, and did external and internal finishing work, too.

From April 1951 to October 1953 (when he was finally released), Sturm worked side by side with Russian engineers on a steadily expanding project: building the 'new Stalino' between the site of the original Stalino and Makijewka. Only Germans worked on this from the spring until the autumn, some 400 men all in all.

The Russians transported materials to the twenty Germans on the site, an empty field, by truck. It was wet, cold, windy, and muddy. April weather! The previous year, there had been sunflowers growing. No tools were brought, not even a shovel to dig a hole for the first fence post to surround the project site. An attempt to build a fire failed. Sturm, growing angrier by the minute, eventually cursed that he was 'finished with this shit-freezing meadow' and was going back to camp. The two Russians were happy to take the Germans back there on the basis that it would be Sturm who faced the consequences.

As time went on, the restriction on the number of words permitted on each postcard home was dropped, though the number of cards remained restricted. Sturm therefore learned to write in the smallest script imaginable.

By 1950, the German prisoners were all hoping for a quick release and return to freedom. But as time dragged on, despair set in. In 1953, several professed themselves ready to join the 'underground' organisation. As a sign of its capabilities, Sturm was told ahead of time exactly when the highest ranking police official of Stalino would be assassinated. The following day, newspapers carried reports of his death and the shooting of two of his assistants. However, none of the Germans did actually join. This was just as well, because a rumour began to circulate that release was imminent. One NKVD officer, nicknamed the 'Boxer' because he so enjoyed beating up prisoners during interrogations, showed Sturm a list of names of those to be released. It contained the names of all the officers sentenced with Sturm in Tiflis. At first, they feared it was but a cruel ruse and that they would all be carted even further into the Soviet hinterland. But when the transports did eventually collect them, they were indeed taken to Germany, and freedom. After his release, Sturm made regular trips to reunions of the last Germans to be released from Soviet captivity, the *Spätheimkehrer*.

On his return to Germany in October 1953, he was reunited with Hilde and finally able to see his son for the first time. On 14 November 1954, Hilde presented Sturm with twin daughters.

Sturm returned to his trade as an engineer and worked for Rheinstahl Union Brückenbau AG until his retirement in 1979 after which he lived in retirement in his native Dortmund. A devoted husband and father, Hans Sturm was blessed with a large and close knit family.

Although much of his time was dedicated to tending to Hilde, whose health was consistently poor until her death in 1998, Hans Sturm still found time to answer the large number of letters he received from those with an interest in military history. He died on 11 December 2004.

Sturm (wearing white scarf) is greeted by Hilde and numerous well-wishers on his release from Soviet captivity.

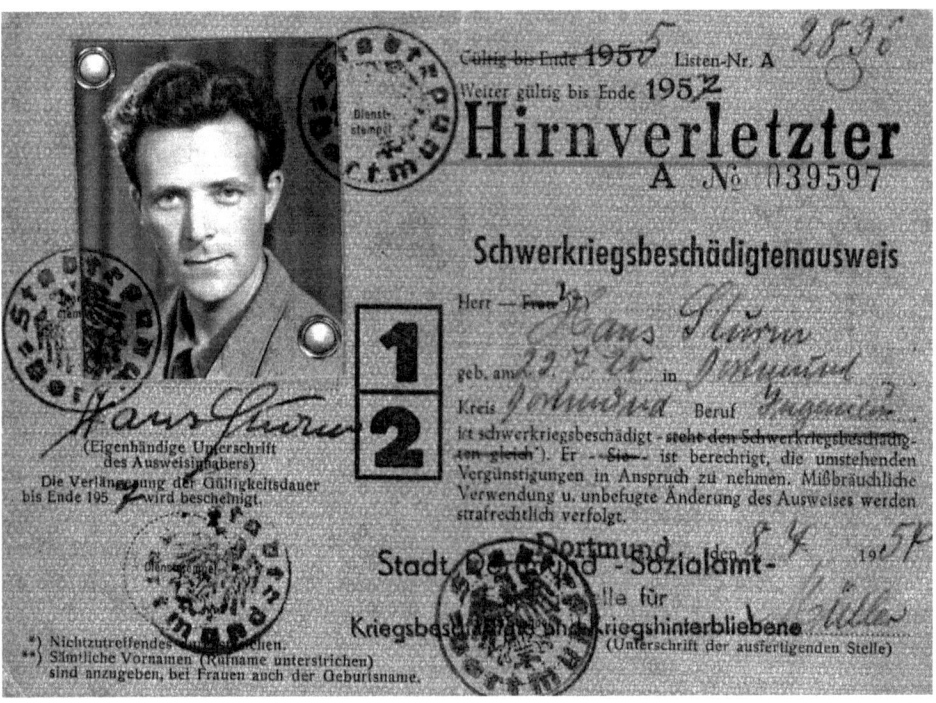

Sturm's certification as war-disabled.

Sturm's membership card for the *Verband der Heimkehrer* (the Association of 'Homecomers', those who were held in Soviet captivity for many years).

Sturm with a presentation certificate rewarding twenty-five years' service with Reinstahl Union Brückenbau AG after his return from Russia.

Only after his release did Sturm finally meet the son born while he was held prisoner in the Soviet Union.

Sturm at his desk at Rheinstahl Union Brückenbau AG.

Sturm and his wife at a reunion meeting of holders of the Knight's Cross of the Iron Cross. Note the Knight's Cross worn at Sturm's neck.

Sturm (far right) with fellow Knight's Cross bearers at a post-war reunion.

Endnotes

1. Enlistment

1 *Schlipsträger*: a derogatory term referring to the wear of a shirt and tie as part of the service uniform of the Luftwaffe. Being the youngest of the armed forces, the Luftwaffe's dress was least affected by Prussian tradition and was in fact closely modelled on that of the RAF. Many thought the Luftwaffe uniform was the least 'military' in its appearance.

2. Infantryman

1 *Landser*: slang for 'soldier'. Used in much the same way as a US soldier would be referred to as a 'GI', or a British soldier as a 'Tommy'.

3. Baptism of Fire

1 *Sanitäter*: medical orderly.
2 *Zeltbahn*: a triangular section of waterproof cotton duck material in camouflaged colours; this had a slot cut in the centre through which the head could be poked, and the material formed into a poncho. Alternatively, several *Zeltbahnen* could be joined together to form a tent.

5. The Iron Cross

1 *König*: king.
2 The Iron Cross Second Class was normally only worn on the day of the bestowal. Thereafter, only the ribbon was worn from the tunic buttonhole, the medal itself reserved for wear on formal occasions, parades *etc.*

6. The Battle Continues

1 *Stuka zu Fuss*: 28-cm rocket launchers. Later, these would be mounted on half tracks to give mobility; initially, however, they were fired from wooden frames set up on the ground. Thought to be as devastatingly effective as the notorious Stuka dive bombers, they were affectionately known as the 'Stuka on foot'.

7. Return to the Front

1 Reference to 'Sie'.

8. Welikije Luki

1 *Sturmbannführer*: an SS rank equivalent to major.

13. The Attack of Moscow Fails

1 The winter conditions on the Eastern Front were such an advantage to the Soviets that they equated to them having a superhuman general, jokingly referred to as '*General Winter*', on their side.

15. The Russians cross Lake Seliger

1 *Oberleutnant* Winter plays on the German word for leaf, '*Laub*', and leave, '*Urlaub*'.

19. 3 and 6 Companies merge

1 *Spiess*: a position held by the senior available NCO in a company. Although in theory, and very occasionally in practice, the post could be held by a rank as low as *Unteroffizier*, it was more often a senior sergeant or warrant officer equivalent. The post was roughly equivalent to that of company sergeant major.

24. Evacuation to Germany

1 Nazi Party officials in their tan-coloured uniforms, decorated with much gold braiding and the red Swastika armband, were generally known by the derogatory term 'Golden Pheasants'.
2 The central motif of the German Cross was a large, black enamelled Swastika, the Swastika itself being the 'German' Cross. Because of its obviously Nazi origins, it was considered by some a political award of sorts. This was most certainly not the case—it was a highly respected military decoration.

25. Incident at Brest-Litovsk

1 *Feldgendarmerie*: the German military police. Although their basic tasks were much the same as the military police in any other army, the *Feldgendarmerie* had considerable powers, and it was a brave and foolhardy soldier indeed who would seek to resist this authority. They were known to the German soldier as 'Chain Dogs' because of the gorget plate worn on a chain around the neck when on duty.

2 *Sicherheitspolizei* (or *SiPo*): an umbrella term for the entire security police apparatus of the Third Reich, of which the SD (*Sicherheitsdienst*) was just a part, along with the Gestapo. In fact, the SD and Gestapo wore almost identical uniforms.

27. Return to Dortmund

1 The Nazi Party leader of the *Kreis*, or district.

29. A Busy Week in Bonn

1 The Blood Order was a political decoration given to those who had personally taken part in the Munich Putsch alongside Hitler on 9 November 1928, though it was later also used as an honorary award to non-participants.

34. The Premiere of 'Baron von Münchhausen'

1 The story was expanded upon by August Bürger, a university professor and jurist in Göttingen. The real Baron felt himself defamed by his spurious additions. Unfortunately, he hadn't the means to set the record straight where necessary. Embittered, impoverished, and in a real Münchhausen-like relationship with a 17-year-old girl, he died at the age of 76 on 22 February 1797 in Bodenwerder. The 'Liar Baron' of August Bürger's imagining is the one remembered today.

38. Visit to the Mountain Troops at Garmisch-Partenkirchen

1 *Gebirgsjäger*: mountain troops.

43. The Visit

1 *Jäger zu Pferd*: Mounted Rifles.

46. Partisans

1 The tank destruction slip consisted of a strip of aluminium braid with a small metal tank motif pinned to it. It was awarded for the single-handed destruction of an enemy tank using only hand-held infantry weapons: thus, anti-tank gunners, for instance, were not elegible. It was a very highly respected award and took considerable personal bravery to earn.

2 *Frontkämpfer* (or 'Front Fighter'): a term of respect used to describe a genuinely battle-hardened combat soldier, as opposed to rear echelon elements.

3 *Bandenkampfabzeichen* (or Anti-Partisan War Badge): see Appendix 2. Although the badge could be awarded to men from all three branches of the armed forces, it is primarily considered an SS and police award and was conferred to some particularly unpleasant SS units involved in atrocities on the Eastern Front, where little mercy was shown to captured partisans. Although many such badges were honourably earned, its association with SS security units meant that many ordinary soldiers considered it distasteful, though few if any others showed Sturm's pluck in refusing to wear it.

48. *Kriegsschule*

1 Whereas 'high treason' is committed against the state or the regime, 'treason' alone entailes violating the security of your country irrespective of its current administration.

2 On 10 October 1953, after the 22.00 hours roll-call, *Feldwebel* Anton Sturm was informed that he was to be released from Soviet captivity. He was one of the last in a long list of names in alphabetical order. Sturm's parents, Hilde, and all who knew him listened intently to the radio for mention of his name among those due for release to the reception camp in Friedland. When his name was finally announced, a flurry of telephone calls passed between Dortmund and Brünen. Their joy and relief was immense. Sturm was finally reunited with Hilde on the morning of 11 October 1953 on the road to the Friedland camp. They had waited almost nine years for this moment.

3 *Jabo*: short for *Jagdbomber*, or 'fighter bomber'.

49. *Leutnant* Sturm

1 Later, in Soviet captivity, Sturm would be in a position to return the favour to *Hauptmann* Conrad. The prisoners were forced to do heavy work in the mines, where they were expected to achieve 100 per cent of their work target each month to receive the full bread ration of 600 g, rather than the 400 g they would otherwise receive. In his third year of captivity, Conrad was seriously injured and allowed lighter, office work. He was released in 1949 and Sturm met him once again in Cologne after his own release in 1954.

2 'If the soldiers march through the town, the young girls will throw open the windows and doors.'

50. Return to Barracks

1 The business still exists today, but in bigger, more modern premises on the other side of the street.
2 *Ordensburgen*: training establishments run by the party as preparatory schools for future NS soldiers.

52. *Volkssturm*

1 One of the Nazi administrative 'Gaue' or 'regions'. *Mark Brandenburg* comprised a large part of the old Kingdom of Prussia, with Berlin as its centre.
2 Gottlob Berger was chief of staff of the *Waffen-SS* and head of the *SS-Hauptamt* ('main office'), a figure with immense power and influence.
3 *Generalfeldmarschall* Ferdinand Schörner was a fanatical Nazi and one of Hitler's most trusted field marshals. A strict and brutal disciplinarian, he was personally responsible for ordering the execution of numbers of German troops on trumped-up charges of desertion or cowardice.

53. The End

1 Albert Graf (Count) von der Goltz was an *Oberst* in command of a mountain troop regiment and, like Sturm, a *Ritterkreuzträger*. He died of wounds received in battle in March 1944
2 'War Over! Everything OK, go home soon!'
3 'No good, political scoundrel!'

Appendices

1. Infantry divisions

Infanterie Division 253: This, the parent division of Sturm's first regiment, was a new unit created during the mobilisation of the German Army in 1939. Its home base was *Wehrkreis XI* in Aachen. The division missed the Polish campaign and first saw action during the invasion of France in 1940. On the successful conclusion of hostilities in France, it remained there on occupation duties until the summer of 1941, when it moved to occupied Poland as a jumping-off point for the commencement of Operation Barbarossa. The division served as part of *9 Armee* on the northern edge of the central sector of the Eastern Front. Attached in the area between Rschew and the *Seeliger See*, it was opposed by the Soviet 22 Army. After Sturm's departure, the division remained in the central sector of the Front right up until May 1945. During this period, it was involved in almost all of *9 Armee*'s major battles, with the exception of the ill-fated Kursk offensive. At that time, *253 Infanterie Division* formed part of *9 Armee*'s reserve. The division ended the war encircled in a defensive pocket east of Prague, and its survivors went into Soviet captivity.

Infanterie Division 356: The unit with which Sturm served in Italy was another freshly formed division. It was raised in occupied France at the start of 1943, drawing mostly on personnel from reserve units. The division served predominantly in a defensive role in Italy, performing coastal defence duties during which it spent much of its time fending off attacks by Italian partisans. In May 1944, the division was committed to combat duties following the allied landings at Anzio and remained in front-line service in Italy until January 1945, when it was transferred to the Eastern Front in Hungary. Here it was committed to battle as part of *I SS-Panzerkorps*, part of *6 SS-Panzerarmee*. It fought with *6 SS-Panzerarmee* in the retreat into Austria and in the battle for Vienna. On the conclusion of hostilities, its survivors went into Soviet captivity.

2. The awards and decorations of Hans Sturm

The photographs included within this book show Hans Sturm wearing almost all of his military decorations, with the significant exception of the Anti-Partisan Badge, which he refused to wear. A full list of his awards runs as follows:

The Wound Badge (*Verwundetenabzeichen*)

Instituted in September 1939, this badge was closely modelled on its imperial predecessor. It comprised a vertical wreath of laurel leaves with, in its centre, a steel helmet superimposed over a pair of crossed swords. The Third Reich version differed in that it depicted a more up-to-date M35 pattern helmet, and of course the ubiquitous Swastika emblem. The badge existed in three basic grades (a special version was later produced for those injured in the attempt to blow up Hitler on 20 July 1944). These consisted of a hollow stamped version painted in black for one to two wounds; a silver grade, usually struck from a solid sheet of metal for three to four wounds; and a gilded version for five wounds or more. The numerical criteria could be waived in cases of particularly severe injury. For instance, a soldier who lost a limb or was blinded on his first wound could immediately receive the gold grade. Hans Sturm qualified for all three grades, though the gold grade was awarded on paper only, the chaotic conditions in the defence of Berlin precluding the issue of the actual insignia.

Infantry Assault Badge (*Infanterie Sturmabzeichen*)

Designed by the firm of C. E. Juncker in Berlin, this award was instituted by *Generalfeldmarschall* von Brauchitsch on 20 December 1939. It consisted of a vertical oval of oakleaves surmounted by a *Wehrmacht* pattern eagle and swastika (exactly the same design, in fact, as that carried on the helmet escutcheon). Lying

The Wound Badge, awarded in three grades, Black, Silver and Gold. Due to the chaotic conditions at the end of the war, Sturm never actually received the gold grade that he had earned.

The Infantry Combat Badge.

diagonally across the badge, from right to left, is a detailed representation of the Mauser Kar 98k rifle with fixed bayonet. The badge was awarded to soldier who had taken part in at least three seperate infantry combat actions on three seperate dates. The badge had a silvered finish for infantry proper, though a bronzed version was later introduced for motorised or armoured infantry.

The Iron Cross

A military decoration with a long history, the Iron Cross was first instituted in 1813 to reward Prussian soldiers for gallantry in the war against Napoleon. It was a temporary award, which meant that it had to be re-instituted each time the country found itself in a state of war.

The 1939 version followed the traditional design of a blackened iron cross pattée held within a silver metal frame. The design carried upon the iron core of the 1939 version featured a Swastika as the central motif, with the instituted year of 1939 in the lower arm. The reverse was plain, apart from the original institution year of 1813 in the lower arm. The Iron Cross came in several grades, to reward varying levels of distinguished service or gallantry.

The Iron Cross Second Class had a small suspension ring attached to the upper arm to allow suspension from a ribbon in the national colours of red, white, and black. In fact the award itself was only ever worn on the day of its bestowal (unless worn on a ribbon bar for formal dress occasions). Thereafter, only the ribbon was worn, either in full size from the second buttonhole of the tunic or in miniature on

The Iron Cross Second Class.

a ribbon bar above the left breast pocket. The Second Class tended to be awarded for a single act of bravery or distinguished service beyond the normal requirements of duty, but not such as would merit the award of the First Class or higher. The Iron Cross First Class featured an obverse design identical to the Second Class, but the reverse face was totally plain, featuring only a hinged pin fixing attachment to allow the award to be worn from the left breast pocket of the tunic. The First Class would be awarded for continued acts of gallantry or distinguished service after the award of the Second Class, but not such as would merit the award of the *Ritterkreuz*. It was a prerequisite of the First Class that the recipient already hold the Second Class. In some cases, this rule would be circumvented by awarding both on the same day.

The *Ritterkreuz* was virtually identical in design to the Second Class but was very slightly larger and featured a genuine silver frame. It also had the ribbon suspension loop slightly modified to allow it to be worn from a neck ribbon. (In fact, many *Ritterkreuzträger* wore a Second Class as a substitute for the *Ritterkreuz* to avoid its damage or loss). The *Ritterkreuz* was awarded only for acts of gallantry or distinguished service well over and above the call of duty. It was a requirement that the recipient already held the Iron Cross in its Second and First Classes. *Ritterkreuzträger* were accorded the status of national heroes, their exploits being widely reported in newspapers and magazines of the day. Collectors' albums were published to allow youngsters of the day to collect various series of photos of their favourite *Ritterkreuzträger*.

The Iron Cross First Class.

The Knight's Cross of the Iron
Cross.

East Front Medal (*Ostmedaille* or, more formally, *Medaille 'Winterschlacht im Osten'*)

This campaign decoration was instituted on 26 May 1942 and was based on a design, not by some medal making firm, but by a serving soldier—*SS-Unterscharführer* Ernst Kraus. It consisted of a circular medallion topped by a German St el Helmet sitting on a stick grenade. This motif, and the edge of the medallion was finished with a bright silver plate or anodised finish. The central field had a black or dark gun-blue finish. On the obverse was featured an eagle with swastika in its talons, over a sprig of laurel. On the reverse face was the inscription 'Winterschlacht im Osten 1941/42' over a sword and sprig of laurel. Like the Iron Cross, the award was only worn on the day of its bestowal, thereafter only the ribbon being worn. The East Front Medal was awarded to all those who had served during the first winter of the war on the Eastern Front, providing they had undertaken at least two weeks of combat action, or had served at least 60 days in the combat zone, or had been wounded or suffered a degree of frostbite for which the Wound Badge had been awarded. The award criteria were altered in January 1943, however it was under these original criteria that Sturm qualified for the award.

The East Front Campaign
Medal.

German Cross in Gold (*Deutsches Kreuz in Gold*)

Although the name of this award at first seems anomalous for a decoration in the form of a radiant sunburst, the title is in fact related to the Swastika (*Hakenkreuz* or hooked cross) which forms the central motif. Designed by Prof. Dr. Klein of Munich, it was instituted on 28 September 1941 and was one of the most complex military awards issued under the Third Reich in terms of its manufacturing process, comprising five basic components.

It consisted of a large silver outer star, over which was laid a slightly smaller, blackened star. In the centre was a large matt silver disc with an inlaid ring of red enamel near its circumference. Onto this red ring was set a wreath of gold laurel leaves with the year of institution, 1941, at its base. In the centre was a large black-enamelled Swastika with silvered edges. The whole assembly was held together with a mixture of concealed prongs and rivets. The reverse face featured a large, flat tapering-hinged pin and retaining clip. The award was quite heavy, and although an embroidered version was authorised and widely worn, the majority of recipients seemed to prefer to wear the original metal version. The German Cross was awarded for outstanding achievement in combat on numerous occasions, and it was required that the recipient already held the Iron Crosses Second and First Class.

The German Cross
in Gold.

The Anti-Partisan Badge (*Bandenkampfabzeichen*)

This award was instituted by *Reichsführer-SS* Heinrich Himmler on 30 January 1944. It was awarded to members of all branches of the armed forces, the police, and the SS, who had been employed in combating partisans. It consisted of a vertical oval wreath of oakleaves with a skull and crossbones at the base of the wreath. In the centre was sword, plunged into a mass of writhing snakes. The sword hilt featured the Germanic sunwheel-type Swastika. The award was produced in three grades: bronze for twenty days' participation in anti-partisan operations, silver for fifty days, and gold for 150 days. It was worn on the left breast pocket, just below the position of the Iron Cross First Class. Due to the nature of anti-partisan warfare, especially on the Eastern Front, some particularly brutal and unsavory SS police units were involved in eliminating the threat from these guerrilla fighters. More often than not, summary justice was meted out on the spot with little or no effort being made to establish genuine guilt or innocence. The fact that German army personnel were prepared to act in such a manner with the summary execution of suspected partisans in Italy sickened Sturm and in protest he absolutely refused to wear the Anti-Partisan Badge that he had been awarded. This could have had extremely serious consequences for Sturm, but once again luck was on his side, and due to the transfer

The Anti-Partisan Badge, an award which Sturm steadfastly refused to wear.

of his commanding officer at just that time he escaped any disciplinary action. As he steadfastly refused to wear this badge, there are no period photographs in existence to show it being worn by Hans Sturm.

The Golden *Hitlerjugend* Badge

Basically a Hitlerjugend membership badge, but with an oakleaf border, this was bestowed to members who had done something special—like win a military decoration. Sturm did not so much 'earn' this as receive it as a formality upon the award of his *Ritterkreuz*.

THE FONTHILL
THIRD REICH
LIBRARY

A selection of Fonthill titles relating to the Third Reich
and the Second World War, but excluding
most of the military topics.

For more information visit
www.fonthillmedia.com

SS ELITE: THE SENIOR LEADERS OF HITLER'S PRAETORIAN GUARD

(Volume 1 A-J)

Max Williams

ISBN 978-1-78155-433-3 | £45.00 | $75.00

hardback | 656 pages | 1,078 illustrations

For more information visit
www.fonthillmedia.com

THE FONTHILL THIRD REICH LIBRARY

THE RISE AND FALL OF THE LUFTWAFFE
Hauptmann Hermann
ISBN 978-1-78155-006-9
£14.99 $21.95
paperback, 224pp
90 illustrations

ADOLF HITLER: THE CURIOUS AND MACABRE ANECDOTES
Patrick Delaforce
ISBN 978-1-78155-073-1
£12.99 $19.95
paperback, 192pp
336 illustrations

THE NAZIS GO UNDERGROUND
Curt Riess
ISBN 978-1-78155-121-9
£16.99 $25.95
paperback, 224pp
76 illustrations

GUARDING THE FÜHRER: SEPP DIETRICH AND ADOLF HITLER
Blaine Taylor
ISBN 978-1-78155-387-9
£18.99 $32.95
paperback, 256pp
572 illustrations

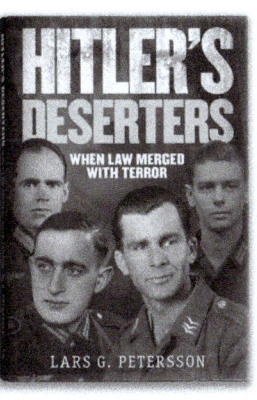

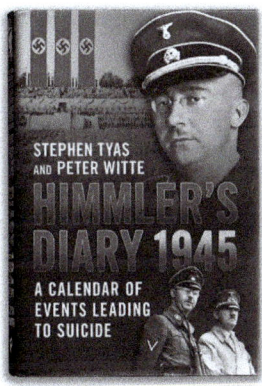

HITLER'S DESERTERS WHEN LAW MERGED WITH TERROR
Lars Petersson
ISBN 978-1-78155-269-8
£18.99 $29.95
hardback, 176pp
37 illustrations

HEINRICH HIMMLER 1945: A CALENDER OF EVENTS LEADING TO SUICIDE
Stephen Tyas and Peter Witte
ISBN 978-1-78155-257-5
£25.00 $40.00
hardback, 272pp
35 illustrations

HITLER'S BERCHTESGADEN: A GUIDE TO THIRD REICH SITES IN THE BERCHTESGADEN AND OBERSALZBERG AREA
Geoffrey R. Walden
ISBN 978-1-78155-226-1
£14.99 $24.95
paperback, 160pp
180 colour illustrations

BEHEADED BY HITLER: CRUELTY OF THE NAZIS, CIVILIAN EXECUTIONS AND JUDICIAL TERROR 1933-1945
Colin Pateman
ISBN 978-1-78155-343-5
£20.00 $29.95
hardback, 240pp
50 illustrations

For more information visit
www.fonthillmedia.com

THE FONTHILL THIRD REICH LIBRARY

HEINRICH HIMMLER:
A PHOTO HISTORY OF THE REICHSFÜHRER SS
Max Williams
ISBN 978-1-78155-405-0
£40.00 $65.00
hardback, 768pp
1,228 illustrations

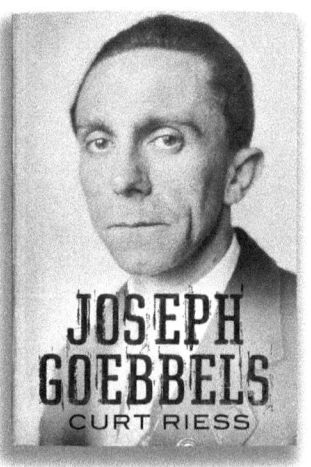

KETTENHUND! THE GERMAN
MILITARY POLICE IN THE SECOND
WORLD WAR
Gordon Williamson
ISBN 978-1-78155-332-9
£30.00 $50.00
hardback, 336pp
450 illustrations

JOSEPH GOEBBELS
Curt Riess
ISBN 978-1-78155-323-7
£16.99 $29.95
paperback, 368pp
93 illustrations

MUNICH PLAYGROUND: THE NAZI
LEADERSHIP AT REST AND PLAY
Ernest R. Pope
ISBN 978-1-78155-454-8
£18.99 $32.95
paperback, 256pp
83 illustrations

For more information visit
www.fonthillmedia.com